Sacrificed Wife/Sac

Sacrificed Wife/Sacrificer's Wife

Women, Ritual, and Hospitality in Ancient India

Stephanie W. Jamison

New York Oxford
OXFORD UNIVERSITY PRESS
1996

Oxford University Press

Oxford New York
Athens Auckland Bangkok
Calcutta Cape Town Dar es Salaam Delhi
Florence Hong Kong Istanbul Karachi
Kuala Lumpur Madras Madrid Melbourne
Mexico City Nairobi Paris Singapore
Taipei Tokyo Toronto

and associated companies in
Berlin Ibadan

Published by Oxford University Press, Inc.
198 Madison Avenue, New York, New York 10016

Library of Congress Cataloging-in-Publication Data
Jamison, Stephanie W.
Sacrificed wife/sacrificer's wife : women, ritual,
and hospitality in ancient India / Stephanie W. Jamison.
p. cm. Includes bibliographical references and index.
ISBN 0-19-509662-2 (cloth). — ISBN 0-19-509663-0 (paper)
1. Women—India—Social life and customs. 2. India—Social life
and customs.
HQ1742.J36 1996
305.4'0954—dc20 94-45729

1 3 5 7 9 8 6 4 2

Printed in the United States of America
on acid-free paper

For Stanley

ācāryasattamaḥ

ACKNOWLEDGMENTS

It is my pleasure to thank the many people who have contributed, directly or indirectly, to this book. As with all my work, chief among them are my teacher, Stanley Insler, and my husband, Calvert Watkins. Both of them have discussed, read, criticized, and lived through this work since its inception. They both, in their different ways, also serve for me as enduring and inspiring models of how to combine meticulous textual scholarship with an instinct for posing truly exciting questions involving ancient languages and cultures. I cannot possibly repay my debt to them except by attempting to emulate this model.

Although I have been puzzling over many of the issues raised in this book for a number of years, most of the research and writing of the crucial part III on ritual was carried out during 1992–93, while I was a research associate and visiting lecturer in the History of Religion in the Women's Studies in Religion program at the Harvard Divinity School. I gratefully acknowledge this program not merely for granting me the leisure to conduct the research but also for giving me the opportunity to learn much from my colleagues in the program, from Dean Constance Buchanan, director of the program, and particularly from the students in my course on gender patterns in the ancient Indian religious tradition, given at the Divinity School in the fall of 1992.

Other students, colleagues, and friends have contributed much. I cannot name them all but would especially like to thank Joel Brereton, Jo Ann Hackett, Rosemary Hale, Chris Minkowski, Hanns-Peter Schmidt, Oktor Skjærvø, the various Harvard students with whom I have read texts over the years, the anonymous reader for Oxford University Press, and Henry Krawitz, my painstaking and very patient manuscript editor at Oxford University Press.

CONTENTS

SANSKRIT PRONUNCIATION AND TYPOGRAPHICAL CONVENTIONS

The following section describes approximate English equivalents for the various Sanskrit sounds and discusses the production of unfamiliar sounds.

Vowels

Short and long *a*'s differ in length and quality:

a	corresponds to the vowel in b*u*t
ā	corresponds to the vowel in f*a*ther

Short and long *i* and short and long *u* differ from each other only in length:

i, ī	The *i*'s resemble the vowel in b*ea*t.
u, ū	The *u*'s resemble the vowel in b*oo*t.

The following four count as "long" vowels or diphthongs, just as ā, ī, and ū do:

e	b*ai*t
ai	b*i*te
o	b*oa*t
au	b*ou*t

ṛ	('syllabic r') is equivalent to the final syllable of fath*er* or the interior sound of p*er*t. There is also (rarely) a long syllabic ṝ.

Consonants

Stops

Sanskrit stops consist of four types: plain voiceless (vl. e.g. *t*), voiceless aspirate (vl. asp. e.g. *th*), plain voiced (vd. e.g. *d*), and voiced aspirate (vd. asp. e.g. *dh*). These are further classified into five series according to where they are produced in the mouth, as diagramed in the following table:

	vl.	vl. asp.	vd.	vd. asp.
velar	k	kh	g	gh
palatal	c	ch	j	jh
retroflex	ṭ	ṭh	ḍ	ḍh
dental	t	th	d	dh
labial	p	ph	b	bh

Remarks on the vertical columns: The aspirated stops (cols. 2 and 4) differ from their plain counterparts by having a small puff of air following the articulation of the stop. The voiceless aspirates (col. 2) are closest in sound to English voiceless stops that are initial in their words. For example, Sanskrit *th* is equivalent to the *t* in English *t*en. It is important to remember that Sanskrit *th* is *not* equivalent to *th* in English words like *th*in, *th*ought, or *th*at. Similarly, Sanskrit *ph* is equivalent to English *p* in *p*en, not the *ph* in *ph*ilosophy.

For our present purposes, the plain voiceless set (col. 1) can be pronounced like the voiceless aspirates (col. 2), though a more exact equivalent would be the type of consonant that appears after *s* in English words: English s*t*op contains a Sanskrit *t*, but *t*op contains a Sanskrit *th*.

The plain voiced set (col. 3) is equivalent to English voiced stops (d, etc.), while the voiced aspirates (col. 4) have a little breathy murmur after the articulation of the stop. There is no English equivalent for the voiced aspirates; for our purposes we can pronounce the voiced aspirates much like plain voiced stops.

Remember that the two aspirate sets (cols. 2 and 4) contain single consonants, not combinations of two consonants. Each is written with one letter in devanāgarī (the current writing system of Sanskrit), not two, as in their English transliterations.

Remarks on the horizontal rows: The *k/g* series is equivalent to English velars *k* and *g* (e.g. *k*eep, *g*uess), also spelled with the so-called hard c in words like *c*at. English *g*'s in words like *g*em are *not* equivalent. The *c/j* series is equivalent to English *ch* (e.g. *ch*eese, *ch*at) and *j* (e.g. *j*udge, *j*eep; also English *g*'s in words like gem). The ṭ/ḍ series, the retroflexes, are pronounced like *t/d*, but with the tongue tip pointed back toward the roof of the mouth. There is no equivalent in English. The *t/d* series corresponds roughly to English *t/d* (and even better to their French equivalents). The *p/b* series corresponds to English *p/b*.

There are also five different *nasal* consonants corresponding to the five horizontal rows:

velar	ṅ	corresponds to English *ng* in si*ng*, etc.
palatal	ñ	like the *ny* in words like ca*ny*on (or the Spanish equivalent *ñ*)
retroflex	ṇ	no English equivalent; pronounced with the tongue tip turned back

dental	n	like English *n*
labial	m	like English *m*

Other Consonants

Sanskrit *y*, *r*, *l*, and *v* are pronounced like their English counterparts. There are three types of sibilants: palatal *ś*, retroflex *ṣ*, and dental *s*. The last corresponds to English *s*, while the other two can be pronounced like English *sh* (*sh*ould, *she*), since English does not make a distinction between palatal and retroflex sibilants. The Sanskrit *h* is a voiced *h*, with no English equivalent. The *ḥ* ('visarga'), ordinarily occurring at the end of words, is voiceless, like the English *h*, and is now often pronounced with a brief vowel following it, which echoes the vowel that precedes it (e.g. devaḥ would end *aha*, but agniḥ *ihi*). Sanskrit ṃ ('anusvāra') may conveniently be pronounced as nasalization of the preceding vowel (e.g. French vin, son).

Accents

The accents marked in the Vedic passages in this work are pitch accents, not accents of intensity, but the complexities of the Vedic accent need not detain us here. In current practice Sanskrit words are conventionally pronounced as if following the "Latin" rules: Words whose penultimate or next-to-last syllable is long (i.e. contains a long vowel or is followed by two consonants) are accented on that syllable (e.g. aśvamédha, praghā́sa, paśubándha). Those that have a short penultimate syllable are accented on the third syllable from the end (e.g. váruṇa, rā́kṣasa). Words of two syllables are accented on the initial syllable, whether long or short (e.g. pátnī, mánu). (N.B.: The accents just marked on these examples are for illustrative purposes only and do not reflect the actual inherited pitch accent found in Vedic.)

Typographical Conventions

Quotation Marks

I have used single quotes for glosses of single Sanskrit words even when the English gloss results in a substantial phrase. Double quotes are used for translations of phrases and utterances.

Parentheses and Brackets

In the numerous translations of Sanskrit quotations, I have used parentheses to indicate material that must be supplied in the English, for the passage to make sense. Brackets are used to further identify or define the preceding referent.

Italics

I use italics for emphasis or to single out crucial words in long quotations. Otherwise Sanskrit words ordinarily are not italicized even in running text.

Sanskrit Quotations

I have excerpted numerous passages from both prose and verse texts. These two types have been differently formatted. Prose extracts have an indented first line and then continue flush left, though for each new section the text is again indented. Verse extracts begin flush left, with subsequent lines slightly indented and run-on lines indented still further.

I

Introduction

1. *Gender, Philology, and Ancient India*

The conceptual universe of ancient India is difficult of access. Though later India has been almost obsessively mapped by anthropologists, folklorists, ethnomusicologists, sociologists, scholars of religion, feminist scholars, and the like, and consequently is reasonably well represented in cross-cultural studies, ancient India—the Vedic and early epic period—remains relatively little known to the wider scholarly world. Even works devoted exclusively to India tend to give a slightly nervous (and often distorting) nod in the direction of the ancient period at the beginning of chapter I and then settle comfortably down to discussion of the familiar.

Ancient India remains the province of the philologists—among whom I am proud to number myself. It can only be approached through its texts, and the philological methods employed to investigate these texts may, to the outsider, appear to approach the status of a mystery religion, to be even more esoteric than the contents of the texts they study. As a philologist, a practitioner of this cult, I am certain that the intricacies of the method are necessary. But I also regret the result: that the knowledge we gain too often remains walled off from the rest of the scholarly community, that the process of gaining it is so consuming that we often lack the energy to communicate it to others—and that others will not invest *their* energy in attending to the unfamiliar details that must be grasped in order to understand the whole. Instead, the picture of ancient India presented by those who do not work primarily in this area tends to be a projection of fantasy, a golden age, or a leaden one, created from shards of later India reflected in a distorting mirror.

The relative neglect of this period in the general scholarly literature is particularly unfortunate because it is potentially of such enormous interest. This period of approximately twelve hundred years[1] provides us with some of the most extensive records extant from any ancient culture. It reflects the turmoil of transition from the small-scale, mobile, pastoral society of the Indo-European peoples who entered northern India to the very different social and political organization of "classical" Indian civilization. It records, with amazing detail, complex religious practice, as well as the religious challenges and accommodations to these challenges that occurred through the period. It establishes canons of knowledge in a number of different areas—law, medicine, statecraft, astronomy, and linguistics, among others. And it does all this in texts often of remarkable literary sophistication and narrative power.

This book seeks to make accessible to a wider audience some of the riches that investigation of this period affords us, while at the same time making a contribution to, not merely a secondary distillation from, Vedic and epic studies. As such, it requires a bit of acrobatic balancing on my part and, perhaps at times, some sympathetic indulgence on the part of both of the audiences to which it is directed. To earn this indulgence I will begin by setting forth briefly what the book is about, directly addressing the distinct set of skeptical attitudes each audience will probably have toward this topic and my treatment of it (and toward each other).

The general subject of the book is the conceptual position of women in early Indic culture, but it is not designed as an inclusive overview of "Women in ancient India" and all the institutions and attitudes affecting them. Rather it focuses on a single, apparently marginal female role—the activities of the wife in solemn ritual—and, through an exhaustive treatment of this somewhat technical material, isolates a set of conceptual functions the wife fills in ritual practice. These functions can then be observed in other cultural institutions in which women participate. Examining these institutions from this point of view turns out not only to inform us about attitudes toward women and gender but also to force us to reassess radically the nature of the institutions themselves.

In addition to filling in a large gap in our understanding of ancient India, this work aims to make a general contribution to the study of women and gender, not merely by supplying information about a place and time poorly represented in these studies, but also by suggesting some methodologies to employ in approaching women and gender in other ancient cultures—new places to look for information and new ways to evaluate it.

This last claim requires me to address the major source of skepticism and doubt that scholars of women and gender will probably raise to my approach: the distrust of texts. I have been told by a number of people that many feminist scholars believe that *no* trustworthy work can be done on gender issues for cultures we know only or primarily through texts, especially "institutional," not private texts. Ancient India confronts us with this problem in its most acute form, for we possess no *other* evidence, as we will see when we discuss sources in more detail. Our investigations must all take place in what may seem like the most unpromising of verbal territory: texts preserved by men for men as the foundation and support for an elaborate, well-organized, institutionalized religious system. How can we even hope to glimpse women's experience in these structures, and if we do glimpse something, how can we tell what it represents? We must make the texts tell us things that their composers did not think they were saying; we must read between the lines. Methods for conducting these investigations will be discussed later.

In contrast to the feminist scholars' principled distrust of texts, philologists live by them, and most philologists have no doubt that texts will yield secrets when interrogated in the proper fashion. What philologists may question is whether a "proper fashion" of approach is the use of gender as a category of analysis. My philological colleagues are wary of imposing analytic levels between the researcher and the text, of reading the text through a directed lens. We are more comfortable posing what appear to be limited technical questions—what does this word really mean, how is the genitive being used in this passage? Though most of us are aware, at least some of the time, that *any* question, no matter how innocent it seems, imposes some level of external analysis on the text, some types of questions appear to have more potential to distort the results than others.

Questions that appear to be part of a social or political agenda, whether "trendy" or the reverse, seem the most distorting: they may possibly lead to seeing in the text only what the observer expects. The lens of gender may seem a particularly dangerous one: since gender concerns are overtly so little represented in the texts, there is too much opportunity for "creative" and ideological reading of the scanty evidence, with insufficient controls on interpretation. My answer to this is that the philological method itself exerts this control. The very stodginess of the first-order questions we ask of the text[2] tends to rein us in from ideological leaps, forces us to *listen* to the text, word for word, not impose our mental will on it.

But every good philologist also knows that sometimes answering the technical questions requires having first addressed the conceptual and interpretive ones. It is often necessary to understand what a passage is *about* before one can figure out the grammar, and knowing what it is about means fitting it into the conceptual structures we have created to explain patterns of ideas that recur from passage to passage. Ah, we say, this particular passage makes sense if it concerns the rebirth of the sun—or the three ritual fires—or some other semantic construct abstracted from the comparison of a number of textual passages. In other words, good philological technique often *requires* the directed lens, the imposition of an analytical level.

In paying attention to gender, I simply seek to add to the stock of available conceptual structures, interpretive schemata, and to do so through the application of common philological methodologies: collection, confrontation, and context-sensitive reading of a variety of texts. I am not a theoretician, and I will not engage with the extensive theoretical literature in gender studies—nor that having to do with other concepts, like gift-exchange, that will come up in the course of this work.

2. *Hospitality, Ritual, and Gender*

Let me begin by sketching out what a concern with gender will gain us in analyzing some ancient Indian institutions that are ordinarily discussed without reference to gender. This book is in many ways about the relationships obtaining in ancient Indian (Ārya̅n) society, especially the relationships between virtual strangers who nonetheless share societal bonds—between (male) members of the human Ārya̅n community, but also between human beings and their gods, and living humans and their ancestors. As has been frequently discussed both in specifically Indic and more generally Indo-European context, these relationships are regulated by an elaborate code of guest-friendship, hospitality obligations, carefully calibrated reciprocity, and mutual gift-exchange.[3] Despite the extensive literature on this subject, several features of these relationships deserve further investigation.

First among these is the connection between ritual and hospitality. Though the similarities between the solemn (śrauta) ritual of early India and the (human) guest reception required by hospitality obligations have been noted, principally by Thieme,[4] the pervasive parallels between these two institutions, even in nonobvious places, seem to have been insufficiently appreciated.

Nor, I think, has proper notice been taken of what must have been the central emotion evoked by these relationships, namely *anxiety*. The elaborate codes of hospitality exist in order to exert some measure of control over potentially dangerous contact between strangers. Contact between men and gods is even more perilous, since the gods hold most of the cards. The fantastic intricacy of śrauta ritual can be interpreted again as a control mechanism, to regulate the damage that can result from such meetings.

The nature of the contact—and its inherent anxieties and rewards—are cast in an interesting and unexpected light when we focus on a figure not usually considered in this connection. Though we tend to think of these relationships as forged between males (and indeed they are, in some sense), the pivotal, mediating figure between the males is frequently a woman. She often dispenses hospitality and, perhaps more important, she is often the means of making alliances—through marriage. She performs this mediating role not only between *human* males but also between men and gods. Though her activity in the human sphere has occasionally been noted, her linkage of human and divine has heretofore been unnoticed, as far as I know. In the body of the book I will use the woman as a lens to examine anew the crucial relationships that bound Ārya society, and in the process we will learn more about the women themselves and their conceptual position in that society.

I will begin (in part II) by examining a brief but emblematic story from the middle Vedic period, whose key figure is a woman and which dramatizes both divine (ritual) and human (narrative) relationships. In certain ways the rest of the book will simply pursue the questions raised by this little tale.

I will then turn, in the heart of the book (part III), to an extended consideration of women's roles in solemn Vedic ritual. The vast amount of textual material on śrauta ritual (to be discussed later) is an almost entirely unutilized resource for the study of women in ancient India, but it presents an ideal laboratory for this investigation. The very constriction of focus, the importance of the forces (gods and divine powers) assembled and unleashed, the removal from everyday life and the practicalities that rule behavior there—all this contributes to a very dramatic and starkly outlined picture of women and their functional roles in a realm where abstract relationships are enacted and encoded.

Having formed our views in this world of pure concept, we can then apply them to the messy sprawl of everyday life, primarily as depicted in epic narrative and as regulated in the legal literature. The two areas we will primarily explore here will be that of hospitality and gift-exchange on the one hand (part IV), and marriage (also as an exchange relation) on the other (part V).

Before embarking on the real topic of the book, however, it is necessary to situate readers unfamiliar with the territory in the universe of ancient India—by giving a brief survey of our sources, some of the methodologies we use to investigate them, and some of the central concepts about women we identify in these sources.

3. Materials for the Study of Women in Ancient India

What follows is not intended as a general overview of Vedic literature and religion. Such a survey is found in the introduction to my 1991 book, *The ravenous hyenas and the wounded sun: Myth and ritual in ancient India*, as well as in Jamison and Witzel (forthcoming a and b). Rather, it will concentrate on the *types* of materials available for gender studies and their problems and possibilities. As I noted above, the problems appear at first glance to be rather serious.

First we must acknowledge what we lack, and perhaps first among these is the absence of any utilizable material remains that can be definitely identified with the people of our texts. Our materials are entirely verbal, and so we lack access to the visual, to the sort of imagery and iconography of women and their activities that have been so sensitively interpreted by investigators of other historical periods. There are no pictures, only words. Needless to say, we also completely lack the evidence of direct testimony and observation of women that has made the study of women and gender in non-Western cultures more often an anthropological than an historical enterprise.

Moreover, the nature of the texts—indeed their sheer bulk—is the symptom of another problem. The texts are entirely religious (though with "religion" quite broadly defined), chronicling an elaborate institutional religion, requiring significant material resources and social organization, privileged in its socioeconomic class. The texts owe their preservation to diligent oral transmission over many generations, spanning centuries—indeed, millennia—and the procedures of this oral transmission skew the types of texts preserved. In order to transmit these holy texts unaltered, intricate systems of mnemonic devices were devised that acted as self-checking mechanisms to ensure that not a syllable was lost or changed. These mnemonic devices were only as good as the next generation, however. The transmission of these texts was managed through "schools," passed from teacher to student in each generation. Herein lies the curse of oral tradition from our point of view. Correct transmission required highly structured, quasi-official organizations, with the economic leisure to devote the lives of countless people to the task of being mnemonic automata, impersonal channels of transmission century after century. Such organizations are unlikely to have been in the hands of women, or to include women much if at all. Though we may think of oral traditions as "folky," "informal," "noninstitutional"—hence a potential haven for women's lore—in fact for such a tradition to endure for very long, it must be the opposite: regimented, institutionalized, and purposeful, qualities not likely to be available to groupings of women in the ancient world, especially over many generations.[5] A text needs to be accepted into this tradition to survive: be orthodox or be forgotten.

From the beginning we must face the fact that we are not going to hear an authentic woman's voice—or at least not without tampering by those who have inserted it into the tradition for their own reasons. There will be no forgotten diaries unearthed in the attic, no cache of letters that can serve as a private and direct channel to women's experience. The types of texts often considered especially useful for research on women, those stemming from the "little tradition" and including folklore and religious texts from loosely structured and heterodox sects, were not preserved per se.[6] Folkloric and nonorthodox elements that are found in our preserved texts have no doubt undergone some processes of adaptation to conform better to orthodox norms and aims.

Examining more closely the *types* of texts we do have, we must admit to another series of gaps. For the period in question there are no historical texts—neither narrative history, such as chronicles, nor the historical raw material so ably exploited by social historians in recent years, such as censuses, birth and death records, private contracts, and land grants.

So what do we have and what good does it do us? As already noted, all our texts from this period are "religious" texts in some sense, but each type of text illuminates (or obscures) a different aspect—legal, literary, ritual—of that all-encompassing religion. I will describe the two chronologically latest types of texts first, as being the most familiar to nonspecialists.

Legal: There exist a number of treatises on dharma or customary law, of which the most famous, though not the earliest, is that of Manu, the Mānava Dharma Śāstra (MDŚ). The texts agree in broad outline, in many of their provisions, and often even in wording, but differ (and even contradict each other and themselves) in many details and in the elaboration and length of treatment. The various codes, though not linguistically very old, obviously are reworkings of older, traditional material. As I have shown elsewhere,[7] we must assume a code with fixed verbal formulae at least by the time of our earliest Sanskrit prose texts (before 1000 B.C.E.). Interestingly enough, the evidence on which I based this argument involves legal provisions affecting women: the killing of a potentially pregnant woman, abortion, and female infanticide.

These so-called law codes are not legislative or judicial codes in the ordinary sense. Though penalties, often severe, are set for various infractions, it is not clear exactly what body would judge the case or enforce the sentence.[8] Rather, the texts are idealized codes of conduct; the notion of dharma includes 'duty' as well as 'law', and many aspects of life that we would not consider part of the legal domain are regulated in the codes.

Literary: The Sanskrit epics, particularly the Mahābhārata (MBh), also traditionally qualify as dharma texts. In fact, large parts of the MBh (particularly Books 12 and 13) consist of strings of legal maxims (identical or close to those in the dharma śāstras) or learned discussions of legal questions. But more interesting is the use of narratives overtly or covertly to illustrate dharmic issues. The narratives show dharma in action, how law/duty is fulfilled or transgressed in particular cases. These cases are often limiting or difficult ones—illustrating the conflict between two dharmically enjoined actions, the sometimes unfortunate results of dharmic requirements, the gray areas where the application of law is uncertain, the manipulative use of dharmic authority to further morally questionable ends, and so forth.

Needless to say, this is not "case law" in any modern sense. We are in the realm of heroic epic, of mythic exaggeration, and in any event the text serves a number of purposes (not the least being entertainment) other than the dry working out of legal puzzles. Nonetheless, it is misleading to read the narratives without an awareness of the legal and religious duties that the participants enact or ignore.

There are a few recent discussions of women in India of which I am aware that make at least some use of the legal and epic material I have just discussed, but almost never in the context of ancient India.[9] Most such studies are concerned with modern religious practice or at least with classical or medieval Hinduism, and they retrospectively quote the same few verses of Manu on the legal status of women, or the epic stories about the heroines Sītā or Sāvitrī, for what they mean or may have meant to a culture several hundred to several thousand years later.[10] The disagreements and contradictions within the legal tradition are not addressed, nor is the important interrelation between the idealized *rules* of conduct in the law codes and the idealized *narratives* in which dharmic principles are applied. In particular, the epic narratives tend to be treated stripped of their dharmic skeletons.[11] Though this use of older materials may be illuminating about the attitudes and underlying assumptions of later India, it gives a disappointingly superficial and anachronistic picture of ancient India.

Moreover, there is an entire textual type, of vast dimensions, that remains entirely unutilized in this area, that of our oldest texts, the ritual texts.

Ritual: Our very earliest texts, the four Vedas themselves,[12] consist of formulae to be pronounced during rituals, not only the solemn semipublic rituals, but also life-cycle rituals (e.g. marriage, funeral, and even such events as the appearance of a baby's first tooth), healing rituals (and those intended to inflict disease), and white and black magic generally (e.g. charms to ensure safe birth, to secure the love of a man).

In addition to these ritual-internal texts, we have an enormous body of ritual-external texts, which describe in minute detail every action to be undertaken by every participant in the whole ritual structure. (Vedic India seems to have been about as highly ritually governed as a culture can get, at least in its upper social strata.) These ritual manuals describe not only the solemn (śrauta) rites, requiring a number of priests (in the śrauta sūtras), but also in the gṛhya sūtras the domestic (gṛhya) rituals to be performed within the household as a part of daily life and at prescribed stages of life.

There is also an earlier stratum of exegetical texts (the Brāhmaṇas) that presuppose the rituals more or less as described in the śrauta sūtras and comment on the meaning and purpose of various details in the ritual and of individual rituals themselves. Besides providing us with our first Indic theology, these texts are also rich sources of mythological and folkloric material.

Now, of course, given the means of textual preservation, these ritual texts do not describe "women's rituals."[13] But women are necessary ritual participants not only in the domestic but also in the solemn rites, and their functions and activities in the ritual realm are therefore described on a minute-by-minute basis.

Unfortunately these ritual texts are rather inaccessible, or at least difficult to use, for the nonspecialist. Many of them have not been translated, and even for those scholars with some Sanskrit, the language of ritual texts is especially enigmatic and condensed. Even translations do not help much: one needs a familiarity with the seemingly endless minutiae of Vedic ritual to make sense of the details. And in the end it is this fullness of detail that makes the texts so valuable: though women participants do not dominate in ritual performance, the comprehensive and objective[14] reporting of every ritual action ensures that women's ritual contributions will make their way into the record.

Yet these texts have hardly been exploited for what they can tell us about women in ancient India.[15] This is another reason that this study mines the ritual material so extensively: these are precisely the types of texts that tell us things they do not know they are saying. The women acting in the ritual are not the point of the texts; as we will see, they are fairly marginal at least in terms of the composers' focus. They are neither demonized nor divinized as fictional exemplars so often are. They simply sit in the background, waiting to perform their little tasks—to carry a pot of water or exchange glances with a priest. But when we assemble these little tasks, they produce a remarkably telling conceptual portrait.

4. Some Methods for the Study of Women in Ancient India

As I have mentioned in notes 9 to 11, though some of the texts discussed earlier occasionally make their appearance in discussions of "Indian women" or "women in Hinduism" or the like, the material is usually not treated with much sophistication. Legal maxims or narrative skeletons are abstracted out of context and strung together like so many beads on an ideological necklace. The richness of each individual text, the effect on the text of its genre and intent, the ambivalence and internal contradictions, both deliberate and unconscious, that complicate the text—all of these are often ignored. So perhaps the most important "methodology" to emphasize is the simple aim of the good philologist, to engage as fully as possible with each text on all levels and to try to understand it as an entity on its own terms as far as possible, rather than subordinating it to the purposes of the investigator. This aim should not have to be stated, but in recent decades skepticism about the possibility of achieving it fully has led many scholars to reject the aim itself (as theoretically naive) and to substitute the unconstrained, idiosyncratic "reading" of the modern interpreter. I continue to believe that we must respect the integrity of each text and to endeavor to model ourselves, in the first instance, on the original audience for this text—to try to hear with ancient ears.

This is not to say that separate texts should not be compared, or that passive and uncritical "appreciation" should be substituted for analysis. Indeed, the different types of texts can act as limiting or correcting mechanisms for each other to some degree. The submissive woman of (some parts of) the legal texts is not the aggressively active one of many epic narratives nor the punctilious ritual partner of the ritual texts. All these images are mediated through male mentalities—they are, of course, not direct images of real ancient Indian women, nor even the idealized portraits that such women would have had of themselves. But the dialogic confrontation of the varying images gives us an opening, to peer behind the relatively homogeneous facade that each text type presents individually.

In addition to these fairly obvious procedures—those that I would hope any reasonably sensitive reader would employ—let me bring up a powerful method that has been neglected (and indeed viewed with suspicion) in feminist studies, that of linguistic analysis, especially close attention to the semantic nexus of words and grammatical constructions. Let me put this more broadly: close attention to *language* in all its uses can be a powerful tool in gender studies because it can give us access to levels of expression that are not the overt intent of a text. All words have a complex nexus of associations, of primary and secondary meanings, of habitual collocations available to the speakers of the language and the inhabitants of the culture it expresses. By careful attention to the original language of a text, we can gain at least partial access to this associational nexus and begin to see the conceptual links between apparently separate notions that are particular to the culture.

Let me give two related English examples. The word 'porridge' is a fairly rare one for American English speakers, and for most of us—however long removed from childhood—it has one strong semantic association. This single word, no matter what context we hear it in, can instantly evoke the whole narrative complex of Goldilocks and the Three Bears, the bowls of steaming porridge, the messy beds. The word 'oatmeal' on the other hand does not. Alertness to the different associational ranges of two apparent synonyms can give a window on the cultural knowledge of the speakers who have these unconscious distinctions. But marginal vocabulary is not the only source of this knowledge. The same instant access to the same narrative is given by the perfectly well-formed, syntactically uninteresting English sentence, "Who's been sleeping in my bed?" Formulaic language of this sort binds a speech community with invisible semantic fetters that close attention to language will bring to light.

By detailed examination of the usage of words and constructions in ancient texts—their rarity or frequency, their habitual contexts, the level of discourse they inhabit, their potential shock value in unusual contexts—we can begin to construct the kinds of associational semantics that native speakers had, begin to imagine what sprang unbidden to their minds when they heard the Sanskrit equivalent of 'porridge'. This linguistic sensitivity requires a relatively high level of engagement with the language. We must aspire to (even though we will never achieve) the knowledge about the language that a native speaker had.[16]

Why is this of particular value to women's studies? Because of the textual bind we are in. Our preserved texts provide us with a very limited segment of the whole discourse of the society in which they were composed, and this limited segment is not random in content: it represents high culture from an official and institutional point of view. It is the tediously proverbial tip of the iceberg, and what we are after—women's discourses—are way below the waterline. But the composers of our texts of limited content participated in many different discourses in their lives, only one type of which has been preserved. And the stuff of discourses—words and syntactic constructions—travel through many levels of discourse and do not shed all their associations when going from one to another. In other words, linguistic levels are not watertight. We can use language as a sort of periscope to peer below the waterline, if we can tap into the associational nexus that the elements of language are part of.[17]

Language, more than most cultural institutions, is the property of all its speakers, both female and male, who will have similar, though not identical sets of associational complexes, associations that are usually below the level of consciousness and so less subject to political and social manipulation than overt cultural structures.[18] To work only with translations, or to know only enough of a language to stumble through the text with a translation as crutch, is willfully to ignore the potentially most fruitful source of information about the forgotten and marginalized segments of society.

5. Some General Observations on Women's Conceptual Position in Ancient Indian Society

Before embarking on the main section of the book, where full textual documentation will be offered (to the point, perhaps, of the reader's exhaustion), I would here like to introduce, without extensive argumentation, some observations on general attitudes toward women found in the texts, and particularly on the unresolvable tensions among these attitudes. These observations will provide a foundation for the more detailed discussion to follow.

It is easy—much too easy—to assemble a set of misogynist maxims from ancient Indian literature. The collection that follows was made in the course of a desultory afternoon and could easily be expanded.

Rig Veda X.95.15 ná vái stráiṇāni sakhyā́ni santi sālāvṛkā́ṇāṃ hṛ́dayāny etā́

There exist no friendships with women. They have the hearts of hyenas.

RV VIII.33.17 índraś cid ghā tád abravīt striyā́ aśāsyám mánaḥ
utó áha krátuṃ raghúm

Even Indra said that the mind of woman is ineducable, and her understanding is weak.

Maitrāyaṇī Saṃhitā I.10.11 (151: 3) (etc.) ánṛtaṁ strī́
Woman is untruth.

MS III.6.3 (63: 12) trayā́ vái náirṛtā akṣā́ḥ stríyaḥ svápnaḥ
Three things belong to disorder: dice, women, dream(s).

Mānava Dharma Śāstra VIII.77 strībuddher asthiratvāt
Because the understanding of women is unsteady . . .

MDŚ IX.3 pitā rakṣati kaumāre bhartā rakṣati yauvane
rakṣanti sthavire putrā na strī svātantryam arhati
Her father guards her in girlhood; her husband guards her in youth;
Her sons guard her in old age. A woman does not deserve independence.

MDŚ IX.18 nirindriyā hy amantrāś ca striyo 'nṛtam iti sthitiḥ
Because they lack virile strength and Vedic mantras [i.e. women's rituals aren't so accompanied], women are untruth—this is firmly established.

Mahābhārata I.68.72 asatyavacanā nāryaḥ
Women are speakers of untruth.

MBh V.36.56 saṃbhāvyaṃ strīṣu cāpalyam
Fickleness is the norm in women.

MBh V.38.39 ye 'rthāḥ strīṣu samāsaktāḥ prathamotpatiteṣu ca
ye cānāryasamāsaktāḥ sarve te saṃśayaṃ gatāḥ
All business that's dependent on women, impetuous people, or non-Aryans is prone to uncertainty.

MBh V.38.40 yatra strī yatra kitavo yatra bālo 'nuśāsti ca
majjanti te 'vaśā deśā nadyām aśmaplavā iva
Countries where a woman, a gambler, or a child rules sink helplessly like stone rafts in a river.

MBh V.39.59 strīdhūrtake 'lase bhīrau caṇḍe puruṣamānini
caure kṛtaghne viśvāso kāryo na ca nāstike
Don't put confidence in a woman or a coward, a lazybones, a violent man, a self-promoter, a thief, an ingrate, much less an atheist.

MBh XIII.38.1 striyo hi mūlaṃ doṣāṇāṃ laghucittāḥ
Women are the root of faults and have weak understanding.

MBh XIII.38.12 na strībhyaḥ kiṃ cid anyad vai pāpīyastaram asti vai
Nothing else more wickeder[19] exists than women.

Jātaka I.155 dhi-r-atthu taṃ janapadaṃ yatth' itthī pariṇāyikā
Fie on the country where a woman is the leader.

J. I.289 sabbitthiyo kare pāpaṃ
All women do evil.

J. I.295 musā tāsaṃ yathā saccaṃ saccaṃ tāsaṃ yathā musā
For them (fem.) falsehood is like truth and truth like falsehood.

J. I.295 itthiyo nāma akataññū mittadūbhā
Women are ingrates and betrayers of friends.

It is not my intention to deny the emotional accuracy of the attitudes here expressed. I have no doubt that women were often regarded with the deep suspicion and fear that many of these maxims reflect. Much of the legal system[20] is designed to control the weak or dangerous features of woman's character, while valuing her life (except when fertile) at the meanest level.[21] Her religious life was also circumscribed. Women were barred, at least theoretically,[22] from studying the Veda, though their presence at and participation in Vedic solemn ritual attests to the fact that they were not prevented from hearing it or indeed from speaking Vedic mantras.

As an example of the careful regulation of all aspects of women's lives, it is instructive briefly to examine the taboos relating to menstruation. As we will see, a menstruating woman is very polluting and must be at least partially removed from ritual.[23] Other activities that must be shielded from the sight of a menstruating woman include Veda study (Gonda 1980, pp. 97, 201) and the eating of a Śrāddha dinner[24] (MDŚ III.239), and she should not look at heavenly bodies (Gonda 1980, 309). A man should not have sex with his menstruating wife or even lie in the same bed (MDŚ IV.40–42); a Brahman should not talk to a menstruating woman (MDŚ IV.57) or eat food touched by one (MDŚ IV.208). Cleansing is prescribed for one who has touched a menstruating woman (MDŚ V.85).

But a famous episode with a menstruating woman as its central character points up the contradictions in the treatment of women. One of the best-known scenes in the Mahābhārata is the outrageous assault on the Pāṇḍavas' wife Draupadī after her husband Yudhiṣṭhira, the oldest Pāṇḍava brother, has gambled her away (MBh II.59ff.). She is dragged while menstruating into the Sabhā, the 'assembly' of men, which her polluting state precludes her from attending. But while many have noted this exclusion, the implications of the *grounds* for her exclusion seem to be overlooked: if it is menstruating women that are barred from the Sabhā, this suggests that *non*menstruating women are not. Indeed, later in the MBh (V.127) the venerable Gāndhārī is specifically summoned to the Sabhā to talk some sense into her wayward son Duryodhana, and she delivers to him and the whole assembly a powerfully reasoned argument against going to war.[25] We should also remember that though Draupadī strongly protests her presence in the Sabhā, she stays—to display more sense and knowledge of the law than anyone else has so far shown.

The preceding short discussion is organized as a series of "yes, but" statements. The negative sentiment expressed in a maxim or embodied in a legal restriction is certainly true and can be paralleled in other texts in other fashions, *but* a set of prominent examples can be adduced that seem to attest to exactly the reverse. It is thus my contention that though we should not ignore or downplay the attitudes expressed in the snappy adages we can so easily pile up in maxim-mad India, we should always look for evidence of the exactly countervailing attitude. This evidence is somewhat more difficult to assemble because often it is found embodied in narratives or acted out in ritual practice, not wrapped up in a tidy four-line śloka that advertises its point. The maxims thus define *areas of anxiety* about women—their fickleness or constancy, their "untruth" or fidelity, their weakness or power, their stupidity or intelligence—and the texts in general provide a set of meditations on these areas, with figures, narrative patterns, and religious procedures that affirm one or the other of the polarities of the attitude in question.

Let us briefly examine one of the most stubborn and illuminating of these polarities. The maxims quoted above harp tediously on the weakness of women and their unfitness for thought or leadership. The oft-cited MDŚ IX.3 assigns the inherently incompetent female to an unbroken series of guardian males:

MDŚ IX.3 pitā rakṣati kaumāre bhartā rakṣati yauvane
rakṣanti sthavire putrā na strī svātantryam arhati

Her father guards her in girlhood; her husband guards her in youth;
Her sons guard her in old age. A woman does not deserve independence.

Other legal texts constrain her freedom on the same grounds.[26] But anyone with a passing acquaintance with Sanskrit literature, indeed anyone who has studied first-year Sanskrit in the traditional way with the story of Nala and Damayantī, has met an entirely contradictory pattern—what I will call, with a nod to the modern self-help movement, the Smart Woman/Feckless Man syndrome. The Vedas and epics abound in stories of resourceful, energetic, and verbally and dharmically accomplished women, coupled with weak or dilatory men.[27] Other examples besides Damayantī in the epic include Sāvitrī, Śakuntalā (in her epic form, not that of the famous play of Kālidāsa), and Draupadī (especially in the aftermath of the dicing scene).[28] Already in the Rig Veda, our earliest Sanskrit text, the same pattern is found, with Urvaśī, Yamī, and Lopāmudrā.[29] In story after story women see what needs to be done, take command, and order the bewildered, hand-wringing male participants into their supporting roles—and the enterprise fails only when one of these ninnies messes up his part of the woman's plan. (Nala is a prime example.)

These fearsomely able women and the women who "don't deserve independence" do not seem to inhabit the same conceptual planet. What is the source of the narrative pattern that contradicts the explicit doctrine of female weakness? I do not have space here for a full investigation of this issue, but, as some aspects of it will be relevant to the body of this book, let me briefly set forth my surmises. I think the topos of woman as independent agent is an almost accidental byproduct of another major tension in ancient Indian ideology: conflicting (male) religious goals.

On the one hand, as is well known, a man must have sons (and his sons must have sons) in order to ensure not only the continuity of the line, but his own continuance in heaven, as he is maintained after death by the ancestor (pitṛ) worship performed by his own male line. On the other hand, the idealization of asceticism so characteristic of later Hinduism is present, in one form or another, from the earliest period, and one of the most powerful forms of ascetic practice is the control of sexuality, the retention of semen. So males are confronted with a conundrum: they do not want sex but they need its products.[30]

There are several ways to solve the problem. One is to locate the contradictory goals in different chronological strata. Such is the practical and durable solution of the later āśrama system (or system of life stages), in which chastity and austerity are a requirement of the earlier and later stages of a man's life, but sexual activity and procreation are a duty of the middle stage, that of householder (gṛhastha).[31] Similar temporal restriction is found in regularly recurring periods of chastity enjoined on even the householder: during certain parts of the wife's menstrual cycle the husband *must* 'approach' her; during other parts he is forbidden to.[32] In the same way, temporary chastity is required during rituals or parts of rituals, as we will see presently, and the more rituals a man performs, the stricter the controls on his sexual activity become. Thus sexual abstinence can be regularly reaffirmed as a goal in the midst of a busy procreative life.

These regulations make it easier for the man to reconcile the conflicting goals by allowing him to fulfill them one at a time. But I think there is a conceptual component to the solution as well, which removes sexual responsibility (or some of it) from the male. The ideal situation for a man who has both goals is to practice his asceticism (an individual and private pursuit) *actively*, as it were, but to acquire sons from sexual activity in which he is a *passive* and accidental participant.[33] Thus, this ideal male figure is the victim of sex, never seeking it or even welcoming it when it is offered. But, then, for sex to take place at all, we need an aggressor, and who is left? The ideological effort to preserve the image of man as the desire-less ascetic leads to locating *active sexuality* in the female, who chooses her unwitting partner, pursues, badgers, and seduces him, and enjoys sex all by herself.

The Seduced Ascetic is a common topos in the epic; the seductress is usually an Apsaras (nymph) sent by a god (usually Indra) jealous of the seer's extreme austerity.[34] But this narrative pattern is not a novel feature of the epic: it appears fully formed already in the Rig Veda, our earliest Sanskrit text. In RV I.179 the seer Agastya is urged to put aside his ascetic labors and engage in sex by his wife Lopāmudrā and seems finally to succumb. In RV X.10 Yamī tries to persuade her priggish brother Yama to have sex with her and populate the world, but he rejects her, afraid of what the gods will say.

The sexual temptress is, of course, a stock figure in many cultures, but our ancient Indian version is slightly different from those most familiar to us. The Indic seductress seems to me a genuinely sexual being, not someone who through innocence or cold calculation enflames sexually susceptible men with purely external charms, without sexual feelings of her own. The non-Indic pattern ordinarily posits a sexually eager man whose sexual drive is the cause of his downfall; the woman is merely an instrument, though sometimes a conscious one. In the Indic pattern, the man is not eager; his drive must be created, and the woman must work hard.[35] She is an *agent*, capable of independent action and resourceful contrivance in the face of resistance. She also wants sex and enjoys it when she finally gets it.[36]

These qualities are responsible, in my opinion, for the strong female figures with which we began. Once you conceive of women as independent actors, as initiators, in one sphere (the sexual), this conception may well spill over into other spheres. The energy, decision, and intelligence necessary for prodding a reluctant and passive partner into sex cannot be ideologically confined to the sexual arena alone. And so we have the spectacle of a culture that professes to believe women are weak and silly embracing fictional females whose control of legal niceties or strategic planning far surpasses that of the men who surround them.[37]

Thus, we should examine each female figure and each feminine role with skeptical delicacy, for we immediately discern that each feature will, quite possibly, be accompanied by its opposite, will encompass its own contradiction. Women in ancient India are "the bearers of all paradox,"[38] and the first figure we will encounter is one of the most paradoxical of all. Let us turn to the Sacrificed Wife/Sacrificer's Wife of my title.

II

Sacrificed Wife/Sacrificer's Wife: The Myth of Manu's Cups

The intertwined themes of this book—women, ritual, and hospitality—find a remarkably condensed, powerful, and regrettably, elliptical expression in a short tale found in several different versions in the Yajur Veda, a narrative I will call "Manu's Cups." We will begin by examining the texts of this story, in order to establish its thematic parameters, and then in subsequent chapters explore the issues that emerge from this examination.

The story we begin with concerns Manu, here the first man and the first sacrificer, not necessarily the same Manu of the famous legal code.[1] Yajur Veda prose contains several nearly identical narratives in which an "Asura-killing voice" (asuraghnī́ vā́c) enters various belongings of Manu (his ritual cups, his bull, his wife) and destroys all Asuras who hear it.[2] In order to stop this ongoing slaughter, two Brahmans of the Asuras approach Manu, ask for each offending vessel containing the voice, and either smash it or sacrifice with it. But the voice, liberated, enters another vessel and continues to cause destruction.

There are two main strains of this story. The more familiar one is found in ŚB I.1.4.14ff., easily accessible in J. Eggeling's translation. Unfortunately, this appears to be an abbreviated and reworked version, adapted for a newer ritual purpose. In this ŚB version the order of the elements in which the "voice" takes refuge is bull (ṛṣabhá)—wife (jāyā́)—cups (yajñapā́trāṇi), and the sacrifices of the bull and even of the wife are accomplished without fanfare. The voice lodges finally in the cups, where it still remains, keeping the Asuras away from the sacrifice.

The earlier version appears in nearly identical passages in MS (IV.8.1) and KS (XXX.1), in other words in the earliest Sanskrit prose we possess. In this version the order of invasion is more sensible: cups (MS pā́trāṇi/KS kapālāni)—bull (ṛṣabhá)—wife (pátnī),[3] with an obvious progression up the scale of importance of the object to be surrendered. (Or so I would hope.) In both MS and KS the cups are destroyed and the bull sacrificed, but the killing of Manu's wife is averted, just barely, by the intervention of Indra. Indra disguises himself as a Brahman and sacrifices (or threatens to) the two Asuric Brahmans in place of Manu's wife, who is then released.

In both MS and KS the narration of this story is both remarkably coherent and remarkably full, given their usual practice. It is not interrupted by ritual exegesis (though of course it has a ritual application), and it includes a fair amount of dialogue, including some that is riddling and sophistic. Since the exact details of the vocabulary and syntax of the narratives will be crucial in what follows, I give here the texts and translations of all three versions.[4]

In the MS[5]

MS IV.8.1 (106: 6) mánor vái pā́trāṇy āsāṁs téṣāṁ samāhanyámānānāṁ yā́vantó 'surā upā́śṛṇvaṁs tā́vantas tád áhar nā́bhavann átha vā́ etáu tárhy ásurāṇāṃ brāhmaṇā́ ā́stāṃ tṛṣṭā́várutrī tā́ abruvaṁś cíkitsataṃ nā íti tā́ abrūtāṃ máno yájvā vái śraddhā́devo 'sīmā́ni nau pā́trāṇi dehī́ti tā́ni vā́ ā́bhyām adadāt tā́ny agnínā sámakṣāpayatāṃ tā́n jvālā́n ṛṣabháḥ sámaleṭ tā́ṁ sā́ menír ánvapadyata tásya ruvató yā́vantó 'surā upā́śṛṇvaṁs tā́vantas tád áhar nā́bhavaṁs tā́ abrūtāṃ máno yájvā vái śraddhā́devo 'sy anéna tva [*sic*] ṛṣabhéṇa yājayāvéti téna vā́ enam ayājayatāṃ tásya śróṇim ánavattāṁ suparṇá údamathnāt sā́ *manā́yyā upástham ā́padyata tā́ṁ sā́ menír ánvapadyata tásyā vádantyā yā́vantó 'surā upā́śṛṇvaṁs tā́vantas tád áhar nā́bhavaṁs tā́ abrūtāṃ máno yájvā vái śraddhā́devo 'sy anáyā tvā pátnyā yājayāvéti tā́ṃ prókṣya páryagniṃ kṛtvédhmā́barhír áchaitāṁ sá índro 'ved imé vái té asuramāyé mánuṃ pátnyā vyàrdhayatā íti tám índro brāhmaṇó bruvāṇá upáit sò 'bravīn máno yájvā vái śraddhā́devo 'si yājáyāni tvā katamás tvám asi brāhmaṇáḥ

kíṃ brāhmaṇásya pitáraṃ kím u pṛchasi mātáram
śrutáṃ céd asmin védyaṁ sá pitā́ sá pitāmaháḥ

kénéty ābhyā́ṃ brāhmaṇā́bhyām ítī́śe 'háṃ brāhmaṇáyor ítī́śiṣe hī́ty abravīd átithipatir vā́vā́tithīnām īṣṭā íti sá dvitī́yāṁ védim úddhantum úpāpadyata tā́ idhmā́barhír bíbhratā áitāṃ tā́ abrūtāṃ kím idáṃ karoṣītīmáṃ manuṁ [*sic*] yājayiṣyāmī́ti kénéti yuvā́bhyām íti tā́ avittām índro vā́véti táu nyásyedhmā́barhíḥ pálāyetāṃ [Bb] táu yád adhāvatāṃ parástād evéndraḥ pratyáit táu vṛ́śaś cáivāṣaś cābhavatāṃ tád vṛ́śasya cáivāṣasya ca jánma sá mánur índram abravīt sáṃ me yajñáṁ sthāpaya mā́ me yajñó víkṛṣṭo bhūd íti sò 'bravīd yátkāma etā́m ā́labdhāḥ sá te kā́maḥ sámṛdhyatām áthótsṛjéti tā́ṁ vā́ údasṛjat

Manu had (some) cups. When they crashed together, as many Asuras as heard them ceased to exist on that day. But at this time there were two Brahmans of the Asuras, (named) Tṛṣṭa and Avarutri. (The rest of the Asuras) said to them, "Heal us!" They two said, "Manu, you are a worshiper with Śraddhā[6] as your deity. Give us these cups." He gave them to them. They burned them with fire. A bull licked up the flames. "Meni"[7] came after/entered him. As many Asuras as heard him bellowing ceased to exist on that day. They two said, "Manu, you are a worshiper with Śraddhā as your deity. We will perform worship for you with this bull." With it they performed worship for him. An eagle stole its haunch, (still) unoffered. It dropped in the lap of Manu's wife. "Meni" came after/entered her. As many Asuras as heard her speaking ceased to exist on that day. They two said, "Manu, you are a worshiper with Śraddhā as your deity. We will perform worship for you with this wife." Having sprinkled her, having performed the circuit of the fire, they went for firewood and barhis. Indra realized, "These two of Asuric magic power will deprive Manu of his wife." Indra, calling himself a Brahman, approached him. He said, "Manu, you are a worshiper with Śraddhā as your deity. I will perform worship for you." "How much of a Brahman are you?"

"Do you ask about the father of a Brahman, about his mother?
If sacred knowledge is in him, that is his father, that is his grandfather."

"With what (will you perform the worship)?" "With these two Brahmans." "Am I master of the two Brahmans?" "Indeed you are master," said (Indra), "A lord of guests [host] is master of his guests." He went to dig up the second vedi. They two came bringing firewood and barhis. They said, "What is this you're doing?" "I am going to perform worship for this Manu." "With what?" "With you two." They knew, "(It's) Indra." Throwing down the firewood and barhis, they fled. When they ran, Indra went toward them from behind. They became *vṛśa* and *evāṣa* [noxious animals or worthless plants]. That is the origin of *v.* and *e.* Manu said to Indra, "Complete my worship. Don't let my worship be destroyed." He said, "Whatever you desired in binding her [the wife] for worship, let that wish be fulfilled. But set her free." He set her free.

In the KS[8]

KS XXX.1 (181: 5)/KapS XLVI.4 manor vai kapālāny āsaṁs tair yāvato-yāvato 'surān abhyupādhāt te parābhavann atha tarhi triṣṭāvarutrī āstām asura-brahmau tā asurā abruvann imāni manukapālāni yācethām iti tau prātaritvānā abhiprāpadyetāṃ vāyave 'gnā3i vāyava indrā3 iti kiṃkāmau stha ity abravīd imāni nau kapālāni dehīti tāny ābhyām adadāt tāny araṇyaṃ parāhṛtya samapiṁṣṭāṃ tan manor gāvo 'bhivyatiṣṭhanta tāny ṛṣabhas samaleṭ tasya ruvato yāvanto 'surā upāśṛṇvaṁs te parābhavaṁs tau prātaritvānā abhiprāpadyetāṃ vāyave 'gnā3i vāy-ava indrā3 iti kiṃkāmau stha ity abravīd anena tvarṣabhena yājayāveti tat patnī yajur vadantī pratyapadyata tasyā dyāṃ vāg ātiṣṭhat tasyā vadantyā yāvanto 'surā upāśṛṇvaṁs te parābhavaṁs tasmān naktaṁ strī candrataraṃ vadati tau prātarit-vānā abhiprāpadyetāṃ vāyave 'gnā3i vāyava indrā3 iti kiṃkāmau stha ity abravīd anayā tvā patnyā yājayāveti sā paryagnikṛtāsīd athendro 'cāyan manuṁ śraddhā-devaṃ triṣṭāvarutrī asurabrahmau jāyayā vyardhayata iti sa āgacchat so 'bravīd ābhyāṃ tvā yājayānīti nety abravīn na vā aham anayor īśa ity atithipatir vāvātither īśa ity abravīt tā asmai prāyacchat sa prativeśo vediṃ kurvann āsta tā apṛcchatāṃ ko 'sīti brāhmaṇa iti katamo brāhmaṇa iti

> kiṃ brāhmaṇasya pitaraṃ kim u pṛcchasi mātaram
> śrutaṃ ced asmin vedyaṁ sa pitā sa pitāmahaḥ

iti tā avittām indro vā iti tau prāpatatāṃ tayor yāḥ prokṣaṇīr āpa āsaṁs tābhir anuvisṛjya śīrṣe acchinat tau vṛṣaś ca yavāṣaś cābhavatāṃ tasmāt tau varṣeṣu śuṣyato adbhir hi hatau tāṃ paryagnikṛtām udasṛjat tayārdhnot

Manu had (some) cups. As many Asuras as he covered (?) with them perished. But at this time there were two Brahmans of the Asuras, (named) Triṣṭa and Avarutri. The Asuras said (to them), "Beg these cups of Manu." They two approached (as) Prātaritvans,[9] (saying) "Ahoy Agni, for Vāyu; ahoy Indra, for Vāyu." "What do you desire?" said (Manu). "Give us these cups." He gave them to them. Having taken them to the wilderness, they smashed them. Manu's cows were dispersed there. A bull licked these (cups). As many Asuras as heard him bellowing perished. The two (Asuras) approached (as) Prātaritvans, (saying) "Ahoy Agni, for Vāyu; ahoy Indra, for Vāyu." "What do you desire?" said (Manu). "We will perform worship for you with this bull." Then his wife approached, speaking a yajus. Her voice went to heaven. As many Asuras as heard her speaking perished. Therefore women speak more brilliantly at night. The two (Asuras) approached (as) Prātaritvans, (saying) "Ahoy Agni, for Vāyu; ahoy Indra, for Vāyu." "What do you desire?" said (Manu). "We will perform worship for you with this wife." She had (already had) the fire-circuit made around her. Then Indra realized, "Triṣṭa and Avarutri, the Asuric Brahmans, will deprive Manu, who has Śraddhā as deity, of his wife." He came and said, " I will perform worship for you with these two." (Manu) said, "No. I am not master of these two." "A lord of guests [host] is master of his guests," said (Indra). He [Manu] handed them over to him [Indra]. He (as) neighbor was making the altar. The two (Asuras) asked (him), "Who are you?" "A Brahman." "How much of a Brahman?"

> "Do you ask about the father of a Brahman, about his mother?
> If sacred knowledge is in him, that's his father, that's his grandfather."

They realized, "It's Indra." They ran off. Releasing the sprinkling waters after them, he [Indra] cut off their heads with these (waters). They became *vṛṣa* and *yavāṣa*. Therefore those two (plants?) dry up in the rains, for they were killed with waters. He released her [Manu's wife], who had had the fire-circuit made around her. With it [the ritual]/her [the wife] he succeeded.

In the ŚB

ŚBM I.1.4.14 [= ŚBK II.1.3.17] mánor ha vā́ ṛṣabhá āsa / tásminn asuraghnī́ sapatnaghnī́ vā́k práviṣṭāsa tásya ha sma śvasáthād raváthād asurarakṣasā́ni mṛdyámānāni yanti té hā́surāḥ sámūdire pāpám vata no 'yám ṛṣabháḥ sacate kátham nv imám dabhnuyāméti kilātākulī́ íti hāsurabrahmā́v āsatuḥ

15 táu hocatuḥ / śraddhā́devo vái mánur āvám nú vedāvéti táu hāgátyocatur máno yājáyāva tvéti kénéty anénarṣabhéṇéti táthéti [ŚBK táṁ hā́lebhire] tásyā́labdhasya sā́ vā́g ápacakrāma

16 sā́ mánor evá jāyā́m manāvī́m práviveśa / tásyai ha sma yátra vádantyai śṛṇvánti táto ha smaivā́surarakṣasā́ni mṛdyámānāni yanti té hā́surāḥ sámūdira itó vái naḥ pā́pīyaḥ sacate bhū́yo hí mānuṣī́ vā́g vádatī́ti kilātākulī́ haivócatuḥ śraddhā́devo vái mánur āvám nv èvá vedāvéti táu hāgátyocatur máno yājáyāva tvéti kénéty anáyaivá jāyáyéti táthéti [K tā́ṁ hā́lebhire] tásyā ā́labdhāyai sā́ vā́g ápacakrāma

17 sā́ yajñám evá yajñapā́trāṇi práviveśa / táto hainām ná śekatur nírhantum . . .

Manu had a bull. In it an Asura-killing, rival-killing voice entered. The Asuras and demons kept being crushed because of its [bull's] snorting and roaring. The Asuras consulted together: "Alas, evil pursues us (as) this bull. How shall we trick / destroy him?" There were two Brahmans of the Asuras (called) Kilāta and Ākuli.

They two said, "Manu has Śraddhā as his deity (they say). Let us two find out." They went (to him) and said, "Manu, we will perform worship for you." "With what?" "With this bull." "OK." [K: They took it (for sacrifice).] When it had been taken (for sacrifice), its voice departed.

It entered Manu's wife Mānavī. When they heard her speaking, the Asuras and demons kept being crushed. The Asuras consulted together: "Greater evil than before pursues us, because the human voice speaks more." Kilāta and Ākuli said, "Manu has Śraddhā as his deity (they say). Let us two find out." They went (to him) and said, "Manu, we will perform worship for you." "With what?" "With this wife." "OK." [K: They took her (for sacrifice).] When she had been taken (for sacrifice), her voice departed.

It entered the ritual itself, the ritual cups. Those two were not able to expel it from there.

The story is a shocking one, but a paraphrase may be necessary to make clear just how shocking it is. Two strangers come to a pious man and imperiously demand to destroy/sacrifice first his possessions and then *his wife*. The pious man agrees without question and stands by watching without intervention while his wife is tied to the victim's stake and all ceremonial necessities are completed for her sacrifice. She is only rescued when another stranger comes by and suggests substituting the first strangers as sacrificial victims in place of the wife, to which further human sacrifice the pious man again agrees.

This story raises many questions, which cluster around the following issues:

(1) Why does Manu meekly and unprotestingly hand over precious possessions when these strangers demand them? What is the source of the strangers' power, and why do they so suddenly lose their power over him? (2) Why is the wife so prominent in the story? Why does she both wield murderous power and serve as victim, given that the wife is usually considered to be marginal to religious practice? And how does Manu have the right to give away a human being, his wife, with as little ceremony as when he disposed of inanimate and animate property?

I raise these questions now only to abandon them for some time, or at least to postpone demonstrating the answers to them within the context of the story itself. But let me anticipate my later treatment of the story by providing the short answers to both questions. Manu surrenders his possessions and his wife to strangers because of his obligations to *hospitality* and to the exchange relations on which hospitality depends. The source of the strangers' power and their loss of power is the same: the ambiguous and dangerous qualities intrinsic to the roles of both host and guest. This story expresses succinctly the real *anxieties of hospitality* that must have accompanied the inherited and dharmically enjoined host-guest relation. The story contains two gross violations of proper host-guest behavior: (1) The guests set about sacrificing the host's wife, surely both an impolite and impolitic piece of conduct. (2) The host agrees to the sacrifice, the killing of his guests, by another guest. (He has, of course, been sorely tried.)

The wife is so prominent in the story because she in some sense embodies exchange relations. She is a mediating figure between different realms, and whenever ancient Indian ritual or mythology requires or depicts the perilous contact between realms, a woman is often the central figure. This mediating quality is responsible both for *her* power in the story and for her near sacrifice. And her role as mediator, as exchange *token*, allows her to be treated as an alienable chattel, to be given at will.

We will explore both hospitality and exchange relations and women's role in them later. At this point, however, I will begin somewhat obliquely by presenting a detailed examination of the other female role implied by this story, specifically by her role as sacrificial victim at the end of it. In the narrative she is cast as *Sacrificed Wife*; the relation depicted is between woman and ritual. Though it is hardly a comfortable relationship for the woman in question, it establishes her as a participant, if unwilling, in the elaborate śrauta rites.

But a small detail in the KS version shows that even before she assumes the role of victim, Manu's wife already has a ritual role. In the KS she says a yajus ('sacrificial formula': tat patnī yajur vadantī pratyapadyata), the speech that causes the Asuras' demise. Such an utterance only makes sense in the context of solemn ritual. Mānavī is functioning here in the standard ritual role of *Sacrificer's Wife*. The story hints to us that women have another relation to Vedic ritual besides victim, and this narrative hint opens to us the technical ritual literature, which provides us with a rich compendium of textual evidence about Vedic conceptions of women's nature and role, as I noted above. For the *Sacrificer's Wife* is a necessary participant in all the śrauta rituals, and her movements and activities are chronicled as exhaustively as those of the other actors on the ritual scene. Taken episode by separate episode, the impact and value of this chronicle may seem small, but when it has all been excerpted and analyzed, the picture is very different. It gives us not only what it literally purports to—a view of woman's position in Vedic ritual—but also a detailed conceptual map of the ideology of women in ancient India, which we can use to explore other types of texts from other eras and, perhaps, from other cultures, since the coherence and detail of the results can be used as models to evaluate the scattered and often fragmentary evidence from the documents of other ancient societies.

In the next section of this book I will assemble and evaluate this ritual evidence at great length. Afterward I will turn to an examination of the hospitality relation, as depicted in both the narrative literature and the texts of domestic ritual and customary law. Using the conclusions I reached in the section on women in ritual, I will look especially at women's functions in the system of hospitality, and at her role in other exchange relations, particularly marriage. This joint focus on women and on hospitality will allow us to return to our narrative point of departure, Manu's Cups, and see the complexities of relationships and representations that this little story so skillfully expresses.

III

The Wife in Ritual

A. The Wife and the Other Ritual Actors

1. Śrauta Ritual and Its Participants

The system of solemn, or śrauta, ritual in ancient India[1] is perhaps the most elaborate of any ritual system textually preserved from any ancient culture—and, quite possibly, of any observed since. The number and complexity of the rituals themselves, the number and complexity of the texts that describe and explain them, the pervasiveness of ritual in daily life (at least theoretically) are all staggering, especially to a society like ours where ritual is, at best, marginal and is often scorned. I do not intend to give here an introduction to or overview of śrauta ritual. (Brief introductions can be found in e.g. Jamison 1991, pp. 5–32; Jamison and Witzel, forthcoming a and b; extremely detailed treatments can be consulted in Hillebrandt 1897, Kane *HDŚ* Vol. II.2, and in a number of publications devoted to individual rituals [such as Hillebrandt 1879 on the Darśapūrṇamāsa; Caland and Henry 1906–7 on the Agniṣṭoma; P.-E. Dumont 1927 on the Aśvamedha; Einoo 1988 on the Cāturmāsyāni] or to particular features of the śrauta system [such as Minkowski 1991 on the Maitrāvaruṇa priest]. Moreover, nothing yet surpasses the description and analysis of the śrauta system found in Lévi's 1898 groundbreaking study *La Doctrine du sacrifice dans les Brāhmaṇas*, and the more general work of Hubert and Mauss [1898], which depends in great part on Lévi's treatment.)

Indeed, comparatively little work of this type has been done since. So much energy is required simply to assemble and organize descriptively accurate accounts of individual rituals that little second-order work—analyzing the rituals thus presented—is to be found. What follows seeks to make a contribution to this genre by examining the *conceptual structures* that seem to shape the baroquely detailed ritual realizations. I will attempt to make as clear as possible the precise ritual context in which are embedded the particular details discussed below, but if a general, minute-by-minute account of each ritual is wanted, the secondary literature mentioned here and elsewhere in this book should be consulted.

One of the underappreciated features of śrauta ritual is what a *social* feat it represents, testifying to a culture with sufficient resources to allow a not inconsiderable portion of its population to devote a good deal of its time to behavior that was not (at least directly) economically productive—and, more important for our purposes, showing a society that regularly fostered contact and collaboration between different social groups.[2] Every śrauta ritual demands the participation of members of several different priestly groups: the representatives of the four Vedas and their assistants, and the more elaborate rites require what seems like a small army of actors from all walks of life, from kings to, as we will see, prostitutes.

The impresario of the whole, the person who gathers the participants and produces the spectacle (and rewards the company at the end), is known as the 'Sacrificer' or *yajamāuna*. The term is somewhat misleading. As noted, the Sacrificer is the man who sets the whole ritual in motion: arranges for the performance, chooses the priests, and pays for the "gifts" that are equivalent to priestly wages. He also receives all the benefit (or malefit) of the ritual: there are no rites performed purely for social or public ends. What he does not do is *sacrifice*, in the narrow sense. Most of the action, both physical and verbal, is the province of the various priests he has assembled. At their prompting the Sacrificer goes from place to place and occasionally says something or makes an offering, but his participation consists primarily of being there and, in some rituals, undergoing a preliminary consecration.

2. *Sacrificer's Wife and Her Presence in Ritual*

One of the main technical requirements for being a Sacrificer is that he must be a householder (gṛhastha); he must be *married*. Not only that but the presence and participation of his wife is required at all the solemn rituals. Sacrificer's Wife (patnī in Sanskrit) is a *structural role* in ritual with particular duties and activities that cannot ordinarily be performed by anyone else. Though treatments of (or rather references to) the Sacrificer's Wife in modern secondary literature tend to minimize the importance of her role,[3] there is much evidence to suggest the opposite.

We might begin by noting the term by which she is invariably referred to. Though there are a number of words for 'wife' current in Vedic Sanskrit of the period (e.g. jāyā, bharyā [lit. 'the one to be supported']), only one is used of her in her ritual role:[4] patnī, the feminine counterpart of pati 'master'. If the English word did not have misleading connotations, 'Mistress' would be a better rendering than 'Sacrificer's Wife'. Her husband is not mentioned in her nomenclature: she is simply the female 'Master' of the rites.[5] Though for clarity I will continue to use the term 'Sacrificer's Wife' in what follows, keep in mind that the 'Wife' is not actually indexed by an explicit reference to her Sacrificer-husband.

The exegetical texts specifically mention her importance to ritual performance. It is often stated that she is half of the ritual, as in

> ŚB I.3.1.12 jaghanārdhó vā́ eṣá yajñásya yát pátnī
> The wife is the back half of the ritual

and half of oneself, as in

> BŚS XXIX.9 (381: 2) vijñāyate cārdho vā eṣa ātmano yat patnīti.
> It is known from tradition that half of oneself is the wife.

A ritual without a wife is not a ritual at all, according to the TB (II.2.2.6 áyajño vā́ eṣáḥ/yò 'patnī́kaḥ). The first major duty of a wife is to serve as ritual partner,[6] and this requirement is so strong that, according to some legal authorities, a wife may not be repudiated once the couple has jointly kindled the fires that establish them as Sacrificers:

> ĀpDS II.11.12 dharmaprajāsaṃpanne dāre nānyāṃ kurvīta
> 13 anyatarābhāve kāryā prāg agnyādheyāt
> 14 ādhāne hi satī karmabhiḥ saṃbadhyate yeṣām etad aṅgam
>
> If his wife is capable of (practicing) dharma and (begetting) offspring, he should not take another.
> If either of these qualities is absent, (another) is to be taken, (but) before the Establishment of the Fires.
> For (a woman) who is present at the Establishment becomes bound to the rituals of which that (Establishment) is a part.

Compare also MBh XII.258.34.

The MŚS makes a particularly strong statement about the ritual partnership of a married couple (in the discussion of the widow's ritual responsibilities to which I will return later), also emphasizing the importance of the Establishment of the Fires:

> MŚS VIII.23.10 sahāvad etau mithunau saṃbhavataḥ sahāgnīn ādhattaḥ saha prajāḥ prajanayataḥ . . .
> 12 . . . tasmād ardhabhāginī bhavati
> 13 yājyāḥ striyo 'rdhabhāk patnī yajñe yajamānasya
>
> This couple comes together mutually; together they establish the fires; together they produce offspring. . . .
> Therefore she is half-sharer (in the ritual).
> Women are fit for ritual. The wife is half-sharer in the ritual of the Sacrificer.

In a similar vein BŚS speaks of the "nondifferentiation of a husband and wife who have established the fires" (BŚS XXIX.9 [381: 2] aviśeṣāj jāyāpatyor āhitāgnyoḥ).

The structural importance of the wife in ritual may perhaps be clearer when we consider rituals with more than one wife. On the one hand, polygamy was common, at least in theory, and the law texts establish various rules about which wife or wives function as ritual partner(s).[7] Later I will discuss the royal rituals, in which a multiplicity of wives is not only allowed but required. But even in the case of an ordinary Sacrificer, the question of additional wives can come up. For example, with regard to the various actions centering around the girding of the wife at the model ritual, BŚS XX.10 reports a debate among four different teachers about whether a group of wives should perform the actions all together or one by one.

A slightly different problem is created by the ritual type known as the Sattra, which possesses multiple Sacrificers: all the participating priests jointly count as Sacrificers in a Sattra and share the benefits from its performance. As they are all yajamānas, they all need wives. The śrauta sūtras in their meticulous (and argumentative) way treat the order and manner in which the wives are consecrated in this type of ritual, whether separately along with their respective husbands or as a group.[8]

We can see from the presence of this crowd of women that the point is not just that every ritual needs a female around, and the Sacrificer's wife is a convenient source for one. Rather, the Sacrificer cannot get access to the full benefits of ritual perfomance without his ritual partner. Each Sacrificer needs to have his own wife acting for and with him in the ritual realm, even if this made for crowding in the "wife's place."

3. *The Wife's Absence from Ritual*

Given that the wife's presence is required at śrauta ritual, a whole ritual machinery has been developed to deal with any temporary inability to take part because she is menstruating or in childbirth. It probably comes as no surprise that menstrual blood is too polluting to be allowed in the ideal world of the ritual ground,[9] and the wife must therefore be excluded if she is menstruating. As BŚS says,

> BŚS XXIX.11 (384: 2) vijñāyate brahmahatyāyai hy eṣā varṇaṃ pratimucyāsta iti tasmād dhavir nānvīkṣeta na spṛśed iti
>
> As is known from tradition, she is in the state of having put on the color of Brahman-murder. [On this concept, see B.2a.] Therefore she should not look at or touch the oblation.

On the other hand, her departure is a grievous loss to the efficacy of the sacrifice. In a well-known passage TB states

> TB III.7.1.9 [= KS XXXV.18 (64: 17)] ardhó vā́ etásya yajñásya mīyate / yásya vrátyé 'han pátny anālambhukā́ bhávati
>
> Half of the ritual is destroyed if on the Vow-taking day his wife is 'untouchable'.[10]

The solution to this dilemma requires much ingenious contrivance in the course of the development of śrauta ritual. The solution suggested in TB/KS is rather stark and unsatisfactory. Both texts continue

> tā́m aparúdhya yajeta / sárveṇaivá yajñéna yajate
>
> Having excluded her, he should worship. Thus he worships with a whole worship.

Here 'whole' should presumably mean 'sound, healthy', not 'entire', since we know half of the ritual has been destroyed. When the worship is finished—and she is pure again—he invites her back, for sex and procreation:

> tā́m iṣṭvópahvayeta . . . tā́v éhi sáṃbhavāva / sahá réto dadhāvahai / puṁsé putrā́ya véttavai

Having worshiped, he should invite her, (saying) ". . . Come here! Let us two 'come together'. Together let us deposit semen, to acquire a male child."

This is the 'expiation' (prāyaścitti).

But this Brāhmaṇic solution is clearly insufficient, since it involves a logical contradiction: the sacrifice is both half-destroyed and whole. The śrauta sūtras improve on, or at least complicate, the solution, by devising various ways in which the wife can be both present and not present. ĀpŚS IX.2.1–3 banishes her with the same words as above (tām aparudhya), but she leaves behind a token of her presence, the bond with which she was yoked at the beginning of the ritual:[11]

ĀpŚS IX.2.1 yasya vratye 'han patny anālambhukā syāt tām aparudhya yajeta
2 jaghanena vedim antarvedi vodakśulbaṃ saṃnahanaṃ[12] stṛṇīyāt

If on the Vow-taking day his wife is 'untouchable', having excluded her, he should worship.

West of (/behind) the vedi ['altar': on this term see discussion to follow] or within it he should spread her tying band, with its strings toward the north.

KŚS (XXV.11.13–16) requires that the wife remove all the consecratory equipment with which she was invested (daikṣārūpāṇi) and sit on sand (sikatā) for the duration of the discharge; during the pressing days of a Soma Sacrifice this sand must be 'in the vicinity of the vedi [altar]' (vedisamīpe). After three days she is bathed with water mixed with cow's urine and may resume her ritual garments and her tasks.

BŚS (XXIX.10–11) has similar, but more complex provisions, depending on what ritual is being performed and what stage it has reached when the wife becomes 'untouchable'. It also specifies that she sit on sand; on pressing days this should be scattered at the mārjālīya, a mound of earth where sacrificial utensils are cleaned. Since this is located half inside, half outside the vedi, it is a notably appropriate place to situate the menstruating wife, who should be both present for and absent from the ritual. On other days she stays in the patnīśālā (the 'wife's hut'), again near the ritual ground but not entirely part of it. She is not to enter the main hall.[13] The waiting period is again three days, the purificatory medium water and cow's urine.

By good fortune (at least for me), at the 1975 performance of the Agnicayana described in Staal (1983), the Sacrificer's Wife began to menstruate on the second day of this twelve-day ritual. The ritual was suspended for the following two days, which were occupied in expiations (prāyaścitti), but two additional days were not added to the ritual. Instead, the actions planned for Days 3 and 4 were for the most part combined and performed on Day 5 (in scrambled order), along with the rites appropriate to Day 5. Activities of Days 3 and 4 that could be conveniently postponed were performed some days later (see esp. p. 236). Unfortunately Staal gives no details on where the wife spent those two days, or how (indeed whether) she was purified for her readmission to the ritual ground.

Childbirth is more polluting than menstruation, and requires a waiting period of ten days (no doubt welcome to the woman!) before she can participate again (KŚS XXV.11.17; BŚS XXIX.11 [384: 3]). Indeed, Kātyāyana toys with the possibility that pregnant women cannot be consecrated at all, because the *fetus* is not ritually fit, a provision he ascribes to "some (teachers)" (KŚS XXV.11.18 na garbhinīṃ dīkṣayed ity eke 'yajñiyā garbhā iti śruteḥ). But he rejects this view (XXV.11.19). Certainly it would not be a very practical restriction, since the wife of a Vedic householder was probably pregnant a good deal of the time.

What happens to her ritual duties when she is thus excluded? Though in certain cases the ritual can be postponed, as in the modern example just discussed, the performance of many rituals is regulated by the calendar, and in any case once set in motion, a particular ritual would be hard to suspend for a period of days.[14] BŚS suggests substitutes for an absent woman, at least in the case of childbirth:

> BŚS XXIX.11 (384: 5) tatkarma putro brahmacārī vā kuryāt tanmantra[ṃ] yajamāno japed eṣā patny akuśalī yadi syād evam eva kārayet
>
> Her actions her son or a student should perform; her mantra(s) the Sacrificer should mutter. If the wife should be indisposed, he [priest] should have it done thus.

In another part of the same text, there is debate about what to do in the case of the wife being absent[15] when her usual yoking (patnīsaṃnahana) is to take place:

> BŚS XX.10 (23: 7) patnyām avidyamānāyām iti / sa ha smāha baudhāyano yajamānāyatana āsīno yajamāna evaitān mantrān nigaded ity atro ha smāha śālīkiḥ patnīsaṃyojakāḥ khalv ete mantrā dṛṣṭā bhavanti tasyām avidyamānāyāṃ naivainān ādriyeteti
>
> Now, in the case of a wife not being available: Baudhāyana says that the Sacrificer, sitting in the Sacrificer's place, should say the mantras. But Śālıki says that the Wife-yoking mantras are "revealed," and if she is not available, he should not go over them.

Even the performance of the simplest śrauta ritual, the daily Agnihotra, gives rise to debate about what to do in the absence of the wife. ĀpŚS offers a material substitute:

> ĀpŚS VI.12.5 yadi patnī nānuṣyād devānāṃ patnībhyo 'mṛtaṃ juhomi svāheti patnyāyatane ninayet
>
> If the wife should not be there, he should pour (water) on the place of the wife, (with the mantra) "I pour nectar to the wives of the gods. Hail!"

A more permanent lack of wife is debated in the AB:

AB VII.9 apatnīko 'py agnihotram āhare3t / nāhare3d iti

Should a man without a wife undertake the Agnihotra or not?

It is emphatically decided that he should (āhared ity āhuḥ), but when, in a section of uncertain textual authenticity (see Keith's note, ad loc.), the question of *how* arises, no answer is provided:

AB VII.10 niviṣṭe mṛtā patnī naṣṭā vāgnihotraṃ katham agnihotraṃ juhoti

If, after (a Sacrificer) has commenced the Agnihotra, his wife dies or disappears, how does he perform the Agnihotra?

The text at this point wanders off into mystical identifications, as the only means to remedy or evade the stubborn problem of his lack of ritual partner.[16] In general, the legal literature requires the widow(er)ed husband to remarry, in order to be able to continue his ritual life (see esp. MDŚ V.167–69 and discussion later in this section).

This problem is dealt with in a novel way in a famous makeshift in the Rāmāyaṇa, in which Rāma makes a golden image of the absent Sītā to substitute for the required patnī and allow him to perform ritual. See Kane *HDŚ* II.558, 683–85; F. M. Smith 1991, pp. 42–43, who also discusses other material substitutes allowed in later ritual texts.

On a very few occasions the wife is specifically excluded or segregated from a particular ritual or part of a ritual not because of the state of her health/body but because of the nature of the ritual. That her exclusion must be specified demonstrates again that her presence and participation are the unmarked state.

One of the occasions for her exclusion is a segment of one of the seasonal rituals (the Cāturmāsyāni), which is considered to pose a danger to her (and probably her unborn children). This is the Mahāpitṛyajña, the great offering to the ancestors, which is made at the Sākamedha, the third of the seasonal rituals. As KŚS flatly announces (V.8.5), this ritual is apatnīkaḥ 'wifeless', and a number of other śrauta sūtras specify that the command (praiṣa) to bind the wife, the preliminary action that makes her a participant in ritual (see below), is to be omitted. Compare, for example,

ĀpŚS VIII.14.1 saṃpraiṣakāle patnīvarjaṃ saṃpreṣyati

At the time of the commands, (the priest) gives the commands except for the one about the wife.

Moreover, the usual joint offering to the wives of the gods (Patnīsaṃyājas [for which see III.B.3a]) that ordinarily closes a ritual of this nature (an Iṣṭi) is also omitted.

The TB suggests the reason:

> TB I.6.9.11 ná pátny ánvāste / ná sáṃyājayanti / yát pátny anvā́sīta / yát saṃyājáyeyuḥ / pramā́yukā syāt / tásmān nā́nvāste / ná sáṃyājayanti / pátniyai gopīthā́ya
>
> The wife does not sit by (during the ritual). They do not perform the joint offerings (to the wives of the gods). If the wife should sit by, if they should perform the joint offerings, she [wife] would be liable to die. Therefore she does not sit by; they do not perform the joint offerings—for the protection of the wife.

Though the ancestors deserve and require honor from the living, this worship involves contact with the dangerous forces of the realm of the dead. The ritual is not held in the ordinary ritual ground, but south of it. The verbal part of the ceremony is done in a low voice, and in some texts the offering ground is fenced from view. The delicate reproductive apparatus of the wife might be harmed by these dread forces that the ritualists take such pains to confine, and so she does not take part.[17]

Yet at least one text finds her presence so important that it gives her a task to do in the safety of her own home:

> HirŚS V.4 (479: 24) . . . na patnīṃ saṃnahyati nā́nvāste gṛheṣv evāsīnājyam avekṣate
>
> He does not bind the wife. She does not sit by. (But) sitting at home, she looks down at the melted butter.

As we will see, the wife's looking at the melted butter is a crucial part of the ordinary Iṣṭi—an act that she usually performs at her place in the ritual ground. Here she is still required to do so, but separated and insulated from the actual ritual itself.[18]

4. *The Wife as Independent Ritual Actor*

It is not difficult to establish that the wife is necessary to the ritual and her absence, either temporary or permanent, poses difficulties to correct ritual performance. It is more difficult to determine to what extent (if any) she is considered and can perform as an independent ritual actor. The legal texts expressly forbid independent ritual action, as in MDŚ V.155 nāsti strīṇāṃ pṛthag yajñaḥ "There is no ritual for women separate (from their husbands)." (Cf. ViSmṛ XXV.15, etc.)

Yet a number of gṛhya sūtras allow the wife to offer the daily offering in the domestic fire,[19] though some prohibit it. On the other hand she does not seem to be officially permitted to act by herself in any śrauta ritual, even the simple Agnihotra, the śrauta version of this daily offering.[20] Of course, technically a man cannot act independently either; he needs a female partner, though as we have just discussed ritual fictions were developed to aid the man who lacked one.

The treatment of the widow of an Āhitāgni (a man who 'has established fires', a śrauta Sacrificer) is instructive. As noted, an Āhitāgni whose wife dies is encouraged to marry again in order to continue his ritual life. In fact, when his wife dies, he cremates her with the fire used for the Agnihotra offering and burns the ritual implements at the same time (MDŚ V.167). When he marries again, he establishes *new* fires, since he has 'given' to his dead wife the fires they jointly established (MDŚ V.168). In other words, the Sacrificer's Wife is not simply an interchangeable part: one slips away and a substitute is inserted. The widower must start his ritual life over again with a new wife, since the old ritual partnership depended on the particular identity of the woman with whom he entered it. We saw above the importance of the Establishment of the Fires in the context of marriage.

Now a widow cannot remarry (at least by the time of the śrauta sūtras and dharma texts), and *her* ritual partnership is also dissolved on the death of her husband, who is cremated with the fires they established. However, at least one śrauta sūtra has devised a gṛhya copy of śrauta rites for the widow to follow—an apparent acknowledgment of her previous importance in the joint ritual life of the married couple. According to MŚS the widow of an Āhitāgni receives a fifth part of the fires and tends this remaining fire with gṛhya rites (MŚS VIII.23, esp. 7). In fact this text allows the pious widow what seems to me considerable ritual latitude, though only within the gṛhya system. She has her own fire drawn from the fires she and her husband established together (MŚS VIII.23.22–23); the Adhvaryu instructs her (presumably in her ritual responsibilities, MŚS VIII.23.3); she can offer not only the daily morning and evening oblations, but also at the time of the new and full moon (in śrauta ritual, the Darśapūrṇamāsa Iṣṭi) and at the change of seasons (in śrauta ritual, the Cāturmāsyāni) (MŚS VIII.23.8). Her offering medium (ghee) and the deities she is to offer to at the latter times (Soma, Tvaṣṭar, the wives of the gods, Rākā, Sinīvalī, and Agni Gṛhapati) are prescribed (8–9). These are exactly the personae who receive worship at the so-called Patnīsaṃyājas ('joint offerings to the wives [of the gods]'), which occur at the end of all śrauta Iṣṭis. These offerings will be discussed later; the important point here is that there are clear śrauta analogues to the gṛhya rites allowed to the widow of a śrauta sacrificer. She lives, as it were, a shadow śrauta ritual life.

Moreover, there are some tantalizing but slender hints that women could undertake more ritual responsibility than the official party line allowed. For example, Manu forbids a Brahman to eat at a sacrifice offered by (among other people) a woman (MDŚ IV.205 na . . . yajñe . . . striyā . . . hute bhuñjīta brāhmaṇaḥ kva cit). If such a provision was necessary, it suggests that women had been known to offer independently. Even more striking is the following passage from Manu:

> MDŚ XI.36 na vai kanyā na yuvatiḥ . . . hotā syād agnihotrasya . . .
> Neither a maiden nor a young woman should be Hotar of an Agnihotra-(ritual).

This law restricts *young* (and in the case of the kanyā, unmarried) women from *serving as priest* in the Agnihotra.[21] As Bühler points out (ad loc.), the next law makes it clear that this is the *śrauta*, not the gṛhya form of the Agnihotra. Again the implication is that some women do perform the Hotar's role, and furthermore that the only disqualifications for this priestly function are youth and virginity: a sufficiently mature woman would do.

Unfortunately, as far as I know, female Hotars are nowhere depicted in the narrative or ritual literature. But, as we will see in V.C.2, under extreme circumstances fictional women, indeed girls, can sometimes undertake solemn rituals all by themselves. For example, the maiden Apālā performs a private soma pressing in the Rig Veda.

Even within the orthodox śrauta system there are tiny indications of occasional independent roles for the wife. ŚŚS I.15.6, in treating the Patnīsaṃyājas, mentions the possibility of changing the command "Called is this Sacrificer" to "Called is this female Sacrificer" (upahūteyaṃ yajamānī), if circumstances require it, that is, if the Sacrificer has died during the performance of a Sattra (see Caland's note, ad loc.). This would indicate that even in the most solemn rites a wife could assume some of her husband's duties *in extremis*.[22] It is probably not an accident that this substitution is allowed in a rite, the Patnīsaṃyājas, that happens in the wife's own realm, at the Gārhapatya, and that has particular ties to the wife, as we also saw in the discussion of widows' rituals.

B. Situating the Wife in Ritual

Before looking at the wife's ritual roles in detail, I must start with a warning: in terms of sheer bulk her role is very small indeed, and her activities are circumscribed. One can read dozens of pages of śrauta ritual at a stretch without finding a single mention of the wife—while the priests and the Sacrificer scamper around the ritual ground reciting and offering. Her movement around the ritual ground is more restricted than her husband's, and for long periods of the ritual she does nothing at all but sit in her assigned spot. Because what follows will generally concentrate on her *presence* in ritual, not her absence, it is possible to forget that for large portions of any particular ritual, she is silent and immobile. I do not wish, by focusing on the wife, to imply that she is the most visible and important participant.

Yet even while issuing this caveat, I want to temper it. Though the wife's activities are comparatively few, they are almost always extremely interesting. She acts independently of her husband; she is not merely his double or shadow in ritual performance. Furthermore, though she is inactive for much of most rituals, when she does act it is often at crucial turning points in the ritual or especially symbolic moments. Indeed, the few incidents in Vedic ritual that have become famous outside the field are ones involving the wife.

It is remarkable enough that the wife's presence was required at the solemn ritual performances, when so much of the legal and cultural system seems devoted to denying women access to higher level institutions. When not only her presence but her active participation is needed, it is not surprising that the ritual moment is often extraordinary. It is always worth paying attention to where this little but dramatically utilized figure shows up, as it tells us not only about the wife but also about the ritual.

In what follows, rather than giving a mere catalog of the wife's activities, arranged in the order of each ritual, I want instead to arrange her actions according to what I see as her *thematic roles*, the functions she performs, overtly or covertly, in the ritual. This will entail some jumping from ritual to ritual, between the simple and the complex, the royal and the nonroyal, the required and the optional, but I hope by this approach to bring out the underlying similarities in superficially very different activities, and to show that some of the extravagant episodes in the complex occasional rites are simply elaborated and dramatized versions of actions in the simpler, regularly repeated rituals.

The three major areas in which the wife operates are the *domestic*, the realm of *sexuality and fertility*, and that of *hospitality and exchange*, but as we will see, these areas cannot really be separated. Before we examine these areas we must situate the wife in the ritual ground and bring her to a state capable of sacral activity, through initiation and consecration.

1. The Wife's World: Her Place in the Ritual Ground

The demarcated place of the ritual, the ritual ground, is a conceptually complex geography bounded especially by three functionally distinct sacred fires. These three fires technically define this as śrauta ritual.[23] The Āhavanīya or 'Offering Fire' in the east and the Gārhapatya or 'Householder's Fire' in the west are aligned on the central axis of the ritual ground, with the vedi or sunken 'altar' between them. The Dakṣiṇāgni or 'Southern Fire' is south of this axis, toward the western end (see diagram).

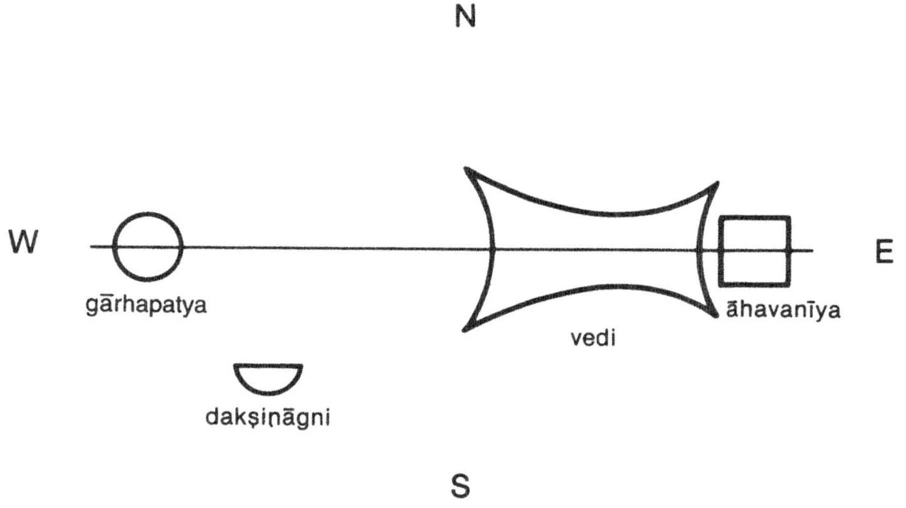

The various parts of the ritual ground have rich symbolic associations, and moving from place to place in this little cosmos is as significant an action as pouring a libation or reciting a mantra. The 'world' or place of the wife (patnīloka) is southwest of the 'Householder's Fire' (Gārhapatya). This is where she stays throughout the ritual except when she is led elsewhere to perform some specific task. The hut built for her in the elaborate rites like the Soma Sacrifice, the patnīśālā that we have already met, is constructed in this part of the ritual ground. Her husband's seat is also on the south side of the ritual ground, but slightly to the east of hers. The positioning of wife and husband is so commonly specified in the ritual texts that it is almost superfluous to cite passages, but compare for example

> MŚS I.2.1.3 dakṣiṇā vedyaṁsād brahmaṇe saṁstṛṇāty aparaṁ yajamānāya paścārdhe patnyai
>
> On the southern shoulder of the vedi he strews (grass for a seat) for the Brahman, to the west (of this) one for the Sacrificer, on the western half (of the vedi) (one) for the wife.

> BŚS I.12 (17: 5) athaitāṃ patnīm . . . jaghanena dakṣiṇena gārhapatyam udīcīm upaveśya
>
> Then having made the wife sit down southwest of the Gārhapatya facing north . . .

Many of the actions performed with regard to the wife happen here at the Householder's Fire. As we will see later, her binding and, when relevant, her consecration occur here. Moreover, it is a general rule that offerings in the Gārhapatya are made on behalf of the wife:

> MŚS VIII.23.14 yad āhavanīye juhoti tad iṣṭaṁ yajñaṁ yajamānasya gārhapatye hutaṃ patnyāḥ
>
> What (the priest) offers in the Āhavanīya is a sacrifice performed for the Sacrificer; what is offered in the Gārhapatya is for the wife.[24]

There are several subrites made specifically to the "wives of the gods": the Patnīsaṃyājas or 'joint offerings to the wives (of the gods)', which are among the final acts of every Iṣṭi, and the Pātnīvata animal sacrifice, the sacrifice '(to Tvaṣṭar), accompanied by the wives (of the gods)'. Both of these also take place at the Gārhapatya and are linked to the wife.

This seat by the Householder's Fire clearly links the wife to the domestic and mundane sphere, but we must examine more closely how this linkage affects the rest of the ritual.

Most of the sacral activity occurs elsewhere, around the Offering Fire to the east. While the wife remains in the west, the priests and the Sacrificer take the sacrificial equipment eastward and pour their libations and speak their mantras at the Āhavanīya. So, in one sense, the wife is physically marginalized in her 'wife's world'. But the Householder's Fire is not only the "home" of the wife, but it is also the *home base* of the whole ritual procedure: the male participants begin there, fare forth to the east for the crucial actions in the middle of the performance, but return to the west to wind down with a series of actions that in some ways reverse the opening activities.[25] Indeed, the Gārhapatya is the literal source of the cardinal points of the ritual ground, in that the other two fires are "taken out" of it whenever a new ritual is undertaken (cf. e.g. KŚS I.3.27).[26] So, though not geographically central, the Householder's Fire and the wife anchor the Sacrificer and the priests to the human world and provide a means of reentry at the end of the ritual. We will return to the wife's function as linkage presently.

The Gārhapatya and the wife who is stationed there provide not merely a spatial foundation but also a *temporal frame* for the ritual. Though the major libations and other devotional actions occur in the busy focal area of the ritual ground, the Āhavanīya fire at the eastern end of the vedi, the whole performance begins and ends at the Gārhapatya—with actions centered on the wife. The ritual starts with the yoking of the wife and ends with her unyoking. The aforementioned Patnīsaṃyājas are performed just before the loosening of the wife, and several other wifely activities to be discussed later open and close the ritual. Thus, though many ritual activities associated with the wife occur at the temporal margins of the ceremony, not at the center of the nested ritual boxes, this temporal placement need not be seen as an indication of the wife's comparative unimportance. Rather, the frame provided by the wife's activities stabilizes the ritual, locates it within the ongoing life of the community, and provides a safe transition into and out of the sacral realms.

Moreover, the wife's position in the ritual ground has another set of associations, besides the domestic and mundane, which will show the unavoidable interlinkage of the wife's functional roles. Because of the east-west orientation of Vedic geography (in which, for example, the same word dakṣiṇa means both 'south' and 'right'), the western part of the sacrificial ground is also called the 'hind end' (jaghana). (See e.g. BŚS I.12 [17: 5] cited earlier.) Because of her seat there, the wife also gets this epithet, as we already saw in a passage quoted in another connection:

> ŚB I.3.1.12 [cf. I.9.2.3, II.5.2.29, V.2.1.8] jaghanārdhó vā́ eṣá yajñásya yát pátnī
>
> The wife is the back(/hind) half of the ritual.

Although this may not seem the most flattering designation, it connects her directly with one of her most important functions, that of bringing fertility into the ritual realm: the hind end (jaghana) of an animal contains its generative organs.

> TS VI.4.1.1 jaghanārdhā́d dhí prajā́ḥ prajā́yante
>
> For from the hind-half offspring are born.[27]

This word (and its derivatives jaghanyà, jāghana, both lit. 'what belongs to the hind end') also refers to human, specifically female anatomy. Women are praised for the sexiness of their behinds (e.g. the 'broad-backsided' [pṛthujāghanā] Indrāṇī in RV X.86.8; the jaghana of a Mahānagnī 'great naked [courtesan]' in AV XIV.1.36; the 'honied' [madhumat] jaghana of a woman in AVP I.55.4), and this part of the woman's body is connected with generation.

ŚB III.8.5.6 jaghanārdhád vái yóṣāyai prajā́ḥ prájāyante

From the hind half of a woman offspring are born.

Indeed, in the MS the connection between a woman's behind and the ritual ground is explicitly made. The prose part of the passage concerns the measurements of the vedi, with the quoted verse indicating the sexual purpose of these dimensions.

MS III.8.4 (96: 15) ṣáṭtriṁśat prakramā́ḥ prā́cī cáturviṁśatir ágreṇa triṁśáj *jaghánena* . . .
. . . / triṁśád yásyā *jaghánaṁ* yójanāny upásthā índraṁ stháviram bibharti

(The vedi) is 36 paces toward the east, 24 along the front, 30 *along the hind part*. . . . "She whose *behind* (measures) 30 leagues holds Indra firm in her lap."

So the wife is seated in a place associated by nature with sex and generation, as well as with the household and domestic sphere.[28]

2. *Making the Wife Ritually Fit*

2a. The Yoking and Unyoking of the Wife

In the next few sections I will discuss several of the actions associated with the wife that provide the temporal frame already mentioned. Most of these, in one form or another, are part of every śrauta ritual,[29] and receive their fullest description in the treatment of the Darśapūrṇamāsa ritual ('Full and New Moon ritual'), which takes place twice monthly.[30] The Darśapūrṇamāsa serves as the model for the class of rituals known as Iṣṭi: the required parts of all Iṣṭis (nonsanguinary rituals) are set forth in the description of the Darśapūrṇamāsa, and only deviations from and additions to the Darśapūrṇamāsa paradigm are noted when other Iṣṭis are described. Iṣṭis are also embedded in other, more elaborate rituals, and so the actions to be presented below are constants in all śrauta rituals.

The most important is the yoking and unyoking of the wife. Before the wife can undertake any sacral duties,[31] she must be girded, in the action known as the patnīsaṃnahana 'the girding of the wife'. While she sits with knees raised, or stands, in her place by the Gārhapatya fire, one of the priests (Āgnīdhra or Adhvaryu) ties a cord (yoktra) of (triple strands [KŚS II.7.1] of) muñja grass around her waist, beneath her upper garment but on the outside of her lower one. Or, according to some texts, she does so herself.[32] There is much discussion in the various texts as to how exactly the cord should be arranged: whether the one loop should go through the other facing upward or downward (BŚS XX.10 [23: 4]), which side of the navel the knot should go on (ĀpŚS II.5.6), and indeed whether there should be a knot at all (the WYV texts seem opposed, the BYV in favor). These details need not detain us, but it is worth noting in one of our first encounters with the ritual manuals to what level of detail they will reach.

This action is accompanied by a number of mantras, which, among other things, describe the action as it is being performed [TS I.1.10.1 sáṃnahye sukṛtā́ya kám[33] "I gird myself for good action."]; identify the wife with several important female divinities, viz. Aditi, the prototypical mother [KS I.10 (5: 7) aditir iva tvā suputropaniṣadeyam "Like Aditi, possessing good sons, I would do honor to you."] and Indrāṇī, the militant wife of the great god Indra [KS I.10 (5: 8) indrāṇīvāvidhavā "Like unwidowed Indrāṇī."];[34] call upon Agni, the domestic lord, and the wives of the gods for invitation to the ritual [KS I.10 (5: 7) agne gṛhapata upa mā hvayasva devānāṃ patnīr upa mā hvayadhvam "O Agni, household lord, invite me here; o wives of the gods, invite me here."]; and express the benefits desired from the performance [KS I.10 (5: 5) āśāsānā saumanasaṃ prajāṃ saubhāgyaṃ rayim "Hoping for benevolence, offspring, good fortune, wealth."].

These mantras may be recited on the wife's behalf by one of the priests, but some texts explicitly state that she is made to say them.[35] What is striking about these mantras is that they are in the first person, as if from the mouth of the wife, whether or not she actually utters them. Here we encounter a discrepancy that we will find time and time again: though it is an article in the law codes (MDŚ II.66) that women's rites lack mantras, in fact much of what the wife does in ritual *is* accompanied by mantras, which she often speaks herself. Indeed, as we saw above, Manu's wife speaks a yajus, to the detriment of the Asuras.

Despite the wealth of detail we have just noted, the girding takes rather little space in any text, a few constricted sūtras with the appropriate mantras usually indicated only by their first words (pratīka). But this girding has a number of resonances with actions elsewhere in the Vedic ritual universe, and how we interpret it will significantly affect what sort of actor/participant we consider the wife in ritual to be.

In fact, the yoking of the wife has recently been discussed by F. M. Smith in this connection.[36] Since he comes to conclusions almost exactly the opposite of those I will present shortly, in examining some (though not all) of the same textual material, it seems worthwhile to investigate in some detail these differing views and the methods that produced them.

Smith sees the yoking of the wife as an act of "restriction" (p. 23), which symbolizes her loss of independence and responsibility, her "limited participation" (p. 27) in ritual. He feels that this restrictive binding has been given a mythological justification: Indra transferred some of his blood guilt for Brahman-murder onto women, as menstrual blood.[37] "Indra's curse" caused them all to be bound by "Varuṇa's noose" (varuṇasya pāśa), embodied in the cord around the wife's waist: "Eternally cursed, she participated in religious affairs bound" (p. 43). This is certainly a seductive scenario. If the first thing that happens to a woman in ritual is to get tied up, it is hard to resist the impulse to interpret this as an almost too obvious symbol of patriarchal domination. There is only one thing wrong: the evidence points the other way. On the one hand, there is very little reason to connect Indra's curse to Varuṇa's noose, or Varuṇa's noose exclusively to the cord around the *wife's* waist. On the other, there is abundant evidence from other rituals and from the mantras used in this one that the yoking had very different associations.

Let us take up these points in turn. Smith presents no arguments for linking Indra's curse to Varuṇa's noose mythologically. He simply asserts the relation, so I will not explore this further beyond pointing out that the two mythic complexes are never associated to my knowledge and that, in general, Varuṇa does not carry out punishments decreed by Indra—if anything, quite the reverse.[38]

Since Smith does make an effort to establish the identification between Varuṇa's noose and the wife's cord, we should therefore examine what he says, and does not say, about this linkage. As it turns out, there is some connection, but it points in a very different direction from his conclusions.

There are only two pieces of evidence for this equation. At the time of the yoking, the ŚB in an exegetical passage explains why the cord goes on the outside of the wife's lower garment, with the typical Brāhmaṇic technique of homologies among ritual, natural, and divine realms:

> ŚB I.3.1.14 sá vā́ abhivā́saḥ sáṃnahyati / óṣadhayo vái vā́so varuṇyā̀ rájjus tád óṣadhīr eváitád antárdadhāti tátho hainām eṣā́ varuṇyā̀ rájjur ná hinasti
>
> He binds (her) over the garment. The garment is plants. This (cord) is a Varuṇian rope. In this way he interposes plants (between her) and this (cord), so the Varuṇian rope does not harm her.

Smith cites this passage (p. 26), but he fails to quote the immediately following one, which *rejects* this identification and substitutes another, more benign one.

> ŚB I.3.1.15 sá sáṃnahyati / ádityai rā́snāsī́tīyáṃ vái pṛthivy áditiḥ séyáṃ devā́nāṃ pátny eṣā́ vā́ etásya pátnī bhavati tád asyā etád rā́snām evá karóti ná rájjum
>
> He binds (her) (with the mantra), "Thou art the girdle of Aditi." Aditi is really this earth, and this (earth) is the wife of the gods. This (woman) is the wife of this (Sacrificer). Thus he makes this (cord) her girdle, *not* a rope.

With this identification, the wife now appears to be wearing the same fashion accessory as a beloved goddess, not an endangering noose.

Why was the first, rejected identification even tried in the first place? Presumably because of the second piece of evidence, the mantra used at the *releasing* of the cord at the end of the sacrifice, the first half of which is

TS I.1.10.2 imáṃ ví ṣyāmi váruṇasya pā́śaṃ yám ábadhnīta savitā́ sukétaḥ
I release this noose of Varuṇa, which benevolent Savitar bound.

The first thing to notice is that the binder is not a punishing Varuṇa, but "benevolent" Savitar, though the noose is undeniably Varuṇa's. But the important features about this mantra are its source and its ritual employment, to which we will return in a moment.

When we examine the girding with more care, we find that instead of signifying the restriction and domination of the wife vis-à-vis the other (male) ritual participants, the act of girding her deliberately recalls two important ceremonial events in Vedic life-cycle rites, one undergone by the Sacrificer, one a previous event in her own life. The girding connects the wife with both of them in a positive way and enhances her status by establishing this linkage.

The watershed event in an Aryan boy's life is his initiation, the upanayana, when he is received by a guru and begins his formal studentship (brahmacarya). This constitutes his second birth and allows him to assume 'twice-born' (dvija) status. Needless to say, like all Vedic rituals the upanayana is complex, with many separate subrites, and differs in details in the different schools, as described by the gṛhya sūtras. But it has two somewhat overlapping features that are especially relevant to our purposes. A *girdle* (mekhalā) is bound onto the new student (brahmacārin). Some texts specify that the girdle is to be made of three strands of muñja grass for a Brahman; others allow muñja grass for all varṇas (cf. Hillebrandt 1897, p. 52; Kane, *HDŚ* II.280–81). Remember that the cord for the wife was likewise three strands of muñja grass. As with the wife's cord, there is elaborate discussion of the types and placement of knots and other details of arrangement.

The student wears this mekhalā throughout his years of study, and ceremonially disposes of it, by throwing it in the water or hiding it in the roots of a tree (cf. Hillebrandt 1897, p. 62), only when he takes the ritual bath (snāna) that signifies the end of his studentship and frees him to marry. In most texts (e.g. KhGS III.1.22; JGS I.19, etc.) the girdle is removed with this mantra, originally from the RV:

RV I.24.15 úd uttamáṃ *varuṇa pā́śam* asmát
Re(lease) the highest *noose* (/fetter) from us, o *Varuṇa*,

which, with its mention of Varuṇa's pāśa 'noose', recalls the very words that accompany the release of the wife's yoke at the end of the Iṣṭi. Though Smith used that mantra as evidence for the wife's particular accursed and restricted status, it is clear that the Sacrificer, while a student, was bound with a cord also identified with Varuṇa's noose. The identification of cord and noose cannot therefore signify a curse directed exclusively against women.

It might be objected that the Sacrificer has long since been released from his fetter, while the wife must wear hers during the ritual, but this brings us to the other crucial part of the student's initiation. At this time he also assumes the sacred cord (upavīta, on the history of which see Kane, *HDŚ* II.287ff.), an emblem of his twice-born state, which he is to wear henceforth at all times, but especially when performing ritual. So, in effect, the initiate receives two bonds, one temporary (though of some years' duration), the mekhalā, one permanent, the upavīta. When the Sacrificer enters the ritual realm, he is wearing the upavīta. He is *already bound* and does not require further yoking. The girding of the wife, then, does not set her apart from her husband and other men, but rather establishes her ritual equality with her husband for the purposes at hand, giving her the temporary status of an initiate.[39] The TB makes this quite explicit:

TB III.3.3.2 etád vái pátniyai vratopanáyanam
3 ténaiváinām̐ vratám úpanayati

This (yoking) is the initiation (upanayana) of the vow of the wife.
With it he [the priest] initiates her into her vow.[40]

When we reexamine the mantras used in the wife's girding and ungirding, we also find resonances with a different ceremony, and these connections in turn help illuminate the complex parallels between men's and women's religious life in this society. When the wife is girded (or girds herself), she says (or a priest for her, see above):

MŚS I.2.5.12 āśāsānā saumanasaṃ prajāṃ puṣṭim atho bhagam
[TS I.1.10.1, ĀpŚS II.5.2, BŚS I.12 (17: 6) . . . saubhāgyaṃ tanūm]
[KS I.10 (5: 5) . . . rayim]
agner anuvratā bhūtvā saṃnahye sukṛtāya kam

Hoping for benevolence, progeny, prosperity, and fortune [/good fortune, body / wealth]
Having become avowed to Agni, I gird myself for good action.

This mantra is a variant of one first found in the AV:

AV XIV.1.42 āśā́sānā saumanasáṃ prajā́ṃ sáubhāgyaṃ rayím
pátyur ánuvratā bhūtvā́ sáṃnahyasvāmṛ́tāya kám

The variants in the first line are unimportant, but the second line translates "Having become avowed to (your) *husband*, gird yourself for the immortal one." AV XIV.1 is the *wedding* hymn.[41] In the ritual sūtras verse 42 is employed at the beginning of the marriage ceremony, when the bride is *yoked with a cord*, also called a yoktra, as in the girding ceremony we have been discussing.[42]

This yoktra is released when the wedding is over, just before the couple is to leave the house (see e.g. ĀpGS II.5.12). The mantra accompanying the release, quoted in the Āpastambhan version, is

ĀpM I.5.16 prá tvā muñcāmi váruṇasya pā́śād yéna tvā́badhnāt savitā́ sukétaḥ

I release you from the noose of Varuṇa, with which benevolent Savitar bound you.[43]

This is a variant of the exact mantra releasing the yoke from the wife in the Iṣṭi. Here too the śrauta ritual has adopted a verse from the marriage ceremony, this one occurring not only in AV (XIV.1.19, 58), but already in the RVic marriage hymn (X.85.24). In a wedding context it makes sense that "benevolent" Savitar fastened the bond. The mythic prototype of earthly marriage is that of the maiden Sūryā with Soma, a description of which opens the RVic marriage hymn. Sūryā's father is Savitar, who would then naturally perform the yoking at the beginning of the ceremony. The loosing of this bond frees her for her husband.

Given the evidence of these mantras, the wife in *our* ritual is not only undergoing a symbolic *initiation*, upanayana, parallel to the Sacrificer's, but she is also likened to the bride in a symbolic *wedding*. These two identifications are not as contradictory as they may appear. Manu states that marriage is the equivalent of upanayana for women

MDŚ II.67 vaivāhiko vidhiḥ strīṇāṃ saṃskāro vaidikaḥ smṛtaḥ

The marriage ceremony is traditionally held to be the Vedic rite of passage for women

in a context where the upanayana is the clear comparandum. In GobhGS II.1.19 the bride is actually said to be wearing the upavīta at her wedding. (On women and the upavīta, see Kane, *HDŚ* II.293ff.) The upanayana and the wedding share other features besides the symbolic yoking. For example, both the initiate and the bride are made to stand on a stone and recite the same mantras about firmness. In fact, we can view the marriage ceremony as a very abbreviated period of "studentship" for the bride, in which she is transferred from parents to husband by way of a liminal period where she is in the charge of the famous series of immortal bridegrooms.[44] These divine bridegrooms may substitute for the guru, who is in charge of the male student in his passage from childhood to marriage.

There is another way in which the period between the yoking and unyoking of the wife in the Iṣṭi resembles the period of studentship following upanayana. One of the restraints on the behavior of both the Sacrificer and his wife during the ritual is a ban on sex,[45] just as a major requirement of a student (brahmacārin) is chastity.[46] The releasing of the student's girdle frees him for marriage; the release of the bride's yoktra sends her on her way to the groom's house and the loss of her virginity. So, the release of the wife's yoktra in the Iṣṭi signals an end to the temporary chastity, one might almost say the temporarily renewed virginity[47] of the ritual.

The sexual abstinence required in all these states may help account for the epithet "Varuṇa's noose" applied to the student's mekhalā, the bride's yoktra (or hair ornament, see n. 43), and the Sacrificer's Wife's yoktra. In the mythological sphere Varuṇa, the moral overseer among the gods, seizes those who transgress against his commands, especially by speaking untruth. His mythological noose is especially invoked during the seasonal sacrifice known as the Varuṇapraghāsa. Thus, the binding of the initiate and the wife may simply be a sort of preventive threat, to remind them to uphold Varuṇa's laws during this sacralized period.

But I think it also may symbolize the restrictions imposed on them, particularly the sexual restrictions. The disease inflicted by Varuṇa's noose is dropsy: swelling caused by retention of fluid. Creatures seized by Varuṇa are often said to "swell up." Sexual abstinence may also be considered a sort of fluid retention,[48] and "Varuṇa's noose" in the ritual realm may simply make reference to the chastity imposed on all, male or female, who are so girded. In this connection we might note that the unyoking of the wife in our ritual occurs simultaneously with a clear sexual and fertility rite, in which the ritual broom, a male sexual symbol, is thrown in her lap or put between her thighs, with the explanation that she will thus conceive a son. I will return to this part of the ritual later.[49]

2b. Consecration (Dīkṣā)

Though his original upanayana and its enduring relic, the upavīta thread, are sufficient to make the Sacrificer ritually fit in the simpler ceremonies known as Iṣṭis, something more is required for the great rituals, particularly the Soma Sacrifice, whose paradigm is the Agniṣṭoma. Here the covert parallelism between the ritual status of Sacrificer and wife becomes overt, in the preliminary consecration known as the Dīkṣā. The two undergo identical purificatory procedures, don similar garments, are vested with similar accoutrements, and endure the same privations with regard to food, speech, freedom of movement, and sleeping arrangements. In the consecratory procedures each is tended by a different priest, the Sacrificer by the Adhvaryu, the wife by the Pratiprasthātar, a sort of assistant Adhvaryu. They then stay in separate huts, the śālā [/prācīnavaṃśa] and the patnīśāla respectively, and each has a separate cow assigned to him/her to provide them with its milk as their sole food, with the portion of each cooked on a different fire. (See e.g. ĀpŚS X.17.6; KŚS VII.4.24.)[50] This separate but equal treatment seems to underscore their relative independence. The wife does not just tag along with her husband, sharing his lot, but has her own dwelling, priest, and cow. The major difference between their experiences is that the actions undertaken for the husband are accompanied by mantras, while hers are done silently (tūṣṇīm; see esp. MŚS II.1.1.33; KŚS VII.2.18, 3.11). Here the often quoted (and, as we have seen, often violated) provision of Manu's concerning the absence of mantras in women's rites is observed.

The actual procedures of the Dīkṣā are well discussed in the standard secondary literature (e.g. Caland and Henry 1906–7; Hillebrandt 1879; Kane, *HDŚ* II), and we need not tarry over them. There is first a preliminary cleansing called the Apsudīkṣā (consecration in water), which involves for both parties washing, cutting the nails, trimming the hair, shaving,[51] adorning with salves and new clothes. Then the pair enter the main enclosure separately, by different doors, and take their usual places. In the Dīkṣā proper they are invested with almost parallel equipment (though made of different materials) in terms of headgear, garments, pegs for scratching themselves, and, most important, girdles. The normal girding of the wife occurs at this point, rather than independently,[52] and at the same time the Sacrificer is bound with a mekhalā of triple-strand muñja grass, as in the following passage:

> ĀpŚS X.9.13 śaramayī mauñjī vā mekhalā trivṛt pṛthvy anyatarataḥpāśā / tayā yajamānaṃ dīkṣayati / yoktreṇa patnīm
>
> There is a mekhalā made of reeds or muñja grass, threefold, broad, with a noose at each end. With it he consecrates the Sacrificer. With the yoktra (he consecrates) the wife.

The parallelism I suggested between the mekhalā of the upanayana and the wife's yoktra in the simpler ritual is here made explicit. The extra solemnity of high ritual has required a species of reinitiation for the Sacrificer, and he dons the mekhalā of his student days.

Both Sacrificer and wife remain girded and in a state of consecration until the very end of the ritual, which lasts some days. In fact together they undergo an Intermediate Consecration (Avāntaradīkṣā, or 'consecration interior [to the ritual]') in the middle, in which they pull their bonds tighter, mekhalā and yoktra respectively, and clench their fists more closely (see e.g. MŚS II.2.1.8; KŚS VIII.2.4–5). When all the principal components of the Soma Sacrifice are completed, the two release the mekhalā and yoktra. The Sacrificer does so with a mantra again referring to the "noose of Varuṇa":

> vicṛtto varuṇasya pāśaḥ
>
> Released is Varuṇa's noose (e.g. MŚS II.5.4.34, ĀpŚS XIII.20.13),

while the wife does so either silently (MŚS II.5.4.34) or with the same mantra used in the Iṣṭi (imaṃ viṣyāmi . . . : ĀpŚS XIII.20.13).

Immediately afterward they descend into the final bath (avabhṛtha), where, without submerging completely (anupamajjantau: BŚS VIII.20 [261: 14]), they wash each other's back (anyo'nyasya pṛṣṭhaṃ prakṣālayataḥ: MŚS II.5.4.35; cf. BŚS VIII.20 [261: 15]). This bath corresponds nicely to the bath that the brahmacārin takes at the end of his studentship, which releases him from the restraints of the initiatory period and releases him to marriage. That bath is likewise immediately preceded by the disposal of the mekhalā (see preceding discussion).

The Iṣṭi paradigm has a simpler version of the avabhṛtha, performed only by the wife—just as only she is girded and ungirded. Immediately after the ungirding and the byplay with the broom, she wipes her face (mukhaṁ vimṛṣṭe/vimṛjya [MŚS I.3.5.18; ĀpŚS III.10.9; BŚS I.20 (31: 14)], etc.) and immediately leaves the scene. This is called the "image of the avabhṛtha" (avabhṛthásyaivá rūpám) by the TB (III.3.10.4; also quoted by BŚS I.20 [31: 16]).

The joint Dīkṣā of the great rituals and the shared restrictions that the Sacrificer and his wife live under in all types of śrauta ritual are the only actions they undertake completely in parallel. Otherwise, though they sometimes act in concert, each has a complementary task in such cases, and they often operate independently, inhabiting different parts of the ritual ground and interacting with different priests. I will now turn to these tasks.

3. *Other Framing Actions Associated with the Wife*

3a. The Patnīsaṃyājas

Remember that when the wife is bound at the beginning of the ritual, she calls upon several divinities to invite her to participate, including Agni as domestic lord and *the wives of the gods*:

> KS I.10 (5: 7) agne gṛhapata upa mā hvayasva devānāṃ patnīr upa mā hvayadhvam
>
> O Agni, household lord, invite me here; o wives of the gods, invite me here.

These divinities also return at the end of the ritual, contributing to the frame, and receive a special set of oblations at the Gārhapatya, offerings known as the Patnīsaṃyājas or 'joint offerings to (Agni, etc., with) the wives (of the gods)'.

When the priests and the Sacrificer return, with carefully described ceremony, from their activities at the Āhavanīya fire in the eastern part of the ritual ground, their first act is to make the Patnīsaṃyāja offerings into the Gārhapatya fire in the wife's portion of the ritual area. This oblation functions as a link between these two realms, the male and the female, and between the human and divine.

The Patnīsaṃyājas actually consist of four oblations: one to Soma, one to Tvaṣṭar, one to the wives of the gods (devānāṃ patnīḥ), and a final one to Agni Gṛhapati 'Agni, Lord of the Household'—the last pairing is the one we met at the wife's yoking.[53] The male deities were not randomly chosen. As a number of texts make clear,[54] the purpose of these oblations is procreation, and each of the gods has his role in this. Soma deposits the semen (and, as we will see often in the course of this book, is frequently *identified* with semen), while Tvaṣṭar shapes this poured-out seed. The wives of course are the receptacles of the seed, and Agni, Lord of the Household, puts this fertile pairing into an appropriately domestic setting for the benefit of the Sacrificer, who is also a gṛhapati.

Either before or after the oblation to the wives, there may be optional offerings to several minor female divinities, on behalf of those with particular wishes: for someone desirous of sons, an offering to Rākā, for one desirous of cattle, one to Sinīvālī, and for one desirous of prosperity, one to Kuhū.[55]

Notice that the oblation to the wives (along with the optional oblations to the other female divinities) is neatly hemmed in by those to the male gods. This confinement is acted out in another way in this ritual: before the oblation to the wives a screen or fence of some sort is erected or held up east of the Gārhapatya to conceal the offering into that fire from the Āhavanīya and the eastern end of the ritual ground.[56] The screen is removed before the next oblation, to Agni Gṛhapati.[57] As we will also see, the female contribution is both crucial to the success of the ritual and poses dangers to it that require it to be under strict controls. The screen serves to confine the 'wives' who receive the oblation: they are present but kept within limits.

While the oblation to the divine wives is being made, the human wife 'takes hold from behind' of the Adhvaryu, who is making it.[58] This ritual posture will be discussed later in detail. Suffice it to say here that this action establishes a linkage between the divine wives and their human counterpart.

The mantra pronounced during the oblation to the wives is also telling:

> MS I.4.3 (51: 4) sáṃ pátnī pátyā sukṛtéṣu gachatām̐ yajñásya yuktáu dhúryā abhūthām
> āprīṇānáu vijáhatā árātiṃ diví jyótir uttamám ārabhethām
>
> Let the wife come together with her husband among the well-performed (ritual actions?).
> You two have become the yoked team of the worship.
> Pleasing each other, leaving behind hostility, you two have grasped the highest light in heaven.

The first action on the men's return to the western end of the ritual ground is thus to reestablish, or reaffirm, the ritual partnership between Sacrificer and wife, and to do so by invoking—indeed creating—divine patterns for it. The wives of the gods, though nameless, provide our human wife with a superhuman model and assert her importance in the ritual schema. Though she has been neglected during the long period of activity at the Āhavanīya, she is now reincorporated into the ritual by this oblation to her divine counterparts, and further activities involving her participation now unfold with the added authority conferred by her connection with the divinities.[59]

3b. The Grain for the Offering

One of these activities involves closing the frame on the first ritual action of the wife in the Iṣṭi—a duty that seems simply a sanctified version of real-life housekeeping tasks, though other conceptual associations spill over onto this simple job. I have not yet discussed this initial action. The grain for the offering cakes at an Iṣṭi is often threshed (ava √han), winnowed (phalī √kṛ), and ground (√piṣ) by the wife. This preparation takes place before the girding (on a previous day, in fact), but in the vicinity of the Southern Fire, with the mortar placed on a black antelope skin (cf. e.g. ĀpŚS I.7.10).[60] Some texts optionally allow an alternate to the wife to perform the action: a 'female slave' (dāsī VārŚS I.2.4.69, ĀpŚS I.21.8), a female Śūdrā (ĀpŚS I.21.9), or just someone else (anyo vā KŚS II.4.14). The reason for the optional performer in all these cases is probably given by ĀpŚS:

> ĀpŚS I.20.12 yā yajamānasya patnī sābhidrutyāvahanti
> 13 yo vā kaś cid avidyamānāyām
>
> The wife of the Sacrificer, having come up, threshes (the grain).
> Or someone else[61] if she is not there.

As usual, her absence is probably occasioned by menstruation or childbirth,[62] and a substitute must be found for this nonoptional task.

The ritual box opened by her preparation of the grain at the beginning of the ritual is closed at the end, in the same complex of actions occurring at the Gārhapatya to which we have had occasion to refer before: the Patnīsaṃyājas, the ungirding of the wife, and the transfer of the broom (for which, see III.C.3). The chaff (phalīkaraṇa) and the remains of the dough (piṣṭalepa) are offered into the Dakṣiṇāgni. As discards and leftovers they are presumably not sanctified enough for the Gārhapatya. The accompanying mantra makes their residual status quite clear:

> ĀpŚS III.10.1 ulūkhale musale yac ca śūrpe āśiśleṣa dṛṣadi yat kapāle
> avapruṣo vipruṣaḥ saṃyajāmi viśve devā havir idaṃ juṣantām
> yajñe yā vipruṣaḥ santi bahvīr agnau tāḥ sarvāḥ sviṣṭāḥ suhutā juhomi svāhā
>
> What is stuck to the mortar, the pestle, what to the winnowing basket, the millstone, the potsherd [on which offering cakes are baked],
> the drippings down, the drippings away—(these) I offer all together. Let the All Gods enjoy this oblation.
> The many drops (that dripped) away in the worship, in the fire I offer them all (so that they are) well sacrificed, well offered. Hail!

Though the wife does not actually make this oblation, the fact that it takes place in her part of the ritual ground, while she is ritually active, links it to her sphere of performance. The household has become tidy again; the dishes have been done, as it were, and the leftovers put away.

It is clear that a desire for domestic order is not the only stimulus for this offering. On the one hand, since even the leavings of the grain and dough have been to some extent sacralized, they must be disposed of properly, or they may fall into the wrong hands and jeopardize the success of the ritual. As ritual material they cannot simply be discarded in the profane realm. On the other hand, as we will see, the notion of 'leftover' is a powerful one in ancient India. In particular, a woman who consumes leftovers is likely to become pregnant—on the mythic model of the goddess Aditi, who conceived a series of twins after eating the leftovers of her oblation.[63] So here as well, the offering of the leftovers may be designed to promote fertility in the Sacrificer's wife, just as the Patnīsaṃyājas are meant to.

There are several other actions involving the wife that frame the ritual, especially the tying and untying of the broom, but these are better discussed in the next section, which treats the wife's sexual roles. The symmetrical and framing structure of the wife's roles in the model Iṣṭi will be laid out after these other actions have been discussed.

C. Sexuality and Fertility: Symbolic Representations

One of the wife's most important roles is that of injecting sexuality into the perfect, ordered world of the ritual. As we have already seen, even her domestic activities often have an undercurrent of sexual meaning. One of the abiding concerns of all Vedic rituals, no matter what else they are directed toward, is fertility, the increase of prosperity through the generation of offspring and cattle and the assurance of good pasturage and crops through abundant rain. This fertility, on whatever level, is often conceived of as sexual in nature, as resulting from sexual activity. Indeed, many other desirable events and states in the natural and social world, like the rising of the sun, are also considered to be the direct result of sexual activity. Now, as we have seen, women are perceived as the primary locus of active sexuality in ancient India. Therefore they act as the conduit to introduce sexual energy into the potentially sterile world of the orderly ritual. Their very presence traps sexuality and its power for ritual use.

This is not an ideological construct of my own. The Brāhmaṇas explicitly state this tediously often. It is the only reason for women in ritual that they consistently recognize. Over and over it is repeated

> yád vái pátnī yajñé karóti tán mithunám
> What the wife does in ritual is sexual pairing.[64]

And activities with the most banal and innocuous aspect can be exegetically tortured into bearing sexual meanings—giving one great respect for the ingenuity of the exegetes.

1. *'Taking Hold of from Behind'*

How is this injection of sexuality manifested ritually? There is a continuum from the most attenuated and subtle suggestions to the most dramatic displays. Let us begin with the subtle ones. There is a ritual posture that we have already met known as 'taking hold of from behind' (anvārambha[ṇa]). This involves touching someone or something from behind, either with the hand or with some intermediary material like a grass blade, while the other person is performing some action like pouring an oblation.[65] The purpose seems to be on the one hand to increase the power and effectiveness of the libation (or other action) by making available to it the power of a second performer, who is linked to the first through physical contact. On the other hand, it also spreads the sacrality of the action or object back to those in contact with it.

In ritual performance this posture is the special province of the Sacrificer, as KŚS stipulates:

> KŚS I.10.12 dānavācan*ānvārambhaṇa*varavaraṇavratapramāṇeṣu *yajamānaṃ pratīyāt*
>
> It is to the Sacrificer that one should refer with regard to . . . touching from behind. . . .

In other words, unless otherwise specified, he is the unmarked performer of 'taking hold of from behind'. Perhaps the most dramatic example of *his* enactment of anvārambhaṇa occurs in the Animal Sacrifice when the sacrificial animal is being led to its death. There is much debate (e.g. TS VI.3.8.1–2; ŚB III.8.1.9–10) about whether the Sacrificer should take hold of the animal from behind at this point. If he fails to do so, he will be cut off from the heavenly world, but if he does touch the victim, he risks sharing its death. In other words, contact is both desirable and dangerous. The ritual solution is ingenious: by interposing material between the Sacrificer and the animal, direct contact is avoided. He both grasps and does not grasp the victim.

In the TS he makes the contact with the two skewers on which the omentum of the victim is to be cooked (vapāśrápaṇī). This must have seemed still too immediate to the WYV, for in the ŚB several other priests lengthen the chain between animal and Sacrificer:

> ŚB III.8.1.9 táṃ vapāśrápaṇībhyāṃ pratiprasthātā́nvā́rabhate pratiprasthātā́ram adhvaryúr adhvaryúṃ yájamānaḥ
>
> The Pratiprasthātar touches him [the victim] from behind with the two omentum-skewers; the Adhvaryu (touches from behind) the Pratiprasthātar; the Sacrificer the Adhvaryu.[66]

This is called a 'mysterious' or 'obscure' touching from behind (ŚB III.8.1.10 etád u *parókṣam* anvā́rabdhaṃ bhavati).

Besides the Sacrificer, the priests also on occasion perform anvārambhaṇa, an example of which we have just seen with the animal victim. The wife is specified as doing so as well, as in the Soma Sacrifice at the so-called Ātithya oblation made by the Adhvaryu:

> BŚS VI.16 (174: 15) ātithyaṃ nirvapaty anvārabdhāyāṃ patnyām
>
> (The Adhvaryu) scatters the Ātithya-offering while the wife holds on from behind.[67]

But the wife's actual, physical performance of anvārambhaṇa is less common than another connection she has with this procedure. The exegetical texts consider almost every task of the wife—looking at some melted butter, conversing with her husband—as *mystically equivalent* to "taking hold of the ritual from behind," as in the following examples:

> MS IV.1.12 (15: 7) pátny ávekṣate 'nvārambhó vā́ eṣá yajñásya pátnyā yajñám enām anvā́rambhayati
>
> The wife looks at (the melted butter). This is the taking hold from behind of the ritual by the wife. Thus he makes her take hold of the ritual from behind.

> MS I.11.8 (169: 15) pátnyā sáṁvadaté 'tho anvārambhó vā́ eṣá yajñásya pátnyā
>
> (The Sacrificer) converses with his wife. This is the taking hold from behind of the ritual by the wife.[68]

Her various actions, however minor they may appear and however far from the center of ritual activity they may occur, are thus classified as physical contact—and not merely with one participant or object in the ritual, but with the very ritual itself. She encompasses the ritual in some sense whenever she performs the smallest sacral action. Thus, though she is physically marginalized during the ritual performance, her forces can be brought into contact with it, through this theoretical 'touching from behind'. Such reclassification of action is not made for any other participant.

Why must it be done for her? The texts provide the answer. Most of the passages cited, having defined her action as 'touching from behind', then continue with a characterization of her ritual role as quoted above:

> yád vái pátnī yajñé karóti tán mithunám
>
> What the wife does in ritual is sexual pairing.

By defining her actions as physical contact, her sexual potential is clearly being both tapped and enhanced. On the one hand, her sexuality and fertility are being spread to the entire ritual by this theoretical contact. On the other, the power unleashed by the ritual because of *its* contact with the divine is spread back to her, to increase her generative capacity. Although the posture itself is not sexual, it enables sexual energy to be communicated.

Again the ritualists have solved a nasty little problem caused by two conflicting principles:[69] the wife's scope of actual activity must be restricted, because she embodies danger and 'untruth',[70] but she must also pervade the ritual, in order for it to achieve the goals of its performance, fertility and increase. Just as the Sacrificer both touches and does not touch the sacrificial victim, in a mysterious (parokṣam) fashion, so the wife both touches and does not touch the ritual performance.

2. Looking at Melted Butter or Boiling Milk

Let us now examine more closely one of the wife's actions that was classified as anvārambhaṇa, namely looking at the melted butter.[71] The ambivalent attitude toward women is quite clear in this simple action, which is one of the early parts of the model Iṣṭi. Immediately after the wife has been girded, while the Sacrificer and the priests are still clustered at the Gārhapatya, they bring a pot of melted butter (ājyasthālī) which has been heating on the Dakṣiṇāgni, set it down by the Gārhapatya, and have the wife look down into it:

> MŚS I.2.5.12 adabdhena tvā cakṣuṣāvekṣa iti patny ājyam avekṣate
>
> (Saying) "With an undeceivable eye I look down at you," the wife looks down at the melted butter.[72]

This is the ghee that will be used to make offerings during the remainder of the ritual, and, as we saw, the wife's looking at it was likened to 'grasping from behind',[73] and given a sexual interpretation.

> MS IV.1.12 (15: 7) pátny ávekṣate 'nvārambhó vā́ eṣá yajñásya pátnyā yajñám enām anvā́rambhayaty átho yát pátnī yajñé karóti mithunáṁ vā́ etát kriyate prájātyai
>
> The wife looks at (the melted butter). This is the taking hold from behind of the ritual by the wife. Thus he makes her take hold of the ritual from behind. Moreover, what the wife does in ritual is made into a sexual pairing, for procreation.

What happens to this butter next? Having melted it on the Gārhapatya, a priest (the Āgnīdhra) then carries it eastward to heat it again on the Offering Fire, the Āhavanīya.[74] Then the Adhvaryu and the Sacrificer look at it, and it awaits its use in the libations to come. This may seem like just so much more ritual frippery, but as usual it has a serious purpose. The Brāhmaṇa texts already cited have made the wife's contribution clear: her glance conveys sexuality into the butter, or rather, as the ŚB explains, makes a sexual pair with it:

> ŚB I.3.1.18 áthā́jyam ávekṣate / yóṣā vái pátnī réta ā́jyaṃ mithunám eváitát prajánanaṃ kriyate tásmād ā́jyam ávekṣate
>
> Then she looks at the butter. The wife is really a woman, the butter semen. A generative sexual pairing is thus made. Therefore she looks at the butter.

The wife thus infuses the butter with sexual capacity while it is still in the more or less profane realm of the Gārhapatya. When it is removed to the divine area of the Āhavanīya, it retains this power and also its connections with the human world for which it must act. The wife does not stir from her patnīloka, but her effect is felt at the other end of the ritual ground, where, from now till nearly the end of the ritual, all action will take place.

But her effect is not entirely positive, as the Brāhmaṇic texts point out. The MS passage quoted earlier continues:

> MS IV.1.12 (15: 9) amedhyáṁ vā́ etád ayajñiyáṁ yát pátny avékṣata āhavanī́yé 'dhiśrayati punā́ty *eváinan[75] médhyam enad yajñíyaṃ karoti

What the wife looks at (becomes) impure and ritually unfit. He puts it on the Āhavanīya. Thus he purifies it. Thus he makes it pure and ritually fit.[76]

The very act that endows the butter with sexuality also pollutes it, and before it can be put to ritual use, it must receive treatment in the sacral realm—reheating on the Offering Fire and glances from priest and Sacrificer—to partially reverse the potentially too virulent sexual strain injected by the wife's gaze.

Let us examine another, more elaborate ritual episode dramatizing the sexual and procreative effects of visual contact between the wife and an oblation. This is in the mystical Pravargya ritual, from which the wife is partly excluded. Though this ritual has its place in the ordinary Soma Sacrifice (on the so-called Upasad days that precede the Pressing Day), it may have been adapted from elsewhere and is often considered an especially esoteric ceremony, which receives more than its share of exegetical puffery.[77] The mystical associations of the Pravargya, the importance attributed to it, and the conditions imposed on its performance[78] are all rather surprising given the elementary nature of the actual ritual activity. The Pravargya simply involves the preparation of a boiling milk drink (gharma) in a pot called the Mahāvīra, which has previously been ceremonially fashioned.

Unlike the exclusion of the wife discussed above, when she is utterly banished from the ritual ground and kept at home during the Mahāpitṛyajña, the position of the wife in the Pravargya is more ambiguous. She is present on the ritual ground, indeed is girded and actively participating in the other parts of the Soma Sacrifice that surround the Pravargya. But for much of its performance she is confined in her own hut (patnīśālā) with the doors of the enclosure where the ritual activity is happening closed against her.[79]

ĀpŚS XV.5.1 pravargyeṇa pracariṣyantaḥ saṃvṛṇvanti dvārāṇi
2 pariśrayanti patnyāḥ

When they are about to proceed with the Pravargya, they close the doors and enclose (it) from the wife.

In the texts of the WYV, which do not specify her confinement, her head is covered by a garment when the crucial parts of the ceremony occur (KŚS XXVI.3.2; ŚB XIV.1.3.16). The wife is not allowed even to watch the pot being made (e.g. ĀpŚS XV.2.9; see van Buitenen 1968, pp. 58–59).

The major effort seems to be to keep the wife from *seeing* the pot, and this is accomplished either by keeping her physically out of the enclosure and/or by covering her eyes.[80] But in some texts this visual prohibition is dramatically reversed. When the kettle has been heated to glowing, her head is uncovered (if relevant) and she *looks* at the pot:

KŚS XXVI.4.12 aporṇauti patnī śiraḥ
13 . . . tvaṣṭṛmanta ity enāṃ vācayati mahāvīram īkṣamāṇām

The wife uncovers her head.

He [the Adhvaryu] makes her recite "Accompanied by Tvaṣṭar . . . ," while she looks at the Mahāvīra pot.[81]

MŚS IV.2.37 tvaṣṭrimantas tveti yajamānaḥ patnyā sahāvekṣate

(Saying) "Accompanied by Tvaṣṭar, thee . . . ," the Sacrificer along with his wife looks at (the Mahāvīra pot).

The reason for this dramatic reversal, the requirement for the wife abruptly to stare at an object which has heretofore been carefully screened from her gaze, is the familiar one: to effect a sexual pairing, as the ŚB explains.

ŚB XIV.1.4.16 vṛ́ṣā vái pravárgyo yóṣā pátnī mithunám eváitát prajánanaṃ kriyate

The Pravargya is male, the wife female. A procreative sexual pairing is thus created.

The sexual and procreative nature of the contact is also signaled by the mantra ("Accompanied by Tvaṣṭar . . . "), which, as we will see, is used at a similarly sexually charged moment in the Soma Sacrifice.

But the BYV texts forbid even this contact: the wife recites the mantra while still confined away from the pot:

ĀpŚS XV.8.17 anuvākaśeṣaṃ tu pariśrite pratiprasthātā patnīṃ vācayati tvaṣṭīmatī te sapeyeti

The Pratiprasthātar has the wife in her enclosed area recite the rest of the anuvāka: "Accompanied by Tvaṣṭar, may I be of service to thee."[82]

Discussions of the Pravargya in the secondary literature usually suggest that the wife is banned from contact with the rite because she might profane its mystical essence.[83] But the texts suggest something different: the ritual is a dangerous one, particularly the great heat, both actual and mystic, of the glowing pot.[84] It threatens physical harm to those in contact with it. According to the ŚB, the wife covers her head lest she should go blind:

ŚB XIV.1.3.16 . . . tásmin pravṛjyámāne pátnī śíraḥ prórṇute taptó vā́ eṣá śúśucānó bhavati nén me 'yáṃ taptáḥ śúśucānáś cákṣuḥ pramuṣṇā́d íti

While (the pot) is being heated, the wife covers her head, (thinking) "This heated (pot) is glowing. (I cover my head) lest this heated and glowing one should steal my eye."

The TĀr sees this as a danger for all:

TĀr V.3.7 īśvaró vā́ eṣò 'ndhó bhávitoḥ / yáḥ pravargyàm anvī́kṣate

He is likely to become blind who looks upon the Pravargya.

And though this text finally allows the male participants to look at it, it (as a BYV text) still forbids it to the wife, for the following reasons.

TĀr V.6.12 . . . ná pátny ávekṣeta / yát pátny avékṣeta / prájāyeta / prajā́ṃ tv àsyai nírdahet / yán nā́vékṣeta / ná prájāyeta / nā́syai prajā́ṃ nírdahet / tiraskṛ́tya yájur vācayati / prájāyate / nā́syai prajā́ṃ nírdahati / tváṣṭīmatī te sapeyéty āha

The wife should not look at (it). If the wife should look at (it), she would produce offspring, but it would burn her offspring. If she should not look at (it), she would not produce offspring, and it would not burn her offspring. Having screened her, he makes her recite the yajus. She produces offspring, (but) it does not burn her offspring. "Accompanied by Tvaṣṭar, might I be of service to thee," she says.

This passage lays out with great clarity the dilemma posed by this ritual: some contact between the wife and the pot is desirable because such contact is procreative. But it is also risky to the embryos thus produced. On the other hand, no contact at all is simply sterile. The texts cited earlier (KŚS, ŚB, MŚS) are willing to take the risk: they grant the wife a single controlled glance at the end of the period of heating. But the BYV is more cautious (and more ingenious). The wife avoids physical contact with the pot, and also the visual contact that is its equivalent, but by participating in the verbal portion of the ritual from a safe, screened distance, she gets access to the power of the ritual without the risks.[85]

I have discussed elsewhere[86] the early Indic notion that the embryo in the womb is especially threatened by heat/fire and the common visualization of this danger as a glowing pot, indeed often the Mahāvīra pot itself. The evidence I adduced there was mythological, but the same concept here finds a ritual embodiment.

In both cases of the wife's exclusion discussed—exclusion from the Mahāpitṛyajña[87] and from the Pravargya—the motive seems not to be to shield the ritual from a woman's profaning presence, as is sometimes suggested, but to protect her from the dangers posed by these particular rituals: the sinister forces of the world of the dead, or the too powerful energy of the glowing Mahāvīra pot. But in each case there is some effort made, at least by some schools, to ensure her partial participation—or some substitute for it. Once again the wife is vital to the success of the ritual.[88]

3. *The Broom*

Let us turn from these rather indirect associations of the wife and sexuality to some in which the symbolic relations are more explicit, incidents in which the wife ceremonially receives from her husband or a priest objects with sexual meaning, for example, a broom, a bow, a fire-drilling apparatus. Though such items may not seem especially suggestive to us, they are culturally freighted in the world of our ritual.

The most elaborated of these token exchanges is that of the broom (veda), a bunch of grass tied together and used to keep the altar tidy, to sweep coals around the fire, and also to serve as support for various pots when they are being carried. We have in fact already met the broom in this last capacity. When the priest brings the butter pot to the wife to look at, it is supported by the broom:

> ĀpŚS II.6.1 ājyam . . . vedenopayamya patnyā upaharati
>
> He brings up the butter to the wife, supporting it with the broom.[89]

After this the broom is removed to the east with the other equipment, but it too returns to the vicinity of the Gārhapatya at the end of the ritual.[90]

When the various offerings at the western end of the ritual ground have been made (the Patnīsaṃyājas and the offering of the remnants of the sacrificial food just discussed), the wife is ungirded—another action already treated at length. At the same time the broom is untied. Indeed in some texts the wife performs both actions, nearly simultaneously:

> KŚS III.8.2 patnī vedaṃ muñcati vedo 'sīti yoktram / pra mā muñcāmi . . .
>
> The wife releases the broom, (saying) "You are a broom," and her girdle, (saying) "I release myself . . . "

The connection between these actions is not accidental. In fact, I would suggest that the broom here is a representation of her husband, a substitute for him, and that their joint unyoking symbolizes the return of husband and wife to the mundane world, newly imbued with fertility acquired from the ritual. Recall in the discussion of the girding of the wife that in the simple Iṣṭis the husband is not specifically girded for the occasion, since his initiatory sacred thread suffices. But the broom *is* tied up at the beginning of the ritual and is now untied, providing a symbolic male girding and ungirding parallel to the wife's—as well as another framing episode.

The broom as male sexual symbol is not an extravagant invention of my own: the symbolism is explicitly spelled out in ritual activity. In some schools the Hotar throws the broom into the wife's lap three times, especially if she wants a son:[91]

> MŚS I.3.5.15 patnyai vedaṃ prayachati . . .
> 16 . . . pratigṛhṇāty upasthe putrakāmā nidadhīta
>
> He hands the broom to the wife.
> She takes hold of it. (A wife) desirous of a son should put it in her lap.

ĀpŚS III.10.3 vedaṃ hotā patnyā upasthe triḥ prāsyati

The Hotar throws the broom into the lap of the wife three times.

Or she puts some of the blades extracted from it between her thighs (BŚS III.30 [104:12]; ŚŚS I.15.14; KB III.9).[92] Again the Brāhmaṇic texts are quite certain of the reason:

ŚB I.9.2.22 átha yát pátnī visraṁsáyati / yóṣā vái pátnī vṛ́ṣā vedó mithunám eváitát prajánanaṃ kriyate

Now, as to why the wife unties (the broom). The wife is a woman/female, the broom is a man/masculine. In this way a procreative sexual pairing is made.

After the broom is untied and symbolically couples with the wife, the Hotar strews the grass blades of which it consisted from the Gārhapatya fire east to the Āhavanīya (cf. MŚS I.3.5.19; TB III.3.9.11) or up to the vedi (KŚS III.8.3; ŚB I.9.2.24; ŚŚS I.15.15).[93] Immediately afterward a last offering (the Samiṣṭayajus or 'completed ritual offering') is made into the Āhavanīya. The lines of force have been reversed again: the sexuality created by the coupling of wife and broom is physically returned to the sacral east, through an unbroken strewing of grass from the broom. The wife is again exercising her power from a distance, but through a chain of representational contact.

4. *Summary: The Wife in the Iṣṭi*

In the last few sections I have examined all the wife's principal actions in the model Iṣṭi, as set forth in the treatments of the Darśapūrṇamāsa ritual. It might therefore be worthwhile to step back briefly, summarize her participation, and see how it fits into the overall shape of the ritual. The incidents we have examined are the following:

1. the threshing and grinding of the grain
2. the yoking
3. the looking at the melted butter
4. the Patnīsaṃyājas
5. the offering of the leftovers
6. the unyoking of wife and broom, and the strewing of the broom

The first thing to note is how marginal these actions are. Most of the ritual, the principal oblations and recitations, happen between nos. 3 and 4; 1–3 are simply part of the preparations, 4–6 of the tidying up. In Hillebrandt's 1879 treatment, containing 186 pages of text detailing the minute-by-minute progress of the ritual, nearly 100 pages elapse between 3 and 4. So it would not be honest or useful to claim that the wife is in the thick of things, a leading actor on the ritual stage.

However, it would be misleading to dismiss or minimize the significance of her participation. As I have repeatedly emphasized, she exists not merely in the margins but in the *frame* of the ritual. The performance begins and ends geographically in her world; the melted butter used in the offering is infused with her force at the beginning; the vital path created at the end between the mundane west and the holy east is made with grass with which she has mated. Her actions, so apparently trivial, are all richly symbolic.

It is also important to keep in mind that this simple ritual is one of the major building blocks of larger ritual complexes. Iṣṭis of various sorts are embedded in the great rituals like the Soma Sacrifice, and so-called Kāmyā Iṣṭis, optional Iṣṭis performed for particular desires, are common. So even in the elaborate rituals I will discuss elsewhere, even in rituals in which the wife has no separate dramatic role, the Iṣṭi pattern sets up a ritual rhythm, continually flowing from and returning to the Gārhapatya and the wife located there. We should not forget these smaller but regular ritual tides as we proceed.

5. *Other Tokens of Fertility: Agni's Mother(s)*

Let me now turn briefly to several other instances in which the wife manipulates an object charged with sexual or fertile meanings. The first, in which a token of sexuality changes hands, is limited to a single text (that I know of). In the Āgnyādheya, the original 'Establishment of the Fires', the Sacrificer and his wife, having bathed and dressed in new clothes, keep vigil the night before establishing the three fires that allow them to perform śrauta rituals.[94] In the evening the Adhvaryu hands the Sacrificer the two fire sticks (araṇī) to be used to churn the fire, with several highly suggestive mantras.

MŚS I.5.2.2 yajamānāyāraṇī prayachati

3 mahī viśpatnī sadane ṛtasyārvācī etaṃ dharuṇe rayīṇām
antarvatī janyaṃ jātavedasam adhvarāṇāṃ janayataṃ purogām

iti pratigṛhṇāti

4 ṛtviyavatī stho 'gniretasau reto dhattaṃ puṣṭyai prajananaṃ
tat satyaṁ yad vīraṃ vibhṛto vīraṃ janayiṣyataḥ . . .

He hands the two fire sticks to the Sacrificer.

(Saying) "You two great ladies [N.B. patnī] of the clan, bearers of wealth, come near to the seat of truth. Pregnant, give birth to Jātavedas [an epithet of fire], belonging to men, the leader of the ceremonies," (the Sacrificer) accepts them.

"You two are in your fertile season. Having fire / Agni as semen, deposit generative semen for thriving. This is the truth, that you two bear a male; you two will give birth to a male."

This text (MŚS) then specifies that the *wife* receives the two fire sticks for the churning of the Dakṣiṇāgni (MŚS I.5.2.5 dakṣiṇāgner araṇī patnī pāṇau kurute) – those in the Sacrificer's possession are for the Gārhapatya. However I have found no other text in which the wife holds any fire sticks, and I assume that the supercharged sexual atmosphere created by the mantras addressing the pregnant female fire sticks (araṇī is grammatically feminine) has suggested this modification of the usual practice to the followers of the Mānava school.[95]

This modification may also have been reinforced by the next incident to be discussed. In the much more elaborate ritual devoted to creating a new fire, the Agnicayana or 'Laying of the Fire(-altar)', the wife fashions the fire pot (ukhā), in which the new fire will be kindled and then carried forward to the new, ceremonially laid fire altar, according to some texts (e.g. MŚS VI.1.2.4–12; ĀpŚS XVI.4.5). Just as the fire *sticks* are considered the mothers of the fire in the Agnyādheya and thus belong appropriately to the wife, the fire *pot* in the Agnicayana serves as Agni's womb and is appropriately created by the wife.

Though the fashioning of pots can be classified in part with the wife's other domestic tasks, both in the general Vedic conceptual realm and in this specific ritual context the pot is clearly symbolic of a womb. I have discussed at length elsewhere[96] the pot as womb-substitute in Vedic and epic mythology: a number of heroes whose original births were mismanaged undergo second gestations in pots. In the śrauta sūtras the actual shaping of the pot, the mantras accompanying the fashioning, and involvement of the wife all contribute to an atmosphere charged with fertility, and for good reason: the new, infant fire will literally be born in it.

Let us examine one account of the fashioning. Even before the events narrated in what follows, the clay to be used has been ceremonially chosen, fetched, and prepared by mixing it with water and other substances.

> MŚS VI.1.2.4 saṁsṛṣṭāṁ vasubhir iti tisṛbhir abhimantrya patnyai prayachati
>
> Addressing her with the three (verses) beginning "Brought together by the Vasus," he [priest] hands (the lump of clay) to the wife.

These three verses are worth quoting in full: they invoke the aid of several goddesses both in the actual fashioning of the pot and in making it fertile:

> MS II.7.5 (80: 7)[97] sáṁsṛṣṭāṁ vásubhī rudráir dhī́raiḥ karmaṇyā̀ṃ mŕ̥dam
> hástābhyāṃ mṛdvī́ṃ kṛtvā́ sinīvālī́ kṛṇotu tā́m
> sinīvālī́ sukapardā́ sukarīrā́ svopaśā́
> sā́ túbhyam adite mahy ókhā́ṃ dad[h]ātu hástayoḥ
> ukhā́ṃ kṛṇotu śáktyā bāhúbhyām áditir dhiyā́
> mātā́ putráṁ yáthopásthe sā́gníṃ bibhartu gárbhā ā́
>
> The clay fit for the rite, brought together by the Vasus, by the wise Rudras—let Sinīvalī,[98] having made it pliable with her two hands, make it (into a pot).
> Sinīvalī of the beautiful braids, beautiful headdress (?), beautiful curls (?)—let her place the pot in your hands for you, o great Aditi.
> Let Aditi make the pot with skill and thought with her two arms. As a mother (bears) a child in her lap, let it [pot] bear Agni / fire in its womb.

The pot-fashioning rite continues:

> MŚS VI.1.2.5 makhasya śiro 'sīti piṇḍam abhimṛśati
> 6 patny ukhāṃ karoti . . .
>
> (Saying) "Thou art the head of Makha," (the priest) touches the lump.
> The wife makes the pot . . .

The next sūtras prescribe the shape of the pot in detail: it has three elevations and four corners, a girdle two fingers below the opening, and some number (two, four, or eight) of breasts (stana). Aditi is connected with the girdle through mantras. Finally,

> MŚS VI.1.2.12 ikṣuśalākayā nilipya kṛtvāya sā mahīm ukhām iti viṣajati
>
> Having smeared it with a sugarcane stalk, she suspends it, (saying) "Having made the great pot, she . . . "

Again the mantra connects the pot quite firmly with Aditi, in her role as archetypal mother:

> MS II.7.6 (81: 5) kṛtvā́ya sā́ mahī́m ukhā́ṃ mṛnmáyīṁ yónim agnáye
> tā́ṃ putrébhyaḥ prā́yachad áditiḥ śrapáyān íti
>
> Having made the great clay pot as womb for Agni,
> Aditi handed it to her sons, (thinking) "They will fire it."

The priest then takes charge of the firing of the pot, again accompanied by mantras connecting the action to Aditi, the wives of the gods, the divine women, the protectresses, the women 'with uncut wings' (achinnapātrāḥ), and other female figures. The mythic landscape is thus overpopulated with femininity, a rather unusual situation in Vedic ritual.

Even in schools in which the wife does not make the pot, the same mantras are employed and so create the same atmosphere of charged feminine fertility. In such texts the Adhvaryu or the Sacrificer seems to be the unmarked fashioner of the pot. ĀpŚS specifies either the Mahiṣī ('principal wife') or the Adhvaryu, for reasons that are not clear to me.

> ĀpŚS XVI.4.5 . . . mahiṣy ukhāṃ karoti bahubhāryasya / adhvaryur ekabhāryasya
>
> The Mahiṣī makes the pot if (the Sacrificer) has many wives; the Adhvaryu if he has one wife.

In most texts the wife fashions the first brick for the fire altar from the same clay the pot is made of,[99] and so perhaps a single wife is not enough to take care of all those tasks.

In any case, the birth metaphor is the controlling one in this ritual episode, and both human and divine women are required to ensure that the birth is a success.

D. Sexuality and Fertility: The Aśvamedha

1. The Dead Horse and the Queens

Such are some of the symbolic representations of sexuality. We come now to actual ones, to the lurid, in fact to a ceremony so striking that it has become notorious even outside the field of Vedic studies (though not particularly far outside).[100] It occurs in the great royal ritual, the Horse Sacrifice (Aśvamedha), which is performed for an already powerful king, to extend, consolidate, and display his power. In royal rituals the king is Sacrificer, and his wives act as patnī, particularly his chief queen, the Mahiṣī or 'Great Female Buffalo'. At the climax of this lengthy and elaborate ritual (the preliminaries take a year), the chief queen copulates with the just slaughtered horse. Though she is covered by a linen garment, the texts leave no doubt as to what physically she is supposed to do, and it is not merely symbolic.

As she lies there, she taunts the horse about his sexual performance, and she and the lesser wives of the king engage in obscene banter with the priests, while hundreds of female attendants of the queens, their hair half unbound, circle the horse and the unfortunate lady, singing, dancing, and slapping their thighs. The verbal part of the ceremony is extremely explicit, and in fact tested the limits of tolerance of our scholarly predecessors. Eggeling, for example, resorts to suspension dots or inserts the untranslated Sanskrit (ŚB XIII. 5.2.2ff.); Keith simply omits TS VII.4.19 d–k in his translation, with the comment "the next verses are hardly translatable"; while Griffith 1899, omitting VS XXIII.20–31, says rather huffily: "the . . . stanzas are not reproducible even in the semiobscurity of a learned European language."[101] Even Caland opts for Latin when he encounters the root √yabh 'fuck'.[102]

It is hard not to see this showcasing of extreme public sexuality, not only physically enacted but verbally encoded, as an attempt to capture sexual power in order to enhance the ritual effect and to promote fertility. In fact, this aspect of the Horse Sacrifice has been so exhaustively discussed, by ancient commentators and modern ones, that I need have less to say about this extravaganza than about the covert sexual representations discussed above.[103] What I hope to have shown, however, is that this is not a freakish and aberrant spectacle, as it is sometimes presented, but the logical, if extreme, fulfillment of woman's function in ritual, as seen earlier in its less dramatic forms.

We know this ritual episode not only from the thorough treatments in the śrauta sūtras, but also, in abbreviated fashion, from the epics. When Yudhiṣṭhira holds his Aśvamedha after the end of the great war, Draupadī does the honors:

MBh XIV.91.2 tataḥ saṃjñāpya turagaṃ vidhivad yājakarṣabhāḥ
upasaṃveśayan rājaṃs tatas tāṃ drupadātmajām
kalābhis tisṛbhī rājan yathāvidhi manasvinīm

When the bulls among priests had made the horse agree [killed it] according to rule,
they caused the wise Draupadī to lie down beside it for three minutes according to rule, o king.

Three minutes sounds about right. For whatever reason, at the Aśvamedha depicted in the Rāmāyana a whole night is required.

R I.13.27 patatriṇā tadā sārdhaṃ susthitena ca cetasā
avasad rajanīm ekāṃ kausalyā dharmakāmyayā

Then with determined mind and desire for dharma, Kausalyā spent one night with the horse.

Kausalyā is the wife of Daśaratha and will be the mother of Rāma. This Aśvamedha is in fact undertaken because of childlessness, and Rāma is the desired result. Another unusual feature is that the other, lower wives of the king also mate with the horse:

R I.13.28 hotādhvaryus tathodgatā hayena samayojayan
mahiṣyā parivṛttyātha[104] vāvātām aparāṃ tathā

The Hotar, Adhvaryu, and Udgātar had the horse unite with the Mahiṣī, the Parivṛktī [Avoided Wife], and finally the Vāvātā [Favorite Wife].

It will be useful now to examine the śrauta sūtra version(s) of the crucial episode, if only to see the unapologetic and unbowdlerizing fashion in which the ritual sūtras present it.[105] What follows is something of a composite. Texts differ on how much detail they give (e.g. MŚS is rather minimal), the exact form and order of the mantras, who says them, and exactly what actions the mantras accompany, but the general structure of the ritual is shared across the texts. Much given below is tentative and uncertain, especially in the translation of the mantras.[106] Though their purport is usually clear, the exact meanings of the words are often not, since they are rare (often confined just to these mantras) and are clearly slangy and crude names for sexual organs and activities—a stratum of language rare in the dignified hieratic diction of most of our oldest texts.

After the horse has been killed, the chief queen (Mahiṣī) is led up to it, usually accompanied by the other wives with roles in the drama: the 'favorite' (Vāvātā) and the 'rejected wife' (Parivṛktī), and, in some texts (e.g. ŚB, ŚŚS), the fourth, lower-class wife (Pālāgalī)—each accompanied (or not) by a hundred attendants. The following mantra is used in the ushering in, according to most texts:[107]

TS VII.4.19.1ab ámbe ámbāly ámbike
ná mā nayati káś caná
sasásty aśvakáḥ

O Mummy, Mummikins, little Mummy.
No one is leading me (to matrimony).[108]
The horsikins is sleeping.

The wives then go around the dead horse, fanning and glorifying it, in a dance-like procession:

ĀpŚS XX.17.13 tā dakṣiṇān keśapakṣān udgrathya savyān prasrasya dakṣiṇān ūrūn āghnānāḥ sigbhir abhidhūnvatyas triḥ pradakṣiṇam aśvaṃ pariyanti

Tying up the right side of their hair and loosening the left, slapping their right thighs and fanning with their hems, they go around the horse three times to the right.[109]

They reverse the action and go three times to the left, and finish with a final three rightward circuits. The mantras of praise are extracted from the RV and exhibit solemn diction and extremely archaic stylistic figures,[110] beginning

RV II.23.1 gaṇā́nāṃ tvā gaṇápatiṃ havāmahe

We invoke you, troop-lord of troops.

The stateliness of the discourse is meant, I think, to contrast pointedly with the coarseness to come.

At this point the Mahiṣī lies down beside the horse and invites it to stretch out its forefeet along with hers:

TS VII.4.19.1e táu sahá catúraḥ padáḥ sáṃ prásārayāvahai

Together let us two stretch forth our four feet.

The activity now becomes very intense, and different texts apportion the accompanying mantras differently. Following ĀpŚS, the Adhvaryu covers the Mahiṣī and the horse with a linen garment (kṣaumeṇa vāsasā), saying[111]

TS VII.4.19.1cd súbhage kā́mpīlavāsini
suvargé loké sám prórṇvāthām
ā́hám ajāni garbhadhám
ā́ tvám ajāsi garbhadhám

O lucky one, clothed in kāmpīla-cloth, may you two be entirely covered in the heavenly world.
I will drive the impregnator; you will drive the impregnator.

and further addresses her with

TS VII.4.19.1f vṛ́ṣā vāṁ retodhā́ réto dadhātu

Let the bullish seed-placer of you two place the seed.[112]

The wife now takes the dead horse's penis and puts it in her vulva or vagina (or, at least, nearby). It is important to make this clear, because some discussions of this ritual refer to it as a *symbolic* copulation (e.g. Puhvel 1970, p. 161). It *is*, of course, symbolic insofar as the horse is dead, but it is not simply a brief and perfunctory moment under the sheets with the wife squirming as far away from the corpse as possible.[113] Consider some of the prescriptions in the ritual texts:

ĀpŚS XX.18.4 prajananena prajananaṃ saṃdhāya

Putting (its) generative organ together with (her) generative organ.

KŚS XX.6.16 aśvaśiśnam upasthe kurute

(The Mahiṣī) takes the penis of the horse in her lap.

BŚS XV.29 (234: 9) athaiṣā mahiṣy upasthe śepham ādhatte

Then the Mahiṣī places the penis in her lap.

VārŚS III.4.4.15 saṁhitaprajananayoḥ

When their two generative organs have been put together . . .

ŚB XIII.5.2.2 áśvasya śiśnáṃ máhiṣy úpasthe nídhatte

The Mahiṣī puts the penis of the horse in her lap.

We should also remember that death by suffocation induces "reflex-conditioned tumescence and emission,"[114] and since she is dealing with an animal not long dead, the Mahiṣī's experience may have been even less symbolic than we tend to hope.

The mantras now become crude; the abstract, semieuphemistic, and high-toned vocabulary of the preceding mantras (garbhadhá 'impregnator' [lit. 'embryo-placer'], retodhá 'seed-placer') gives way to racier terms (many of which we do not fully understand). And women's sexual pleasure is the theme—a rather startling one in light of what is occurring:

TS VII.4.19.1–2g út sakthyòr gṛdáṃ[115] dhehy
añjím údañjim ánv aja
yá strīṇā́ṃ jīvabhójano
yá āsāṃ biladhā́vanaḥ
priyá strīṇā́m apīcyàḥ
yá āsāṃ kṛṣṇé lákṣmaṇi
sárdigṛdim parā́vadhīt

Put the penis up between the two thighs.
Drive the sleek one, adorned at the end,[116] along (the thighs)—

Which is the living pleasure-maker for women,
Which is their hole-runner/cleaner,[117]
The dear secret of women,
Which has hit[118] their sardigṛdi[119] in the black mark.

In some texts (e.g. BŚS XV.29 [234: 12]) this text seems to be in the mouth of the Adhvaryu, but most assign this to the Sacrificer (KŚS XX.6.17; ŚŚS XVI.3.35; ŚB XIII.5.2.3). In other words the husband of the Mahiṣī, watching his wife manipulate the dead horse into some sort of copulatory position, addresses the two with the most coarsely explicit verse in the ritual (though the Parivṛktī's exchange below comes close). Meanwhile, the Mahiṣī is also required to share the coarseness, by mocking (abhimethati) or scolding (garhate) the horse with

TS VII.4.19.2h ámbe ámbāly ámbike
ná mā yabhati káś caná
sasásty aśvakáḥ

O Mummy, Mummikins, little Mummy.
No one is fucking me.
The horsikins is sleeping.[120]

The other bystanders are busy as well, exchanging a set of derisory verses.[121] Again texts differ on the identity of the particular speakers, but the general parameters are clear. The other wives[122] are the main verbal participants. According to ĀpŚS (XX.18.5–6) the other wives mock the Mahiṣī in chorus with the four verses we will discuss shortly, in answer to her repetitions of the mantra just cited. BŚS (XV.30) also has the wives address the Mahiṣī, first individually, one verse for the Vāvātā (Favorite) and one for the Parivṛktī (Avoided Wife), then the entire group (sarve gaṇāḥ).[123]

Other texts (e.g. ŚB, KŚS, ŚŚS), however, depict a more complex (and, I think, more original) procedure. The wives engage in individual dialogues with the priests. A priest addresses a wife with a verse, and she[124] replies with a variant of it. Again there is disagreement about the pairings. Both ŚB (XIII.5.2.4–8) and ŚŚS (XVI.4.1–6) include the fourth, low-caste wife (Pālāgalī), and ŚB adds a maiden (Kumārī) of uncertain affiliation.[125]

ŚB		*ŚŚS*	
Adhvaryu	Kumārī	Hotar	Mahiṣī
Brahman	Mahiṣī	Brahman	Vāvātā
Udgātar	Vāvātā	Udgātar	Parivṛktī
Hotar	Parivṛktī	Adhvaryu	Pālāgalī
Kṣattar	Pālāgalī		

The verses they exchange are clearly erotic, but not in quite as direct a way as those we have just examined. They are full of bawdy slang and riddling images, so that though the sexual intent is clear, the precise references are anyone's guess (and were probably meant to be, even at the time). Let us examine the way such exchanges proceed, as given in the ŚB, before looking at the verses more closely:

> ŚB XIII.5.2.4 áthādhvaryúḥ kumārīm abhímethati / kúmāri háye-haye kúmāri yakā́sakáu śakuntikéti tám̐ kumārī́ pratyabhímethaty ádhvaryo háye-hayé 'dhvaryo yakó 'sakáu śakuntaká íti
>
> Then the Adhvaryu derisively addresses the maiden (with the verse beginning) "Maiden, hey hey. Maiden! Which little (female) birdikins yonder . . ." The maiden derisively replies to him (with the verse beginning) "Adhvaryu, hey hey. Adhvaryu! Which little (male) birdikins yonder . . ."

It is worth looking at the verses in detail not only for their erotic content, which is rare in Vedic literature, but also for their style, which will allow us to connect this whole ritual playlet with material that superficially seems quite distant. We can begin with the verse whose pratīka we have just seen:[126]

> VS XXIII.22 yakā́sakáu śakuntikā́hálag íti vā́ñcati
> ā́hanti gabhé páso nígalgalīti dhā́rakā
>
> The little (female) birdikins[127] yonder, which moves crookedly along saying 'āhalak',
> knocks the penis into the slit. The 'holder' gulps it down.

The reply:[128]

> VS XXIII.23 yakó 'sakáu śakuntaká āhálag íti vā́ñcati
> vívakṣata iva te múkham ádhvaryo mā́ nas tvám abhíbhāṣathāḥ
>
> The little (male) birdikins yonder that moves crookedly along saying 'āhalak'—
> it's like your mouth when you want to 'speak'.[129] Adhvaryu, don't you speak to us.

Following the order of the ŚB, the next verse is that addressed by the Brahman to the Mahiṣī:[130]

> VS XXIII.24 mātā́ ca te pitā́ ca té 'gram̐ vṛkṣásya rohataḥ
> prátilāmī́ti te pitā́ gabhé muṣṭím ataṁsayat
>
> Your mother and your father climb to the top of the tree.
> (Saying) "I am passing over," your father shuttled his 'fist' back and forth in the slit.

Her reply (VS XXIII.25) is identical in the first half-verse, but with krīḍataḥ 'they two *play*' for rohataḥ; the second half-verse is essentially that of verse 23, with address to the Brahman rather than the Adhvaryu.

Next the Udgātar to the Vāvātā:[131]

> VS XXIII.26 ūrdhvā́m enām úcchrāpaya giráu bhārám̐ hárann iva
> áthāsyai mádhyam edhatām̐ śīté vā́te punánn iva

Prop her up, like one carrying a burden up a mountain.[132]
Then let her middle thrive, like one winnowing in a cool breeze.

The verse may be especially appropriate for the Vāvātā because, as we will see, she has charge of the *middle* of the sacrificed horse. The Vāvātā's reply (VS XXIII.27) changes the genders: "prop *him* up," "*his* middle," and in the third pāda substitutes the phonologically similar verb ejatu for edhatām. The result is, of course, gender appropriate: "let his middle stir."

These last few verses have kept their erotic tone coy. Though their sexual nature is fairly clear, the references are veiled. But the next pair, the exchange between Parivṛktī and Hotar (ŚŚS Udgātar), is raw, though the style is still riddling:[133]

VS XXIII.28 yád asyā aṁhubhédyāḥ kṛdhú sthūlám upā́tasat
muṣkā́v íd asyā ejato gośaphé śakulā́v iva

When the stunted, thick (penis) has shuttled from her narrow slit,
her two balls[134] stir like the two splinters (/ fish) in a cow's hoof (?).[135]

VS XXIII.29 yád devā́so lalā́magum prá viṣṭīmínam ā́viṣuḥ
sakthnā́ dediśyate nā́rī satyásyākṣibhúvo yathā

When the gods have favored the (man) with a star-marked, stiffened (penis),
the woman displays with her thigh, like eye-witnesses to the truth (?).[136]

The last exchange in the ŚB (XIII.5.2.8), between Pālāgalī and Kṣattar (ŚŚS Adhvaryu),[137] is by contrast fairly innocuous, though still erotic in nature. It clearly makes reference to the lower-class origins of this wife:

VS XXIII.30 yád dhariṇó yávam átti ná puṣṭám paśú mányate
śūdrā́ yád áryajārā ná póṣāya dhanāyati

When the deer eats grain, it does not consider the nourished beast (or, does not consider itself a nourished beast?).[138]
When a Śūdra woman has an Arya for a lover, she (/ he?) does not need riches to thrive.

The reply (VS XXIII.31) basically switches the genders.

Finally the Mahiṣī is allowed to get up, and they all do the equivalent of washing out their mouths with soap.

BŚS XV.30 (235: 3) dadhikrāvṇo akāriṣam iti caturthīṁ sarva eva surabhimatīm ṛcam japanti ye yajñe 'pūtam vadanti

All those who say impure (speech) in the ritual then mutter the 'fragrant', four-part verse "I have commemorated Dadhikrāvan."

The recital of this verse, RV IV.39.6, accomplishes two goals. It is called 'fragrant' (surabhi-mant) because its third pāda, rabhí no múkhā karat

ur mouths fragrant,

a sort of verbal cleansing. But, more importantly, it returns mediately to the grave and dignified level of Rigvedic discourse, the dead horse through praise of its mythic counterpart Dadhikrāvan. Just as the licentious atmosphere of the middle of this episode exploded abruptly from the solemn Rigvedic verses of glorification with which the wives circled the victim, so we have just as abruptly returned to the rhetorical heights, with the same feeling of verbal dissonance. There follow three more Rigvedic verses (X.9.1–3) in praise of the waters, while they wash with water. The carnival is closed.

It is difficult to know what to say after this. The ritual spectacle is so powerful that analysis seems pallid and in some ways unnecessary. The wallowing in sexuality, the deliberate suspension of all ordinary rules of behavior and discourse at the most critical point in the ritual seem to have a purpose that is almost blindingly obvious. And, in fact, one of its points may be its very obviousness: the subtle suggestions, the veiled representations of sexuality in less important rituals are here allowed to play themselves out, in the open. The wife who usually mates decorously and symbolically with a broom parts the metaphorical curtains and reveals what has really been going on all along.

But it is appropriate now to ask what that "really" really is. One of the ways to explore this question is to look for verbal parallels to the remarkable mantras that so heighten the hectic atmosphere of copulation, that are in some ways more shocking than the act itself. We can characterize these mantras as (1) dialogic; (2) riddling; (3) explicitly sexual. If we concentrate on the first two characteristics, we need not look very far for parallels.

2. *The Aśvamedha and Riddles*

On two occasions in the Aśvamedha, temporally close to the sacrifice of the horse, two priests engage in riddling dialogue. According to ŚB (XIII.2.6.9ff.) the Brahman and the Hotar do so before the victims are bound to the stakes, while all the principal priests do so almost immediately after the wives perform (XIII.5.2.11ff.).[139] The dialogue is specifically called a brahmodya in most texts. This is of course the word for the famous "verbal contest" that has occasioned so much discussion in the secondary literature.[140] In the form we have it in the Aśvamedha, it consists of patterned question and response, as in the pairs

VS XXIII.9 káḥ svid ekākī́ carati ká u svij jāyate púnaḥ
kíṁ svid dhimásya bheṣajáṃ kím v āvápanaṃ mahát

Who indeed wanders alone? Who indeed is born again?
What indeed is the remedy for cold? And what is the great vessel?

VS XXIII.10 sū́rya ekākī́ carati candrámā jāyate púnaḥ
agnír himásya bheṣajám̐ bhū́mir āvápanam̐ mahát

The sun wanders alone. The moon is born again.
Fire is the remedy for cold. The earth is the great vessel.

The use of riddles to inquire about and formulate cosmic truths is familiar from the earliest Vedic: RV I.164, the so-called riddle hymn, presents fifty-two verses of them, with answers rarely as straightforward as those just given. In fact the RVic riddles remind us in style far more of the exchanges we saw between wives and priests. Compare one example:

RV I.164.22 yásmin vṛkṣé madhvádaḥ suparṇā́ niviśánte súvate cā́dhi víśve
tásyéd āhuḥ píppalam̐ svādv ágre tán nón naśad yáḥ pitáram̐ ná véda

In which tree all the honey-eating birds settle and breed,
at its top, they say, is the sweet berry. No one reaches it who does not know the father.[141]

The language is richly metaphorical, as in the dirty riddles, and, as with them, "solving" the riddle does not simply involve identifying a single referent ("Who walks alone?": "*The sun.*") but a complex situation with several referents, possibly working on more than one level at a time—e.g. a riddle may depict both a cosmic and a ritual situation simultaneously.[142]

The priests' brahmodya at the Aśvamedha seems to have been "fixed"—simplified and routinized into an automatic responsive litany, with no possibility of a wrong answer. But it seems likely that this replaced a discussion in which there was some risk. There was intellectual challenge both in formulating a metaphorical representation of a cosmic or mystical truth, and in recognizing the homologies involved in this representation, that is, in solving the riddle. Needless to say, both activities afforded crucial training in exactly the kind of theological speculation that informs Vedic and Upaniṣadic discourse.

The place in the ritual where this more challenging type of dialogue is preserved is precisely in the exchanges with the wives at the horse's deathbed. The style remains complex and allusive, and the answers are not given. Perhaps prudery kept the ritualists from replacing these riddles with more straightforward ones (though prudery did not have much other influence on the proceedings). Perhaps sex and fertility retained more ambivalently viewed mystery than "mere" cosmic truths. Or perhaps at the time when the verbal portions of the ritual were modernized and given fixed form, the women's dialogues were considered simply foolish prattle and were left as they were.

Whatever the reason for their preservation, I think we must treat these riddling dialogues as deeply serious attempts to approach and verbally harness the mysterious forces released in sexual activity. The tepid and simplistic exchanges between the priests that we have just examined are not the real continuators of the ancient brahmodya tradition: this is found in the women's dialogues, where both intellectual and emotional risks are taken. The earnest intent of the formulations contrasts with the deliberate lewdness in which they are cast. The result is verbal material of remarkable, disturbing power, which both repels and draws us even now, in a time when we hardly react to the crude obscenity that daily bombards us.

If the women's exchanges at the Aśvamedha are the true continuators of the ancient brahmodya tradition, this in turn suggests that the *particular* pairs of verses preserved in the extant ritual were not the only possible ones, but that the exchanges reproduced above happen to be the liturgically frozen remains of a single, especially favored version of the ritual. In other words, it seems to me possible that in the early Vedic period, the verbal part of the Aśvamedha was no more fixed than that of any other ritual. In various slots of any ritual there was a regular place for the freely composed hymns the Rigvedic bards turned out in such numbers: a new hymn to Agni, say, or Soma would be commissioned and inserted in the service, just as a new Bach cantata enlivened each Sunday service in Leipzig.

The suggestive exchanges in the center of the Aśvamedha might be a natural place where verbal inventiveness, perhaps even a bit of improvisation, would be appropriate, and one can imagine the Vedic bard welcoming such a "job," as a lively change from the gravitas of his usual assignments. As time went on, the liturgy became fixed, and only one set of dialogues was preserved for us *within the codified Aśvamedha*.

3. The Aśvamedha and Rig Veda X.86

But I think it quite possible that our Vedic texts preserve other remnants from this portion of the ritual. Early Vedic literature contains a few other examples of deliberate bawdiness. Scattered through the RV and AV are individual verses with erotic similes,[143] depictions of mythological couplings (like the incestuous rape of his daughter by Heaven/Sun),[144] and so forth. The last book of the AV contains the so-called Kuntāpa sequence of hymns,[145] much of which is salacious in nature (but badly transmitted and often quite obscure).

Since *all* Vedic texts are religious texts and owe their preservation to membership in a meticulously guarded canon, we must always ask what liturgical purpose an apparently mundane text might serve. This is especially true of the so-called secular hymns of the Rig Veda. No matter how these hymns strike our modern ears, we must not assume that the redactors of this most sacred of texts made room in the tradition for miscellaneous saucy ballads and popular songs, even in the apparently heterogeneous Xth Maṇḍala. I would suggest that some of this material was utilized in the portions of the Aśvamedha just discussed—or in similar ritual situations, like the Mahāvrata Day to be treated later.

In particular, I consider the most sustained and accessible parallel to our Aśvamedha material to be the famous (or, rather, notorious) Vṛṣākapi hymn of the RV (X.86), which contains obscene dialogue rather like what we have recently encountered.

Unfortunately the "accessibility" of this hymn is a relative matter. Though its location in the RV ensures the excellence of its textual preservation and the grammar and vocabulary do not present their common RVic difficulties, the contents and context of the hymn are extremely puzzling. It is a dialogue with three (or four) participants: the great god Indra, his wife Indrāṇī, the monkey companion of Indra Vṛṣākapi (lit. 'virile/bullish monkey'[146]), and possibly *his* wife. The situation depicted is a sort of triangle: Indrāṇī berates Indra for his friendship with Vṛṣākapi, who in turn verbally abuses and sexually taunts Indrāṇī. But why Vṛṣākapi is allowed such license, what the quarrel is really about, how the situation is resolved, and what the ultimate point of the hymn is are among the many open questions. A potential connection between RV X.86 and the Aśvamedha has already been suggested by O'Flaherty (1981, p. 261), but her treatment of the Vṛṣākapi hymn is so eclectic that she did not work out the details of any of the connections hinted at.

I would suggest that reading the hymn with the Aśvamedha in mind may illuminate some (by no means all) of the hymn's dark corners, and this may in turn make the underlying assumptions in the Aśvamedha's ritual copulation somewhat clearer. Accordingly, I will embark here on a lengthy digression, analyzing this difficult hymn in this context.[147]

I think it is possible to read the Vṛṣākapi hymn as a mock-Aśvamedha: the elements of its "plot" can be correlated with portions of the ritual, the dialogue compared to the ritual exchanges we have examined above. In this interpretation Indra fills the role of king and Sacrificer, Indrāṇī of the Mahiṣī, and Vṛṣākapi of the horse/victim. I am not suggesting that there is a one-to-one correlation between every element in the hymn and a feature of the ritual, nor that the chronology of the hymn exactly follows that of the ritual, nor—especially—that we should ignore the delightful tone of domestic squabbling in order to match the hymn solemnly to the ritual. Quite the opposite: its risqué and aggressive teasing captures the mood of that bizarre spectacle.

Let us examine the points of contact between hymn and ritual, verse by verse, but beginning with the hymn's refrain, the line that serves as the fifth pāda of every verse:

> RV X.86.1–23 víśvasmād índra úttaraḥ
>
> Indra above all!

The line does not appear to fit easily into the hymn. Particularly in its early parts Indra seems more like a henpecked (and probably cuckolded) husband than a superior being. However, if the hymn depicts a (mock-)Aśvamedha, with Indra as king/Sacrificer, the refrain makes sense. The point of the Aśvamedha is to consolidate, display, and *declare* the king's supreme power, and "Indra above all" insistently does so, even when it does not seem appropriate. Everything in the hymn is ultimately designed to exalt Indra.

The hymn begins with an apparent exchange[148] between Indra and his wife Indrāṇī about Indra's raffish pal, the monkey Vṛṣākapi, who has been causing trouble by "getting high on the goodies of the ari ('stranger/Aryan')." Vṛṣākapi's 'wavering course' (vyáthiḥ) is referred to in verse 2. Meanwhile, Indra complains of neglect, and Indrāṇī bluntly tells him he must look elsewhere for worshipers.

RV X.86.1 ví hí sótor ásṛkṣata néndraṃ devám amaṃsata
yátrấmadad vṛṣấkapir aryáḥ puṣṭéṣu mátsakhā
víśvasmād índra úttaraḥ

[Indra:] Indeed, they have left off pressing (soma); they have not honored (/stopped honoring) Indra (as) god
(in the places) where my comrade Vṛṣākapi was getting high on the goodies of the ari.
—Above all Indra!

RV X.86.2 párā hī̀ndra dhấvasi vṛṣấkaper áti vyáthiḥ
nó áha prá vindasy anyátra sómapītaye
víśvasmād índra úttaraḥ

[Indrāṇī:] Indeed, o Indra, you run away beyond (/pass over) the wavering course of Vṛṣākapi,
and you do not find anywhere else for soma-drinking.
—Above all Indra!

What could this possibly have to do with the Aśvamedha? I suggest that this is a mocking variant of the great yearlong journey of the sacrificial horse. As we will see below, the chosen animal is ceremonially prepared and then sent off, to wander at will through anyone's territory he wants, eating off the land, guarded by hundreds of armed men supplied by the king. In these verses this grand progress is reduced to the mischievous pilfering of a monkey, which causes his protector to lose some friends.[149]

The worried tone of the first two verses, the possible loss of Indra's worshipers, requires some comment, but, I think, clarifies some aspects of the Aśvamedha that the ritual texts soft-pedal. Though we tend to think of this ritual as a triumphal one, celebrating the supernal power of an especially great king, it seems likely that such a complex and expensive spectacle was undertaken only when a threat to that power, past or present, was perceived.

In the Rāmāyaṇa Rāma's father performs the ritual because he is childless: a threat to the continuance of his line, as well as a sign that he lacks the virile power of a great king (R I.11, esp. vs. 8). In Mahābhārata XIV Yudhiṣṭhira undertakes an Aśvamedha after the Kurus are defeated, but not as a cheerful postwar celebration. Instead it is an attempt to assuage his guilt[150] about the disastrous and divisive war. Vyāsa repeatedly (MBh XIV.3; XIV.70.16; 90.15–16) promises the deeply depressed king that performing the Aśvamedha will make him free from the evil (pāpman) he has accumulated from killing, and the smell of the horse's cooked omentum when the sacrifice is finally offered brings him 'the destruction of all evil' (sarvapāpmāpaham, XIV.91.4). The mood of the Aśvamedhika Parvan is grim, not exultant;[151] the most that the sacrifice produces is a certain release.

Thus the epic examples suggest that it was anxiety or difficulty that motivated the performance of an Aśvamedha, and our possible RVic example conforms to this notion. In RV X.86 Indra is a great god/king, whose transcendence is implicitly challenged and whose support is dropping off. Even his wife mocks him, and for companionship he is reduced to a monkey. He needs the great sacrifice to produce a change in his fortunes.

The next verse introduces the emotional tensions of the domestic triangle that will dominate the middle part of the hymn. Indra berates Indrāṇī for her supposed jealousy of the monkey.

RV X.86.3 kím ayám̧ tvā́m̧ vr̥ṣā́kapiś cakā́ra hárito mr̥gáḥ
yásmā irasyásīd u nv àryó vā puṣṭimád vásu
víśvasmāt . . .

[Indra:] What has this tawny beast Vr̥ṣākapi done to you
—or to the thriving goods[152] of the ari—that you are envious of him?
—Above all . . . !

Note in passing the verbal and thematic echoes of the verse exchanged between Pālāgalī and Kṣattar/Adhvaryu in the Aśvamedha dialogues:

VS XXIII.30 yád *dhariṇó* yávam átti ná *puṣṭám̧* paśú mányate
śūdrā́ yád *árya*jārā ná *póṣāya* dhanāyati

When the *deer* eats grain, it doesn't consider the *nourished* beast (or, doesn't consider itself a nourished beast?).

When a Śūdra woman has an *Arya* for a lover, she (/he?) doesn't need riches *to thrive*.

Here in the first half-verse a different animal is consuming goodies (puṣṭá) that also do not belong to him, and in fact the two animals can be connected. The 'deer' word here literally means 'the tawny one' (hariṇá- [the initial *d* in the verse is sandhi-induced]), and Vr̥ṣākapi is called 'the tawny beast' (haritó mr̥gáḥ) in verse 3.[153] In the second half-verse the goodies, in the form of a lover, are identified as Aryan. Though it is hard to know where a monkey would fit in the varṇa system, I would wager that he would be a Śūdra. In any case, it seems likely to me that these verbal echoes between RV X.86 and the Aśvamedha riddles are deliberate.

Indrāṇī replies to Indra's question of verse 3 with two verses of invective:

RV X.86.4 yám imám̧ tvám̧ vr̥ṣā́kapim priyám indrābhirákṣasi
śvā́ nv àsya jambhiṣad ápi kárṇe varāhayúr
víśvasmāt . . .
5 priyā́ taṣṭā́ni me kapír vyàktā vy àdūduṣat
śíro nv àsya rāviṣam̧ ná sugám̧ duṣkŕ̥te bhuvam̧
víśvasmāt . . .

4 [Indrāṇī:] This dear Vr̥ṣākapi that you protect, o Indra—
the boar-hunting dog will snap at his ear.
(—Above all . . . !)

5 The monkey has spoiled[154] my dear (well-)shaped and decorated things.
I will break his head. I will not be easygoing for a bad actor.
(—Above all . . . !)

The potential sexual double meanings here are fairly obvious, and have been pointed out by others (see e.g. Geldner's and O'Flaherty's notes on this verse). The sexual innuendo is both veiled and comparatively mild; in the Aśvamedha paradigm it might correspond with the teasing introduction of the horse: "No one is 'leading' me. The little horsikins is sleeping," though the tone here is not of affectionate mockery but of petty annoyance.

There may be another level of reference, however. In verse 4 the curse she lays on him

RV X.86.4 śvā́ nv àsya jambhiṣad ápi kárṇe varāhayúḥ
The boar-hunting dog will snap at his ear.

may be a glancing allusion to another early episode in the Aśvamedha. Before the horse is sent on its travels, it stands in water into which a dog is brought and killed (by a whore's son; see III.E.3). The dog is then put under the horse's feet, a symbolic display of the horse's vanquishing powers. Indrāṇī seems to be testily suggesting here that the tables might be turned.[155]

The last pāda of the next verse alludes even more direly to the eventual fate of the sacrificial victim:

RV X.86.5 ná sugáṃ duṣkṛ́te bhuvam
I will not be easygoing for a bad actor.

'Easygoing' (sugá) is an adjective that characteristically modifies 'path' (pánthā). Though it can (and does), of course, have an erotic interpretation, it may also deliberately evoke another RVic verse:

RV I.162.21 ná vā́ u etán mriyase ná riṣyasi devā́ṁ íd eṣi pathíbhiḥ *sugébhiḥ*
You do not die nor are you harmed. You go to the gods along *easygoing* paths.

This verse comes from the RVic Aśvamedha hymn, and it is employed in the ritual sūtras at the moment when the horse is *put to death*. Indrāṇī's railings at the monkey thus contain some rather mean-spirited references to his upcoming demise.

The erotic hints of verse 5 give way abruptly to raw sexuality in verses 6–7, almost surely spoken by Indrāṇī and Vṛṣākapi, respectively:

RV X.86.6 ná mát strī́ subhasáttarā ná suyā́śutarā bhuvat
ná mát práticyavīyasī ná sákthy údyamīyasī

[Indrāṇī[156]:] No woman has a better bottom than me or will be more eager for sex (?).
None is better at counter-thrusting than me, nor raises her thighs higher.[157]

RV X.86.7 uvé amba sulābhike yáthevāṅgá bhaviṣyáti
bhasán me amba sákthi me śíro me vì̄va hr̥ṣyati

[Vr̥ṣākapi:] I see, o mummy easy to get, how it's really gonna be.
My bottom, o mummy, *my* thigh, *my* "head" are getting, like,[158] excited.

We have encountered this wrenching plunge into lewd talk before, exactly at the point in the Aśvamedha when the Mahiṣī lies down with the horse. And it is not merely the tone that is similar. Note the double vocative amba 'mummy', which also introduces both the clean and the dirty versions of the Mahiṣī's address to the horse:

ámbe ámbāly ámbike	
ná mā nayati káś caná	ná mā yabhati káś cana
sasásty aśvakáḥ	
O Mummy, Mummikins, little Mummy.	
No one is leading me.	No one is fucking me.
The horsikins is sleeping.	

Note also that the RV vocative sequence amba su*lābhike* is phonetically reminiscent of the version (VS XXIII.18 [cf. MS III.12.2]) of the vocative ambe . . . *ambālike*, with flipped *lābh/bāl*.

This exchange seems to me to signal the moment of sexual consummation, the equivalent of the Mahiṣī's moment under the blanket with the horse. Indrāṇī first indicates reluctance in her hectoring verses 4 and 5, but then signals her participation by boasting about her sexual charms in verse 6—the willingness readily perceived by Vr̥ṣākapi in verse 7. It is as if the dead horse speaks. Just as in the ritual counterpart, the verbal vulgarity here signals overt sexual action—recall the rawness of the verse addressed to the Mahiṣī when she reaches for the horse's penis.

The function of the next verses is less clear. Verse 8 continues with the praise of Indrāṇī's body, but somewhat less coarsely:

RV X.86.8 kíṃ subāho svaṅgure pŕ̥thuṣṭó pŕ̥thujāghane
kíṃ śūrapatni nas tvám abhy àmīṣi vr̥ṣā́kapim

[Indra?:] Why, o well-armed, well-fingered, broad-braided, broad-backsided one[159]—
why, o wife of a hero, do you vex our Vr̥ṣākapi?

The verse is probably Indra's, and forms half of an exchange with Indrāṇī:

RV X.86.9 avī́rām iva mā́m ayáṃ śarā́rur abhí manyate
utā́hám asmi vīríṇī́ndrapatnī marútsakhā

[Indrāṇī:] This noxious creature has intentions toward me, as if I lacked a man.
And I *have* a man—with Indra as husband and the Maruts as companions.

In part this dialogue is simply a reprise of the similar exchange in verses 3–4, where Indra asked Indrāṇī what she had against Vr̥ṣākapi. But in the context of the Aśvamedha it is possible to see Indra's question as a sly and comic reference to the thrashing around under the blanket. The Mahiṣī's manipulation of the recently dead (and, I would assume, unwieldy) victim could appear more like hostility—deliberate vexation—than sex. Remember also that the Sacrificer/husband led the mockery of the horse and wife in the ritual. Indrāṇī's response maintains the ambiguity between sex and hostility: the verb abhí √man, literally, 'set one's mind on', means both 'desire' and 'persecute'. The English rendering 'have intentions toward' may weakly capture this double meaning.

Indrāṇī also raises the issue that will dominate the next verses (9–11): what is one to think of a woman who will do such a thing? Is she reduced to sex with a monkey (/horse) because she lacks a man? She appears to have behaved like a whore, but in fact she is the glorious wife of a glorious husband: in verse 10 she is again praised as vīríṇī 'having a man/hero' and índrapatnī 'having Indra as husband'. Her apparently unchaste action in fact ensures that her husband will not die, as verse 11 states.

RV X.86.10 saṃhotrám sma purā́ nā́rī sámanaṃ vā́va gachati
vedhā́ ṛtásya vīríṇī́ndrapatnī mahīyate
11 indrāṇī́m āsú nā́riṣu subhágām ahám aśravam
nahy àsyā aparáṃ caná jarásā márate pátiḥ

10 Until now the woman has been accustomed to come down to the joint offering[160] or to the encounter.
(Now) she is magnified as the Ordainer of Truth, as one having a man / hero, having Indra as husband.[161]
11 I have heard of Indrāṇī as (most) fortunate among these women.
For indeed never, even in the future, will her husband die of old age.

Notice her epithet in verse 10: vedhā́ ṛtásya 'the Ordainer of Truth' (vel sim.). Vedhás is an august ritual title, and the "vedhas of truth" appears to be an Indo-Iranian designation, preserved in personal names (e.g. Aves. Ašavazdah; see Mayrhofer, KEWA s.v. vedhā́ḥ). This collocation appears only here in Vedic. To apply a title of such archaic dignity to a female, especially one that a few verses ago was boasting about her sexual tricks to a monkey, is extraordinary. But no more so than the rapid shift in tone at the end of the *ritual* episode, when jokey sexual innuendo gives way to a solemn laud of the dead horse. Indeed, verse 11 indrāṇī́m . . . ahám aśravam "I have heard of Indrāṇī . . . ," with fronted name and first person aorist ceremonial annunciation reminds us exactly of dadhikrāvṇo akāriṣam "I have celebrated Dadhikravan," which inaugurates the praise of the horse.

Here, for once, the much-tried Mahiṣī gets some credit. It is her activity in the Aśvamedha that brings the ritual benefits to her husband, and the verbally extravagant glorification of Indrāṇī in these verses recognizes this fact. *She* is responsible, through this humiliating sexual performance, for the continued fame, indeed the immortality, of her husband.

The next few verses in most interpretations of this hymn have an especially hectic character. Indrāṇī has banished Vṛṣākapi from the house. Indra misses him and slams off after him. He arrives at Vṛṣākapi's house, where Mrs. Vṛṣākapi proceeds to whip up a particularly tasty set of oblations. And so on.[162] This does not strike me as a likely RVic literary tactic. Though RVic hymns often refer to different actions, belonging to different time periods, these actions are not usually arranged in a *plot*, even a plot with the links left out. In recounting mythological narratives there is rather a single focused *event*, to which other mentioned events are related thematically, not chronologically.[163]

In the genre of dialogue hymns, to which X.86 belongs, the focus is even more intense; the dialogue seems bound by a set of almost Classical unities. Hymns like I.179 (Agastya and Lopāmudrā), X.10 (Yama and Yamī), X. 95 (Pururavas and Urvaśī) present only the speaking participants, captured at a single moment in a single place, with no narrative frame,[164] no "action," no movement. Other events, both past and future, can be alluded to by the speakers but not experienced or narrated. I think we should seek an interpretation of X.86 that fits these conventions as closely as possible. That we have no literary theory preserved from this period does not mean that rules of genre did not exist.

Interpreting the hymn as a veiled Horse Sacrifice allows the next verses to form a coherent part of the dialogue already established, without requiring change of venue or speakers. Verses 12–15 concern in part a new series of oblations to Indra. The first two (12, 13) in the sequence of oblation verses both mourn the loss of Vṛṣākapi and promise Mrs. Vṛṣākapi a rich and fertile life. The two verses appear to be addressed to Indrāṇī and Mrs. V., respectively:

RV X.86.12 nā́hám indrāṇi rārana sákhyur vṛṣā́kaper ṛté
yásyedám ápyam háviḥ priyáṃ devéṣu gáchati

O Indrāṇī, I find no pleasure without my friend Vṛṣākapi,
whose watery dear / own oblation goes here and now (idám) to the gods.

RV X.86.13 vṛ́ṣākapāyi révati súputra ā́d u súsnuṣe
ghásat ta índra ukṣánaḥ priyáṃ kācitkarám háviḥ

O wife of Vṛṣākapi, rich, having good sons and daughters-in-law,
Indra will eat your oxen (and) the dear / own oblation that effects whatever (you want).

These are the verses that have Oldenberg sending Indra on the road, leaving Indrāṇī and showing up at Vṛṣākapi's place expecting a meal. There is, I think, a simpler solution within the Aśvamedha framework. Vṛṣākapi has not been banished from the house. He is dead, the sacrificial victim, and the oblation that is now going to the gods is made of himself, hence the priyám: 'dear, own'.[165]

Indra addresses his regret for his sacrificed friend to his own wife, Indrāṇī. And then, by my interpretation, in the next verse he addresses *the same woman* as 'wife of Vṛṣākapi' (vṛ́ṣākapāyi). Indrāṇī qualifies as such, since she just copulated with him, and it was this act that will make her rich and fertile, as the proleptic vocatives say. She is both the "real" wife of Indra and the temporary ritual wife of the victim, and she can pass the benefits from the latter situation to her partner in the former.

Having the same person as referent for both these vocatives in these paired verses solves one of the unacknowledged problems of this hymn. Because of the vocative vṛ́ṣākapāyi, most interpretations have required the existence and participation of this fourth character, but the dynamics of the hymn's interaction seem that of a triangle.[166] Vṛṣākapāyī has little to do and seems dramatically superfluous, and accounting for her presence has been responsible for some of the more twisted portions of previous interpretations.

Indrāṇī's mating with Vṛṣākapi, like the central act of the Aśvamedha, gives access to the previously constricted fertility and ritual fervor, and reestablishes the ritual connections between Indra and his recently reluctant worshipers. The lament with which Indra began

RV X.86.1 ví hí sótor ásṛkṣata néndraṃ devám amaṃsata

Indeed, they have left off pressing (soma); they have not honored (/ stopped honoring) Indra (as) god.

is answered by his exultation in the oblation in the next two verses. Verse 14 contains one of my favorite Rigvedic lines, in praise of a high-cholesterol diet:

RV X.86.14 ukṣṇó hí me páñcadaśa sākám pácanti viṃśatím
utā́hám admi pī́va íd ubhā́ kukṣī́ pṛṇanti me

They cook fifteen oxen at a time for me—twenty.
And I eat only the fat meat.[167] They fill both my cheeks.[168]

The next verse is ritually more important because it announces that Indra is receiving *soma* again.

RV X.86.15 vṛṣabhó ná tigmáśṛṅgo 'ntár yūthéṣu róruvat
manthás ta indra śáṃ hṛdé yáṃ te sunóti bhāvayúḥ

Like a sharp-horned bull roaring within the herd,
the 'stirred' (libation), which the one desiring prosperity presses for you, is weal for your heart, o Indra.

Most interpreters[169] claim that the offering in verse 15 is *not* soma, but a substitute for it, a type of porridge called mantha in the later ritual texts. But this seems unlikely. The first half verse presents a simile for the common action of mixing soma with cows' milk:

vṛṣabhó ná tigmáśṛṅgo 'ntár yūthéṣu róruvat

Like a sharp-horned bull roaring within the herd . . .

The comparandum in the verse is the manthá- or 'stirred' libation, which must at this time refer to soma mixed with milk. Not only does the verse say that it has been 'pressed', the usual preparation for soma

RV X.86.15 mantháḥ . . . yáṃ te *sunóti* bhāvayúḥ

The 'stirred' (libation), which the one desiring prosperity *presses* for you.

but the almost identical term manthín- clearly refers to a mixed soma brew in the RV:

RV III.32.2 gávāśiram manthínam indra śukrám píbā sómam . . .

O Indra, drink the soma, with a bovine admixture, stirred (and also) pure.

The later mantha-porridge of the ritual sūtras is clearly not meant here. This may seem like a minor point, but, as often with ritual minutiae, it actually crucially affects how we interpret the purport of the hymn.

If the purpose of the Aśvamedha is to affirm the power of the king who offers it, the ritual in this hymn can be seen to *re*affirm Indra's power as god, his right to receive the choicest of oblations — bulls and soma — which seems to have lapsed in the early part of the hymn. The ritual is over and has achieved the desired results.

There now follow a pair of bawdy verses which, with their strict verbal responsion, remind us of the exchanges between wives and priests in the Aśvamedha, where only genders and similar grammatical functions were switched. The slighting reference to male sexual performance is also familiar from that ritual.

RV X.86.16 ná séśe yásya rámbhate 'ntarā́ sakthyā̀ kápṛt
séd ī́śe yásya romaśáṃ niṣedúṣo vijṛ́mbhate

He is not master, whose penis hangs between (his) thighs [nonerect].
He is master, for whose (penis), the hairy (vulva) gapes when it [erect penis] has sat down.

RV X.86.17 ná séśe yásya romaśáṃ niṣedúṣo vijṛ́mbhate
séd ī́śe yásya rámbhate 'ntarā́ sakthyā̀ kápṛt

He is not master, for whose (penis), the hairy (vulva) gapes when it [erect penis] has sat down.
He is master, whose penis hangs between (his thighs) [nonerect].

In my opinion, the partners in this dialogue are Indra and Indrāṇī, the only two of our actors left alive under my interpretation.[170] Which one says which verse probably depends on what mood we think Indrāṇī is in after her experience. In any case the first verse expresses what might be considered a universal opinion: the sexually successful male has the power, while his opposite is 'impotent' in both senses. The second verse reverses this statement into a striking paradox. The second speaker both literally and figuratively has the last word, and we are obviously expected to take it as the formulation of a deeper truth than the banal sentiment of the first verse.

As it happens, this truth is *dramatized* by the Aśvamedha, and so it has particular force here. The sexually "successful" male in the ritual is the horse, which mates with the woman. But the horse is *dead*, its real power gone even as it engages in sex.[171] The king is a cuckold, witness to the act and even required to urge it on verbally, while remaining sexually inactive. *But* he is the master, and his power is increased by the sexual act in which he does not take part.

This control (in both senses) on the part of the king is ceremonially enacted earlier in the ritual. During the year when the horse is journeying, the king lies nightly with his favorite wife (Vāvātā), but does not have sex.

KŚS XX.1.17 . . . hute 'gnihotre 'pareṇa gārhapatyam udakśirāḥ saṃviśati
18 ūrvantare vāvātāyā brahmacārī

After the Agnihotra is offered, (the Sacrificer) lies down behind the Gārhapatya, with his head toward the north.

(He) observes chastity between the thighs of the Vāvātā.

KŚS XX.3.5 vāvātāsaṃveśana- . . . saṃvatsaram

(The observances previously mentioned) of lying with the Vāvātā wife (etc.). . . . (continue) for a year.

ŚB XIII.4.1.9 jaghánena gā́rhapatyam údaṅ vā́vātayā sahá sáṃviśati . . . só 'ntaróru̇́ ásaṃvartamānaḥ śete 'néna tápasā svastí saṃvatsarásyodṛ́caṁ sámaśnavā íti

He lies down with the Favorite Wife west of the Gārhapatya. He lies between her thighs without embracing her, (thinking) "May I, by this austerity, reach the end of the year successfully."

Similarly, the horse on its travels is to be kept away from female horses, and if it should mate with one, an expiatory oblation is required.[172]

The sentiment expressed by these proscriptions is the standard one of later India, so frequently found in the epics: retention of semen creates power, which is dissipated by emission. We have discussed this before. The above pair of verses in the Vṛṣākapi hymn is one of its earliest explicit statements.[173]

The verse pair also marks the climactic end to the mock-Aśvamedha, in my interpretation. What follows is a kind of extended pun relating the two journeys of the victim—the yearlong rambling that preceded the sacrifice and the journey to the gods that follows the killing of the victim. This sequence begins with a sort of summary verse of the ritual:

RV X.86.18 ayám indra vr̥ṣā́kapiḥ párasvantaṃ hatā́ṃ vidat
asíṃ sūnā́ṃ návaṃ carúm ā́d édhasyā́na ā́citam

O Indra, this Vr̥ṣākapi found a slaughtered parasvant [ass?],
a knife, a basket, a new pot, and a wagon piled with firewood.

Since von Schroeder (1908, p. 311), this ritual has been identified with an expiatory gr̥hya ritual (PārGS III.12.2) for a student's lapse from chastity. But, as Oldenberg points out (*Noten* ad loc.), perhaps the more important association (already noted by von Schroeder) is one found in the AV (VI.72.2, 3), where the parasvant is identified as having an especially big penis in a charm for virility.[174] Vr̥ṣākapi is in some sense identified with this virile victim, and his 'discovery' of the ritual equipment may refer to the ritual preparations the Aśvamedha victim finds waiting for him at the end of his year's journey.

This journey, alluded to in verses 1–2, is enlarged on in the following verses, where Vr̥ṣākapi[175] asserts its grander purpose:

RV X.86.19 ayám emi vicā́kaśad, vicinván dā́sam ā́ryam
píbāmi pākasútvano 'bhí dhī́ram acākaśam

Here I go inspecting, distinguishing between barbarian and Aryan.
I drink (the offering) of the sincere presser. I have gazed upon the wise.

In the next verse the great distance and varied terrain he has traversed are alluded to, and Vr̥ṣākapi is urged to return:

RV X.86.20 dhánva ca yát kr̥ntátraṃ ca káti svit tā́ ví yójanā
nédīyaso vr̥ṣākapé 'stam éhi gr̥hā́m̐ úpa

The waste place and the precipice—how many yojanas [a measure of distance] are they
away (from here).
O Vr̥ṣākapi, come home, to the nearer houses.

The purpose of the return, the sacrifice of the traveler, is not mentioned.

This interpretation of these verses presents one difficulty that other interpretations evade. It assumes that the hymn does not proceed in absolute chronological order, for while the intermediate verses depict the actual sacrifice, these refer back to the original journey. However, let us remember that most RVic narrative is distinctly *not* chronological, but alludes to events in jumbled and imaginatively reshaped order. Moreover, the reconstructions of the plot of this hymn that assume that it *is* chronological (and all of the standard treatments do) can produce some rather ridiculous scenarios, with the air of a TV sitcom with an overdetermined plot: the main characters quarreling and storming out of the house and making up and returning, all in perpetual motion. I think it is at least worth considering another strategy of interpretation.

The following "journey" verses (21–22) provide a subtle transition to the more permanent journey of death:

RV X.86.21 púnar éhi vṛṣākape suvitā́ kalpayāvahai
yá eṣá svapnanáṃśanó 'stam éṣi pathā́ púnaḥ

Come here again, o Vṛṣākapi. We two will arrange good goings (for you)
who, as sleep-destroyer / -attainer,[176] go home again along the path.

Here I think Indrāṇī is speaking (as do most other interpreters), adding to Indra's invitation (see vs. 20) her own encouragement to Vṛṣākapi to return from his yearlong ramblings. But her verse is sinisterly phrased. She will, in fact, arrange 'good goings' for him—to the world of the dead. (Compare vs. 5, where she initially refused to be 'easygoing' [sugá] for him.) He will not only *destroy* her sleep (temporarily) when they lie together, but he will *attain* permanent sleep in the sacrifice. It is hard not to connect this epithet with the Mahiṣī's mocking refrain in the Aśvamedha, sasásty aśvakáḥ "The horsikins is sleeping."[177] Finally, she suggests he will "go home along the path," which again seems an oblique reference to the mantra that accompanies the slaughter of the horse in the ritual:

RV I.162.21 ná vā́ u etán mriyase ná riṣyasi devā́m̐ íd eṣi *pathíbhiḥ* sugébhiḥ

You do not die nor are you harmed. You go to the gods along easygoing *paths*.

X.86.21 thus unites both the 'path' and a synonym for 'easygoing': su(v)-itá- (√i 'go') vs. su-gá- (√gam 'go'), though not in the same constituent.

The last verse directly relating to the Vṛṣākapi saga is probably spoken by the poet, outside the frame of the story, and it leaves us tantalizingly hanging. It consists of two questions, to which we can supply our own puzzled answers:

RV X.86.22 yád údañco vṛṣākape gṛhám indrā́jagantana
kvà syá pulvaghó mṛgáḥ kám agañ janayópanaḥ

When, o Vṛṣākapi, o Indra, you all[178] went home upward/to the north,
where (was) this beast of many misdeeds, to whom did the remover of men go?

My answers are as puzzled as those of others, but I would point out that the actual place where the horse is slaughtered in the Aśvamedha is *north* of the Mahāvedi ('great altar'), and the horse is led there right before the killing from his place tied to the yūpa[179] ('stake') east of the Mahāvedi. Whatever the answers to the deeper questions, the verse seems to locate the victim in its place of sacrifice. It may then refer obliquely to the great journey of death.

The final verse of this maddening hymn has no apparent connection with what precedes it:

RV X.86.23 párśur ha nā́ma mānavī́ sākáṃ sasūva viṃśatím
bhadráṃ bhala tyásyā abhūd yásyā udáram ā́mayat

Manu's wife / daughter, Parśu ('Rib') by name, gave birth to twenty at once.
(Good) fortune indeed was there for her whose belly (labor-pain) vexed.

This verse seems to function as a Zauberspruch[180] expressing the happy result to be expected from recitation of the hymn or reference to its story. And the desired result is, of course, fertility and the production of many sons. Let us first remember that the Aśvamedha can be directed, at least partially, to these ends. Recall the explicit mantras urging the horse to impregnate the Mahiṣī[181] and also remember that Rāma's father performs this ritual as a remedy for childlessness in Rāmāyaṇa I.

Though the last verse seems at first distant in content from the rest of the hymn, its verbal configuration explicitly echoes phrases found elsewhere in the hymn. The structure of the second pāda

sākáṃ sasūva viṃśatím
She gave birth to twenty at once

exactly matches that of verse 14:

sākám pácanti viṃśatím
They cook twenty (oxen) at once.

In verse 14 the performance of the ritual broke the sacrificial deadlock that had kept Indra from receiving offerings, and produced a welcome overabundance of food and drink for him. In the final verse the explosive abundance is of sons.[182] Ritual plenty induces the same in the mundane world.

The other parallel is between

yásyā udáram *ā́mayat*
. . . Whose belly (labor-pain) *vexed.*

and verse 8

kíṃ śūrapatni nas tvám *abhy àmīṣi* vṛṣā́kapim
Why, o wife of a hero, *do you vex* our Vṛṣākapi?

Here verbs belonging to the same root √am 'vex' (a root of relative rarity in the RV)[183] express two almost complementary actions. As we saw earlier, in verse 8 the 'vexing' of Vṛṣākapi can be interpreted as the Mahiṣī's act of copulation with the victim. This leads, sometime later, to the 'vexing' labor pains of the birth of twenty. In fact, we might even interpret the belly-vexing pain as referring not only to labor, but also to the initial sexual activity that caused it, which vexed the other sexual partner.

So, though neither the personnel nor the central event of the final verse has any apparent connection with the rest of the hymn, verbal echoes reinforce the thematic connections: the fertility to arise from the performance of the Aśvamedha, the ritual covertly depicted in the rest of the hymn.

My reading of the Vṛṣākapi hymn differs radically from those of other commentators and, like theirs, supplies far more context for its verses than is ever made explicit. It may seem far-fetched—indeed it does in part seem so even to me. But I am emboldened to propose it because, on the one hand, the other interpretations seem unsatisfactory—implausible in their reconstruction of events and unfaithful to the conventions of this Vedic genre—and, on the other, because a self-consistent interpretation of the hymn *can* be constructed in the context of the Aśvamedha, taking into account the style and tone of the hymn, as well as the actions and participants. It is especially the diction of the hymn, evoking that of the obscene exchanges in the center of the Aśvamedha, that convinces me that they belong in the same realm.

I suggest that the Vṛṣākapi hymn is a verbal remnant predating the codification of the ritual, a hymn once employed ritually in the Aśvamedha that did not make it into the fixed liturgy of that ritual.[184] The entire hymn may have been acted out by the ritual participants. Or certain pairs of verses, for example 6/7 and 16/17, may have constituted the original liturgy, and a hymn was later created around them, perhaps reshaping a well-known folk tale. Though the hymn, however constituted, did not become *the* orthodox Aśvamedha script of the middle Vedic ritual, it was given a place in the motley Tenth Maṇḍala of the Rig Veda—perhaps because of its artistry, or its clever innuendo, or even its almost impenetrable weirdness. For this we may extend our baffled thanks to the redactors.

E. Sexuality and Fertility—"Negative" Representations

Vedic ritual presents several examples of what, for want of a better term, I will call "negative sexuality": situations in which what appears to be sexual misconduct or disfunction is again used to channel sexual energy into the ritual.

1. The Confession at the Varuṇapraghāsa

Let us begin with a curious incident in the second of the yearly seasonal rituals (Cāturmāsyāni or 'Four-monthly' rituals), the Varuṇapraghāsa 'the devouring [subjective genitive] of Varuṇa', which occurs at the beginning of the rainy season. Varuṇa is, of course, in part a stern god who punishes injustice and untruth, and this character of his accounts for some of the interpretations of the act we are about to examine.

At a point early in the course of this ritual, just before the priest (Pratiprasthātar) is to lead the wife away to make an offering, he asks her either (depending on the text) "Who is your lover?" or "How many lovers do you have?" Let us examine some of the variants of this question:

MŚS I.7.4.11 . . . pratiprasthātā gārhapatyānte pṛchati patni kati te kāntāḥ

The Pratiprasthātar at the edge of the Gārhapatya asks, "Wife, how many beloveds do you have?"

ĀpŚS VIII.6.20 . . . patni kati te jārā iti [= HirŚS V.2 (Einoo 106); BhārŚS VIII.9.4; VaikhŚS VIII.12]

"Wife, how many lovers do you have?"

BŚS V.7 (136: 15) . . . patni kas te jāra iti

"Wife, who is your lover?"

KŚS V.5.5 . . . kena carasīti [ŚB II.5.2.20][185]

"With whom do you go about?"

VārŚS I.7.2.27 . . . katibhir mithunam acara iti

"With how many have you had sex?"

She is supposed to name him or point to him or to hold up as many grass blades as she has lovers. The standard verbal response seems to be

asau me jāraḥ [ĀpŚS VIII.6.22; BŚS V.7 (136: 17)]

"Yonder one / so-and-so is my lover,"

which she should say as she 'indicates' (nir √diś) him.[186] The verb is ambiguous, as is its English translation (and cognate); it may simply mean 'name/ declare', but its root sense is 'point to', and I do not think we can entirely rule out the physical gesture here. As an alternative, KŚS allows the manoeuvre with the grass:

KŚS V.5.6 saṃstutān ācaṣṭe
7 tṛṇāni vodgṛhṇāti pratisaṃstutam

She announces her paramours.
Or she holds up grass blades, (one for) each of her paramours.

The confession is extracted with a certain amount of threat: some member or members of her family will die or be harmed if she does not answer truthfully:

MŚS I.7.4.11 yadi mithyā vakṣyasi priyatamas te saṁsthāsyatīti

(The priest says) "If you speak falsely, someone very dear to you will die."

ĀpŚS VIII.6.22 [= BŚS V.7 (136: 17); HirŚS V.2 (Einoo 106); TB I.6.5.2]
. . . priyaṃ jñātiṃ rundhyāt

. . . she would obstruct a dear relative.

KŚS V.5.8 [cf. ŚB II.5.2.20] anākhyātam ahitaṃ jñātibhya iti śruteḥ

A nondeclaration is harmful to her relatives, according to sacred tradition.

After this very public and presumably humiliating confession, enforced with dire threats, what happens? Very little, in fact, at least right away. In most texts the priest utters what seems a rather perfunctory curse of the lover, unsupported by any ritual action, and then immediately proceeds with the main ritual by leading the wife to the Southern Altar.

MŚS I.7.4.11 yaṃ nirdiśet taṁ varuṇo gṛhṇātv iti brūyāt

Whom she should indicate, (about him the priest) should say "Let Varuṇa grasp him."[187]

Only in one text that I know of is there any attempt at expiatory action: in VaitŚS the priests have the wife wash and say an expiatory mantra:

VaitŚS VIII.20 aticāraṃ pṛṣṭāṃ patnīm idam āpaḥ pra vahateti mārjayanti

They have the wife, when she has been asked about her transgression, wash, (saying) "O waters, convey this away (AV VII.89.3)."[188]

The similarity of this expiatory cleaning to the 'final bath' (avabhṛtha) of various other rituals, in which Sacrificer and wife wash each other (see III. B.2b), the fact that the mantra is adopted from another similar ritual use (the cleansing at the end of the Paśubandha; see ĀpŚS VII.21.6), and that only one text prescribes this action suggests that this particular school noticed the apparently lenient treatment of the wife's offense and created an expiation for it out of already existing ritual materials. It does not seem an original part of the ceremony, especially as there is a displaced expiation later in the ritual, as we will see.

The usual interpretation of the interrogation of the wife is that it represents a need for confession and purification before embarking on important religious duties.[189] This explanation in fact goes back to the earliest texts, where the importance of speaking truth and the doctrine that "confession is good for the soul" hold sway. We cannot blame this interpretation on Western scholars misled by their Christian heritage, as a few extracts from Vedic prose will show:

MS I.10.11(151: 3) [= KS XXXVI.6] ṛtáṁ vái satyáṁ yajñó 'nṛtaṁ stry ánṛtaṁ vā́ eṣā́ karoti yā́ pátyuḥ krītā́ saty áthānyáiś caraty [*sic*] ánṛtam evá niravadā́ya ṛtáṁ satyám úpaiti . . . átha yád vācáyati médhyām eváinām karoti

The ritual is truth and reality. Woman is untruth. Indeed a wife who, though bought by her husband, then goes about with others[190] does untruth. Discharging her untruth, she approaches truth and reality. . . . So when he makes her talk [confess], he thus makes her ritually fit.

ŚB II.5.2.20 . . . átho nén me 'ntáḥśalpā juhávad íti tásmāt pṛchati níruktaṃ vā́ énaḥ kánīyo bhavati satyáṁ hí bhávati

(Worried) "Lest she will offer for me with a dagger within (her)," he therefore asks (the above question). A sin, once uttered, becomes less, because it becomes real.

No doubt there is something to this, as there is to the theory that it banishes evil from the ritual by scapegoating the lover.[191] As we will see, the confession does lead indirectly to a general expiation. But let us note some features of this episode that do not conform to this explanation and suggest that something else is going on as well.

Why does the confession happen only in this ritual? No similar interrogation and confession occur elsewhere in the system. Why after the ritual has started, not at the beginning? Would not the spiritual force of what went before be annulled because impurity had not yet been banished? In fact, since the Cāturmāsyāni rites form a cycle, it would make more sense to exact the confession at the first of them, the Vaiśvadeva, not at the Varuṇapraghāsa, when the cycle is well under way. And why is only the wife involved, when other participants should be equally pure to be effective? One could argue, of course, that the wife is considered the seat of 'untruth' (ánṛta), as in the MS passage cited earlier, but then we still must wonder why her 'untruth' does not trouble the ritual at other times.

We might also wonder, on the purely practical level, why the wife's confession is not more disruptive to the ritual. If her husband is hearing for the first time the name or names of his wife's lover(s) and possibly seeing them, among the spectators, physically pointed out, we might expect him to display some emotion, attempt some retribution, rather than meekly trailing off with his wife to the Southern Altar for the next bit of ritual action, the offering of the karambhapātrāṇi. Ritual imposes powerful restraints on behavior, but it is hard to believe that no outraged husband ever broke up the ceremony to light out after his rival. Or at least one would think that the ritualists would not take this chance.

There is an even more jarring element, however, which no one seems to have commented on: the presupposition at the heart of the question. The wife is presupposed to have a lover; she has no option to announce that she has none.[192] All of the variants of the question cited above ask either "which one?" or "how many?"; none are formulated as yes/no questions: "do you or do you not have a lover?" Indeed, it is possible to read some of the texts as suggesting that the *non*existence of a lover automatically evokes the threat we saw earlier.

ĀpŚS VIII.6.22 [= BŚS V.7 (136:17); HirŚS V.2 (Einoo 106)] yaj jāraṃ santaṃ na prabrūyāt priyaṃ jñātiṃ rundhyāt

Though this is usually interpreted as meaning "if she should have a lover and not declare him . . . ,"[193] it seems to me possible to take the santam as the existential predicate of the embedded clause: "if she should not declare that a lover exists. . . ."[194]

In any case, under the explanation of the confession given above, one would assume that the best state of affairs would be a complete (and honest) denial. Though a sin confessed is better than one unadmitted, no sin at all should be better still. Why is the question so phrased that no well-formed answer allows the wife to affirm her innocence? It is the ancient equivalent of the old trick question "When did you stop beating your wife?"

One could try to counter by asserting that women *regularly* took lovers, that this was the socially expected situation. But there is absolutely no evidence for this. Nothing in the legal system or in the narrative literature suggests that wifely unchastity was the norm. Though the legal texts do treat adultery on the part of the wife (for this see esp. Kane, *HDŚ* II.571–73), the legal reaction suggests that such conduct was neither so socially engrained as to be condoned, nor considered so characteristic of woman's character as to be especially feared and guarded against. According to most legal authorities, an adulterous woman must undergo a penance and loses some authority and privileges, but she cannot be abandoned or divorced simply on those grounds. Moreover, she becomes purified by her next menstrual period.[195] The space allotted to wifely adultery in the legal texts is relatively sparse. Narrative literature[196] of this approximate period does not display a particular preoccupation with adulterous wives, either. The Brāhmaṇas and the Mahābhārata present a series of female types, both positive and negative, but the Adulterous Wife is not in this gallery of archetypes. In fact, considering the frequency of temptresses in this literature, it is remarkable that so few of them are *married* women. I am not claiming that adulterous wives did not exist, nor that husbands never feared this possibility. However, our texts give us no reason to suppose either that wives were regularly adulterous in practice, or that fear of it was an overwhelming psychological component of the general male culture.[197]

We must seek another explanation. All of this leads me to suppose that to serve ritual purposes the wife *needs* to have a lover—or at least the fiction of one. It seems to me possible that eminently respectable, middle-aged Aryan ladies "confessed" to lovers they did not have, for the sake of ritual effectiveness. I think the confession may be a sham, a setup, with the named "lover" a nonspeaking role parceled out to a bit player on the ritual scene.[198] Why? Perhaps because illicit sex may bring a bigger jolt of sexual energy into the arena than proper marital sexual conduct, and the wife, as locus of sexuality, was charged to provide this. A kind of "animal passion" outside of socially sanctioned norms is what is wanted. Further consideration of the nature of the Varuṇapraghāsa will support this hypothesis.

First of all it is probably no accident that the interrogation of the wife takes place at the ritual that ushers in the rainy season, which begins the cycle of fertility. Moreover, we should look again at *where* in the ritual the confession takes place. It is embedded in the middle of another peculiar episode in that ritual, involving the offering of a pair of statuettes of ram and ewe, cunningly fashioned of barley meal with their sexual organs especially prominent. This is a unique oblation in Vedic ritual. One account of the production of these models follows:

> ĀpŚS VIII.5.42 āmapeṣāṇāṃ meṣapratikṛtī bhavataḥ
> 43 meṣam adhvaryuḥ karoti meṣīṃ pratiprasthātā
> 6.1 striyāḥ strivyañjanāni
> 2 puṃsaḥ puṃvyañjanāni
> . . . 11 . . . anaiḍakībhir ūrṇābhir meṣapratikṛtī lomaśau kurutaḥ
>
> There is a pair of sheep models (made) of raw-ground (barley) meal. The Adhvaryu makes the ram, the Pratiprasthātar the ewe.[199] The female has female distinguishing marks, the male male distinguishing marks. . . . They make the pair of sheep models hairy with wool from a non-Eḍaka sheep.

At the same time and using the same mess of barley meal, the wife fashions the 'meal-dishes' (karambhapātrāṇī) for the members (including one unborn) of the Sacrificer's household.

> ĀpŚS VIII.5.40 āmapeṣāṇāṃ patnī karambhapātrāṇi karoti
> 41 yāvanto yajamānasyāmātyāḥ sastrīkās tāvanty ekātiriktāni
>
> The wife makes meal-dishes of raw-ground (barley), as many (dishes) as there are members of the Sacrificer's household, including women, with one extra.[200]

Though in most texts the ewe and ram are fashioned by the Adhvaryu and Pratiprasthātar, ĀpŚS VIII.6.3–4 seems to suggest that it is the wife that fashions them according to the Vājasaneyins.[201]

Once the sheep figurines have been modeled and covered with wool (or kuśa grass in the absence of wool), they are set down in dishes of curds—the ram in curds destined for the Maruts, the ewe in those for Varuṇa—and śami-leaves are scattered in front of them as mock fodder (ghāsa, so explicitly VārŚS I.7.2.20; TB I.6.4.5). Varuṇa's curds go on the Northern Altar (uttarā vedi) along with the other oblations, those of the Maruts alone on the Southern Altar (dakṣiṇā vedi).

It is immediately after this business (in most texts) that the wife is called upon to name her lovers. As we saw, the actual confession occasions relatively little fanfare, and immediately after that, she puts a basket containing the meal-dishes on her head and proceeds to the Southern Altar, where she, jointly with her husband, offers the meal-dishes into the fire.[202] At this point the married couple pronounces a mantra that seems a displaced expiation for her supposed moral deviation:

> TS I.8.3.1 (etc.) yád grā́me yád áraṇye yát sabhā́yāṃ yád indriyé
> yác chūdré yád aryè énaś cakṛmā́ vayám
> yád ékasyā́dhi dhármaṇi tásyāvayájanam asi svā́hā

What wrong we have committed in the village (or) in the wild, in the assembly (or) in Indrian (strength)[war?],
to the Śūdra (or) to the Aryan,
what is against the customary law of (any)one, of that you are the expiation. Hail!

It is significant that *both* parties utter this mantra, though only one of them has supposedly transgressed, and that it is a mantra of the most general application: all errors and sins are covered. If *one* of the reasons for the wife's confession is to purify the entire ritual, then she is operating as a sort of ritual-internal scapegoat. Just as she is the locus of active sexuality, she also serves as the symbol of impure behavior, and she then represents the transgressions of *all* the ritual participants, particularly her husband, when she "confesses" a misdeed supposedly committed by herself alone. Her confession allows her husband to expiate his own misdeeds without implicating himself. This expiation occurs simultaneously with the offering of the 'meal-dishes' that represent the Sacrificer's family. The threat originally made to the wife at the interrogation: "If you speak falsely, someone very dear to you will die" is thus rendered harmless by a blanket (hence almost vacuous) repudiation of wrongdoing.

What happens next? The wife is led back to her patnīloka, and her direct role is over. The principal offerings are now to be made, and with them we return to the barley meal statuettes. First these models are switched: the ram in the Maruts' curds is moved to Varuṇa's dish, and vice versa (see e.g. ŚB II.5.2.36), and the figures, along with lashings of curds and melted butter, are offered.[203]

Though the offering of mock ram and ewe seems at first to have little if anything to do with the wife's confession, the conjunction of these two unique ritual events is surely not by chance. The hypersexed ovine pair, with their exaggerated dough genitalia, are animal stand-ins for the wife and her "lover." Earlier I suggested that "animal passion" was needed for the ritual, and the sheep provide exactly that. The exchange of the two figures from one dish to another in the middle of the ritual may be a sort of mock copulation, and sheep, especially rams, are often symbols of sexual force in Vedic.[204] Even the wool with which they are carefully provided may be symbolic of their fertility, since hair has such associations in early India.[205]

The double pairing of ram and ewe, wife and lover in a way fill out the square that is implied in the skewed pairing of wife and horse in the Aśvamedha:

	Aśvamedha		*Varuṇapraghāsa*	
	human	*animal*	*human*	*animal*
male	—	horse	lover	ram
female	wife	—	wife	ewe

The matching on the vertical axis makes the couplings less shocking than that of the Aśvamedha, but the animal realm is tapped nonetheless, albeit indirectly. At least one other feature of the ewe/ram episode may find its counterpart in the Aśvamedha. As noted, śami-leaves are provided for the figurines as symbolic fodder. At the Aśvamedha after the wives have adorned the horse and before it is killed, they (or in some texts [e.g. KŚS XX.5.18] the Adhvaryu) give fodder to the horse, as in

> MŚS IX.2.3.25 annahomaśeṣaṃ patnyo 'śvāyopakiranti
>
> The wives scatter the rest of the food-oblations for the horse.

This feeding of the horse has the effect of reverse fertility. The wife whose food it eats will get pregnant:

> BŚS XV.26 (229: 12) yasyai hānnam atti tasyai hārdhukā prajā bhavatīti vijñāyate
>
> Whose food it eats, she will have prospering offspring—so it is known from tradition.

Though the wife is not especially associated with the mock-fodder in the Varuṇapraghāsa, its fertility effects may be implicitly referred to—especially in the karambhapātrāṇi offering with its extra cake for the unborn child.

The way in which the sexual symbolism of ram and ewe is utilized in the Varuṇapraghāsa will become clearer when I chart the episodes discussed so far:

1.	making of ram/ewe by priests (represent sexuality)	making of meal dishes by wife (represent family)
	[events occur simultaneously using same material]	
2.	wife is interrogated and confesses to lover(s)	
3.	wife and husband offer meal dishes with expiatory mantra	
4.	priests offer ram/ewe	

The sexual pair of ram and ewe frame the events relating to the household, and the wife is in contact with both thematic complexes. She both shapes and offers the family dishes. But for the family dishes she physically uses the same barley meal that forms the sheep. This contact is not fortuitous or dictated by housewifely economy. Rather, I would suggest, it transfers some of the sexual force of the animals into the household arena and with luck will provide the fertility to add an extra member to the household.

The same sexual "kick" is then provided by the (mock-)confession. She and the lover are human representatives of the oversexed ewe and ram. Her confession both taps this sexual energy and dissipates its menace, and the energy can be immediately and safely transferred to the family through the subsequent offering of the meal dishes, performed with domestic propriety by husband and wife together.[206] As so often, the wife is the lightning rod for forces that the Sacrificer cannot approach directly.

Thus, examining the wife's confession in its ritual context demonstrates that it is not randomly placed, nor does it simply serve generalized purificatory ends, as others have argued. Instead, though it certainly has expiatory functions, it also, almost slyly, does something like the opposite: injecting a controlled version of uncontrolled sexuality into a ritual whose aim is fertility. This sexuality is represented twice, in separate but covertly connected fashion. Both the barley meal figurines and the wife with her quite possibly fictitious lover are tidy and manageable simulacra of rampant sexuality, in a yearly repeated ritual where the real thing, in the mode of the Horse Sacrifice, might be too much.

2. *The Student and the Whore in the Gavāmayana*

A similar jolt of sexuality is delivered at the equivalent of a New Year's Ceremony (the Mahāvrata Day) at the end of a yearlong ritual called the Progress of the Cows (Gavāmayana). The Mahāvrata Day coincides with the winter solstice. The ceremony has something in common with the Aśvamedha, as we will see, but I treat it here because the female who administers the jolt is in some sense a negative figure: a whore (puṃścalī/puṃścalū, lit. 'one who goes after or with men').

The Mahāvrata celebration must have been a very busy rite; in the texts it sounds like a three-ring circus. There are several matched pairs of opponents performing complementary actions, with a great deal of musical accompaniment and choreography in the background. In one part of the ritual ground a śūdra and an Aryan contend over a "white round cowhide" (carma . . . vāśaṁ śvetaṃ parimaṇḍalam MŚS VII.2.7.11).[207] The Aryan is allowed to win.[208] These two also verbally revile each other in some texts, while in others a separate pair of Praiser (abhigara) and Blamer (apagara) do the verbal sparring.[209]

But the pairing of most interest to us is that of the whore and the brahmacārin, a student whose very title, as we have seen, is a watchword for chastity. This shockingly contrastive couple was clearly deliberately matched, and they embody without disguise the twin poles of gendered sexuality that we have seen hinted at elsewhere: the male self-controlled and sexually nonassertive, the female going after men and purveying sex. If anyone is the "locus of active sexuality" I have alluded to before, it is the whore.

The two are stationed such that the student is within the vedi, the whore outside it.[210] They both insult each other, in tones reminiscent of the bawdy dialogues in the Aśvamedha, and copulate.[211] Let us examine several accounts of their activities, as not all texts specify both the physical and the verbal, and some texts are more euphemistic than others:

> MŚS VII.2.7.13 brahmacārī puṁścalī cānāryakarmann avakīrṇi duścaritaṃ nirākṛtam iti bahirvedi puṁścalī dhik tvā jāraṃ parasya janasya nirmārjani puruṣasya-puruṣasya śiśnapraṇejanīty antarvedi brahmacārī

(There are) a student and a whore. The whore, outside the vedi, (says) "O you doer of un-Aryan things,[212] you spiller (of semen). Bad conduct is (to be?) rejected."[213] The student, within the vedi, (says) "Fie on you, o wiper-off (/masturbator?) of the lover of other people,[214] o washer of the penis of man after man."

KŚS XIII.3.6 puṃścalūbrahmacāriṇāv anyonyam ākrośataḥ
. . . 9 mārjālīyaṃ dakṣiṇena parivṛte mithunaṃ sambhavati

A whore and a student shriek at each other. . . .
In an enclosure south of the mārjālīya there takes place a sexual coupling.[215]

BŚS XVI.21 (267: 10) atha dakṣiṇe vedyanta [*sic*] kaṭaparivāre mithunau saṃpravādayataḥ
. . . 22 (268: 10) saṃvartete mithunau

Then in a grass enclosure on the south end of the vedi the sexual pair hold conversation.
. . . The sexual pair "roll up together" [euphemism for sex].

ĀpŚS XXI.17.18 nikalpete brahmacārī puṃścalī cāgreṇa sadaso dakṣiṇāṃ dvārbāhum ārtiṣyamāṇau
19 uttarasyāṃ vediśroṇyāṃ puṃścalyai māgadhāya ca pariśrayanti
. . . 19.5 ṛtīyete brahmacārī puṃścalī ca dakṣiṇāṃ dvārbāhum āśliṣyamāṇau
19.6 saṃvartete puṃścalī māgadhaś ca

In front of the right doorpost of the shed, a student and a whore get ready to quarrel.
On the northern hip of the vedi they make an enclosure for the whore and the Māgadhan.[216] . . .
The student and whore quarrel (at) the right doorpost while embracing each other.[217]
The whore and the Māgadhan roll up together.

VārŚS[218] III.2.5.30 purastād āgnīdhrīyasyāntarvedi brahmacārī bahirvedi puṁścalī
31 [sā] brahmacāriṇam āha anāryakarmann avakīrṇin duścaritinn iti
32 dhik tvā jālmi puṁścali parasyāryajanasya mārjanīti brahmacārī pratyāha
. . . 36 pariśrayati mithunacāribhyāṃ dakṣiṇāparāṃ prati vediśroṇiṃ bahirvedi
37 tau mithunaṁ saṃbhavataḥ

East of the Āgnīdhrīya (there are) a student within the vedi and a whore outside the vedi.
She says to the student, "O doer of un-Aryan things, spiller (of semen), doer of misdeeds." The student replies, "Fie on you, vile whore, wiper of Aryans (and) others (?)."[219]
. . . On the south side of the vedi, outside the vedi, he [a priest, vel sim.] makes a fenced enclosure for the two practicing sex.
The two perform a sexual coupling.[220]

JB II.405 māgadhaṃ ca puṃścalūṃ ca dakṣiṇe vedyante mithunīkārayanti

They make a Māgadhan and a whore have sex on the southern end of the vedi.

KS XXXIV.5 (39: 11) brahmacārī ca puṁścalī cartīyete sarvā hi bhūte vāco vadanti mithunaṃ caranti

A student and a whore quarrel. They (plural) indeed speak all manner of speech when this happens. They (plural) practice sex.[221]

TS VII.5.9.4 antarvedí mithunáu sámbhavataḥ

There is a sexual pairing within the vedi.

AiĀr V.1.5 . . . bhūtānāṃ ca maithunaṃ brahmacāripuṃścalyoḥ sampravādaḥ . . .

There is sex among creatures and a dialogue between student and whore.

The lewd and insulting dialogue and the ritual copulation between a shockingly mismatched couple remind us of the Aśvamedha (so also Hauer 1927, p. 264). The titillated shudder produced by interspecies sex in the Horse Sacrifice is here achieved[222] by pairing two people who inhabit the extreme ends of the human sexual scale.

But, though the Sacrificers' Wives have been spared the sexual indignities of the Aśvamedha by the substitution of a whore, they are present and, quite literally, add to the din. Though this is not a royal ritual (like the Aśvamedha), there are multiple wives, because the Gavāmayana is a Sattra, a type in which all the priests simultaneously serve as joint Sacrificers.[223] As noted above, in Sattras all the priests' wives must serve as multiple patnīs. In an elaborate ritual like this, this requirement ensures quite a band—and that is in fact what the wives form. While the various events discussed above are going on, the wives play musical instruments: lutes and flutes of assorted types.[224]

Meanwhile a group of eight female slaves (dāsī) carrying water jars circle the mārjālīya (close to where, in some texts, the copulation occurs) singing, making ritual exclamations, slapping their thighs, and stamping their feet.[225] This is clearly a low-budget version of the four hundred female attendants of the queens in the Aśvamedha. Though their songs are not bawdy (at least superficially)—rather a joyous celebration of cows, bees, soma, and other good things—they are punctuated with exotic cries (e.g. hillu hillu), apostrophes (hai mahā3), and announcements (idaṃ madhu "here is honey"). The net effect must have been rather like that of the great crowd of women at the Aśvamedha: to create a swirling, resounding, disorienting spectacle that heightened the impact of the little playlets—Aryan and Śūdra, Praiser and Blamer, Student and Whore—that were happening at the same time.

Thus the Gavāmayana reshuffles the elements of the Aśvamedha, but still deploys them to similar effect. The shocking sex is displaced from the chief queen to a more appropriate female figure, the whore—but a female one would hardly expect to see on the ritual ground. The horse is gone, but the frisson of forbidden sex is produced by replacing it with the very symbol of (male) chastity, the student. The wives and their attendants are relieved of overt participation in the sexual aspects of the ritual, but sing and dance in a way that could only contribute to the atmosphere of bacchanal. What a New Year's Eve!

3. The Whore's Son at the Aśvamedha

A whore participates in ritual peripherally in the Horse Sacrifice as well. At the beginning of the ritual, before the horse is released for its long ramble, it is led to water, and a preventive sacrifice is performed, clearly to anticipate and ward off potential harm to the horse on its travels. Collateral relatives of the king and queen[226] lead a 'four-eyed' dog to the water (supposedly one with blazes around its eyes), and a 'whore's son' (puṃścaleya), who follows this procession, kills it with a wooden club:[227]

> MŚS IX.2.1.19 śvānaṃ caturakṣaṁ saidhrakeṇa musalena pauṁścaleyo 'nvaiti . . . 23 saidhrakeṇa musalena pauṁścaleyaḥ śvānaṁ hanti
>
> A whore's son follows the four-eyed dog with a club made of sidhraka wood. . . . With the sidhraka club the whore's son kills the dog.

The accompanying mantra is (MS III.12.1 [160: 7], etc.) yó árvantaṃ jíghāṁsati tám abhyàmīti váruṇaḥ "Who wishes to harm the steed, him Varuṇa vexes." Afterward the horse is made to put its right foot on the dead dog, with the pronouncement (MS III.12.1 [160: 8], etc.) paró mártaḥ paráḥ śvā́ "Away the man, away the dog!"—thus presumably banishing danger arising from hostile humans and animals.[228] I referred to the killing of this dog earlier, in my discussion of RV X.86.4.

It is not entirely clear to me why the killing is assigned to a whore's son, who otherwise does not figure in this ritual at all (or in fact any other). Perhaps it is simply to confine especially inauspicious action to a person of low origins, though in that case the generic Śūdra should do as well. Perhaps instead the whore's son indirectly puts the horse in contact with the same power of forbidden sex at the beginning of the ritual which it will meet at the end, while at the same time dramatizing the range of female sexual figures from the despised whore to the highly placed chief wife of the king.[229]

4. The Avoided Wife

A mirror-image figure to the lady and her phantom lover in the Varuṇapraghāsa (see section 1) is a wife who plays an important part in several royal rituals. Recall, in my discussion of the Horse Sacrifice, that while the chief queen is under the linen with the horse, several other wives of the king stand by making dirty jokes. These subsidiary wives have other roles. In the ceremonies immediately preceding the sacrifice of the horse, they join the chief queen in anointing the horse and adorning it by weaving hundreds of beads into its hair. After it is killed and the copulation is over, they insert needles into the dead animal, to guide the paths of the knives in cutting up the victim. Let us briefly examine these episodes, which occur just before and after the ritual copulation I treated at such length. First the adornment of the horse:

ĀpŚS XX.15.7 patnayo 'śvam alaṃkurvanti / mahiṣī vāvātā parivṛktīti . . . 10 vāleṣu maṇīn āvayanti / bhūr iti sauvarṇān mahiṣī prāg vahāt / bhuva iti rājatān vāvātā pratyag vahāt prāk śroṇeḥ / suvar iti sāmudrān parivṛktī pratyak śroṇeḥ . . . 12 athāsya svadeśān ājyenābhyañjanti . . . gaulgulavena mahiṣī . . . kāsāmbavena vāvātā . . . maustakṛtena parivṛktī

The wives adorn the horse—the Mahiṣī, the Favorite, and the Rejected Wife. . . . They weave jewels into its hair. The Mahiṣī gold ones (into the hair) in front of the shoulders, with "Bhūḥ!"; the Favorite silver ones between the shoulders and the hips, with "Bhuvaḥ"; the Rejected Wife marine ones [pearls or shells?] behind the hips, with "Suvar!" . . .

Then each anoints her part of it [horse] with melted butter—the Mahiṣī with (butter) mixed with bdellium; the Favorite with (butter) mixed with kasāmbu, the Rejected Wife with (butter) mixed with mustakṛt.

Now the needles for the paths of the knives:

ĀpŚS XX.18.7 . . . sauvarṇībhiḥ sūcībhir mahiṣy aśvasyāsipathān kalpayati prāk kroḍāt . . . rājatībhir vāvātā pratyak kroḍāt prāṅ nābheḥ . . . lauhībhiḥ sīsābhir vā parivṛktī śeṣam

With golden needles the Mahiṣī arranges the paths for the knives forward of the horse's breast; with silver (needles) the Favorite behind the breast and in front of the navel; with copper or lead (needles) the Rejected Wife the rest.

One of these wives is the Rejected or Avoided Wife (parivṛktī/parivṛktā), whom we have met before. Her verbal exchange with the priest at the copulation was one of the coarser ones:

VS XXIII.28 yád asyā aṁhubhédyāḥ kṛdhú sthūlám upā́tasat
muṣkā́v íd asyā ejato gośaphé śakulā́v iva

When the stunted, thick (penis) has shuttled from her narrow slit,
her two balls stir like the two splinters (/ fish) in a cow's hoof (?).

VS XXIII.29 yád devā́so lalā́magum prá viṣṭīmínam ā́viṣuḥ
sakthnā́ dediśyate nā́rī satyásyākṣibhúvo yathā

When the gods have favored the (man) with a star-marked, stiffened (penis),
the woman displays with her thigh, like eyewitnesses to the truth (?).

The Rejected Wife seems to be one no longer favored by the king, perhaps because she has failed to bear a son, as the ŚB explicitly says (ŚB V.3.1.13 yā́ vā́ apútrā pátnī sā́ párivṛttī [*sic*]). This may be supported by an AV passage directed against a female rival:

AV VII.113.2 párivṛktā yáthā́sasy ṛṣabhásya vaśéva

. . . so that you will be 'avoided', like a vaśā-cow by a bull.

As Falk has shown,[230] the vaśā is a cow that has been mated but has so far failed to calve. The speaker of this hymn seems to be wishing at least temporary barrenness on her rival. Notice that the particular part of the horse the Parivṛktī has charge of in the Aśvamedha is the hind end, which, of course, contains the generative organs and is connected with sexuality. This curious paradox must be deliberate.

The Rejected Wife also appears in the ritual of the Consecration of the King (Rājasūya): an offering is made in her house, one of a series performed in the dwellings of a set of important social figures known as the 'Bejeweled' (Ratnin). The number and identity of the Ratnins varies from school to school, but it usually ranges from eleven to thirteen, and it always includes both the Mahiṣī and the Parivṛktī, the only two females on this list (except in some texts the Vāvātā). A typical group is that of TS I.8.9:

Brāhmaṇa	member of priestly class
Rājanya	member of warrior class
Mahiṣī	chief wife
Parivṛktī	rejected wife
Senānī	leader of army
Sūta	equerry (?)
Grāmaṇī	village headman
Kṣattar	chamberlain (?)
Saṃgrahītar	charioteer (?)
Bhāgadugha	distributor
Akṣāvāpa	dice-thrower[231]

The two wives form an obvious pair, following after the paired Brāhmaṇa and Rājanya. The whole group seems designed to encompass globally the range of social leaders, to secure their support and the forces they command for the consecrated king.

Each Ratnin offering is made to a different divinity, out of different material, and rates a different Dakṣiṇā (gift to the priest). Note the pointed contrast between those of the Mahiṣī and the Parivṛktī:

> KS XV.4 (211: 16) adityai carur mahiṣyā gṛhe dhenur dakṣiṇā nairṛtaś caruḥ kṛṣṇānāṃ vrīhīṇāṃ nakhanirbhinnānāṃ parivṛktyā gṛhe śyenī kūṭā vaṇḍāpasphurā dakṣiṇā
>
> There is a caru for Aditi [the benevolent mother goddess] in the house of the Mahiṣī. The Dakṣiṇā is a milch-cow. There is a caru of black rice grains, broken by the (finger)-nails, to Nirṛti [goddess of 'disorder'] in the house of the Avoided Wife. The Dakṣiṇā is a white, crumple-horned,[232] tailless, kicking (cow).

The bland, generic caru oblation at the Mahiṣī's house, with its generic if desirable Dakṣiṇā of a productive cow, sets off the gleefully devised negative specificity of the Parivṛktī's offering. It is also a caru, but made of black rice—black often has sinister associations in Vedic, as in so many cultures. The rice grains are 'split by the fingernails', a provision that recurs across texts.[233] The picture this may conjure up, to modern sensibilities, is that of the Parivṛktī as a scarlet-nailed harpy, driven by jealous rage, systematically assassinating rice grains, one by one. Though we should distrust this too easy crosscultural image making, it is worth noting that nails are inauspicious in Vedic. At the beginning of the Dīkṣā, the Sacrificer (and his wife) have their nails trimmed (cf. e.g. Hillebrandt 1897, p. 125), and some ritual actions are specifically prohibited from being performed with the nails (cf. e.g. MS IV.1.10 [14: 10]; ĀpŚS II.3.3).

Even the Dakṣiṇā has its share of bad associations. The cow in question is deformed: in the cited passage[234] it has ill-shaped horns (or none at all) and lacks a tail, though at least it is white. Most other texts, on the contrary, require a black animal:

> BŚS XII.5 (92: 2) [cf. TS I.8.9.1; TB I.7.3.4] kṛṣṇāṃ kūṭāṃ dadāti
>
> (She) gives a black, crumple-horned (cow).
>
> KŚS XV.3.21 kṛṣṇā vatsatary apahatottamasya
>
> A black, broken-down heifer (is the Dakṣiṇā) of the last (Ratnin oblation).
>
> ŚB V.3.1.13 tásya dákṣiṇā kṛṣṇā́ gáuḥ parimūrṇī́ paryārī́ṇī
>
> The Dakṣiṇā for this (oblation) is a black, decrepit, diseased cow.[235]

This cow is not only physically marred. According to the KS passage [= MS IV.3.8 (47: 15)], she also has behavior problems: she is a cow that kicks (ápasphurā). A *non*kicking (án-apasphur(ant)-) milch-cow (dhenú/sudúghā/ duhānā) is a common symbol for tranquil prosperity in Vedic texts (esp. numerous passages in AVP), as in

> AVŚ XII.1.45 [= AVP XVII.5.3] sahásraṃ dhā́rā dráviṇasya me duhāṃ
> dhruvéva dhenúr ánapasphurantī
>
> Let (the earth) give as milk for me a thousand streams of wealth,
> like a steady nonkicking milch-cow.

Everything connected with the Parivṛktī in the Rājasūya thus has sinister associations. Why is such a presumably inauspicious person alloted important roles in rituals that affect not only the king but the security, power, and fertility of his kingdom, the Rājasūya and the Aśvamedha? She is a person whose very title names her despised position. Is this simply a case of inviting the bad fairy to the feast, so she will not crash and spoil it? This may be part of it, but I think there must be more.

The Avoided Wife fills an important *structural role* in both these rituals. It is not just that a particular king *happens* to have a wife he does not like much anymore, but *happens* to feel sorry enough for or nervous enough about to give her a little something to do at the festival. There *has* to be an Avoided Wife—to perform her Ratnin offering, to take charge of her end of the horse, to participate in her obscene verbal exchange—and if there does not happen to be one, presumably she has to be invented, or some perfectly well-liked wife has to play her part. This reminds us of the Varuṇapraghāsa, where the adulterous wife and her scapegoat lover are roles that must be filled one way or another. In the Varuṇapraghāsa I determined that the confession of adultery served ritual ends: it was not the solution of a personal and practical problem—a particular wife who happened to have strayed—but a means of infusing the ritual with sexuality.

I would suggest that it is useful to think about the Rejected Wife in the same way, as a potential *ritual tool*. What does such a figure, apparently so negative, provide the ritual; what can she do that no one and nothing else does? The detailed treatment of her Ratnin oblation, glorying in all its unattractive aspects, contrasts with the bland description of the Mahiṣī's. The verbal behavior of the Parivṛktī at the Aśvamedha is matched in lewdness only by the exchanges involving the copulating Mahiṣī. She has charge of the hind-end of the horse, source of both defilement and fertility. All this suggests that the ritualists had given great thought to her position and felt she had access to important forces. Why?

I would suggest that, like the "adulterous" wife, the Rejected Wife is a woman who lives outside of sociosexual norms and who therefore has access to more charged sexual energy than others do. In her case, sexual frustration/rejection is felt to build up unreleased passion—to see that this is a widely held view we need look no further than modern models like the movie *Fatal Attraction*, not to mention the old cliché, "Hell hath no fury like a woman scorned." This passion can be channeled into the ritual and utilized in two important ways. On the one hand, as the Ratnin oblation to 'Disorder' (Nirṛti) shows, the Parivṛktī's power can be apotropaic: she repels the dangerous and unwelcome force of 'Chaos' by her very similarity to this dangerous goddess, as the Brāhmaṇa texts make clear:

> ŚB V.3.1.13 yā́ vā́ apútrā pátnī sā́ nírṛtigṛhītā tád yád evā́syā átra nairṛtáṁ rūpáṃ tád eváitác chamayati tátho hainaṁ sūyámānaṃ nírṛtir ná gṛhṇāti
>
> A wife without a son [the ŚB's definition of the Parivṛktī; see preceding discussion] has been seized by 'Disorder'. In this way whatever disorderly nature there is in her he thus propitiates. So Disorder does not seize him while he is being consecrated.[236]

But there is a more interesting employment of the Parivṛktī. The effort seems to be not to banish her dangerous power, but to harness it, in order to increase the king's own power in battle and other hostile activities. Her sexual fury can be ritually transformed into martial fervor. Let us now assemble some evidence for this rather more subtle use of the Parivṛktī.

We might start with an indirect piece of evidence. As we saw earlier, the Dakṣiṇā at the Parivṛktī's Ratnin oblation is a 'kicking' (ápasphurā) cow, who contrasts negatively with her desirably docile cousins. But not always. As the following RVic passage shows, a beast that kicks is sometimes wanted:

> RV VIII.69.10 ā́ yát pátanty enyàḥ sudúghā ánapasphuraḥ
> apasphúraṃ gṛbhāyata sómam índrāya pā́tave
>
> When the variegated, easy-to-milk, nonkicking (cows) fly hither,
> do ye grasp the kicking Soma for Indra to drink.

This verse describes, as so often, the mixture of soma, the intoxicating drink, with milk, and the contrast between the behavior of the cows and the soma suggests that the 'kick' in this intoxicating drink (exactly the English metaphor) is one of its desirable characteristics. The root √sphur is used for other positively viewed actions as well, as when Indra 'kicks out' Vṛtra (RV II.11.9, VIII.3.19, again a familiar turn of phrase) or the bow gives the arrow a kick (RV VI.67.11, VI.75.4). In other words, though the behavior of the Parivṛktī's Dakṣiṇā may not be what you want from Bossy, it does have its place, and that place is in the martial sphere.

Let us turn now to direct evidence for the Parivṛktī's martial character. First recall the Parivṛktī's position in the list of Ratnins. In most of the lists she comes between the Mahiṣī (or Vāvātā) and the *Senānī* 'leader of the army'. Even in the WYV list, which isolates the Parivṛktī at the end, the other figures have been rearranged, so that the Senānī comes first—a polar opposition which may carry as much significance as adjacency.

Other evidence for the Parivṛktī's identification with militant action comes from mythology, in the figure of Indrāṇī, whom we have met before. In the Vṛṣākapi hymn (RV X.86) Indrāṇī seemed to fill the role of the Mahiṣī in the Aśvamedha, apparently copulating with the monkey/victim. But even in that hymn her relation with her husband Indra was prickly. Though her good fortune in having Indra as husband was proclaimed, the marriage did not seem a happy one, and he berated her on several occasions in the hymn for her jealousy and ill-treatment of the monkey. This is the behavior one might expect of a husband toward a Parivṛktī, or toward a wife who is about to become one.[237]

And indeed Indrāṇī is elsewhere specifically called Indra's Parivṛktī.

> KS X.10 (136: 12) eṣā vā indrasya parivṛktī jāyā
>
> She is the Avoided Wife of Indra.

The context of this remarkable announcement is perhaps even more important than the identification itself. The occasion is an oblation made to Indrāṇī under particular circumstances, with particular ends in view:

> KS X.10 (136: 8) indrāṇyai caruṃ nirvapet senāyām utthitāyāṃ rājño gṛhe senā vā indrāṇī brahmanaivaināṃ vittyai saṁśyati balbajā idhme ca barhiṣi cāpi-

bhavanti śakno vā ete jātā nyāyenaivainām abhinayati yat sā vindeta tato dakṣiṇā samṛddhyā indrāya cendrāṇyai ca caruṃ nirvapet senāyām utthitāyāṃ rājño gṛhe eṣā vā indrasya parivṛktī jāyā goṣv evainām adhinayati balbajā idhme ca barhiṣi cāpibhavanti śakno vā ete jātā nyāyenaivainām abhinayati yat sā vindeta tato dakṣiṇā samṛddhyai

He should offer a caru to Indrāṇī in the house of the king when an army/weapon[238] has been raised. Indrāṇī is an army/weapon. With a formulation he thus sharpens her [simultaneously Indrāṇī and the army/weapon] to acquire (spoils). There are balbaja grass blades on the firewood and strewn grass (at this caru offering). These (balbaja blades) arose from shit. In an appropriate manner he thus leads her off. What (spoils) she should acquire, from that the Dakṣiṇā (is made up). (This is) for prosperity.

He should offer a caru to Indra and Indrāṇī in the house of the king when an army/weapon has been raised. She [Indrāṇī] is the Avoided Wife of Indra. He thus leads her among the cows. There are balbaja grass blades on the firewood and strewn grass (at the caru offering). These (balbaja blades) arose from shit. In an appropriate manner he thus leads her off. What (spoils) she should acquire, from that the Dakṣiṇā (is made up). (This is) for prosperity.

This passage exhibits the typically incomprehensible surface of Saṃhitā prose exegesis: the logical connections between Indrāṇī, armies, balbaja grass, excrement, and cows—so self-evident to the composers of the text—initially escape us, and it is hard to see why this conjunction of ill-assorted elements leads inexorably to prosperity. But this apparent hodgepodge will repay our close attention, and with the aid of some parallel and related passages we can figure out what the KS is talking about and what relevance it has to our Avoided Wife of ritual.

The passage seems to concern the acquisition of booty, particularly cows, since the Dakṣiṇā will consist of some portion of those gained. The offering is made to bring divine favor to the Sacrificer's cattle-raiding expedition. Let us examine each of the details in turn, to see what each contributes to this mission.

Let me begin by clarifying perhaps the most curious piece of the puzzle: the balbaja grass. Why is it specified for this ritual, and why does it arise from excrement? The TS parallel gives some clue:

TS II.2.8.1–2 bálbajān ápi // idhmé sáṃnahyed gáur yátrā́dhiṣkannā nyámehat táto bálbajā údatiṣṭhan gávām eváinaṃ nyāyám apinī́ya gā́ vedayati

He should fasten balbaja grass blades on the firewood. Where the cow, covered (by a bull), pissed, thence arose balbaja blades. Thus by leading him [Sacrificer] on the way of the cow, he [priest] makes him find cows.

In other words, balbaja grass is the product of some waste product of a mythological Ur-cow, excrement in KS/MS, urine in TS. Including balbaja grass in the ritual is the equivalent of following a trail of droppings left by the herd. It is good tracking procedure and will allow the Sacrificer to return with the desired booty. The nyāyena of the KS passage, translated above 'in an appropriate manner', thus also means 'along the way (of the cows)', i.e. on the trail of their droppings/balbaja grass.

But who is tracking the cows, and why is the success of the expedition tied to the mythological figure Indrāṇī? Why is she the appropriate divinity to ask for help in this armed raid? The TS says she is "the divinity of the senā" (TS II.2.8.1 indrāṇī́ vái sénāyai devátā), but this is essentially repeating what we have already deduced, that she is the proper divinity to approach.

We can begin answering these questions by noting an identification imposed by the structure of the KS passage. In identical positions in the two sections of the passage we find the equations:

senā vā indrāṇī	Indrāṇī is really a weapon/army.

and

eṣā vā indrasya parivṛktī jāyā	She [Indrāṇī] is really the Avoided Wife of Indra.

which suggests a third, covert equation:

*senā vai parivṛktī	*The Avoided Wife is really a weapon/army.

Indrāṇī's power thus seems to derive from her structural role as Avoided Wife, and she infuses this power into the "raised army/weapon" (senāyām utthitāyām) in the control of the Sacrificer.[239] The Sacrificer seeks to provide himself with an effective senā by this oblation—and the senā, as we have just seen, is identified with the Avoided Wife.

Further examination of the KS passage makes clear *how* the power of Indrāṇī, the Avoided Wife, is to be deployed in the raid. The identification with which we began continues

> KS X.10 (136: 12) eṣā vā indrasya parivṛktī jāyā goṣv evaināṃ adhinayati
>
> This (Indrāṇī) is the Avoided Wife of Indra. He thus leads her among the cows.

Interpreting this statement requires reference to a different mythico-doctrinal complex. I have elsewhere[240] discussed the theme of the "Rejected Dakṣiṇā." In this set of stories (or wispy references to stories), a Dakṣiṇā (i.e. a *cow* given as priestly gift) is rejected by the intended recipients. Refusing a gift without cause is a terrible insult and leads to hostile relations, as we will see later, and the rejected cow is transformed into a fierce wild female beast—lioness, tigress, or female hyena depending on text—who ravages the herd. A Rejected Dakṣiṇā is therefore not supposed to be let back into her original herd:

KS XXVIII.4 (159: 1) tasmād dakṣiṇā pratinuttā na pratigṛhyā na goṣu cālayet sālāvṛky evainaṃ bhūtvā praviśati sainaṃ nirdahati

Therefore a Rejected Dakṣiṇā is not to be taken back, nor allowed to wander among the (other) cows. Having become a female hyena, she enters him [Sacrificer?/it = herd?] and burns him/it up.

In KS X.10 Indrāṇī seems to be homologized to the Rejected Dakṣiṇā: she is led among the cows (goṣv evaināṃ adhinayati) as a hostile being and will return victoriously with them as booty. This homology to the Rejected Dakṣiṇā is possible only because she is identified as the Rejected Wife.[241] The same mechanism of rejection creates militant hostility in both cow and wife, in the former case literally making her a new critter. And, though an enraged female in the bosom of the herd/family may bring destruction, she is a useful weapon against the lives and goods of others. Thus Indrāṇī in her character as Avoided Wife is an appropriate figure to pray to for aid in a military endeavor.

If Indrāṇī appears as the prototype of the Avoided Wife in this passage, we can cautiously examine other material about Indrāṇī for further clues to the character of the Avoided Wife in ritual.

Indrāṇī, undefeated, is associated with 'kicking' (remember the kicking Dakṣiṇā of the Avoided Wife) in an, as usual, enigmatic AV passage:

AV I.27.4 prétaṃ pādau prá sphuratam váhataṃ pṛṇató gṛhā́n
indrāṇy ètu prathamā́jītā́muṣitā puráḥ

Go forth, you two feet. Kick forth. Carry the givers home.
Let Indrāṇī go first in front, undefeated, unrobbed.

A militant Indrāṇī is also found in a set of pādas fairly widespread in BYV.[242]

KS VIII.17 (102: 5) indrāṇī́ pátyā sújitaṃ jigāya

Indrāṇī won a well-won (victory) with her husband.

(102: 5) úd áṁśena patividye bibheda

She came out with (her) share in the husband-finding.

(102: 8) indrāṇī́ prāsáhā saṃjáyantī

Indrāṇī winning by force . . .

The ambiguity of the first of these is especially interesting: we cannot tell if she won the well-won victory 'with' in the sense of 'against' her husband or 'with' him by her side. In either case, Indrāṇī emerges as the figure in command, to whom even her powerful husband, the warrior god of ancient India, either loses or defers. Her power may well derive from the fury aroused by sexual rejection, and her victory may lead to victory also in 'husband-finding' (i.e. reacquiring the affection of her husband), as the second quoted pāda suggests.

This set of hypotheses—Indrāṇī as Avoided Wife, who acquires militant force from this state, wins a great battle, and gets her husband back—seems at the moment to be based on rather slender evidence. Let us turn now to a RVic hymn that seems to exhibit the same constellation of features and, despite the great difficulty of its interpretation, may support this mythic reconstruction.

RV X.102, the so-called Contest of Mudgala, is another of those maddening hymns that the Tenth Maṇḍala seems to specialize in, tantalizing us with a story we cannot really reconstruct. The hymn seems to concern a vehicle race undertaken by one Mudgala, without the proper equipment. In particular he seems to have yoked a piece of wood next to his bull to serve as an ill-assorted team, and his wife Mudgalānī is the charioteer. Nonetheless, they win to great acclaim.

There is much about this hymn I do not understand, and I will not attempt a full exegesis here. What I want to do is point out the remarkable similarities, especially verbally, between RV X.102 and the twin figures of Indrāṇī in Brāhmaṇic mythology and the Avoided Wife of ritual. First we might note that Mudgalānī is called 'Indra's weapon' (indra*senā́* X.102.2), just as Indrāṇī is called a senā in KS. Like Indrāṇī's enterprise in the Brāhmaṇas, the race is undertaken for cattle, as is repeatedly reiterated:

RV X.102.2 út sma vā́to vahati vā́so 'syā ádhiratham yád ájayat sahásram
rathī́r abhūn mudgalā́nī gáviṣṭhau bhā́re kṛtám vy àced indrasenā́

The wind blew up her garment when she won the thousand (cows) and the chariot, too. Mugdalānī was the charioteer in the contest for cows. 'Indra's weapon' got the best throw in the game [a metaphor from dicing].

RV X.102.5 téna sū́bharvaṃ śatávat sahásraṃ gávām múdgalaḥ pradháne jigāya

With this (bull) Mudgala won a well-nourished thousand and hundred cows in the battle.

RV X.102.9 yéna jigā́ya śatávat sahásraṃ gávām múdgalaḥ pṛtanā́jyeṣu

With which (hammer) Mudgala won a thousand and hundred cows in the battle-contest.

The piece of wood yoked to the bull is actually a kū́ṭa 'hammer, mallet' (X.102.4). Remember that the Dakṣiṇā at the Avoided Wife's Ratnin oblation was kūṭá 'possessing mallet-like horns'. Neither kū́uṭa nor its possessive derivative is at all common in Vedic, and their appearance in the same thematic complex is notable, despite their different applications.

The bull performs several actions that remind us of passages in which Indrāṇī has figured. For example, he stretches (prá √bhṛ) his legs in his eagerness to win:

RV X.102.4 prá muṣkábhāraḥ śráva ichámāno 'jirám bāhū́ abharat síṣāsan

The one with balls, desiring fame, seeking to win, stretched his forelegs eagerly.

This resembles the AV passage in which Indrāṇī leads a procession, kicking her feet (prá √sphur) in her progress:[243]

AV I.27.4 prétaṃ pādau prá sphurataṃ váhataṃ pṛṇató gṛhā́n
indrāṇy ètu prathamā́jītā́muṣitā puráḥ

Go forth, you two feet. Kick forth. Carry the givers home.
Let Indrāṇī go first in front, undefeated, unrobbed.

The bull also shits and pisses during the contest, and the unlucky charioteer, Mudgalānī, gets splashed in the process:

RV X.102.5 ámehayan vṛṣabhám mádhya ājéḥ

They made the bull piss in the middle of the contest.

RV X.102.6 dúdher yuktásya drávataḥ sahā́nasa ṛchánti ṣmā niṣpádo mudgalā́nīm

The droppings of the frenzied yoked (bull), running with the wagon, reached Mudgalānī.[244]

This reminds us of the balbaja grass, arisen from the piss or shit of the cows, in the caru to Indrāṇī. It should also recall the fact that the Avoided Wife in the Aśvamedha has control of the hind end of the horse, that is, of its organs of generation and elimination.[245] Similarly, Mudgalānī is in literal contact with the potentially fertilizing ordure.

But the most significant parallel between RV X.102 and the material we have been examining is found late in the hymn, in a simile describing Mudgalānī:

X.102.11 parivṛktéva patividyam ānaṭ pī́pyānā kū́cakreṇeva siñcán

Like an Avoided (woman) she achieved husband-finding, pouring out like a swelling (woman) with a bad (water-)wheel.

This verse is quite reminiscent of Indrāṇī's situation in KS VIII.17 (etc.). Like Mudgalānī Indrāṇī won a great contest, and even as Mudgalānī's efforts allowed Mudgala to win cattle (see the passages cited earlier), so Indrāṇī's seem undertaken on behalf of or along with her husband:

KS VIII.17 (102: 5) indrāṇī́ pátyā sújitaṃ jigāya

Indrāṇī won a well-won (victory) with her husband.

(102: 8) indrāṇī́ prāsáhā saṃjáyantī

Indrāṇī winning by force . . .

Also like Mudgalānī Indrāṇī's reward is in the domestic sphere, in fact in exactly the pativídya of Mudgalānī in verse 11.

KS VIII.17 (102: 5) úd áṁśena pativídye bibheda

She came out with (her) share in the husband-finding.

I am not entirely certain what to make of all this, but I would suggest that Indrāṇī *when militant* is a mythological model of the Avoided Wife, with the passion caused by rejection channeled and transformed into battle fury, as suggested earlier. Indrāṇī uses this fury to win victory, with and for her husband. Mudgalānī is a human analogue to this militant goddess; Mudgalānī charges into a messy chariot race, minding neither the inadequacy of her equipment nor the literal filth that flies while the contest rages. She also brings victory to her husband.[246]

Both the mythological model and her human counterpart provide a sort of optimistic practical self-help guide for the wife who finds she has fallen into the Avoided predicament. Use that fury to further your husband's ends, and you will get him back—and you may become a swelling, fertile woman, like the image in the second half of RV X.102.11. If sonlessness is what makes a wife avoided, then this last promise would be especially appealing. Formulated thus baldly, the mythic complex seems like bad advice from American women's magazines of the 1950s. Nonetheless, I do not think the suggestive connections between the title Avoided Wife, the figures of Indrāṇī and Mudgalānī, and their aggressive activity and ultimate success can be explained away. By providing the Avoided Wife with models of power and ability like Indrāṇī, some of the sting may have been removed from her unpleasant position, even as in the meantime her own forces are tapped for ritual effectiveness.

5. Appendix: "Adoption" at the Rājasūya?

The contrastive pair of Mahiṣī and Parivṛktī has recently been examined by Falk (1984) in the context of an episode in the Rājasūya (Consecration of the King), which serves as the point of departure for a searching and speculative reevaluation of the entire Rājasūya ritual.

In the middle of this ritual there are two brief but curious episodes involving the wife and the son of the king. The first of the actions occurs, in most texts, right after the unction (Abhiṣeka) of the king. At this point a ceremonial exchange or 'intertwining' of names takes place between the king and a person known in several texts as a Pratihita, sometimes with the mother of the latter also participating:[247]

ĀpŚS XVIII.16.14 yāṃ bhāryāṃ kāmayeta rāṣṭram asyai prajā syād iti tasyā aupāsane pratihitam ārambhayitvā ye pātreṣu lepā vyavasṛtās tebhyo nāmavyatiṣañjanīyau homau juhuyāt prajāpate na tvad etānīti

15 asāv amuṣya putro 'muṣyā asau putra iti nāmanī vyatiṣajati
16 nāmānīty eke

About whichever wife he should wish that her offspring should have sovereignty, in *her* domestic fire he should offer the two 'name-intertwining' oblations from the leftovers smeared in the cups, having made the Pratihita grasp from behind, (saying) "Prajāpati, not than thee these . . . "

(Saying) "That one is the son of that one (masc.). That one is the son of that one (fem.)," he intertwines the two names.

Or, according to some, the (three) names.

TB I.7.8.7 prájāpate ná tvád etā́ny anyá íti tásyai gṛhé juhuyāt / yā́ṃ kāmáyeta rāṣṭrám asyai prajā́ syād íti

(Saying) "Prajāpati, not other than thee these . . . ," he should offer in the house of her about whom he should wish, "Her offspring should have sovereignty."

MŚS IX.1.4.27[248] patnīloke pratihitasya mātaram upaspṛśya pratihitam anvārabhya prajāpate na tvad ity etayā gārhapatye nāmavyatiṣaṅgaṃ juhoti pālāśasaṃpātam
28 asā amuṣya putro 'muṣyāsau putra iti nāmanī vyatiṣajati
29 vayaṁ syāma patayo rayīṇām iti pratihitaṁ vācayati

In the wife's place (in the ritual ground), having touched the mother of the Pratihita, having grasped the Pratihita from behind, with the (verse) "Prajāpati, not than thee . . . ," he offers in the Gārhapatya (as) the 'name-intertwining' oblation the remains of the palāśa (cup).

(With) "That one is the son of that one; of that one that is the son," he intertwines the two names.[249]

He has the Pratihita say, "May we be lords of wealth."

The ŚB specifies the "dearest son" of the king, rather than the Pratihita, and does not mention his mother. Otherwise the action is similar but more elaborately described than in the texts just quoted. The son also receives a cup containing the leftovers from the king's unction waters:

ŚB V.4.2.8 tád yò 'sya putráḥ priyátamo bhávati / tásmā etát pā́traṃ práyachatīdáṃ me 'yáṃ vīryàṃ putrò 'nusáṃtanavad íti
9 átha pratiparétya gā́rhapatyam anvā́rabdhe juhoti / prájāpate . . . ayám amúṣya pitéti tád yáḥ putrás táṃ pitáraṃ karóti yáḥ pitā́ táṃ putráṃ tád enayor vīryè vyátiṣajati . . .

He hands the cup (containing the leftover unction waters) to whoever is his [king's] dearest son, (with the thought) "This son of mine will extend this manly vigor of mine after (me)."

Then returning to the Gārhapatya, he offers (in it) while being taken hold of from behind (by his son), (saying) "Prajāpati. . . . This is the father of that one." In this way he makes the son the father and the father the son. Thus he intertwines the manly vigors of these two.

Soon after, there is a (mock) cattle raid, which in some versions involves the king's shooting arrows at a Kṣatriya stationed with the cattle (e.g. MŚS

IX.1.3.29; ĀpŚS XVIII.17.6–8).[250] The bow and arrows employed were ceremonially presented to him at the Abhiṣeka (cf. e.g. MŚS IX.1.3.12–14; ĀpŚS XVIII.14.10–13). The Sacrificer/king of course triumphs, and when he drives back to the place of sacrifice, according to some texts[251] he presents the bow to his wife, with a mantra referring to their son:

MŚS IX.1.3.31 eṣa vajro vājasātamas tena nau putro vājaṁ sed iti patnyai dhanvāni prayachati
32 tāny añjalinā pratigṛhṇāti

(Saying) "This is the most booty-winning cudgel. With it may our son win booty," he hands the bow to his wife.
She accepts it with her hollowed hands.

That the exchange of names and the bestowal of the bow are connected seems clear from BŚS, where the bow figures also at the naming ceremony. However, the wife, though present, is not conspicuous. An excerpted version of the elaborate description of both episodes in the BŚS follows:

BŚS XII.11 (102: 3) atraiteṣām abhiṣekāṇāṃ mukhye pātre saṁsrāvān samavanīya pratihitasya gṛhān ety athānvārabdhayoḥ pratihite ca mahiṣyāṃ ca juhoti prajāpate . . . ity atrāsmā eṣa pratihito varaṃ dadāty atha pratihitāya pātraṃ prayacchann āhedaṃ te pātraṃ dāyādyam asad yadā tvābhiṣiñcāmīdaṃ te 'sad iti . . . atrāsmai dhanuḥ prayacchati yadi purastād aprattaṃ bhavati samunmṛṣṭe samutkrośanty abhyaṣecy ayam asāv āmuṣyāyaṇo 'muṣya putro 'muṣya pautro 'muṣya naptā rājasūyeneti

Then, pouring the blended remainders of these unction (waters) into the chief cup, he [the Adhvaryu] goes to the house of the Pratihita. Then, with the Pratihita and the Mahiṣī holding on from behind, he offers, (with) "Prajāpati . . . " Then the Pratihita grants him a boon. Then, handing over the cup to the Pratihita, he says, "This cup will be your inheritance. When I anoint you, it will be yours." . . . Then he hands him the bow, if it has not been previously given. He wipes him. They proclaim: "This one has been anointed—that one, belonging to that family, son of that one, grandson of that one, descendant of that one—by the Rājasūya."

BŚS XII.12 (103: 6) uttarata ete rathā yuktās tiṣṭhanti tān dṛṣṭvaiva pratihito 'vatiṣṭhaty atha pratihitasya dhanur ādāyādhijyaṃ kṛtvā ratham ātiṣṭhati . . . taṃ tadānīm eva pratihito 'nvātiṣṭhati . . . atha pratihitāya dhanuḥ prayacchann āha . . .

To the north the chariots stand yoked. On seeing them, the Pratihita stops. Then having taken the bow of the Pratihita and having strung it, (the king) mounts the chariot. . . . The Pratihita mounts after him. . . . Then handing the bow to the Pratihita, (the king) says . . .

There follows in BŚS a mock attack on a warrior by the son, not the father: the Pratihita shoots an arrow at the warrior, which is designed to miss, and the warrior wipes the arrow on his garment and returns it to its shooter. As we saw earlier, in most other texts it is the king who is the attacking party.

What is all of this about?

The exchange of names occupies very little space in the Rājasūya, but Falk has recently suggested that this episode is the key to the original purpose of the ritual. He considers this an *adoption* ceremony: the Pratihita is the adopted son, the 'substitute'. The adoption is necessary because of the particular circumstances of the king: his "regular" wife is childless, and he must legitimate the son of a woman to whom he is not (yet) married. Falk considers this adoption ceremony most faithfully preserved in the BŚS passage just quoted.[252]

This scenario requires a complete reinterpretation of several key terms for women in the king's entourage, the Mahiṣī (usually considered the chief wife of the king, as we have seen) and the Parivṛktī (the 'Avoided Wife') and the other royal wives. Falk suggests that the Parivṛktī herself is the regular but childless wife of the king.[253] The Mahiṣī, in contrast, is not (yet) married to the king but has borne a child. This is the Pratihita, whom the king adopts in the course of the Rājasūya (see esp. Falk 1984, p. 120). The other wives of the king, the Vāvātā and the Pālāgalī who are found in so many texts, are simply the figments of ritual exegesis and have no real-life counterparts (120, n. 19).

Despite Falk's always ingenious and stimulating argumentation, I find his reinterpretation unconvincing. For one thing, given the size and elaboration of the Rājasūya as we have it, this little episode seems a very small tail to wag a very large dog. Moreover, his textual support is rather fragile. The BŚS passage seems to me to differ from the other texts not in kind, but in the extent of its treatment—a not uncommon feature of BŚS.

Falk lays much emphasis on the fact that the Pratihita is proclaimed as anointed (abhi √sic) in the BŚS, and considers that his new parentage is being announced in the phrase beginning asāv āmuṣyāyaṇaḥ. But we must remember that this is the *second* unction ceremony of the Rājasūya and is performed with the leftover waters from the first. It is at least as possible to see this part of the ceremony as the appointment and proclamation of the 'heir apparent', the king's chosen successor among his sons. On such an occasion the ceremonial announcement of the son's full name and ancestry would be entirely appropriate, and the presence of his mother, as guarantor of the nobility of his maternal lineage, is also not surprising. The 'intertwining' (vy-ati √saj) of the names of father, son, and, in some texts, mother simply strengthens the continuity of the line by interlocking the principals. The identifications of father as son/son as father is a standard strategem to deny that there will ever be disjunction or interruption in the succession.[254] Using the water from the first unction for the second also stresses the continuity of the royal line.

To support his interpretation Falk is required to attribute more to the literal interpretation of the term pratihita than I think is justified. He claims that the word means 'replacement, substitute', but this is not the ordinary usage of the idiom prati √dhā, which simply means 'fix, establish' and is often used of the 'fixing' of the arrow to the bow string, just prior to shooting. The heir apparent as 'fixed', 'appointed', or even 'aimed' is semantically unimpeachable. Falk must also consider the ŚB's putráḥ priyátamaḥ "dearest son" a functionally distinct, later substitution for the pratihita found in the other texts. And he must tacitly reject the universal interpretation of Mahiṣī as 'chief wife of the king': he offers no arguments for this lexical departure.

The business with the bow, especially in the BŚS version of events, seems exactly analogous to the intertwining of names. The bow, symbol of warrior activity, passes back and forth between father and son.[255] Indeed the father even prepares the bow (adhijyam kṛtvā) for the son's ritual shot at the Rājanya stationed to receive it. Again father and son are identified, and the son is initiated as well into his warrior role. Those texts in which the king performs the cattle raid and then hands the bow to his wife emphasize, as at the name-intertwining, her role as progenitor of the heir apparent, as the mantra accompanying the transfer shows:

> MŚS IX.1.3.31 eṣa vajro vājasātamas tena nau putro vājaṁ set
>
> This is the most booty-winning cudgel. With it may our [dual] son win booty.

It may not be entirely fanciful to suggest that the term for the heir apparent, Pratihita, is partly responsible for the symbolism of the bow. Since, as noted earlier, this lexeme is often used of arrows fixed or aimed just prior to shooting, the king's appointed successor can be seen as the aimed arrow and the wife, as source of the child, perhaps as the bow—ready to propel her child to his appointed target.

It also seems possible that the exact shape of this part of the ritual may depend on the age of the Pratihita: if he is old enough, he follows his father onto the chariot and shoots the arrow himself. But if he is too young, he may not participate in the cattle raid at all, and the handing of the bow to the wife, after the king has performed his role in the cattle raid, may substitute for the exchange of bow between father and son. As so often the wife would serve as a mediator, but here she would be the mediating link between two people who are also identified with each other. Indeed, this is another occasion that MS (IV.4.5 [56: 1]) calls "the taking hold of the ritual by the wife": her roles as proxy in the transfer of dynastic power and wife/mother of the two participants may account for this ascription of global control to the wife here. Without the proper harnessing of her sexual powers, the legitimate continuance of the royal line would not be possible.

F. Hospitality and Exchange Relations: The Soma Sacrifice

Let us now leave the sexual realm and turn to an area where the role of the wife seems to me at least as important, though not as explicitly recognized by contemporary exegetes. This is the area of hospitality and exchange relations—a crucial mechanism in ancient India, governing the relations between people (or rather, to be realistic, men) as well as those between the human and the divine, the living and the dead. Hospitality—its obligations and dangers—

and gift exchange, the delicate negotiations involved in giving and receiving presents, are endlessly repeated themes throughout Indian literature and religious practice, as already discussed. Women figure prominently in both areas, as dispensers of hospitality on the one hand and, more important, as the ultimate exchange token in the most fundamental exchange relation, that of marriage. Needless to say, her importance in these areas is symbolically represented in the ritual, again in a continuum from subtle to dramatic.

Many of her activities in these spheres are especially clearly highlighted in the most elaborate of the nonroyal rituals, the Soma Sacrifice—a ritual in which the *plant* soma, made into the inspiriting *drink* soma, is both ceremonially received as king and god and then as ceremonially sacrificed. The complex of exchange relations in this ambivalent treatment of the central substance, soma, is reflected in the wife's several roles.

There are, of course, many varieties of Soma Sacrifice, whose ritual paradigm is given in the so-called Agniṣṭoma.[256] Though I cannot treat the whole multiday ritual in detail or chronologically, there are several complexes of activity that will draw our attention in this ritual. Let me schematize the relevant ones briefly before I focus on any one in particular.

Consecration (see B.2b)

Purchase of soma (see F.2)

Guest reception of soma (see F.1)

Driving soma in a chariot to the place of sacrifice (see F.3)

Pressing and offering of soma (three times in one day) (see F.4)

Closing rites, release of consecration, and final bath (see B.2, B.3a, C.3, C.4)

We have already discussed the consecration (Dīkṣā) undergone by both Sacrificer and wife. This occupies the beginning of the ritual, while other preparations are also being made. The period between the consecration and the actual offering of the soma is occupied by the acquisition and the honoring of the plant/king and its transport to and installation in the place where it will be pressed. We will begin by examining the middle of this sequence of events, the guest reception.

1. *The Hospitality Rite*

First let us note that when King Soma is ritually received as guest in the hospitality rite (Ātithya),[257] the wife—unusually—participates in the oblation. This rite is conducted exactly as if the dry bundle of sticks from the soma plant were an especially distinguished human visitor: he is brought in on a cart, solicitously taken down, offered a seat and comestibles. The exegetical texts make the homology between plant and visiting king quite clear, as in the following ŚB passage:

ŚB III.4.1.2 átha yásmād ātithyáṃ nā́ma / átithir vā́ eṣá etásyā́gachati yát sómaḥ krītás tásmā etád yáthā rā́jñe vā brāhmaṇā́ya vā mahokṣáṃ vā mahājáṃ vā pácet tád áha mānuṣáṁ havír devā́nām evám asmā etád ātithyáṃ karoti

Now as to why (this oblation) is called the 'Guestly' one: Soma, after it is bought, comes as his [Sacrificer's] guest. So, even as one would cook a great ox or great goat for a king or Brahman—that is the human (equivalent) of the oblation to the gods—even so for this one [soma] he makes a Guestly offering.

Once soma has been comfortably settled, they proceed to perform an Iṣṭi of the same general type as the Darśapūrṇamāsa we have examined before. But here the wife is a part of the main offering, though the texts differ slightly on her exact role. According to MŚS she holds out her hand, and the Adhvaryu uses her hand to strew the grains for the offering cake (MŚS II.1.5.3 patny avadhārayed yasmān nirvapet). ĀpŚS gives a set of choices, some involving her hand as offering medium:

ĀpŚS X.30.5 nirvapaṇakāle patnīṃ śakaṭam anvārambhayitvātithyaṃ nirvapati

6 patnyā vā hastena

7 hastād vā / hastān nirvapan haste sarvāñ chakaṭamantrāñ japet

At the time for the (grain-)strewing, having made the wife take hold of the cart from behind, (the Adhvaryu) strews the Guestly offering.

Or he strews (it) with the wife's hand.

Or from (her) hand. If he strews from her hand, he should mutter all the "cart" mantras over (her) hand (instead).

In MS III.7.9 (88: 5) the strewing also happens from her hand (pátnyā hástān nírvapati). Other texts stipulate rather that she 'touch from behind' (anv-ā √rambh) the Adhvaryu[258] (BŚS VI.16 [174: 15]; KŚS VIII.1.2; KS XXIV.8 [98: 13]; TS VI.2.1.1; ŚB III.4.1.6), while he is performing the strewing.

The lack of agreement about just what her action is seems to me an indication of the ritualists' discomfort with her unusual participation. In particular, the awkward phrasing of the provisions concerning her hand seems designed to avoid awarding her *agency* in this action: her hand is an instrument almost detached from her person that the Adhvaryu is making use of. The 'taking from behind' of the several texts may be a later measure to distance her further from this ritual action. This recasting may rest on a text like MS, which specifies that her hand be used and then interprets this use as a *symbolic* 'taking from behind' of the ritual,[259] of the type I have discussed before.

But, clearly, she cannot be banished from this ritual action completely—precisely because her role here is, in many ways, just a ritual enactment of a wife's household duty. As we will see, the wife is often a dispenser of hospitality, and for this most eminent of visitors her absence from the guest reception would be insulting. But this is not all. The Saṃhitā prose texts (MS, KS, TS) explain the need for her participation in a stronger way, which raises questions to which I do not have complete answers. They state that she "has control of the household goods," and so her *permission* to give them away to a guest is required:

> MS III.7.9 (88: 5) pátnī vái pā́rīṇahyasyeśe pátnyaivá rātám ánumataṃ kriyate
>
> The wife is master of the household goods. Thus the gift (of them) is made with the approval of the wife.[260]

There are several curious features in this passage. Let me briefly mention one to which we will return: immediately after this statement the passage turns to the usual sexual explanation for the wife's ritual participation. MS III.7.9 continues without interruption:

> MS III.7.9 (88: 6) yád vái pátnī yajñé karóti tán mithunáṃ mithunatvā́ya vái pátnyā hástān nírvapati
>
> What the wife does in ritual is a sexual pairing. It is for sexual pairing that he strews from the hand of the wife.[261]

Though this may simply be an independent explanation for the wife's participation, signaling a return to the usual preoccupations of the ritualists, I will later suggest a different avenue for the introduction of this sentiment.

Another peculiar feature is the rather startling statement that she is master over material goods. The verb employed (√īś) is a strong statement of control: it is a standard verb for ruling and the same verb used in the Manu's cups story for Manu's life-or-death power over his guests, in the exchange between the disguised Indra and Manu that seals the Asuras' fate:

> MS IV.8.1 (107: 11) *ī́śe* 'háṃ brāhmaṇáyor ítī́śiṣe hī́ty abravīd átithipatir vā́-vā́tithīnām *ī́ṣṭā* íti
>
> [Manu:] "*Am I master* of the two Brahmans?" "Indeed *you are master*," said (Indra), "A lord of guests [host] *is master* of his guests."

It is striking that similar control over goods is attributed to the wife here,[262] especially as in most legal texts her right to ownership of property is extremely restricted, usually to adornments and small presents from her family and husband, what was given her at marriage, and a share in her mother's goods. See, for example, MDŚ IX.192–200, with the especially succinct

> MDŚ IX.194 adhyagnyadhyāvāhanikaṃ dattaṃ ca prītikarmaṇi
> bhrātṛmātṛpitṛprāptaṃ ṣaḍvidhaṃ strīdhanaṃ smṛtam
>
> What is given at the (nuptial) fire, on the (bridal) procession, and in token of affection, and what was received (as presents) from brother, mother, and father—these are known as the six types of women's property.

The other odd feature is the word for 'household goods', the very rare pā́rīṇahya. Outside of these three parallel passages I am aware of only one other occurrence (of the variant pāriṇāhya), in a passage in Manu also concerning the wife:

> MDŚ IX.11 arthasya saṃgrahe cainām vyaye caiva niyojayet
> śauce dharme 'nnapaktyāṃ ca pāriṇāhyasya vekṣaṇe
>
> He should employ her [the wife] in collecting and spending money,
> in cleanliness, in duty, in cooking food, and in looking after the household goods.

The word is a transparent vṛddhi derivative of slightly more common parīṇáh-, which seems to refer to a container or (traveling) box in some of its occurrences.[263] So the 'household goods' may be literally 'those belonging to the cupboard' (vel sim.) or 'those belonging to the trunk' (vel sim.). If the latter is the source, the striking attribution of property ownership to the wife might be explained. The pā́rīṇahya might originally have been the moveable goods that the bride brought to her new home at marriage (as expressed by the first two types of property in MDŚ IX.194 quoted earlier). These she would have control of, and even when pā́rīṇahya came to refer to household goods in general, the old notion of the wife's ownership of what she literally brought to the marriage may have been preserved. This may in turn help explain why the wife's permission is needed to give away what she does not really own, hence part of the reason why she is so necessary to the exercise of hospitality. The wife's tacit approval of the Sacrificer's gifts may also be alluded to at the time of the bestowal of the Dakṣiṇās (at the Midday Pressing), when KŚS for example says "The wife also gives" (KŚS X.2.36 patnī ca dadāti).

The word parīṇáh- is also used at least once to refer to female genitalia (by a semantic transference too common to comment on), in a charm for safe childbirth:

> KS XIII.9 (191: 5) vi te bhinadmi takariṃ vi yoniṃ vi parīṇaham
>
> I split apart your takari (?), apart your womb, apart your 'box'.[264]

If this was a common Vedic vulgar idiom, it may be that the expression "the wife is master of 'what belongs to the box'" conveyed a sexual meaning as well as a housekeeping one in the passages in question, and the transition from the cupboard to the bed in all three passages would be easier to understand. Even as she is innocuously giving permission to give the guest, King Soma, "her" food and drink, there may be a sense that she is offering herself to him (and by extension to the ritual) sexually, hence the remark in MS III.7.9 quoted above. This combination of sex and hospitality is not uncommon in ancient India, as we will see,[265] and indeed the sexual pairing of wife and soma forms the climactic end of the Soma Sacrifice (see III.F.5).

One must, of course, beware of reading too much into the details of our often terse texts. However, this seems to me another instance in which sensitivity to language—not merely the immediate semantic content of a word, but its relation to other words, and its frequency or rarity in the type of context at issue—enriches our interpretation of an apparently straightforward statement. There were many ways in Vedic to say that the wife dispenses hospitality along with her husband. That three (related but not duplicate) texts did not say this at all, and, in what they did say, chose two unlikely words, one of which is extremely rare, would indicate that what is being expressed is not quite as straightforward as we may think.

In any case, whatever other associations are evoked, the wife plays a specific part in this hospitality Iṣṭi different from her usual ritual role, partly because of her importance in domestic hospitality observances. We see this crossover from domestic guest reception to ritual in other parts of the Soma Sacrifice, where again, however, something more than the enactment of simple hospitable behavior is involved. "Hospitality" can be used to symbolize different types of relationships and responsibilities. Later I will examine a particularly complex use of hospitality as symbol in the wife's involvement with the so-called Foot-washing water (pannejanī). In the secular realm a major requirement for the reception of a guest is to provide him with water to wash his feet, as we will see. In the ritual realm this simple element of ordinary guest reception is deployed in a remarkable fashion, as part of a tangle of representations and mediations so complex that I must postpone discussion of it for some time.

In the meantime, let us move back chronologically in the Soma Sacrifice to the major event that immediately precedes the hospitality rite I have just examined, to the formal 'purchase of soma'. Here we will see women's role as exchange token quite remarkably enacted, but through such a series of transfers that I think it has previously escaped notice.

2. *The Soma-Cow*

The situation is this: before Soma the king can be received as a guest, soma the plant must be purchased. The purchase is part of the ritual—even the bargaining is scripted—and the purchase price is a cow, called the Soma-krayaṇī ('Soma-purchasing one [female]'). Needless to say, given the elaboration of every other part of the procedure, the cow is not just produced and handed over. A series of actions prepare her, too, for the exchange. These actions connect her both with the wife and with the Sacrificer in a bizarre sort of switch.

On the one hand, the wife and the cow participate in two nearly simultaneous exchanges. They are made to look at each other, to exchange glances, and the wife is given the sand from a footprint of the cow, sand which she will later distribute ritually. Though there is no physical contact by our standards, both gazes and footprints are symbolically charged in this culture, as has been amply demonstrated by others. Mutual gazes "count" as physical contact and are frequently used in ritual to transfer forces, as we saw earlier with the melted butter in the paradigm Iṣṭi. Footprints are so representative of the person or animal that made them that they are objects of worship to this day,[266] and, as we will see, this particular footprint is especially significant.

Let us examine a few variants on these two exchanges. In most texts the footprint, which is carefully prepared and honored, changes hands several times.

> BŚS VI.13 (169: 19) athaitasmin pade hiraṇyaṃ nidhāya saṃparistīryābhijuhoti . . . apoddhṛtya hiraṇyaṁ sphyena vā kṛṣṇaviṣāṇayā vā padaṃ parilikhati . . . athainat sphyenopasaṃgrāhaṃ yāvattmūtaṃ paddharaṇyāṁ saṃvapati . . . yajamānāya prayacchati . . . yajamānaḥ patnyā atha patnīṁ somakrayaṇyā samīkṣayati . . . atha patnī yajamānam īkṣate . . . atha yajamānaḥ somakrayaṇīm īkṣate[267]
>
> Then having put (a piece of) gold down in this footprint and having strewn around it, he [Adhvaryu] offers (ghee into it). Having taken out the gold, he draws a line around the footprint with the wooden sword or a black antelope horn. Then with the sword he scatters into the Footprint-carrying (vessel) (the sand that has been) gathered up, as much as has been soaked by the ghee.[268]
>
> He gives (it, i.e. vessel) to the Sacrificer. The Sacrificer (gives it) to the wife. Then he [probably Adhvaryu?] makes the wife exchange glances with the Soma-cow. Then the wife looks at the Sacrificer. Then the Sacrificer looks at the Soma-cow.

This set of exchanges can be schematized as follows:

Soma-cow('s)	footprint taken	by priest (in pot).
Priest	gives pot	to Sacrificer.
Sacrificer	gives pot	to wife.
Wife	looks at	Soma-cow.
Wife	looks at	Sacrificer.
Sacrificer	looks at	Soma-cow.

Though other texts present slight variants on this pattern,[269] the cycling between cow, priest, Sacrificer, and wife is present in all.

The reason for this elaborate choreography will be clear when I identify the particular footprint from which the sand has been extracted. Just previously the priests have caused the cow to take seven steps. It is the footprint from the seventh step that provides the sand that the wife receives.

> BŚS VI.12, 13 (169: 15 [immediately before passage quoted above]) tasyai ṣaṭpadāny anuniṣkrāmati . . . saptamaṃ padam abhigṛhṇāti
>
> He [Adhvaryu] strides following her six footsteps. The seventh footstep he takes hold of.

What is the significance of this seventh step?[270]

Let us consider an important ritual belonging to the domestic (gṛhya) sphere, the marriage ceremony. This ritual has a number of parts, but the climactic moment is the "seven steps," which the bride makes, led or accompanied by the groom,[271] as in

ŚGS I.14.5 prāgudīcyāṃ diśi saptapadāni prakramayati

He makes (her / them?) stride forward in a northeastern direction for seven steps.

According to the legal texts after this action the marriage is legally irrevocable:

MDŚ VIII.227 pāṇigrahaṇikā mantrā niyataṃ dāralakṣaṇam
teṣāṃ niṣṭhā tu vijñeyā vidvadbhiḥ saptame pade

The (performance of the) mantras of the marriage ceremony is the sure sign of a lawful wife.
Wise men recognize the decisive conclusion of these (mantras) at the seventh step.[272]

So when the Soma-cow makes the seven steps, she becomes symbolically a bride; she *marries* the Sacrificer. The exchange of the glances and of the sand between wife and cow simply cements their interchange of roles. Wife becomes cow, cow wife. Indeed, in at least one text the Sacrificer addresses the cow with a variant of the same mantras the groom addresses to the bride under the same circumstances at the wedding. In the marriage ceremony the groom rather tersely expresses a different wish at every step, beginning

ŚGS I.14.6 (etc.) iṣa ekapadī ūrje dvipadī rāyaspoṣāya tripadī . . .

Step one for liquid nourishment; step two for solid nourishment; step three for thriving of wealth . . .

The bridegroom's standard injunction at the seventh step is

ŚGS I.14.6 (etc.) sakhā saptapadī bhava

Become a companion of the seventh step.

In ĀpŚS X.22.12 the Sacrificer addresses the cow for the first six steps with exactly the sequence found in the corresponding gṛhya treatment of the marriage ceremony, ending with

ĀpŚS X.23.1 sakhāyaḥ saptapadā abhūma . . .

We have become companions at the seventh step.[273]

So the cow now represents the Sacrificer's wife, and as soon as she does so, he sets out to *exchange* her for the soma plant that is to become successively Soma the king, honored guest, and soma the drink, the sacrificial victim. The wife, both directly and in the guise of the cow, mediates between the Sacrificer and his guest and the Sacrificer and his victim. It is worthwhile formulating this action as baldly as possible: the Sacrificer is about to *buy* soma *with his* (symbolic) *wife*. The purchase price is, of course, the cow, but cow has been transformed into wife by the mock marriage that has just taken place. Put thus, the transaction seems a shocking one—selling your wife for a bunch of twigs—but ritual exists in some ways to interpose filtering screens between ritual activity and the "reality" it seeks to represent, and the cow here is such a screen. In fact, she has functioned so effectively that the import of this ritual business seems not to have struck other scholars.[274]

The bargaining and purchase that follow are no simpler than what precedes, and though the human wife is not on the scene, we should follow the fortunes of her bovine surrogate. After the measuring and selection of the soma stalks, the Soma-seller and the Adhvaryu engage in formulaic haggling, which has, nonetheless, a ring of mundane verisimilitude about it.[275] The dialogue in BŚS begins

> BŚS VI.14 (172: 1) athopotthāya pṛcchati somavikrayin krayyas te somā3 iti krayya itītaraḥ pratyāha mūjavatā3 iti mūjavato hītītaraḥ pratyāha
>
> Then going up to (him), (the Adhvaryu) asks, "Soma-seller, is your soma for sale?" "It is for sale," answers the other. "(Is it) from Mt. Mūjavant?" "From Mt. Mūjavant indeed," answers the other.

But the buyer begins with an insulting offer: one-sixteenth (kalā) of the cow. To which the seller responds:

> ĀpŚS X.25.5 (etc.) bhūyo vā ataḥ somo rājārhati
>
> King Soma is worth much more than this.

The bargaining proceeds through eighth-, fourth-, and half-portions of the cow—with the seller's impassive rejection remaining the same—until finally the whole cow is offered, sometimes with additional items to sweeten the deal. This time the seller accepts.

In most of the ritual sūtras this ends the focus on the sale. We turn to the soma that has been purchased, and one is left to assume that the Soma-seller takes the Soma-cow away. But in some (see Caland and Henry 1906–7, p. 47; Kane, *HDŚ* II.1143) the Soma-cow is then further exchanged for another cow, and she herself is returned to the Sacrificer. The Soma-seller is also sometimes physically abused and even deprived of any of the purchase price (cf. ĀpŚS X.26.16; KŚS VII.8.25).

It may not be fanciful to see in this retention by the Sacrificer of the original Soma-cow some anxiety on the part of the ritualists about the implications of her sale. They may have seen a little too clearly that the Soma-cow stands in for the wife and so her sale is tantamount to a sale of the patnī. Effecting a further sleight of hand, by substituting another cow for the first one, would enable the Sacrificer not only to keep his wife in reality—a result already ensured by substituting cow for wife—but also symbolically, by bringing the cow back to the Sacrificer's own stall.

However, this was presumably not the only reason for the switch (or the cheating of the seller). There was also the pleasure of driving the harder bargain (so, approximately, Hillebrandt 1897, p. 126) and, as well, the dramatization of the evils of selling a sacred substance, as Caland and Henry suggest (1906–7, p. 48).

This whole little theme has its mythic prototype, as Keith (1925, p. 327) has pointed out. The usual story told in the Brāhmaṇas apropos of the soma purchase is the familiar one of bringing soma from heaven.[276] On his journey hither he is stolen by the Gandharvas, and the gods decide to ransom him—with a woman, because Gandharvas are 'fond of women' (strīkāma). They send the goddess Vāc 'Speech', and after she has ransomed the soma, the gods engage in a verbal contest with the Gandharvas over her. The gods woo her back by singing to her. (The Gandharvas are foolishly and uncharacteristically earnest and speak mystic formulations [bráhman] to her, for which she has no taste.) So the gods end up with both the soma and what they had exchanged for him. This bit of divine dirty dealing presumably served as foundation myth to allow the ritualists to overcome any twinge of conscience they might have had about cheating on a contractual agreement—otherwise a serious offense for the legally punctilious Aryans.

3. The Soma-Cow's Footprint

We have recently been following the trail of the Soma-cow after her seven steps. But what, in the meantime, has happened to the physical remains of the seventh step, which we saw made into an object of veneration? We last saw it in a pot in the possession of the wife. What does happen to it is a challenge to our interpretive imagination and involves some strain to our attempts to see the hidden connections between seemingly arbitrary ritual events. Indeed, even the ancient comments on this particular part of the ritual betray a certain incomprehension. But I believe the chain of ritual reasoning can still be followed.

After the series of exchanges centering around the cow and her footprint, the sacralized sand or dirt from the seventh step is afforded different treatment, depending on the text. According to MS (III.7.7 [84: 5]) and KS (XXIV.6 [95: 6]) the sand is scattered beside the Gārhapatya fire, but both recognize the possibility (which they argue against and reject) of scattering it also by the Āhavanīya. Indeed, TS VI.1.8.5 actually does scatter the sand by both fires. The ŚB (III.6.3.6) agrees with the MS/KS procedure of confining the sand entirely to the Gārhapatya, but rather disapprovingly cites some authorities who divide the sand into four parts, only one of which ends up at the Gārhapatya (ŚB III.6.3.5; cf. KŚS VIII.6.31). ĀpŚS suggests a threefold division:

> ĀpŚS X.23.9 . . . padaṃ traidhaṃ vibhajya tṛtīyam uttarato gārhapatyasya śīte bhasmany upavapati / tṛtīyam āhavanīyasya / tṛtīyaṃ patnyai prayacchati
>
> Having divided the (sand of the) footprint into three, he scatters a third in the cold ash north of the Gārhapatya, a third (in the cold ash) of the Āhavanīya, and he gives a third to the wife.

This last third presumably remains quietly in the wife's safekeeping for several days, while other ritual events draw the focus: the buying and guest reception of the soma and some days of ancillary rites (the Pravargya and the Upasads).

But this butter-soaked dirt reemerges at what at first seems an utterly irrelevant moment. The wife uses the remains of the cow's footprint to anoint the axles or linchpins of the two Soma-carts.

> ĀpŚS XI.6.4 athaine patnī padatṛtīyenājyamiśreṇopānakti
> 5 ā no vīro jāyatām iti dvir dakṣiṇām akṣadhuraṃ dakṣiṇena hastenottānena prācīnam
> 6 na ca hastam āvartayati
>
> Then the wife anoints these two (carts) with a third of the footprint mixed with butter. (Saying) "Let a hero be born to us," (she anoints) twice the right linchpin with her right hand, palm upwards, eastwards [i.e. making the hand movements only toward the east]. She does not turn her hand back.[277]

This action certainly should have a firm conceptual foundation because its practical value seems extremely dubious: whatever advantage the grease might bring to the smooth running of the cart, the sand introduced into the works would surely offset it.

We have seen the footprint put to several apparently unrelated uses, the last mentioned of which is surely the most bizarre. Indeed when the exegetical texts attempt to account for the wife's anointing the wheels of the Soma-carts, they seem rather at a loss and for the most part fall back on their standard interpretive strategies. Both MS (III.8.7 [103: 16]) and KS (XXV.8 [113: 13]) suggest, as usual, that this is both a sexual pairing (mithuná) and a "grasping from behind of the ritual" (yajñásyānvārambhá). The TS (VI.2.9.2) does likewise, but also claims that

> TS VI.2.9.2 pátnī hí sárvasya mitrám mitratvā́ya
>
> The wife is a friend / ally to all. (The action) is for friendship / alliance.

The ŚB is more creatively explicit about the sexual aspects of the action:

> ŚB III.5.3.16 átha yát pátny ákṣasya saṃtāpám upānákti / prajánanam eváitát kriyate yadā́ vái striyái ca puṁsáś ca saṃtapyáté 'tha rétaḥ sicyate tát tátaḥ prájāyate
>
> Then, in that the wife anoints the heated-up part of the axle, procreation is thus done. When there is heating up of woman and man, then semen is poured out and subsequently birth takes place.

I think, in fact, that these various explanations are correct, but perhaps for the wrong reasons. Producing the right reasons requires us to consider all the potential uses of the cow's footprint as conceptual variants of each other.

Remember the simplest employment of this sand (MS, KS): it was all scattered next to the Gārhapatya. As we are well aware, the Gārhapatya is the 'wife's world' (patnīloka). Depositing the entire footprint of the Soma-*cow*, which has become the surrogate *wife of the Sacrificer*, returns her symbolically to her own world, even as she is led forth to be swapped for the soma. Like the makeshifts that represent the wife when she is banished from the ritual ground by menstruation or childbirth, the sand from the wifely Soma-cow's footprint gives her a literal foothold in the wife's world that she is supposed to inhabit.

The TS solution, to scatter it both at the Gārhapatya and the Āhavanīya, can be understood with regard to another ritual complex we have already examined. Recall that, at the beginning of the paradigm Iṣṭi, the wife, situated at the Gārhapatya, looks at melted butter, which is then taken to the Āhavanīya to serve as the oblation material for the rest of the ritual. This looking at the melted butter was also called a 'sexual pairing' and a 'taking from behind of the ritual', and I explained this action as a means of introducing woman's sexual force into the pure ritual world of the eastern end of the ritual ground. The use of the Soma-cow's footprint at the Āhavanīya can serve the same function.

With these fairly straightforward uses of the footprint in mind, we can now understand the anointing of the cartwheels as doing exactly the same thing, but in order to see this we must know something more about the carts and the part of the ritual in which the anointing occurs.

All the preliminary actions of the Soma Sacrifice (which, by now, have occupied some days) have taken place on a fairly restricted ritual ground essentially identical to that used for an ordinary Iṣṭi. But the ritual geography is about to expand considerably. A much larger Mahāvedi ('great altar') is measured out to the east. At its extreme eastern end a place for a new Āhavanīya fire is readied, to which the actual fire is ceremonially carried. The old Āhavanīya then is recategorized: it becomes the new Gārhapatya.[278] Several temporary structures are built within the Mahāvedi, including a shed to house the two Soma-carts.

Just as the journey to the new Āhavanīya has its ritual procession, so the driving of the Soma-carts to their garage in the middle of the Mahāvedi is accompanied with some fanfare. The wife's anointing of the linchpins and the oblation in the wheel-tracks immediately precede the start of their eastern progress. Despite the brevity of the journey, it is treated in some ways as if it were a pioneering expedition to the unknown east[279]—as is dramatized by the wife's anointing the pins in only one direction, toward the east, thus giving the wheels a preliminary warm-up spin.

I would suggest that the new vedi to the east needs the symbolic presence of the wife, just as the more restricted ritual ground did, and this is supplied when the "pioneering expedition" of the two carts sets off to take possession of it. This womanly presence is supplied doubly: the human wife performs the anointing, and she does so with substance from the bovine wife.

Furthermore, the journey recalls a different but equally momentous trip, taken in the mundane world: the wedding journey, on which the bride is transported with great ceremony and exaggerated care to her new home.[280] All the gṛhya sūtras treat this with some attention, starting with the preparation and mounting of the bridal chariot, a preoccupation also already visible in the RVic wedding hymn (X.85). In at least one gṛhya sūtra the new wife performs a remarkable task, entirely parallel to what she does here: she anoints the axles of the chariot:

> ŚGS I.15.3 atha rathākṣasyopāñjanaṃ patnī kurute
>
> Then the wife performs the anointing of the chariot axles.

After which she continues to smear the rest of the chariot with the same substance. Thus, in the Soma Sacrifice when the wife anoints the wheels, she is acting like a bride—with soma, the occupant of the chariot, her bridegroom.

This gṛhya parallel will help us to explain why the presence of the wife is not extended all the way to the new Āhavanīya, as it was in the paradigm Iṣṭi recently mentioned. There are several answers to this. One is that it actually is: in the texts that suggest a fourfold division of the footprint (ŚB III.6.3.5; cf. KŚS VIII.6.31), one quarter ends up as support for the new Āhavanīya. But there is a more interesting answer. The crucial ritual substance, soma itself, will spend the day before its pressing in these very Soma-carts (hence their name). Soma is often conceptualized as semen. It is also, in the Third Pressing, mixed with milk, in a pairing that is often likened to a sexual mating, as we will see. The Soma-cow is, in several texts, explicitly called a representative of the milk with which soma will ultimately be mixed:

> TS VI.1.10.2 dhenvā́ krīṇāti sā́śiram eváinaṃ krīṇāti
>
> He buys (soma) with a milch-cow; he thus buys him provided with the mixing milk.[281]

When *the wife* anoints the cart for *soma* with the footprint of the *Soma-cow*, she is setting the stage for the implied sexual union of soma and cow('s milk) that will be effected some time hence, at the end of the pressing day, and the fertility that should spring from it. I will return to the complexity of the Third Pressing later.

The episodes just outlined, starting with the Soma-cow's little stroll before the purchase, passing through the wife's anointing of the linchpin of the Soma-cart, and looking forward to the final pressing of the soma, occur on different days and are separated from each other by many different ritual events. Even without those distractions, the conceptual connections I have suggested between these episodes may seem rather tenuous, and when viewed in the mass of occurrences of the ritual as a whole, the tracery of connections may be almost invisible. I will produce further evidence for these crucial relationships presently, but let us now just consider some of the mantras that accompany the first two events, mantras which in their immediate context seem incongruous, but which make sense if the pattern I have suggested obtains.

At the time of the exchange of footprint and glance, the wife says to the Soma-cow (so ĀpŚS X.23.7) or to her husband (BŚS VI.13 [170: 7]):

tvaṣṭ[r]īmatī te sapeya suretā reto dadhānā
vīraṃ videya tava saṃdṛśi

Attended by Tvaṣṭar, may I serve you. Possessing good semen, becoming pregnant [lit., placing semen within myself],
may I obtain a hero in your regard.[282]

Recall also the mantra with which the wife performs the anointing of the cart wheels: ā no vīro jāyatām "Let a hero be born to us." Though neither mantra has a clear connection with the action being performed, they establish a verbal link between the two episodes through the focus on the impregnation and birth of a hero, just as the Soma-cow's footprint creates a physical link, and both mantras express the deeper purpose of the actions, whose fruit is some way off.

4. The 'Foot-Washing' Water and the Third Pressing

The wife has ritual dominion over the so-called Foot-washing water (pannejanī). In the ritual realm the term pannejanī refers to two, differently employed containers of water. On the one hand, rather uncommonly, the term is used in the Animal Sacrifice to refer to the water with which the wife washes the limbs of the dead animal victim (see e.g. ŚB III.8.2.1; KŚS VI.6.1), an action I will discuss later. Much more commonly it is used of some particular water in the Soma Sacrifice that never gets near anyone's feet (or at least not too near). If the 'Foot-washing' water never washes feet, it must be so called for some other reason. As we explore this reason, we will see that it is the connection with hospitality that gives it its name, but hospitality with the peculiar twist that ritual application brings.

Let us trace the course of this Foot-washing water through the ritual. It is a phenomenon only of the Pressing Day, though it is related to water fetched earlier. Before sunset on the night before the Pressing Day, a vessel is filled with waters from a stream. These are the so-called Overnight waters (vasatīvarī), which will be utilized in the pressing the next day. These waters are fetched with due ceremony, and then paraded around the margins of the ritual ground with even more ceremony, before being deposited for their overnight vigil. The most striking feature of this circumambulation is that the entire Mahāvedi and the adjoining śālā (hut) are cleared of personnel for this action. Only three people remain: the Adhvaryu, who will carry the waters, and the Sacrificer and his wife, who sit in their usual seats while the circuit is accomplished.[283] The banishment of the other ritual participants—priests, their various assistants, and whatever spectators may be about—gives the parade and the 'Overnight waters' a particularly private and domestic focus. In the texts of the WYV it is also specified that the wife touches the water jar in the middle of the procession (KŚS VIII.9.18; ŚB III.9.2.14).

In the morning new waters are collected (ekadhana), and several vessels are filled – including both the pressing tubs (savanīyakalaśa) and the vessel for the Foot-washing water (pānnejana).[284] For this latter action the wife is led forward, carrying the tub, by the Neṣṭar, and according to some texts (e.g. ĀpŚS) she performs the ladling of the water herself.

> ĀpŚS XII.5.3 prehy udehīti neṣṭā patnīm udānayati / ehy udehīti vā / pānnejanīṃ sthālīṃ dhārayamāṇām . . .
> 12 patnī pannejanīr gṛhṇāti pratyaṅ tiṣṭhantī vasubhyo rudrebhya ādityebhya iti
>
> (Saying) "Come forth, come up!" or "Come, come up!" the Neṣṭar leads up the wife, who is carrying the vessel for the Foot-washing waters. . . .
> The wife, standing west/behind (?), ladles the Foot-washing waters, (saying) "For the Vasus, the Rudras, the Ādityas . . ."

The full text of her mantra is

> TS III.5.6.2 vásubhyo rudrébhya ādityébhyo víśvebhyo vo devébhyaḥ pannéjanīr gṛhṇāmi
>
> I ladle you (as) Foot-washing waters for the Vasus, the Rudras, and the Ādityas, for the All Gods.

Though the Foot-washing waters consist of newly fetched water, these new waters are soon brought into contact with the Overnight waters,[285] and function in some ways as their continuators. Besides contributing the Foot-washing water, the newly collected waters also serve the central ritual task of the pressing of the soma. So, the Foot-washing water has an historical connection with the water that formed a magic circle around the ritual pair, the Sacrificer and wife, the night before, and it is identical in source with the water that will be in contact with the soma on this Pressing Day.

The Foot-washing waters themselves are not physically employed until the end of the day, at the Third Pressing, and they need a home for the interval. They remain in the wife's charge. She carries them away from the ladling place and into the sadas (shed) in the Mahāvedi, where she deposits them in an out-of-the-way location until they are needed – according to most texts behind the hearth of the Neṣṭar, who is the wife's usual leader.[286] BŚS VII.15 (225: 13) specifies that place be asaṃcare sāmapathe "not frequented (but) on the path of the sāman," in other words where the Udgātar priest can see the waters, as Caland and Henry suggest (1906–7, p. 223). She does so with a variant of the original mantra:

> TS III.5.6.2 yajñáya vaḥ pannéjanīḥ sādayāmi
>
> I deposit you Foot-washing waters for the ritual.

This is the last important task of the wife until the end of the day. The first two pressings of the soma, with all the intricate physical business, the many libations and the attendant recitations and chanting, essentially proceed without major participation on the part of the wife. She returns in the Third Pressing, which has a number of peculiar features—many of which can be understood with reference to the wife's role. Indeed the relative prominence of the wife in the Third Pressing is the first remarkable aspect of this ritual to note.

The Third Pressing (Tṛtīya Savana) on initial inspection seems a rather anticlimactic end to the grand spectacle of the Soma Sacrifice. In fact, it has a mingy and ungenerous air: it does not even have its own soma. Each of the first two pressings has a separate stock of soma, which is pressed afresh. But in the Third Pressing they take the dregs (ṛjīṣa) left over from the previous pressings and re-press them—rather like offering the gods a used tea bag. The result is, it seems, eked out with filler, with sour milk or curds mixed into the soma. From our point of view it seems like offering your guests leftovers after a weary weekend of entertaining and hoping they get the message: it's time to go.

But, as usual, we must beware of the superficial impression. The very features that seem the least inviting turn out to convey the most powerful messages. The Third Pressing finally unites the separate forces that are deployed in the ritual, and it in some sense encodes in its sequence of episodes the desired result of all of this elaborate ritual behavior. Before examining this in detail, we might note some clues that our first impression needs to be modified.

First, the milk mixture (āśir) that may seem like a mere soma-extender is actually a constant and exalted theme in religious poetry. The Rig Vedic soma hymns continually treat the meeting of soma with the milk, usually couched in erotic terms: the virile bull soma racing eagerly to the equally desirous cows. It is almost superfluous to quote examples:

RV IX.6.6 táṃ góbhir vṛ́ṣaṇaṃ rásam mádāya devávītaye
sutám bhárāya sáṃ sṛja

Release the bullish sap, the pressed (soma), (to be) with the cows, for exhilaration, for the service of the gods, for booty.

RV IX.101.8 sám u priyā́ anūṣata, gā́vo mádāya ghṛ́ṣvayaḥ

The dear cows have roared together, eager for the exhilarating (drink).

RV IX.97.34 gā́vo yanti gópatim pṛchámānāḥ . . .
35 sómaṃ gā́vo dhenávo vāvaśānā́ḥ

The cows come asking for a master / husband of cows—
the milch-cows desiring[287] soma.

RV IX.97.22 ā́d īm āyan váram ā́ vāvaśānā́ júṣṭam pátiṃ kaláśe gā́va índum

The cows came hither by choice, desiring[288] the drop in the cup (as) enjoyable husband.

Alternately, the image is of the milch-cows' maternal tenderness for the infant soma:

RV IX.1.9 abhīmám ághnyā utá śrīṇánti dhenávaḥ śíśum
sómam índrāya pā́tave

The unharmable milch-cows mix this child (with milk),
the soma for Indra to drink.

That the mixture is so often referred to in the hymns would indicate that it was not considered a slightly embarassing economy measure—milk is after all cheaper and easier to obtain than soma—but rather something to be celebrated, and it is significant that the terms in which it is celebrated are both erotic and maternal.

We might also note that the notion of "leftover" does not have the negative connotations in Vedic that it does in modern America. For example, the AV contains a hymn to leftovers (ucchiṣṭa), entitled by Whitney "Extolling the remnant of the oblation" (AV XI.7), of serious and indeed mystical aspect. According to this hymn, almost everything of cosmic import is established in or derived from the leftover. Even more to the point, in the famous story of the birth of Aditi's children, the distinguished group of gods known as the Ādityas, leftovers are the motive force. Aditi gets pregnant with twins whenever she eats the leftovers (again ucchiṣṭa) from an oblation she has made.[289] Disaster (in the form of miscarriage) only strikes when she begins to eat in advance of the oblation.

It is unlikely to be an accident that the first offering at the Third Pressing is made to the Ādityas and that this offering consists of soma that was saved (/left over) from the Morning Pressing, mixed with sour curds (dadhi).[290] The practical reason for the mixture is clearly expressed by the ŚB:

ŚB IV.3.5.14 yád v evá dádhi gṛhṇā́ti / hutocchiṣṭā́ vā́ eté saṁsravā́ bhavanti nā́lam ā́hutyai tā́n eváitát púnar ā́pyāyayati tathā́lam ā́hutyai bhavanti tásmād dádhi gṛhṇāti

Now, as to why he takes sour curds: the poured together (soma) is the remnant (ucchiṣṭa) of an offering. It is not sufficient for an oblation. He swells it up again in this way [by adding the curds]. It thus becomes sufficient for an oblation. Therefore he takes sour curds.

But the mythic model is also invoked explicitly in another text:

KS XXVIII.6 (160: 8) ucchiṣṭād vā ādityā jātās tasmād eṣa ucchiṣṭas somo gṛhyate

The Ādityas were born from the leftover. Therefore this leftover soma is taken (for the oblation).

This opening action of the Third Pressing both announces the "problem"—not enough soma for a libation—and, by connecting it with the Ādityas, who are the fortunate result of leftovers, makes the "problem" one not to be fretted over, but to glory in. We cannot here fully pursue the theme of the leftover;

nonetheless, it is worth remembering the connection between the remnant and fertility as we progress through the Tṛtīya Savana.

After the offering to the Ādityas, the "pressing" proper occurs. The dregs from the two earlier pressings are pressed again, using the Overnight water (rather than the fresh water fetched in the morning, as in the other two pressings), another leftover.[291] The pitiful result (or so one assumes) of this pressing then receives the milk-āśir (lit., 'mix-in'). This milk has been churned and curdled outside the Mahāvedi, according to some texts by the wife herself (ĀpŚS XIII.10.8; cf. Caland and Henry 1906–7, p. 336). She brings it into the hut and pours it, with the assistance of the Pratiprasthātar (MŚS II.5.1.25) or her husband (ĀpŚS XIII.10.10), through the soma strainer into the vessel containing the soma.[292] In other words, the āśir is treated as if it were soma, and by churning and pouring the āśir the wife is acting almost as a substitute soma presser.

The four verses that accompany the mixing in of the āśir among the Taittirīyans[293] emphasize the cooperation of the wife and husband and the benefits they will obtain. Despite their length it is worth quoting these verses in full[294] because of the high rhetorical style of their celebration of the āśir and their unusual concentration on the domestic couple:[295]

TS III.2.8*i* asmé devāso vápuṣe cikitsata yám āśírā dámpatī vāmám aśnutáḥ
púmān putró jāyate vindáte vásu átha víśve arapā́ edhate gṛháḥ

O gods, pay attention to this wonder: what desirable thing the household couple attains with the āśir.
A male child is born. He finds wealth. Moreover everyone in the household prospers unharmed.

TS III.2.8*k* āśīrdāyā́ dámpatī vāmám aśnutām áriṣṭo rā́yaḥ sacatāṁ sámokasā
yá ā́sicat sáṃdugdhaṃ kumbhyā́ sahéṣṭéna yā́mann ámatiṃ jahātu sáḥ

Let the household couple attain a desirable thing through their giving the āśir. Let unharmed wealth follow the two dwelling in the same house.
Who has poured the milk together with the (soma in the) pot, let him through worship leave misfortune on the way.

TS III.2.8*l* sarpirgrīvī́ pī́vary asya jāyā́ pī́vānaḥ putrā́ ákṛśāso asya
sahájānir yáḥ sumakhasyámāna índrāyāśíraṁ sahá kumbhyā́dāt

His wife is fat with butter on her neck, his sons are fat, not skinny,
who, well offering, along with his wife has given the āśir along with the (soma in the) pot to Indra.

TS III.2.8*m* āśī́r ma ū́rjam utá suprajāstvám íṣaṃ dadhātu dráviṇaṁ sávarcasam
saṃjáyan kṣétrāṇi sáhasāhám indra kṛṇvānó anyā́ṁ ádharānt sapátnān

Let the āśir establish in me solid nourishment, good offspring, liquid nourishment, and wealth with splendor.
I (who am) overcoming the fields with strength, o Indra, and putting other rivals below (me).

The close connection perceived among the āśir, the cooperation of the wife, and the fortunes of the household goes back to the Rig Veda. RV VIII.31, which contains two of the twelve occurrences of āśir in that text, is entitled by Geldner "Praise of the Sacrificer and his wife" ["Lob des Opferers und seiner Gattin"]. In this hymn the happiness and prosperity of the couple are tied to their jointly performing ritual duties, including the addition of the āśir:

RV VIII.31.5 yā́ dámpatī sámanasā sunutá ā́ ca dhāvataḥ dévāso nítyayāśírā
6 práti prāśavyàṁ itaḥ samyáñcā barhír āśāte ná tā́ vā́jeṣu vāyataḥ

Which household pair [man and wife] being of the same mind press (soma), and rinse (it), and (mix it) with the prescribed āśir-mixture, o gods,
they two reach (the rewards) reserved for the very punctual. United they two achieve the barhis. They two do not grow weary in (the pursuit of) booty.

The next verses continue to list the blessings that accrue to the couple who have properly performed the ritual actions described in verse 5.

Before proceeding any further into the Third Pressing, it will be useful to sketch the structural pattern that seems to underlie the actions so far enumerated and that will be found also in the later episodes of this pressing. The Tṛtīya Savana seems to be structured as a series of exchanges; these exchanges are carried out by means of "mixtures." These exchanges and mixtures are designed to behave like chemical reactions. The elements that have been fairly inert in their pure state[296] produce, when mixed, some sort of explosive force, which creates, finally, the desired ritual result.

And what are these elements? The essential mixture in this part of the ritual, on all its levels, is that of male and female, and the explosive force is sexual, whose desired result is fertility and procreation. This is, of course, by now a hackneyed theme in the ritual—or at least in my treatment of it—but the enactments of it in this last climactic pressing display a subtlety, variety, and ingenuity that again prove the power of ritual, like poetry, to dramatize and concretize a theme without exhausting or trivializing it—no matter how banal the bald statement of this theme may seem.

Let us examine how the theme has been embodied in the actions I have discussed so far. The stage was set, as it were, by the preliminary oblation to the Ādityas, which consisted of a *mixture* of leftover soma and sour curds and announced the mythological support for the doctrine of the fertility of the remnant. But this oblation is, quite literally, an hors d'oeuvre: as we saw, it is not considered a real part of the Third Pressing, but a mere curtain raiser.

The real sign that something different is going on in the Tṛtīya Savana is the relatively large role alloted to the wife, who participates for the first time in the pressing. Her very presence announces that *mixture* is occurring: the female sexual element she represents has been introduced in the very male atmosphere of the soma pressing. She also presides over the creation (churning) of the physical additive to the milk and over the *mixing* itself: she herself adds the sour milk to the soma in a procedure homologized to the soma preparation. We have already seen that the āśir is strongly linked to the fortunes of the household *couple*.

I have also already noted that this moment of mixture between soma and milk is endlessly and explicitly likened to mating between bull and cow in the liturgical poetry of the Rig Veda. Thus, by adding (female) milk from the human realm to the (male) soma to be offered to the gods, the soma oblation has been fertilized, as it were, made procreative for the divine realm, and mixture, exchange has been set up between the human and the divine.

The more difficult problem that the ritualists face is the opposite one, that of introducing the male divine element into the realm of the human female, in order to produce fertility on the human level. The stumbling block is the ritual fact that women do not consume soma.[297] If they did, one might imagine that the required mixture might be easily enough obtained by handing the wife a cup of the "bullish" soma. Why is this not allowed, beyond habit and custom? It seems that this direct contact was considered dangerous for two reasons. On the one hand, ingesting the powerful soma directly might harm the woman and the reproductive process, a risky business at best.[298] On the other, as we have seen before, though the woman is needed in the ritual, she is also considered to pose dangers to it, and various methods are devised to introduce her power while counteracting the potential bad effects of it.

Such devices are particularly imaginatively deployed in the Third Pressing in the ritual complex we are about to examine: a set of episodes flowing smoothly one to another, involving several different groupings of the participants, and touching on the central themes from a variety of points of view. The complicated interweaving of separate incidents, realms, and attitudes reminds one almost of the sublime act-ending ensembles of Mozart operas.

It begins[299] with the Pātnīvata offering: the oblation to Agni 'with the wives [of the gods]'. This is an offering of soma further adulterated with some ghee left over from the 'unction of the hearths' (dhiṣṇyāghāraṇa). (The offering substances begin to sound like a casserole that slowly acquires leftovers from meal after meal.) The oblation starts unremarkably; it seems in some ways the equivalent in the Soma Sacrifice of the already examined Patnīsaṃyājas ('joint worship of the wives') that comes toward the end of the ordinary Iṣṭi. The mantras encourage Agni, along with Tvaṣṭar, to consume the soma: Agni and Tvaṣṭar are also (two of) the male divinities worshiped in the Patnīsaṃyājas:[300]

TS I.4.27 ágnā3i pátnīvā3ḥ sajū́r devéna tvā́ṣṭrā sómam piba svā́hā

Ahoy Agni, possessing (/along with) the wives—together with god Tvaṣṭar drink the soma. Hail!

What is immediately interesting is what the Brāhmaṇa texts make of this offering. Each in its own way treats it as a foundation myth for women's subordination, and each does so by explaining (indirectly, as usual) how or why women do not drink soma. As I noted just now, the logic of the structure of the Third Pressing should require that the wife drink soma and thereby acquire the divine male essence directly. But she does not, and instead acquires it indirectly through a set of mediations. As this Pātnīvata oblation introduces this set of mediations, it is especially appropriate that the anxieties about the wife's potential contact with soma—anxieties that are responsible for the restrictions on it and substitutes for it—should be brought up at this point.

Perhaps not surprisingly, the explanations given[301] do not entirely agree with each other and are not entirely coherent. They are all based on two somewhat contradictory notions, each the consequence of separate operations of ritual logic. On the one hand, the oblation, with its mixture of soma and ghee, is a pairing, hence procreative.

> MS IV.7.4 (97: 9) mithunáṁ vái ghṛtáṃ ca sómaś ca yát pātnīvatáṃ ghṛténa śrīṇā́ti mithunatvā́ya
>
> Ghee and soma are a sexual pairing. When he mixes the Pātnīvata cup with ghee, (it is) for sexual pairing.[302]

This is, of course, the standard ritual doctrine and the controlling structural metaphor of the Third Pressing.

But on the other hand, in the *particular* myth each text invokes, the ghee added to the soma is a weapon, not a sexual pairing—though the Black and White Yajur Veda texts disagree on the target of this weapon. The wives of the gods wished to go to heaven, and attempted to do so through the Pātnīvata offering. But, as the BYV says, soma would not stand still to be ladled out for women (or could not stand [the thought of] it). The gods made ghee into a weapon and hit soma with it, which made it possible to draw him for the women's cup but also weakened him. The TS has the fullest account, which goes in part:

> TS VI.5.8.2 . . . sá sómo nā́tiṣṭhata strībhyó gṛhyámāṇas táṃ ghṛtáṃ vájraṃ kṛtvā́ghnan táṃ nírindriyam bhūtám agṛhṇan
>
> Soma did not stand being drawn for women. (The gods) having made ghee into a cudgel smashed him. They (then) drew him, who had become without strength.

The result is the female double bind: they get the cup, but it has lost its vigor. This explains women's nature, according to the texts. TS continues

> TS VI.5.8.2 tásmāt stríyo nírindriyā ádāyādīr ápi pāpā́t puṁsá úpastitaram // 3 vadanti
>
> Therefore women lack strength, have no inheritance, and speak more submissively than even a low man.

The MS doctrine is similar:

MS IV.7.4 (97: 16) tásmān nírindriyā strī́ púmān indriyávāṁs tásmāt púmāṁsaḥ sabhā́ṁ yánti ná stríyo yád ítarānt sómāñ śrīṇīyúr ná pātnīvatáṁ stríyaḥ sabhā́m iyúr ná púmāṁsaḥ

Therefore the woman lacks strength, (but) the man is strong. Therefore men go to the assembly, not women. If they should mix the other soma drinks (with ghee), not the Pātnīvata, women would go to the assembly, not men.[303]

Above I posited two possible reasons for restricting women from drinking soma—soma may be dangerous to women, or women drinking soma may be dangerous to the ritual. In these BYV passages we have one version of this justification: the threat came from soma. He was too strong, and also unwilling to be given to women. He could only serve for women after he was so weakened that he became next to useless. The weapon of ghee was directed against him, and soma, thus pacified, became fit for the wives of the gods. Even this adulterated soma may still be too strong for puny human females—such seems to be the implication. Hence the substitutions that will shortly be introduced.

The ŚB gives the other justification, using the same basic mythic material. It is the wives that are the threat, liable to arrogate male characteristics and privileges. The ghee-weapon is used to smash *them*.

ŚB IV.4.2.13 . . . vájro vā́ ā́jyam eténa vái devā́ vájreṇā́jyenā́ghnann evá pátnīr nírākṣṇuvaṃs tā́ hatā́ níraṣṭā nā́tmánaś canáiśata ná dāyásya canáiśata tátho eváiṣá eténa vájreṇā́jyena hánty evá pátnīr nírakṣṇoti tā́ hatā́ níraṣṭā nā́tmánaś canéśate ná dāyásya canéśate

Ghee is a cudgel. With this ghee as a cudgel the gods smashed the wives and castrated them. They, smashed and castrated, had no lordship over themselves and no lordship over inheritance. Even so, with this ghee as a cudgel he smashes the wives and castrates them. Smashed and castrated, they have no lordship over themselves and no lordship over inheritance.[304]

The translation of nir √akṣ as 'castrate' is no more than literal. The shocking effect of this expression in this context would be increased by the relative rarity of the idiom in high discourse (and probable frequency in the ordinary discourse of stock-breeders). Anxiety about women runs throughout this passage. Several times just earlier the text forbids a certain action

ŚB IV.4.2.11, 12 nét strīṣú vīryàṃ dádhānī́ti

(The priest thinking) "Lest I establish virile strength in women."

Soma is forbidden to women because it might strengthen them too much, or, perhaps rather, allow them to hold on to the excessive strength they already have, strength that challenges male power unless it is smashed. Hence the substitutes for soma that are about to be introduced. The net result is the same in both Black and White YV, of course, but the different routes used to get there by related texts using the same story are a nice example of the flexibility of mythic thinking.

We have established that the wife does not consume the soma in this (or any other cup), not even soma weakened by the addition of ghee. When we ask who does consume it, we come to the most peculiar part of this entire offering. An assistant of the Adhvaryu, the Agnīd/Āgnīdhra, has already recited the offering verse for the Pātnīvata. This is not too surprising, as the Agnīd already has some connection to the wives of the gods: he had made a recitation of their names at an earlier time (the first Upasad day) in the ritual.[305]

Then comes the surprising command (praiṣa):

> ĀpŚS XIII.14.11 (etc.) agnīn neṣṭur upastham āsīda
>
> Agnīd, sit in the lap of the Neṣṭar.

A command that, according to some texts, he obeys, while consuming the remains of the soma in the Pātnīvata cup:[306]

> KŚS X.6.22 sapātra āsīdati neṣṭur upastham
>
> With the cup he sits in the lap of the Neṣṭar.[307]

Several texts, however, specifically forbid this action because of the possibly adverse effect it may have on the Agnīd's manhood:

> KS XXVIII.8 (163: 6) nopastha āsīta yad upastha āsīta paṇḍakas syāt
>
> He should not sit in the lap. If he should sit in the lap, he would become impotent (/a eunuch).[308]

These texts suggest a substitute: the Agnīd consumes the cup *in the vicinity* of the Neṣṭar.

The Agnid's lap-sitting sets in motion a whole series of actions. In fact the praiṣa just quoted is the beginning of a string:

> BŚS VIII.14 (254: 13) (etc.) agnīn neṣṭur upastham āsīda neṣṭaḥ patnīm udānayodgātrā saṃkhyāpyāpa upapravartayatād ūruṇopapravartayatān nagnaṃ kṛtvorum upapravartayatāt
>
> Agnīd, sit in the lap of the Neṣṭar. Neṣṭar, lead up the wife. Having had her looked at by the Udgātar, have her then pour water; have her pour (water) along her thigh; having made her thigh naked, have her pour (water) along (it).

We have here almost a chain reaction, a transfer of forces link by link:

Agnīd (sits on lap of) → *Neṣṭar* (leads) → *wife* (looked at by) ↔ *Udgātar*

The Agnīd is the one who directly mediates between divine and human: he drinks the bullish soma. And he does so while seated *in the lap* of the Neṣṭar (or, among the more prudish texts, in his proximity). The sexual representation here is both extremely obvious and extremely obscure. On the one hand, 'lap' (upastha) has more or less the same semantic range in Vedic as in English, from the innocent to the sexually euphemistic. It can refer coyly to the genitals (as we saw in the Aśvamedha[309]) as well as to the comfortable haven where children sit. Here the fear expressed that the Agnīd will become a eunuch (or whatever this obscure word paṇḍaka means) shows that a sexual construction was put upon this action, and that this construction might be the "wrong" one, that it might be interpreted as homosexual activity.

But the action is surely meant as a representation of heterosexual activity, and herein lies the problem. Who is representing which sex? If we look at the chain again, we will see that at least at its beginning, each link must be capable of representing either sex, in order for the transfer of forces to be effective. Of the exegetical texts, the ŚB is clearest about the gender switching (and even its "clearest" leaves the matter still rather opaque). According to the ŚB (IV.4.2.16),[310] when the Adhvaryu hands the Pātnīvata cup to the Agnīd, the latter says, ádhvarya úpa mā hvayasva ("Adhvaryu, invite me [to drink]!"), about which the commentator says:

> ŚB IV.4.2.16 táṃ ná pratyúpahvayeta kó hí hatásya níraṣṭasya pratyupahaváḥ
>
> He should not invite him. For what (sort of) invitation is there for one who is smashed and castrated.[311]

Here the Agnīd is described with the same words as were applied to the *wives* after the ghee-weapon had been used against them. He is identified with the weakened women, and in drinking the soma he represents the human female to be fertilized by sexual mixture with the divine male soma.

But immediately afterwards the Agnīd's gender role is reversed, as is most clearly seen in ŚBK:

> ŚBK V.4.4.13 só 'gníd bíbhrad evá tát pā́traṃ néṣṭur upástham ā́sīdaty agnír vā́ eṣá nidā́nena yád agnī́n néṣṭo [*sic*] vái pátnī nidā́nena yóṣā vái pátnī vṛ́ṣāgnír mithunám eváitát prajánanaṃ kriyate
>
> The Agnīd, carrying this cup, sits in the lap of the Neṣṭar. The Agnīd is, in essence, Agni; the Neṣṭar is, in essence, the wife. The wife is female, Agni male. A procreative sexual pairing is thus made.[312]

The Agnīd has been transformed from the *wives,* for whom the cup was originally drawn in the myth, to the male *Agni,* for whom the cup is drawn in the ritual. This transformation is of course facilitated by his title, which connects him verbally and functionally with Agni/fire. The Neṣṭar can then be identified with the wife because he is her standard escort and caretaker during the Soma Sacrifice.

But the original, if fleeting, identification of the Agnīd with the female element is necessary, because he/she must receive the soma/seed before passing it on, and it is received as seminal fluid in conceptual sexual intercourse. The sexual polarity procedure continues. The Neṣṭar now symbolically passes on the seed he has received to the wife, by leading her up. He thus becomes a representation of masculinity again. As the TS succinctly puts it:

> TS VI.5.8.5–6 ágnīn néṣṭur upástham ā́sīda // néṣṭaḥ pátnīm udā́nayéty āhāgnī́d evá néṣṭari réto dadhāti néṣṭā pátniyām
>
> (The priest) says, "Agnīd, sit in the lap of the Neṣṭar. Neṣṭar, lead up the wife." The Agnīd thus deposits seed in the Neṣṭar, the Neṣṭar in the wife.

The chain has reached its destined end—the wife, who was barred from direct contact with the soma/seed, has received it through two highly abstract simulations of sexual intercourse, which in turn substitute for the wife's drinking soma. KS recognizes as much. When it discusses the Agnīd's consumption of soma in the lap of (or near to) the Neṣṭar, it comments, with apparent irrelevancy since the wife has not yet made her appearance, patnīr eva somapīthaṃ gamayati (KS XXVIII.8 [163: 5]) "thus he makes the wives attain the soma-drinking." The 'soma-drinking' is what this is all ultimately about, as I hypothesized earlier: finding a way to allow the human wife to 'drink' the soma. The chain of gender-switching priests can be schematized as follows:

soma (+ male)
↓
Agnīd (+ female ⇒ + male) → *Neṣṭar* (+ female ⇒ + male) → *wife* (+ female)

The achievement of the end of the chain is signaled by another action, more dramatic than the somewhat abstract representations we have finally been reduced to. This is the wife's business with the Foot-washing water, which we left so long ago. After the Neṣṭar leads the wife into the shed, she sits down with the Foot-washing water, which has been reposing for some hours behind the Neṣṭar's own hearth. She then pours this water along her thigh or thighs:

> MŚS II.5.2.21 prastute patnī pānnejanaṃ kalaśam antarata ūruṇā dakṣiṇena . . . udañcaṃ pravartayati
>
> After this chant, the wife, (putting) the vessel with the Foot-washing water between (her thighs), pours it along her right thigh to the north (/upwards [i.e. from the knee up]?).

ĀpŚS XIII.15.9 specifies that the thigh be naked (nagna), and allows the possibility of pouring along both thighs (XIII.15.10). In fact, it suggests an even more extreme procedure:

> ĀpŚS XIII.15.11 upari dūram udūhed ā vakṣaṇānām āviṣkartoḥ / ahrītamukhy asyā jāyata iti vijñāyate

She should pull (her garment) far up, so as to expose her belly. Her (offspring) will thus be born with unashamed faces, according to the sacred tradition.[313]

The water she pours is clearly representative of both soma and semen: the soma she is not allowed to drink (but whose essence has reached her through the priestly chain) and the semen it also symbolizes. Again the exegetical texts had no trouble recognizing this last obvious identification, as in the TS explanation:

TS VI.5.8.6 apá úpa právartayati réta evá tát siñcaty ūrúṇópa právartayati ūrúṇā hí rétaḥ sicyáte nagnaṃkŕ̥tyorúm úpa právartayati yadā́ hí nagná ūrúr bhávaty átha mithunī́ bhavató 'tha rétaḥ sicyaté 'tha prajā́ḥ prájāyante

She pours out water. Thus she lets semen flow. She pours it out along her thigh. For along the thigh semen flows. Having made her thigh naked, she pours it out. When the thigh is naked, then a couple has sex. Then semen flows. Then offspring are born.[314]

Directly before this highly symbolic (and presumably rather embarrassing, at least in the ĀpŚS scenario) action is performed, the Udgātar is made to look at her three times (according to most texts[315]), with sexually charged mantras as an accompaniment:

BŚS VIII.14 (255: 4) prastute sāmni neṣṭā patnīm udgātrā saṃkhyāpya vācayati viśvasya te viśvāvato vṛṣṇiyāvatas tavāgne vāmīr anu saṃdṛśi viśvā retāṁsi dhiṣīya

When the sāman has been sung, the Neṣṭar, having made the Udgātar look at the wife, makes (her) say: "In the sight of you, who are all, who have all, possessing bullishness, O Agni, might I receive all semen(s), following (the manner of your) dear (wives)."

Despite the fairly clear *general* purport of the activity with the Foot-washing water, there remain a number of particular puzzles in the details. First, why the involvement of the Udgātar? The transference of force would seem to be complete without him: from soma to the Agnīd to the Neṣṭar to the wife. The Udgātar seems a superfluous link hanging beyond the wife, who was the target. Next, why is the husband, i.e. the Sacrificer, never involved in the chaining? Since the ultimate aim is to have the wife produce *his* children, it might seem logical to include him in the sexual linkage. Finally, why the *Foot-washing* water? Wouldn't any other water do as well? In fact, since this water never washes feet in the ritual, but only finally the wife's thigh, why is it consistently *called* Foot-washing water in the texts?

What answers I have to the first two questions are connected, so we will consider them together before turning to the last question. There is both a ritual and a mythological answer to these first two puzzles. With the wife involved directly or indirectly with Agnīd, Neṣṭar, and Udgātar, she is brought into contact with the three Vedas: the Agnīd is an adherent of the Yajur Veda, the Neṣṭar of the Rig Veda, the Udgātar of the Sāma Veda.[316] The wife's triple contact then ensures completeness. All three Vedas contribute to the establishment of fertility, just as they do to the proper cooperative performance of the ritual.

Moreover, the three priests also function as the three immortal bridegrooms, to whom the bride is briefly married during the wedding ceremony, before she is handed over to her mortal husband. I have had occasion to refer to this before, but it is worth quoting the verse again.

RV X.85.40 sómaḥ prathamó vivide gandharvó vivida úttaraḥ
tṛtī́yo agníṣ ṭe pátis turī́yas te manuṣyajā́ḥ

Soma possessed (you) first; a Gandharva possessed (you) next.
Agni was your third husband; your fourth is human-born.

This mythological model may account for the curious absence of the husband that we have just noted. He is not part of the sexual chain precisely *because* he is to be the ultimate beneficiary of the fertility created in this rite. The wife must first pass through the hands of the divine trio, and the three priests represent this trio in the ritual enactment.

There are several additional reasons for involving the Udgātar in particular, however. Some of the exegetical texts[317] explain the Udgātar's involvement by identifying him with Prajāpati, the all-purpose Brāhmaṇic creator god:

TS VI.5.8.6 udgātrā́ sáṃkhyāpayati prajā́patir vā́ eṣá yád udgātā́ prajā́nāṃ prajánanāya

He makes the Udgātar look at (her). The Udgātar is really Prajāpati. (The looking is) for the procreation of offspring.

This identification is fairly common in other contexts as well.[318] Although it would be too much of a digression to inquire why the Udgātar is held to be the equivalent of Prajāpati, we can examine one of the particular facets of this identification.

Let us consider the provision that the Udgātar look at the wife three times. These three glances correspond to the three times that the Udgātar produces the stereotyped opening of the sāman he sings: the opening is the meaningless sound *him*.[319] In fact, ĀpŚS makes the connection between the glances and this syllable quite clear:

ĀpŚS XIII.15.8 hiṅkāram anūdgātrā patnīṁ saṃkhyāpayati

Following the (Udgātar's) *hiṃ*-cry, (the Neṣṭar) makes the Udgātar look at the wife.

And PB gives a reason for this connection:

PB VIII.7.13 hiṅkāraṃ prati saṃkhyāpayanti hiṅkṛtād dhi reto 'dhīyata

They make (him) look (at her) at the *hiṃ*-cry, for after the *hiṃ*-cry semen is deposited.

The *hiṃ*-cry is the key. This noise is especially associated with domestic animals—and humans acting like domestic animals—under two particular circumstances. On the one hand, males utter the *hiṃ*-cry just before they approach females for intercourse. As the following MS passage makes clear, this is considered to be the practice of domestic animals (paśuvrata), which should be adopted by humans who wish to operate in a state of ritual purity (medhya).

MS I.8.7 (126: 5) úpa stríyam eti . . . paśúvratena bhavitavyàṃ tūṣṇī́m iva paśávaḥ sáṃbhavanti té médhyā yát tūṣṇī́ṃ stríyam upáiti médhyataras téna bhavati hiṃkṛ́tyópeyād evám iva hí paśáva upayánti medhyatvā́ya

He 'approaches' a woman. . . . This is to be done according to the practice of the domestic animals. Domestic animals have intercourse silently, as it were. They are ritually pure. When one approaches a woman silently, by that he becomes more ritually pure. After having made the sound *him*, he should approach (her). For thus do domestic animals approach (females). (This practice is) for ritual purity.[320]

Thus, in the ritual we are discussing, when the Udgātar cries *him* just before the wife pours water on her thigh(s), he is symbolically initiating sexual intercourse, announcing the beginning of cohabitation. Hence the somewhat cryptic remark of PB quoted above: "for after the *hiṃ*-cry semen is deposited."[321]

This also explains an apparently trivial ritual fact noted earlier: while the waters remained by the Neṣṭar's hearth, they were to be visible to the Udgātar. Since they represent his semen, it is not surprising that he would want to keep an eye on them. Nor is it surprising that the *physical* representative of semen, the Foot-washing water, only reappears at the point when the Udgātar says *him* and looks at the wife, rather than being passed through the hands of the other priests, for the chain of potential fertility stretching from the soma through the Agnīd and Neṣṭar is only activated by the utterance of the Udgātar.

But *him* has another semantic association in Vedic, attested even earlier than the one just discussed. *Him* is the cry that a mother cow makes over her newborn calf or one that has strayed. This usage is found already in the "riddle hymn" of the RV:

RV I.164.27 hiṅkṛṇvatī́ vasupatnī́ vásūnāṃ vatsám ichántī mánasābhy ā́gāt

Making *him* the Goods-lady of goods has come hither seeking her calf with her mind.

RV I.164.28 gáur amīmed ánu vatsám miṣántam mūrdhā́naṃ híṅṅ akṛṇon mā́tavā́ u

The cow lowed to its calf (just) blinking [opening its eyes for the first time?]. She made *him* over his head (for the calf) to low (back).

Him here is a *maternal* cry, made to animate a newborn, or to locate a lost infant. The animating function of the cry is especially clear in the following passage from KS:

> KS XXVII.9 (150: 3) prajāpatiḥ prajās sṛṣṭvā tā abhihiṅṅakarot . . . tasmād gaur vatsaṃ jātam abhihiṅkaroti
>
> Prajāpati, having created the creatures, made *him* over them. Therefore the cow makes *him* over her calf, just born.

And another PB passage[322] connects the *Udgātar* with this maternal creativity:

> PB VII.10.16 eṣa vai yajamānasya prajāpatir yad udgātā yad . . . hiṅkaroti prajāpatir eva bhūtvā prajā abhijighrati
>
> The Udgātar is the Prajāpati ['lord of creatures'] of the Sacrificer. In that he [Udgātar] makes *him*, having become Prajāpati he sniffs at the creatures (to animate them).[323]

So we have here one last sexual switch. The Udgātar in our ritual not only functions as the male, the releaser of semen, in the mock sexual pairing with the wife, but he may also stand in as a mother figure, proleptically giving a maternal cry to the offspring that will be born from the pairing. Just as Agnīd and Neṣṭar take both female and male roles in quick succession, so also may the Udgātar do so simultaneously, given the double associations of the cry he makes at the beginning of his recitation. The dual presence of erotic and maternal imagery that we noted before, in discussing the mixture of soma and milk, is found here as well.

But why is the substitute for semen in this ritual called 'Foot-washing water'? As we noted above, this particular water never gets near any feet. It has been waiting inactive by the Neṣṭar's hearth since shortly after the wife drew it into the vessel at the beginning of the day. Its name, 'Foot-washing water', must be designed to evoke and apply semantic associations from elsewhere, in order to enhance further the multileveled "meaning" of this ritual episode.

We must first remember that though the water has not washed any actual feet, it has been used for conceptual feet. The literal justification for the name of these waters is the mantra that accompanies the drawing of the waters (and the variant at the deposit at the Neṣṭar's hearth), as cited above:

> TS III.5.6.2 vásubhyo rudrébhya ādityébhyo víśvebhyo vo devébhyaḥ pannéjanīr gṛhṇāmi
>
> I ladle you (as) Foot-washing waters for the Vasus, the Rudras, and the Ādityas, for the All Gods.

The waters are destined for the feet of the gods, and not just any gods. The three specific groups named, i.e. Vasus, Rudras, and Ādityas, are the tutelary deities of the three pressings:

ŚB IV.3.5.1 trayā́ vái deváḥ / vásavo rudrā́ ādityā́s téṣām víbhaktāni sávanāni vásūnām evá prātaḥsavanáṁ rudrā́ṇām mā́dhyandinaṁ sávanam ādityā́nāṃ tṛtīyasavanám

There are three (types of) gods: Vasus, Rudras, and Ādityas. The pressings are divided among them. The Morning Pressing is the Vasus', the Midday Pressing the Rudras', and the Third Pressing the Ādityas'.

So the Foot-washing waters are verbally consigned to the divinities of the entire Pressing Day, with the All Gods thrown in, probably to take care of anyone who might have been inadvertently skipped.[324]

Since the gods come to the ritual as honored guests, they are due the requisites of normal hospitality on their arrival—including the washing of their feet. None of the pressings has an actual foot-washing ceremony for these divine visitors, of course. In the absence of physical images of the gods, it is hard to see how such a rite could have been carried out without farce.[325] Instead the Foot-washing waters stand ready for them, inside the Mahāvedi, all through the day, for the gods' staggered arrival times at the various pressings dedicated to them. Just as the wife was deeply involved in the guest reception of Soma the king, as we saw, so she has charge of this symbol of hospitality.

Once the Third Pressing has begun, the Foot-washing waters have outlived their usefulness, in one sense. All the visitors have arrived and been duly welcomed. The waters are therefore available for another task and are soon pressed into service to be poured over the wife's thigh. But our experience with ritual will not allow us to see this new use as simply a practical economy measure: we need some water to wash the wife's thigh, and here's some extra water. Every object that enters the sacral arena must be properly prepared for its task, accounted for at all times, and when it finishes the task or leaves the arena, disposed of appropriately. Otherwise the forces it has touched or accumulated may go awry.

That the gods' Foot-washing water, which the wife ladled into its container and carried around the ritual ground, now returns to lave her thigh is surely no accident. Rather, it identifies her as the central token of the hospitality exchange relation, as the mediator between the visiting gods and the hosting mortals at this ritual feast. And just as she has symbolically proffered the waters to the gods, transferred the force of her hospitable behavior onto them, by washing their feet (conceptually speaking), so she receives their force in return, in the form of the mediating water that was her instrument of transfer. This water has now been transformed into the fertilizing soma/semen that is the desired human share of the ritual bargain.

This reward for hospitality reminds us of the many epic stories in which a properly hospitable pair receive offspring in return for their hostly trouble. Many of us meet this theme in the first real page of Sanskrit we ever read: the beginning of the Nala episode of the Mahābhārata, when the childless King Bhīma and his wife receive the seer Damana:

MBh III.50.7 taṃ sa bhīmaḥ prajākāmas toṣayām āsa dharmavit
mahiṣyā saha rājendra satkāreṇa suvarcasam.
8 tasmai prasanno damanaḥ sabhāryāya varaṃ dadau
kanyāratnaṃ kumārāṃś ca trīn udārān mahāyaśāḥ

Dharma-knowing Bhīma, desirous of offspring, together with his Mahiṣī, satisfied him
of good lustre [Damana] with hospitality, o best of kings.
To him [Bhīma] together with his wife, Damana, well-satisfied, granted a boon:
a girl-jewel and three excellent boys of great glory.

Hospitality is inextricably linked with sexuality and fertility in ancient India in both ritual and narrative literature, as we have seen and will see again. And the woman, the wife, is in certain ways the embodiment of this linkage.

In the Third Pressing and the role of the wife in it we find perhaps the most complex of the ritual representations we have discussed, as is perhaps fitting for this climax of the most elaborate of the nonroyal Vedic rituals. As we have seen, it is structured as a series of mixtures, of marriages—the human married couple (Sacrificer and wife) perform the mixture of soma and milk, who in some sense represent them. The divine marriages symbolized by the cup of soma offered to Agni and the wives of the gods have their effect on this human marriage, through a different kind of mixture: contact between the divine and the human. This contact is established in two different ways: the soma from the cup offered to Agni et al. is also consumed by a human (the Agnīd) and is indirectly transferred to the wife through a chain of priests. And she is in more direct contact with the gods through their Foot-washing water. The various mixtures and marriages can be diagramed as follows:

Horizontal: "Marriages" Between Male and Female Elements

	male		*female*
divine	Agni	↔	Pātnīvata
ritual substance	soma	↔	milk
human	sacrificer	↔	wife

Vertical (Bottom Up): Benefits the Divine Realm

	male		*female*
divine	gods		
	↑		
ritual substance	soma	←	milk
			↑
human			wife

Translation: wife adds milk to soma (the oblation) destined for gods.

Vertical (Top Down): Benefits the Human Realm

	male		*female*
divine	soma	gods	
	↓	↓	
ritual substance	soma	foot water	
	↓	↓	
human	(priests)	→	wife

Translation: The divine soma is transferred by way of the ritual drink soma, through gender-switching priests, to the wife. Then gods' footwater (as semen) is transferred to the wife.

After this skein of contacts has been created, the ritual purpose has in many ways been achieved. It is not surprising that, after a few further libations and such, the main part of the Soma Sacrifice is over, and they move to the concluding actions that close the ritual box. Every one, divine and human, can go home; they have done their job. Again I would suggest that concentrating our attention on the apparently peripheral figure of the wife has allowed us to discern the covert but controlling structural patterns of the Third Pressing and, in turn, to see its crucial importance within the Soma Sacrifice.[326]

Further evidence for the sexually charged atmosphere of the Third Pressing comes from the recitations prescribed for a particular variant of the Soma Sacrifice. We have had occasion before to refer to the yearlong Sattra known as the 'Progress of the Cows' (Gavāmayana): its finale is the wild Mahāvrata day (discussed in III.E.2), characterized by singing, dancing, mock-fighting, and ritual copulation. The ritual year that precedes this bacchanal consists of numerous smaller ritual units that lead up to and away from the midpoint, the summer solstice (the Viṣuvant Day).[327] Each month is made up of five periods of six days each: four six-day Abhiplava Ṣaḍahas and one six-day Pṛṣṭhya Ṣaḍaha. Clustered around the summer solstice are other special ritual days, including one called the Viśvajit Day, occurring just three days after the solstice. On the sixth day of the Pṛṣṭhya Ṣaḍaha, that is, once a month through the year, the assistants of the Hotar, the Hotrakas, recite special śastras known as the Śilpa Śastras at the Third Pressing.[328]

All the mind-numbing ritual detail just presented is in service of a rather surprising point. One of the Hotrakas, the Brāhmaṇācchaṃsin, recites the *Vṛṣākapi* hymn (RV X.86) and the *Kuntāpa* hymn sequence (AVŚ XX.127–36) at this time. In other words, at the point in the ritual, the Third Pressing, when the wife of the Sacrificer is being impregnated with symbolic semen from two different sources in a set of transparently sexual actions, the verbal accompaniment is also explicitly sexual, consisting of one hymn full of sexual taunts and boasts, dramatizing the interspecies copulation of the Aśvamedha (if I am right), and a series of verses and pairs of verses glorifying sexual organs, sexual penetration, and a remarkable lady known as the Mahānagnī ('great naked [woman]'). Neither Vṛṣākapi nor Kuntāpa has any other application in śrauta ritual of which I am aware.[329]

We have before noted that the verbal portion of ritual is often used to heighten the drama of the actions being performed alongside. The Third Pressing in its ordinary form already presents us with a fairly lurid spectacle: a chain of priestly sexual interchanges, culminating in mock copulation with the wife. At regular intervals in the yearlong performance of the Gavāmayana, this striking dumb show is accompanied not by typical innocuous RVic verses of praise and supplication, but by shockingly obscene riddles and insults. The forthrightly sexual character of the recitation draws attention to what is really happening in the ritual, underscores the somewhat masked sexuality of the Third Pressing, and connects it with the real copulation of the Aśvamedha and Mahāvrata day—without the usual sacral blurring produced by high rhetorical style.

It is not surprising that this intensification of the sexual atmosphere in the Third Pressing happens in the Gavāmayana, which ends with the indecent jeering dialogue and ritual copulation of whore and chaste student at the Mahāvrata. The monthly Vṛṣākapi/Kuntāpa recitation at the Third Pressing of the sixth day of the Pṛṣṭhya Ṣaḍaha serves as a symbolical dress rehearsal for the genuine sexual activity at the Mahāvrata ritual—regularly establishing as the year progresses a mood of heightened sexuality for participants and spectators in anticipation of the explosive action at the end of the year.[330]

5. *Bathing the Victim in the Animal Sacrifice (Paśubandha)*

We can also see the wife's role as mediator in another of her ritual tasks, the tending and preparation of the animal victim, once it has been sacrificed.[331] This is the other place in śrauta ritual in which Foot-washing waters appear. In animal sacrifices all the principal actors stay strictly away from the actual killing of the animal; they physically remove themselves and turn their backs while someone else does the inauspicious deed. But once the animal is dead, it must be rearranged, cut up, cooked, and offered.

In the first step of the process, when the fearful forces bound up in the killing have not yet been dissipated, the wife is led near, to bathe the animal and verbally reinvigorate it. The Pratiprasthātar or the Neṣṭar leads her from her usual spot up to the place northwest of the ritual ground where the animal has been 'appeased'. She carries a vessel of water and before embarking on her duties salutes the sun.

> BŚS IV.6 (118: 6) atha pratiprasthātā patnīm udānayaty udakamaṇḍalum utthāpyāthainām ādityam udīkṣayati namas ta ātāneti

Then the Pratiprasthātar leads up the wife, holding up a vessel of water. Then he makes her look up at the sun, (saying) "Homage to thee, extended one."[332]

As we noted earlier, the WYV texts specifically call the water pannejanī 'Foot-washing water' (ŚB III.8.2.1; KŚS VI.6.1).

After she or the Adhvaryu addresses a mantra to the waters, the two set to work, pouring the water on the victim, bathing the places of the 'breaths' (prāṇa), and reciting encouraging mantras all the while. The particular job each does depends on the text, and in some it is difficult to tell who is doing what. But it is clear that both are in close contact with the dead animal. The verbs describing the actions they perform also differ. Consider a few different versions:

MŚS I.8.4.4 yathāliṅgam aṅgāni prakṣālayati patny āsiñcati

(The Adhvaryu) washes the limbs according to their marks. The wife pours.

ĀpŚS VII.18.6 adbhiḥ paśoḥ sarvān prāṇān āpyāyayati
7 sarvāṇy aṅgāny adhvaryur abhiṣiñcati patny āpyāyayati / etad vā viparītam

S/he swells all the breaths of the animal with water. The Adhvaryu pours on all the limbs; the wife swells them. Or vice versa.

BŚS IV.6 (118: 12) sānupūrvaṃ paśoḥ prāṇān āpyāyayati . . . etān eva punaḥ saṃmṛśati . . . padaḥ prakṣālayati

S/he swells the breaths of the animal in regular succession. . . . (Having done so,) s/he strokes them all again. . . . S/he washes its feet.

KŚS VI.6.2 paśoḥ prāṇāñ chundhati patnī

The wife purifies the breaths of the animal.

VārŚS I.6.5.14 tābhyaḥ patnī paśoḥ prāṇān prakṣālayaty adhvaryur vā
15 anyataro 'bhiṣiñcet

From these (waters) the wife washes the breaths of the animal—or the Adhvaryu. The other should pour.

ŚB III.8.2.4 átha paśóḥ prāṇā́n adbhíḥ pátny úpaspṛśati

Then the wife touches the breaths of the animal with water.

The MS comments about the wife's work:

MS III.10.1 (128: 8) . . . etā́ṃ bahú riprám amedhyáṃ cárantīm ā́po ná hiṁsanti

. . . the waters do not harm her, (though she) performs much that is dirty and ritually impure.

We should focus on two questions about this activity: first, what is actually occurring conceptually, and second, why is it the wife who performs it? In answer to the first question, it is of course obvious that one of the purposes is purification: the cleansing waters remove the impurities acquired in the violence of the sacrificial process. But there seem to be other purposes as well, as signaled by some of the vocabulary employed.

The fact that the WYV texts call the water 'Foot-washing water' and that the BŚS in a separate clause prescribes the washing of the feet suggests that this cleansing is also a perverted hospitality ritual. The victim is treated as a guest and accorded the same ceremonial courtesy the gods received at the Soma Sacrifice we just discussed. The "Sacrificed Guest" is not a new figure in our ritual landscape: Soma was received as guest in the hospitality ritual (Ātithya) and then sacrificed, as we have seen. The order of the elements is simply reversed with the animal victim.

Another detail of the cleansing reveals a further connection between soma and the animal victim. The verb several texts (ĀpŚS, BŚS) use for the procedure is āpyāyayati 'makes swell', not necessarily the most descriptively accurate one for what presumably happens when you pour water on a recently suffocated animal. This idiom, moreover, appears in most of the texts in the mantras addressed to each body part (the seat of each 'breath') in turn:

> BŚS IV.6 (118: 13) vāk ta āpyāyatām iti vācaṃ prāṇas ta āpyāyatām iti prāṇaṃ cakṣus ta āpyāyatām iti cakṣuḥ . . .
>
> "Let your speech [mouth] swell," (s/he says) over his speech (/mouth). "Let your breath [nose] swell" over his breath (/nose). "Let your eye swell" over his eye. . . . etc.

In the Soma Sacrifice, after soma has been purchased and hospitably received, he is 'swelled' with water, using the same verbal idiom as here. The dry twigs expand, gain flesh, as it were—rehydrating the plant in preparation for its own sacrifice by pressing. We can view this rehydration as a reanimation, a bringing back to life of a dry and apparently lifeless substance. If it worked for soma, then it will work for the other victim, the animal, too—such perhaps is the ritual logic—though again the order of elements is reversed. When the animal is killed, it is addressed with the misleading comfort, "You do not die here; you are not hurt" (ná vā́ u etán mriyase ná riṣyase). The 'swelling' with water is the physical equivalent of this cheerful illusion: the animal is revived, reborn; there was no killing really.

Now let us consider why the wife is the central figure in this somewhat grisly scene, recalling also that the scene is played out more dramatically in the Aśvamedha: there, when the time comes to cut up the horse, the wives use needles to prepare the paths of the knives to cut up the victim.

> ĀpŚS XX.18.7 . . . sauvarṇībhiḥ sūcībhir mahiṣy aśvasyāsipathān kalpayati prāk kroḍāt . . . rājatībhir vāvātā pratyak kroḍāt prāṅ nābheḥ . . . lauhībhiḥ sīsābhir vā parivṛktī śeṣam
>
> With golden needles the Mahiṣī arranges the paths for the knives forward of the horse's breast; with silver (needles) the Vāvātā behind the breast and in front of the navel; with copper or lead (needles) the Rejected Wife the rest.

The Brāhmaṇic texts give us one reason for the wife's participation, one that is linked to the discussion of 'swelling' above: the wife as progenitor causes the dead animal to be reborn.

> ŚB III.8.2.5 átha yát pátny upaspṛśáti / yóṣā vái pátnī yóṣāyai vā́ imā́ḥ prajā́ḥ prā́jāyante tád enam etásyai yóṣāyai prā́janayati tásmāt pátny úpaspṛśati
>
> Now, as to why the wife touches (the victim). The wife is a woman. It is from woman that offspring are born here. In this way he [priest] causes him [victim] to be born from this woman. Therefore the wife touches (him).

Again the wife's fertile powers are being tapped.

But there is another reason, I would suggest, related to her general functions in the realm of hospitality. The Sacrificer's Wife, by touching the dead animal, creates the necessary contact between the human and the divine realms, between the living and the dead that is a major aim of the sacrifice. She is the lightning rod for divine power, or, to change images, the point of entry, the channel for it. She gains access to powerful and dangerous forces unleashed by the killing and can direct them to her husband and the success of his ritual, without his putting himself at risk.

The husband himself never touches the animal; even when it was still alive, he made contact only by touching it from behind with a meat skewer, as we saw earlier.[333] During the washing of the victim, the Sacrificer, though present, is essentially inactive. In only one text I have excerpted does he play any role at this point, and it is a fairly distanced one.

> KŚS VI.6.4 śeṣeṇa yajamānaś ca śiraḥprabhṛty anuṣiñcataḥ . . .
> 6 . . . paścāt paśor niṣiñcataḥ
>
> With the rest (of the water) (the Adhvaryu?/the wife?) and the Sacrificer pour along (the victim) beginning with the head. . . .
> They pour (the remaining water) behind the animal.

The wife's general role in the mundane world as both dispenser of hospitality and as mediator, central token in the system of exchanges, allows her to perform this same function in the ritual realm.

This concludes our survey of the roles of the Sacrificer's Wife. Despite, or perhaps because of, the rigid, limited, and esoteric nature of śrauta ritual, our examination has identified several crucial, interconnected functions for the wife, with major implications for ancient Indian culture beyond the apparently narrow world of ritual. We will explore these issues in the rest of the book—in particular the interrelations of gender, hospitality, and exchange, and the anxieties associated with them.

IV

The Anxieties of Hospitality

A. Introduction: Oghavatī and Ahalyā

We have recently seen, especially in the discussion of the wife and the Foot-washing water, the remarkable connection between women, sex, and hospitality, as acted out in a ritual context. There the hospitality was dispensed symbolically, to the unseen gods, through the mediation of somewhat enigmatic sexual representations. Let us now consider two epic narratives in which the connection is depicted quite graphically, without the use of ritual screens, in the unambiguous context of guest reception. After examining these stories I will provide a context for them by treating hospitality more generally, not focusing particularly on women's roles in it, but will return later to women once I have established the parameters of the hospitality relation and its dangers.

The Mahābhārata, as we will see, contains a wide range of hospitality narratives, in which the host or guest (or both) confronts potential abuses of this relationship of trust. We will examine first the Sudarśanopākhyānam (MBh XIII.2). In this episode Sudarśana, Agni's son, has taken a vow of unquestioning hospitality, about which he instructs his wife Oghavatī:

MBh XIII.2.41 atitheḥ pratikūlaṃ te na kartavyaṃ kathaṃ cana
42 yena yena ca tuṣyeta nityam eva tvayātithiḥ
apy ātmanaḥ pradānena na te kāryā vicāraṇā
43 etad vrataṃ mama sadā hṛdi saṃparivartate
gṛhasthānāṃ ni suśroṇi nātither vidyate param
44 pramāṇaṃ yadi vāmoru vacas te mama śobhane
idaṃ vacanam avyagrā hṛdi tvaṃ dhārayeḥ sadā
45 niṣkrānte mayi kalyāṇi tathā saṃnihite 'naghe
nātithis te 'vamantavyaḥ pramāṇaṃ yady ahaṃ tava

41 It is wrong for you not to do everything possible for a guest.
42 By whatever way you might satisfy a guest,
even by the gift of yourself, you should not hesitate to do it.
43 This vow exists always in my heart,
for, o well-hipped one, there is nothing higher than a guest for householders.
44 O fair-thighed one, if my speech is an authority for you, o lovely one,
without confusion you should hold this statement in your heart always.
45 When I am away, just as when I am present, o lovely and faultless one,
no guest is to be scorned by you, if I am your authority.

She assents, and Sudarśana then goes off to collect firewood, followed by Death, who is looking for an opportunity to do him in. Meanwhile a Brahman comes by the hermitage and seeks hospitality:

MBh XIII.2.49 ātithyaṃ dattam icchāmi tvayādya varavarṇini
I seek an act of hospitality given by you today, o fair-faced one.

She innocently offers what we will discover are the usual things for a guest, a seat and water, but then asks a dangerous question:

MBh XIII.2.51 āsanaṃ caiva pādyaṃ ca tasmai dattvā dvijātaye
provācaughavatī vipraṃ kenārthaḥ kiṃ dadāmi te
Having given this twice-born one a seat and Foot-washing water,
Oghavatī asked the seer, "With whom is your business? What can I give you?"

His reply leaves no doubt:

MBh XIII.2.52 tvayā mamārthaḥ kalyāṇi nirviśaṅke tad ācara
53 yadi pramāṇaṃ dharmas te gṛhasthāśramasaṃmataḥ
pradānenātmano rājñi kartum arhasi me priyam
My business is with you, o fair one. Undertake it without hesitation.
If the dharma approved for the householder's state is your authority,
by the gift of yourself, o queen, you ought to do me a favor.

She attempts to offer him other desirable gifts, but he will be satisfied by nothing less than what he had demanded (vs. 54). So, mindful of her husband's charge, she agrees despite embarrassment (vs. 55), and they go off together (vs. 56). Sudarśana in the meantime has amassed sufficient firewood (vs. 57); he returns to the hermitage and keeps calling for Oghavatī (vs. 58). Still in the embrace of the Brahman (vs. 59), she keeps silent out of shame:

MBh XIII.2.59 tasmai prativacaḥ sā tu bhartre na pradadau tadā
karābhyāṃ tena vipreṇa spṛṣṭā bhartṛvratā satī
But she did not reply to her husband then,
true to her vow to her husband, (while) touched by the sage with his two hands.

The phrase bhartṛvratā satī "true to her vow to her husband" is ingeniously ambiguous. She is both a faithful wife and therefore embarrassed to be caught with another man—and true to her particular promise to him, so that she allows the other man to continue to touch her though her husband has returned and summoned her. The next verse expresses her shame more vigorously:

MBh XIII.2.60 ucchiṣṭāsmīti manvānā lajjitā bhartur eva ca
tūṣṇīṃbhūtābhavat sādhvī na covācātha kiṃ cana
Thinking "I am the leftover[1] (of another man)," shamed (before) her husband,
the noble woman was silent and said nothing.

Meanwhile Sudarśana is getting testy (. . . kva sā yātā garīyaḥ kim ato mama "Where is she gone? What is more important than me?" vs. 61). The Brahman, emerging from the hut, acquaints him quite straightforwardly with the facts:

MBh XIII.2.63 atithiṃ viddhi saṃprāptaṃ pāvake brāhmaṇaṃ ca mām
64 anayā chandyamāno 'haṃ bhāryayā tava sattama
tais tair atithisatkārair ārjave 'syā dṛḍhaṃ manaḥ

Know me as a guest arrived here and a Brahman, o Pāvaki.
I am being pleasured by this wife of yours, o best one.
By virtue of these very acts of hospitality to a guest, her mind is firm in rectitude.

As it turns out, this is a test. The hovering Death thinks this is his chance: Sudarśana will falter in his devotion to householder's hospitality. But, like other exploited hosts we will see, Sudarśana is generous spirited and unwaveringly free of jealousy. Citing again his vow of hospitality, he performs an act of truth with regard to his cheerful acceptance of what has happened, and thereby cheats Death.

67 tyakterṣyas tyaktamanyuś ca smayamāno 'bravīd idam
68 surataṃ te 'stu viprāgrya prītir hi paramā mama
gṛhasthasya hi dharmo 'gryaḥ saṃprāptātithipūjanam
. . . 70 prāṇā hi mama dārāś ca yac cānyad vidyate vasu
atithibhyo mayā deyam iti me vratam āhitam
71 . . . tenāhaṃ vipra satyena svayam ātmānam ālabhe

67 Without jealousy, without anger, smiling he said this:
68 "Let your sexual pleasure be my greatest enjoyment, o first of seers.
For the first law of the householder is to honor a guest who has come.
70 'My breath, my wife, and what other goods I possess
are to be given by me to guests'—such is my established vow.
71 By this truth, o seer, I seize myself." [an oath-taking posture?—the act of truth continues for some time].

The libidinous visitor turns out to be Dharma (as often in these stories, as we will see), and all turns out well. Dharma praises Sudarśana for the fortitude of his vow and, incidentally, Oghavatī as well (also assuring her husband of her continued virtue), and promises great rewards for the couple.

Once again, as in several ritual episodes we have discussed, the wife acts as mediator for her husband in a risky or unpleasant situation, and he receives the benefits of her action (and here, annoyingly, acclaim for his forbearance in observing with equanimity the sexual infidelity he himself imposed on her). As in the ritual, she has direct contact with the divine (disguised as human), and the contact is sexual. It involves 'voluntary' exchange (the 'gift of oneself' ātmadāna), and the context of this exchange is dharmically enjoined hospitality. As in the Manu's Cups story the husband is tested, is required to demonstrate the highest virtue, and the pinnacle of his virtuous achievement is *his willingness to sacrifice his wife*—as a token of his devotion to the hospitality relations that obtain between him and other males.

The first book of the Rāmāyaṇa (I.47–48) contains a narrative that is the mirror image of Oghavatī, namely that of Ahalyā.[2] The starkly contrastive deployment of the same thematic elements simply underlines the strong cultural connections among these elements.

Ahalyā is the wife of the great sage Gautama, who, like Sudarśana, has temporarily left his ashram to glean wood and other ritual oddments (R I.47.23). Taking advantage of his absence, Indra comes to the ashram, disguised as Gautama. Ahalyā is not fooled, but is eager for the god, and they make love (I.47.17–20). When Gautama returns, he knows immediately what has happened. He curses both of them—Indra to lose his testicles and Ahalyā to live austerely and invisible for thousands of years, until Rāma comes and *she extends hospitality to him* (R I.47.28–31):

R I.47.30 yadā caitad vanaṃ ghoraṃ rāmo daśarathātmajaḥ
āgamiṣyati durdharṣas tadā pūtā bhaviṣyasi
31 tasy*ātithyena* durvṛtte lobhamohavivarjitā
matsakāśe mudā yuktā svaṃ vapur dhārayiṣyasi

When Rāma, the unconquerable son of Daśaratha,
will come to this dreadful forest, then you will become purified.
By the *Guestly offering* to him, o badly behaved one, you will assume your own body in my presence, freed from lust and delusion, yoked with joy.

When in the fullness of time Rāma does arrive, she gives him the proper guest reception and regains her body and husband (R I.48.18–20). The verse describing the guest reception uses the full vocabulary of hospitality, which I will discuss later.

R I.48.18 pādyam arghyaṃ tadātithyaṃ cakāra susamāhitā
pratijagrāha kākutstho vidhidṛṣṭena karmaṇā

Intently she performed the Guestly offering, the Foot-washing water, the Arghya water.
Kākutstha [Rāma] accepted them by the rite ordained by custom.

In this tale the wife's sexual congress with a visiting stranger is not justified by preenjoined hospitality, as in the Oghavatī story. Rather it is purified by a later (chaste) act of hospitality to an especially deserving guest, also ordered by her husband. The wife literally disappears until the proper connections between sex and hospitality have been established after the fact—the same connections that were set up, in the right order, in the Oghavatī story.

As these stories—and many others we will presently examine—show, any close consideration of women in ancient India ultimately becomes entangled in the vast subject of hospitality and exchange. Similarly, the story with which we began, of the near sacrifice of Manu's wife, is one where hospitality relations trigger all of the action, as I will demonstrate. But in order to understand the mechanisms of that narrative, we must first examine hospitality in general, and see how it is embodied not merely in the legal and domestic texts that spell out its provisions, but also in the narratives, like the Sudarśanopākhyānam and Manu's Cups, that dramatize its risks.

Hospitality, the appropriate behavior between host and guest, is a theme that infuses Sanskrit literature and as cultural behavior remains crucial to the present day. The duties of a host are set forth quite extensively in the offical dharma and gṛhya manuals, and this codification of hostly behavior can be traced back to earlier texts like the AV, as in AV IX.6, entitled by Whitney "Exalting the entertainment of guests." It is also a constantly recurring motif in literary texts in Sanskrit and other Indic languages.[3]

Though the official manuals give little hint of this, Sanskrit literature presents us with many examples of violations of hospitality relations and their dire effects—for example, in the numerous stories in which the anger of an ill-treated guest is what sets the mainspring of the action in motion. Perhaps the most famous example occurs in the Śakuntalā of Kālidāsa: lovesick Śakuntalā is too dreamy and distracted to display appropriate hospitality when the irascible sage Durvāsas comes to the hermitage, so he lays a curse on her that her lover should not recognize her. Like Ahalyā she in essence disappears.

For Vedic, Thieme[4] has amply demonstrated the ambivalent feelings about the ari, the stranger to whom one owes hospitality—potentially either hostile enemy or guest worthy of honor. But he has given less emphasis to the inherent uncertainties within the category of guest: even the hospitality relation may impose strain and danger rather than ensuring safety. In what follows we will focus on the roles of host and guest and their mutual obligations, and especially on the violations of these obligations, unfair advantages taken of either of the assigned roles.

B. Hospitality and Hostly Perils

1. Guest Receptions: Proper and Improper

Let us first consider the nature of the central hospitality rite, that of guest reception. The protocol of guest reception in Sanskrit literature is no doubt familiar to anyone with a passing acquaintance with the texts, at least in its basic outline. The rock-bottom necessities are water for washing the feet (pādya), water for rinsing the mouth (ācamanīya), a seat (āsana), and, usually, food—these for guests of no particular distinction. As the importance of the guest rises—because of rank, learning, or special relationship to the host—the requirements become more exacting. For example, according to GDS V.32–34, the food for a learned Brahman (Śrotriya) should be of superior quality (annaviśeṣa) or at least especially carefully prepared (saṃskāraviśiṣṭa), but a not so learned Brahman gets not so special food (madhyato 'nnadāna "food of middling quality"). Particularly worthy guests are offered the Arghya water

(water perfumed with flowers and grasses), the Madhuparka (a mixture of honey, curds, and sometimes other things), and, as we will see, a cow. Both the dharma texts and the gṛhya texts treat the guest reception quite fully, and they generally make fine rankings of the worthiness of the guest and the calibrated treatment he accordingly deserves.[5]

That this preoccupation with varieties of guest reception was not an invention of hairsplitting Sūtrakāras is clear from the importance it assumes in literary texts. In the MBh for example, even in the most minor and quickly narrated visits, at least one śloka is usually devoted to the guest reception accorded the visitor. The usual elements of hospitality are concatenated in verbal formulae like the following:

pādyam ācamanīyaṃ ca [MBh I.54.13; III.45.2, 197.10, 198.17; V.17.4, etc.]	"Foot-washing (water) and rinsing (water)"
udakaṃ madhuparkaṃ ca [MBh. V.35.20, 21 ≅ V.38.3]	"water and the Madhuparka"
x x gāṃ madhuparkaṃ ca [MBh V.87.19, V.89.9, etc.]	"a cow and the Madhuparka"

The elements in these guest reception scenes may be formulaic, but they are not randomly distributed: the Arghya water, the Madhuparka, and the cow are not proffered to every stray visitor in the MBh, but only to those whom the codes would consider worthy. Many of the guest receptions described in the MBh are qualified with adverbs like yathāvidhi (e.g. MBh II.19.29, V.8.16) 'according to rule' or śāstravat (e.g. MBh III.49.30) 'according to the śāstra'.

Janamejaya's reception of Vyāsa when he comes to the Snake Sacrifice (MBh I.54.10ff.) can represent the typical treatment of a particularly honored guest:

I.54.10 janamejayas tu rājarṣir dṛṣṭvā tam ṛṣim āgatam
sagaṇo 'bhyudyayau tūrṇaṃ prītyā bharatasattamaḥ
11 kāñcanaṃ viṣṭaraṃ tasmai . . .
āsanaṃ kalpayām āsa . . .
12 tatropaviṣṭam . . .
pūjayām āsa rājendraḥ śāstradṛṣṭena karmaṇā
13 pādyam ācamanīyaṃ ca arghyaṃ gāṃ ca vidhānataḥ
. . . tad arhāya nyavedayat
14 pratigṛhya ca tāṃ pūjāṃ pāṇḍavāj janamejayāt
gāṃ caiva samanujñāya vyāsaḥ prīto 'bhavat tadā

10 The royal seer Janamejaya, best of the Bharatas, with his followers,
having seen the seer arrive, got up and approached him quickly, with affection.
11 He prepared for him an extensive golden seat.
12 The best of kings did honor to him seated there with a rite found in the śāstras.
13 He offered to the worthy one Foot-washing (water), rinsing (water), Arghya (water), and a cow, according to rule.

14 Having accepted this honor from the Pāṇḍava Janamejaya
and having dismissed the cow, Vyāsa became pleased.

The more important the encounter, the more elaborate the descriptions of the elements of guest reception. When Kṛṣṇa goes on his embassy of peace to the Kurus in Book V (85ff.), the last major event before the beginning of the war, his reception by each of his hosts or potential hosts is accorded considerable space. At each meeting with the opposing side, for example, the required seat is offered to him—and described to us, not simply indicated by āsana as is usual. At his meeting with Dhṛtarāṣṭra, it is ūrjitaṃ mṛṣṭaṃ kāñcanaṃ mahad āsanam (V.87.18) "a mighty, polished, golden, great seat"; at Duryodhana's it is jāmbūnadamayaṃ paryaṅkaṃ supariṣkṛtam / vividhāstaraṇāstīrṇam (V.89.8) "a golden sofa well-adorned and strewn with various spreads"; and when he finally goes to the assembly, there is an āsanaṃ sarvatobhadraṃ jāmbūnadapariṣkṛtam (V.92.37) "a seat, splendid on every side, adorned with gold" for Kṛṣṇa and āsanāni . . . mṛṣṭāni mahānti vipulāni ca / maṇikāñcanacitrāṇi (V.92.45) "seats, polished, large and commodious, bright with jewels and gold" for the seers that Kṛṣṇa insists be received. The seats of the Kurus in the assembly are likewise described. Thus, the elaboration (or lack of it) in the formulaic description of the guest reception can index the significance of the episode to come.

One short episode demonstrates how the finely graded artifacts of the hospitality reception can become almost a part of the drama. This is the story of a Brahman named Sudhanvan and a Daitya named Virocana, narrated by Vidura to the sleepless Dhṛtarāṣṭra in V.35[6]—perhaps not coincidentally just before the arrival of Kṛṣṇa stirs up a series of hospitality crises, as we will see. In the first half of this story the relative status of the rivals Sudhanvan and Virocana is indicated entirely through byplay about chairs.

At the svayaṃvara[7] of a certain Keśinī, the girl playfully (?) asks Virocana if Brahmans or Daityas are better, then emends her question to atha kena sma paryaṅkaṃ sudhanvā nādhirohati (V.35.6) "Or who will Sudhanvan not climb on a sofa with?" Virocana of course boasts of his greatness, but Keśinī tells him to wait and see. "Sudhanvan will come here early tomorrow, and I would like to see you two together" (V.35.8 sudhanvā prātar āgantā[8] paśyeyaṃ vāṃ samāgatau).

When Sudhanvan arrives, Keśinī offers him a seat and other hostly necessities,[9] in a verse omitted from the Critical Edition, but of quite widespread attestation in the manuscripts:

V.197* sudhanvā ca samāgacchat prāhlādiṃ keśinīṃ tathā
samāgataṃ dvijaṃ dṛṣṭvā keśinī bharatarṣabha
pratyutthāyāsanaṃ tasmai pādyam arghyaṃ dadau punaḥ

Sudhanvan joined (Virocana,) son of Prahlāda, and Keśinī.
Having seen the twice-born one arrive, Keśinī,

having stood up, gave him a seat, Foot-washing (water), likewise Arghya (water), o bull of the Bharatas.

I think it likely that some such verse was always a part of the story; otherwise the next verse, with Sudhanvan's direct speech, is quite abrupt—though perhaps that is the point.

V.35.10 anvālabhe hiraṇmayaṃ prāhlāde 'ham tavāsanam
ekatvam upasaṃpanno na tv āseyaṃ tvayā sahā

O son of Prahlāda [Virocana], I take the golden seat of yours, after (you)—
having obtained it entirely (lit., as a unity). I would not sit with you.

Here Sudhanvan tacitly declines the seat politely offered by Keśinī (if we accept 197*) and usurps Virocana's seat. This is not just simple rudeness (though rude it assuredly is), but constitutes Sudhanvan's assertion of superior status: he and he alone deserves the grand seat that Virocana occupies, which Sudhanvan pointedly calls 'golden'—remember the golden seats offered to distinguished visitors earlier. He answers Keśinī's question of the day before: he will certainly "not climb on a sofa with" Virocana.

Van Buitenen's translation of this verse, "Son of Prahlāda, I accept the golden seat from you, now that I have met you; but I will not sit with you!", rests on two important misconceptions that make the entire passage hard to follow. First, as we will see (and cf. MBh I.54.14 quoted earlier), the standard formula for accepting hospitality is prati √grah, not anu-ā √labh. √Labh here seems to have its full root meaning: 'take (forcibly)', not 'accept'. Indeed, ā √labh is the standard lexeme for grasping a sacrificial victim to bind it for its killing, and the implicit violence of that phrase may be intended to be perceived here. The preverb anu 'after, following' should also be taken literally: Sudhanvan *follows* Virocana as occupant of the seat, displacing him.

I assume that van Buitenen's "now that I have met you" renders ekatvam upasaṃpannaḥ or some variant of it (x x *tvām upasaṃpannaḥ?) [no such variant is found in the manuscripts]. But ekatvam ('in its entirety') is a crucial word here, indicating that Sudhanvan refuses to share the seat, since that might imply equality between the two men.

Virocana is not to be moved. Instead he meets the rude challenge with a calculated insult of his own:

V.35.11 anvāharantu phalakaṃ kūrcaṃ vāpy atha vā bṛsīm
sudhanvan na tvam arho 'si mayā saha samāsanam

Let them bring a board or a bundle of grass or indeed a bṛsī.[10]
Sudhanvan, you are not worthy of a seat equal with mine.

The suggested substitutes are very humble affairs. Virocana is literally trying to put Sudhanvan in his place, defining his status as low by his makeshift seat. Needless to say Sudhanvan is indignant and replies with a shot at Virocana's father, likewise in the realm of sitting arrangements:

V.35.12 pitāpi te samāsīnam upāsītaiva mām adhaḥ

Even your father would sit below me if I were sitting with him.

By this point the quarrel has become so serious—though nothing but seating has been overtly discussed—that the two bet their lives against each other as to which is better, and they go off to Prahlāda, Virocana's father, to ask him the decisive question. The denouement of the story is as tied to the hospitality rite as is its beginning. When they arrive, Prahlāda's first act anticipates the answer he will give to the question he has not yet heard. Prahlāda says

V.35.20 udakaṃ madhuparkaṃ cāpy ānayantu sudhanvane
brahmann abhyarcanīyo 'si śvetā gauḥ pīvarīkṛtā

Let them bring water and the Madhuparka for Sudhanvan.
Brahman, you are worthy of reverence. A white cow has been fattened.

The offerings provided to the most worthy guests are paraded here, including the cow, rather elaborately described.[11] It is no wonder that Prahlāda will soon disappoint his son by proclaiming Sudhanvan better than Virocana (vs. 28), for his choice of guest reception indicates how highly he rates the visitor.

It is also no wonder that Sudhanvan brushes aside Prahlāda's offerings with a curt udakaṃ madhuparkaṃ ca patha evārpitaṃ mama "water and the Madhuparka were prepared for me on the road" (vs. 21). Refusal of offered hospitality carries a very particular message.

An element of the hospitality rite closes this little tale as well. Prahlāda asks for his son's life, which Sudhanvan has won. Sudhanvan gives it to him, but with a condition:

V.35.31 eṣa prahlāda putras te mayā datto virocanaḥ
pādaprakṣālanaṃ kuryāt kumāryāḥ saṃnidhau mama

Prahlāda, this son (of yours), Virocana, is given to you by me.
(But) he must perform the foot-washing for me in the presence of the girl.

Virocana is placed in a humiliating position, serving Sudhanvan in front of the girl they were both courting, but the humiliation is achieved by performing a task that is part of the proper reception of distinguished guests.[12] It is also noteworthy that a woman is the pivotal figure here: she both provokes the quarrel and witnesses the humiliation. She is the catalyst that crystallizes the tensions between the two men through an apparently innocent act of hospitality.

2. The Inconvenient Obligations of Hospitality

What are we to make of this elaborate edifice of hierarchically ranked gestures and offerings? I would suggest that the codification of hostly responsibility was in part a response to the dangerous open-endedness of the hospitality relation, an attempt to limit what could or would be asked of a host, to control the unpredictable quality of this inherently risky relationship. In other words, I would suggest that behind the hospitality relation in general was the unsettling notion that a host might *have to give* whatever a guest demanded, though perhaps only certain guests and certain hosts and only under certain conditions. This vulnerability of the host seems to be what is at issue in the Manu's Cups story with which we began. He *has* to accede to the visiting Asuras' demands; he simply has no choice.

Several episodes in the Mahābhārata demonstrate how much hardship producing even the basic hospitable reception may impose on the host. In the Nakulākhyāna (XIV.93) a destitute and nearly starving Brahman and his family have just managed to get hold of a small amount of barley when a hungry guest arrives as they are about to eat (XIV.93.9–11). They have him enter their hut (vs. 14) and offer him the proper guest reception, including their precious barley groats:

MBh. XIV.93.15 idam arghyaṃ ca pādyaṃ ca bṛsī ceyaṃ tavānagha
śucayaḥ saktavaś ceme niyamopārjitāḥ prabho
pratigṛhṇīṣva bhadraṃ te mayā dattā dvijottama

Here is Arghya (water) and Foot-washing (water), and here is a bṛsī-seat for you, o faultless one.
Here are white barley groats obtained by a vow, o lord.
Accept them, if you please. (These) are given by me, o twice-born.

The guest accepts and eats, but not to satiation, whereupon the old, emaciated, sick wife of the Brahman presses her own portion on the visitor (madbhāgo dīyatām, vs. 18). He recognizes her pitiful condition and initially refuses the offer:

MBh. XIV.93.19 kṣudhāparigatāṃ jñātvā saktūṃs tān nābhyanandata
20 jānan vṛddhāṃ kṣudhārtāṃ ca śrāntāṃ glānāṃ tapasvinīm
tvagasthibhūtāṃ vepantīm

Having realized she was afflicted with hunger, he refused (lit., did not welcome) the groats,
recognizing that the ascetic woman was old, pained by hunger, tired, wearied, mere skin and bones, trembling.

But she ultimately prevails upon him to accept. Again he is not satiated, and the same scene is played through with both son and daughter-in-law. The guest finally reveals himself to be Dharma, and the worthy family is rewarded, as usual. The point here is that the machinery of hospitality constrained both host and guest to act as they did, though the guest had no desire to leave his hosts starving. Neither party had any choice, once the encounter had been set in motion.

Food is provided at even greater sacrifice to the host in the story of the pigeon and the fowler (Kapotalubdhakasaṃvāda, XII.142f.).[13] The fowler, trapped in the woods by a storm, captures and imprisons a female pigeon. When her pigeon-husband laments her capture, she replies with a lesson in manners, ordering him to offer hospitality to her captor (XII.142.14f.). (Notice that the impulse to hospitality comes from the ***abused wife***.) He reluctantly agrees, addresses the fowler with the required welcome, and asks what he can do for him:

MBh. XII.142.23 . . . svāgataṃ te brūhi kiṃ karavāṇy aham . . .
24 tad bravītu bhavān kṣipraṃ kiṃ karomi kim icchasi

Welcome to you. Say what I can do.
Let your worship say quickly which I can do, what you want.

The pigeon then attempts to supply the fowler's needs. He first makes a fire as protection from the cold (vss. 29–32), but when the fowler asks for food (33), the pigeon must make the humiliating admission that he has none (34). After some thought and preparation, twice citing his devotion to atithipūjana ('honoring of guests', 39, 40), he ceremonially enters the fire himself, to make of himself the cooked food he needed to offer the fowler. (The fowler is aghast and repents his evil ways, but that is irrelevant to the story.) Hospitality can hardly exact any higher price than self-immolation.

The first question addressed to the fowler by the pigeon, kiṃ karavāṇy aham, is a trivial variant on the standard question posed by host to guest in the MBh, once the guest's immediate needs have been met: kiṃ karavāṇi (te/vaḥ) "What can I do for you?" (cf. I.3.116; III.61.65, 97.8 ≅ I.65.6; III.71.21; V.94.19, etc.), and it may stand as an emblem of hostly vulnerability. Of course, one should not attribute too much significance to such a conventional question: presumably the speaker usually had as much interest in a sincere answer as we do with a casual "How are you?" But just as we sometimes elicit more than we bargained for, so the Sanskrit question sometimes prompted an undesirable request.

For example, MBh V.94 contains the story of King Dambhodbhava, who wants to challenge the great fighters Nara and Nārāyaṇa, now in ascetic retirement. He approaches them with guestly respect (V.94.18); they offer the appropriate reception with water, food, and a seat (19) and ask another variant of kiṃ karavāṇi te, namely kiṃ kāryaṃ kriyatām, roughly "Let (your) business be done." He replies

MBh V.94.20 bhavadbhyāṃ yuddham ākāṅkṣann upayāto 'smi parvatam
ātithyaṃ dīyatām etat

I have come to this mountain desiring a fight with you two.
Let this *act of hospitality* be granted.

The ascetics try to talk him out of this desire, but ultimately give in (and teach him his lesson). They seem *forced* to give in: the act of hospitality, the guest gift, he demanded in answer to their question could not be denied.

3. *The Exploited Host*

As we saw in the last section, even a guest with benevolent intentions, a "good guest," can bring hardship on his host, and the potential for abuse of the host's mandated generosity is great. A "bad guest" can literally get away with murder. The Manu's Cups story presents us with contrasted good and bad guests: Indra is the longed-for "good guest," using the power given him by the host with propriety and generosity. The two Asuras in the Manu story are by contrast the archetypal "bad guests," who take advantage of the host's open-ended question by making outrageous demands. The figure of the Exploited Host, who patiently and unquestioningly accedes to increasingly onerous and often humiliating demands, is almost a stock character in the Mahābhārata. Sudarśana, Oghavatī's husband, is one. Let us now examine some other Exploited Host narratives.

Some of these stories turn on what seems a mere breach of manners on the part of the guest, who disdains the host's best efforts to entertain him properly. Such, for example, is one of the less violent encounters between the rival seers Vasiṣṭha (or rather Dharma disguised as Vasiṣṭha) and Viśvāmitra (MBh V.104). Vasiṣṭha comes to Viśvāmitra's hermitage hungry and desiring food (V.104.9). While Viśvāmitra fusses over the preparation of a caru, Vasiṣṭha eats already prepared food given him by other ascetics (presumably with fewer culinary pretensions). When Viśvāmitra finally flourishes his finished product, Vasiṣṭha simply says (vs. 12) bhuktaṃ me tiṣṭha tāvat tvam "I have eaten. You stand (there) awhile," and goes away. Viśvāmitra does indeed stand awhile—for a hundred years, holding the food on his head with both hands—until Vasiṣṭha returns and eats the food, which is still hot (vs. 17). It is this trial, successfully met, that allows Viśvāmitra to rise from Kṣatriya to Brahman.

This trouble over food reminds us somewhat of a wrangle between Utaṅka and Pauṣya early in the Mahābhārata (I.3.123ff.). Utaṅka has achieved his errand at Pauṣya's (on which see IV.D.1), and, as he is hurrying off, Pauṣya offers him food. Utaṅka in his haste asks for whatever food is at hand, but when it is offered, he finds it is cold and has a hair in it (I.3.126 śītam annaṃ prakeśam) and curses his host. After a countercurse and some quarreling the issue is resolved, when Pauṣya sees the truth of the complaint and apologizes for the poor quality of his food.

There are several similar stores in the Mahābhārata about what I would term 'the houseguest from Hell'—imperious and capricious visiting Brahmans who take over their host's households and even their lives. These stories contain similar thematic elements, even though the personnel are different. The three we will examine are the familiar story leading up to the birth of Karṇa, in which Sūrya disguised as a Brahman visits Kuntī's father (III.287ff.), and two more elaborate episodes, the visit of Durvāsas to Kṛṣṇa (XIII.144)[14] and that of Cyavana to Kuśika (XIII.52f.).

In the Sūrya-Kuntī story Sūrya begs a meal from Kuntibhoja and asks to stay (III.287.6), demanding free rein in the house:

MBh III.287.8 yathākāmaṃ ca gaccheyam āgaccheyaṃ tathaiva ca
śayyāsane ca me rājan nāparādhyeta kaś cana

I would go and come at will, o king,
and no one should offend against my bed and seat.

Kuntibhoja agrees and sets the maiden Kuntī to wait upon him, cautioning her to do exactly as the visiting Brahman wishes. Kuntibhoja gives the Brahman a lovely white house (III.288.16) and a seat (note the seat again) in his fire sanctuary (288.17), as well as food and so on.

For a year the visitor makes himself as disagreeable as possible.

MBh III.289.2 prātar āyāsya ity uktvā kadā cid dvijasattamaḥ
tata āyāti rājendra sāye rātrāv atho punaḥ
3 taṃ ca sarvāsu velāsu bhakṣyabhojyapratiśrayaiḥ
pūjayām āsa sā kanyā vardhamānais tu sarvadā
4 annādisamudācāraḥ śayyāsanakṛtas tathā
divase divase tasya vardhate na tu hīyate
5 nirbhartsanāpavādaiś ca tathaivāpriyayā girā
brāhmaṇasya pṛthā rājan na cakārāpriyaṃ tadā
6 vyaste kāle punaś caiti na caiti bahuśo dvijaḥ
durlabhyam api caivānnaṃ dīyatām iti so 'bravīt

2 Sometimes the best of the twice-born, having said "I'll come back early in the morning,"[15]
then came back in the evening or at night, o Indra of kings.
3 At all hours the maiden honored him with the ever increasing refuge of all kinds of food (?).
4 Her entertainment of him with food and so forth, her activity with regard to bed and seat
increased day by day and did not flag.
5 Even with his reviling and blaming and his unpleasing speech,
Pṛthā [Kuntī] did nothing unpleasing to the Brahman, o king.
6 He returned at various times, and often the twice-born did not come at all.
Even about food that was hard to find he simply said, "Give (it)!"

At the end of this ordeal the disguised Sūrya is pleased with the ever agreeable Kuntī and grants her a boon, which ultimately leads to his fathering Karṇa. Notice that though Kuntibhoja is the nominal *host*, his daughter Kuntī does all the work. As often women are the actual conduits of the hospitality so blithely offered by their male relatives.

No matter how trying Sūrya may seem in this story, he pales in comparison with both Durvāsas and Cyavana, who have all of Sūrya's bad habits and more. Indeed Cyavana comes to stay with Kuśika because he wishes to destroy Kuśika's family (XIII.52.9), though he simply announces to Kuśika that a desire to visit has come over him (XIII.52.10 vastum icchā samutpannā tvayā saha mamānagha). Kṛṣṇa, on the other hand, should have known what he was getting into, since Durvāsas traveled about the country demanding hospitality in a most unpleasant fashion:

MBh XIII.144.13 sa sma saṃcarate lokān ye divyā ye ca mānuṣāḥ
imā gāthā gāyamānaś catvareṣu sabhāsu ca
14 durvāsasaṃ vāsayet ko brāhmaṇaṃ satkṛtaṃ gṛhe
paribhāṣāṃ ca me śrutvā ko nu dadyāt pratiśrayam
yo māṃ kaś cid vāsayeta na sa māṃ kopayed iha

13 He wandered about the worlds, both divine and human,
singing these Gāthās in squares and assemblies:
14 "Who would have the Brahman Durvāsas to stay, properly honored, in his house?
Who having heard my speech would give me shelter?
Whoever would have me stay had better not anger me!"

Despite this unappealing self-invitation, Kṛṣṇa takes him in.

Both Cyavana and Durvāsas display the same unpredictability about meals and entrances and exits as Sūrya. Here, for example, is Durvāsas:

MBh XIII.144.16 sa sma bhuṅkte sahasrāṇāṃ bahūnām annam ekadā
ekadā smālpakaṃ bhuṅkte na vaiti ca punar gṛhān

Sometimes he ate the food of many thousands.
Sometimes he ate very little. (Sometimes) he did not come home at all.

Cyavana requires that Kuśika and his wife be ready to massage his feet and that they keep vigil while he sleeps; then he proceeds to sleep for twenty-one days, while the householders, fasting, watch over him (XIII.52.31–35). Afterwards he leaves the house without speaking, attended by the famished pair, and magically disappears (36–39); when the despondent couple return to their house they find him asleep in his bed (XIII.53.4). There is another vigil and a bath, before which the two anoint him with oil (5–12).

The climax of this part of the story is Cyavana's abuse of the food provided him—food, as we have seen, is often a focus in hospitality tales. The feast is elaborately described in four ślokas (16–19) and includes not only various meats and vegetables, but also condiments, light drinks, sweets, cakes, and exotic fruits and nuts. All of this food, plus his bed and seat, as well as the serving utensils, Cyavana covers with his cloak and incinerates:

MBh XIII.53.20 tataḥ sarvaṃ samānīya tac ca śayyāsanaṃ muniḥ
21 vastraiḥ śubhair avacchādya bhojanopaskaraiḥ saha
sarvam ādīpayām āsa cyavano bhṛgunandanaḥ

Then the ascetic, assembling all (the food), and the bed and seat,
along with the serving utensils, covering (them) with his bright garments,
Cyavana, delight of the Bhṛgus, set it all on fire.

Durvāsas engages in similar pyromania:

MBh XIII.144.18 so 'smadāvasathaṃ gatvā śayyāś cāstaraṇāni ca
kanyāś cālaṃkṛtā dagdhvā

Having come to our dwelling, having burned the beds and bedcovers and the well-adorned maidens (!)[16] . . .

He also, like Cyavana, wastes the food he demands, though in a novel fashion. Having asked for rice milk and been supplied with it, he addresses Kṛṣṇa:

MBh XIII.144.21 kṣipram aṅgāni limpasva pāyaseneti . . .

Quickly smear your limbs with rice milk.

The unflappable host complies, and his wife is forced into the same condition:

MBh XIII.144.22 avimṛśyaiva ca tataḥ kṛtavān asmi tat tathā
tenocchiṣṭena gātrāṇi śiraś caivābhyamṛkṣayam
23 sa dadarśa tadābhyāśe mātaraṃ te śubhānanām
tām api smayamānaḥ sa pāyasenābhyalepayat

Without hesitation I [Kṛṣṇa] did that then.
I wiped my limbs and head with the remainder.[17]
He then saw nearby your lovely faced mother[18] [Rukmiṇī].
Smiling at her he had her smeared with rice milk.[19]

Both these stories end in the same way, with a dramatic display of the utter degradation of the host. The visitor has one or both of the householding pair yoked to their own chariot and forces them to draw him along the highway in full view of their own subjects. In the Cyavana story the husband and wife are yokemates:[20]

MBh XIII.53.31 tataḥ sa taṃ tathety uktvā kalpayitvā mahāratham
bhāryāṃ vāme dhuri tadā cātmānaṃ dakṣiṇe tadā

Then having said yes to him, having had the great chariot prepared,
my wife at the left shaft, myself at the right . . .

Kuśika remains obedient and obliging, though Cyavana clearly wants the ordeal to be as humiliating as possible:

MBh XIII.53.33 bhagavan kva ratho yātu bravītu bhṛgunandanaḥ
yatra vakṣyasi viprarṣe tatra yāsyati te rathaḥ
34 evam uktas tu bhagavān pratyuvācātha taṃ nṛpam
itaḥprabhṛti yātavyaṃ padakaṃ padakaṃ śanaiḥ
35 śramo mama yathā na syāt tathā me chandacāriṇau
sukhaṃ caivāsmi voḍhavyo janaḥ sarvaś ca paśyatu

33 [Kuśika:] "Sir, where shall your chariot drive? Let the delight of the Bhṛgus speak.
Wherever you say, o priestly sage, there your chariot will drive."
34 Thus addressed, the lord then replied to the king,
"Starting from here it should be driven, little step by little step, very gently.

35 (You two are to) comply with my wishes, so that there will be no trouble for me.
I am to be conveyed pleasantly, and all the people should watch."

As they pull him along, Cyavana sets about giving away all of Kuśika's riches to Brahmans along the road (vss. 36–39), at the same time beating the miserable pair with a sharp-tipped goad (tīkṣṇāgreṇa . . pratodena, vs. 41). They are a sight of extreme pathos:

MBh XIII.53.42 vepamānau nirāhārau pañcāśadrātrakarśitau
kathaṃ cid ūhatur vīrau daṃpatī taṃ rathottamam

Trembling, without food, emaciated by fifty-nights' (fast),
somehow the heroic household pair drew the best of chariots.

In the story of Durvāsas only one of the couple is yoked to the chariot, namely Rukmiṇī, Kṛṣṇa's wife—still dripping with porridge.

MBh XIII.144.24 muniḥ pāyasadigdhāṅgīṃ rathe tūrṇam ayojayat
tam āruhya rathaṃ caiva niryayau sa gṛhān mama
25 . . . pratodenātudad bālāṃ rukmiṇīṃ mama paśyataḥ

The ascetic had her, her limbs smeared with rice milk, yoked quickly to a chariot.
Having mounted the chariot, he drove forth from my house.
He struck the girl Rukmiṇī with a goad, while I watched.

In both cases the hosts have reached the lowest possible point, subjected to a very public, almost symbolic act of humiliation. Their re-elevation happens quickly in both stories. The guest is pleased by their stoic obedience and their lack of anger, and he heals and blesses them and restores their property.

The similarity of these stories to the Manu story is striking. The host's duty of unfailing generosity to a visitor is not limited to the usual food and other accoutrements, but extends to the ceding of control over the persons of the hosting family. Like Manu, Kuśika and Kṛṣṇa and their wives first give their possessions, but when this is not enough, they risk their lives at the abrupt demand of their guests. The Kṛṣṇa-Durvāsas story is especially interesting because—as in Manu's Cups, as in the Oghavatī story—it is only the *wife* Rukmiṇī who is in physical pain and danger, while her husband watches helplessly. The *yoking* of Rukmiṇī resembles the *binding* of Manu's wife prior to sacrifice, and the ascetic's smearing of Rukmiṇī with rice milk seems a ritual, almost sacrificial act, as if a preparation of the woman as an oblation.

One final tale brings us all the way to the ordered killing of a member of the host's family, the story of Śibi and his son (not included in the Critical Edition; B III.198 = CE III, Appendix I 21.6.136ff.). A Brahman comes to Śibi in search of food and orders Śibi to prepare, cook, and serve his son Bṛhadgarbha as his meal. (Again note that the issue is food.) He agrees and sets about doing it, while the Brahman occupies the preparation time by burning down Śibi's house and all its outbuildings. When Śibi finally catches up with him,

Śibi merely says (145) siddhaṃ bhagavann annam iti "Your food is ready, sir." But the Brahman refuses it and orders Śibi to eat instead (148 tvam evaitad aśāneti)—in other words to eat his own son, whom he has already cooked for the Brahman's meal. Even then Śibi begins to comply, but the Brahman finally relents, snatches his hand away, and restores the son to life. Again it is Śibi's lack of anger and willingness to obey that impress and please the Brahman.

I have by now examined enough Mahābhārata stories to demonstrate more than amply the value attached to yielding without complaint to any demand of a guest, no matter how bizarre or painful. All the stories have the same basic structure: a visitor behaves outrageously and makes excessive demands, and when the host has sufficiently demonstrated that he can be pushed much further than seems fair, the visitor reveals himself as a divine figure, often Dharma, and rewards the compliant host.

The disguised divinity of the guests in these stories is a crucial feature. There is more of an incentive to practice unquestioning hospitality if every guest, especially the more trying among them, may actually be a god in disguise—as no doubt the Visiting Brahman lobby was well aware.

The uncertainty about the real identity of a guest is reflected in other texts as well, though in the opposite direction, as it were. If a guest passes himself off as someone grander than he actually is, the host still receives the merit of having given to an especially worthy person, if he is unaware of the imposture:

> ĀpDS II.7.17 asamudetaś ced atithir bruvāna āgacched āsanam udakam annaṁ śrotriyāya dadāmīty eva dadyāt / evam asya samṛddhaṃ bhavati
>
> If someone not entirely exalted should come calling himself a guest, (the host) should give the seat, water, food, (thinking) "I am giving to a learned Brahman." Thus (merit) is accrued for him.

(Compare AV XV.13.6–7, which is less generous.)

The identity of a guest is always uncertain: he can be better or worse than he first appears (and sometimes both simultaneously, like the generous gods disguised as abusive Brahmans). The host's merit comes from respecting the hospitality tie itself, regardless of the actual identity of the guest.

C. Manu's Cups Revisited I: The Cow, the Wife, and the Power of the Guest

We have recently been examining epic narratives demonstrating the frightful results of an assertive guest who takes advantage of the latitude to demand that the host must allow him. The extreme exaggeration of these narratives testifies to the deep anxiety that must have characterized the hospitality relation: the stories represent the worst nightmares of a host.[21] But they also provide a happy resolution to these nightmares. Hostly forbearance will bring a divine reward.

That these stories are exaggerations, but not rank inventions of the guest's power over the host seems clear from a ritual reflection of it. There is a ritualized (hence controlled) survival of the guest's power of command embedded in the Arghya ceremony, the reception of especially worthy guests. I have already mentioned several of the elements of this reception, the Arghya water, the Madhuparka mixture, and the cow. Let us now examine the cow in more detail, especially as presented in the gṛhya sūtras. After the valued guest has been made comfortable in the usual way, a cow is announced to him. He holds the power of life or death over her, can either have her killed for a feast or let loose.[22] With a lengthy formulaic response he pronounces his decision. One account follows:

> HirGS I.13.10 athāsmai / gauḥ // iti prāha
> 11 tasyāḥ karmotsargo vā
> 12 gaur dhenur bhavyā / . . . pra ṇu vocaṃ cikituṣe janāya / mā gām anāgām aditiṃ vadhiṣṭa // pibatūdakaṃ tṛṇāny attu // *om utsṛjata // ity utsarge saṃśāsti*
> 13 gaur asy apahatapāpmāpa pāpmānaṃ jahi . . . / *kuruta // iti kriyamāṇāyām*
>
> Then he announces to him [the guest], "Cow!" [In several of the sūtras this is done three times.]
> There is either sacrifice or release of her.
> *In the event of release,* (having said) "This cow is to be a milch-cow." "I announce this to people who understand, 'Do not kill this sinless cow, (who is) Aditi.'" [= RV VIII.101.15] "Let her drink water. Let her eat grass," (the guest) *orders,* " . . . *Om, Let loose!*"
> *In the event of her being 'prepared'* [killed], (having said) "You are a cow whose evil has been smashed away. Smash away (my) evil . . . ," (*he orders*) " . . . *Prepare!*"[23]

The guest is directly involved in the slaughter. In light of this, we might examine the word go-ghna, lit. 'cow-killing', when used to designate a guest. Pāṇini III.4.73 must treat this word as a semantic or functional exception, with 'datival' rather than agentive value. He thus interprets the word as denoting 'one *for whom* a cow is killed'.

> Pāṇ. III.4.73 dāśa*goghnau* saṃpradāne
> (The words) dāśa (and) *goghna* (are) in datival (function).

But I would suggest that the word was regularly *formed*, just like the feminine asura-ghnī- 'Asura-killing' at the beginning of the Manu story—that the guest was really considered a cow-killer. Though he does not wield the knife, he gives the order, and that is what usually counts. Later the term was reinterpreted and rid of its rather shocking cultural implications, at the cost of substituting grammatical ones.

For our purposes what is most remarkable about this feature of the Arghya reception is that it reminds us uncannily of Indra's command at the end of the

Manu story in the MS. After Indra has eliminated the two Asuric Brahmans, thereby preventing them from sacrificing Manu's wife, the unfortunate woman still remains bound to the stake, as it were. Manu, displaying ritualistic rather than uxorious fervor, asks Indra to complete the worship anyway, so as to avoid bad effects. But Indra promises there will be no bad result from non-completion, and in his role as "good guest," grandly orders the release of Manu's wife, with the same lexeme (ut √sṛj) as is used for the release of the cow in the gṛhya sūtras:

> MS IV.8.1 (108: 2) sò 'bravīd yátkāma etā́m ā́labdhāḥ sá te kā́maḥ sámṛdhyatām áth*ótsṛjé*ti tā́ṁ vā́ údasṛjat
>
> He said, "Whatever you desired in binding her for worship, let that wish be fulfilled. But *set her free.*" He set her free.

This final act of the Manu's Cups narratives has its analogue not only in the gṛhya ritual just described, but also in one additional episode in śrauta ritual, which matches the tale of Manu's Cups so exactly that the ritual and the myth may not be independent. Indeed in the Brāhmaṇas of the BYV, Manu's Cups serves as the foundation myth for this ritual. This is the so-called Pātnīvatapaśu, the 'animal (victim) for (Tvaṣṭar) with the wives (of the gods)', an optional animal sacrifice often incorporated into the very end of the Soma Sacrifice as a part of the sacrifice of eleven other victims.[24] We have, of course, met 'Tvaṣṭar and the wives of the gods' before—in the identically named Pātnīvata *cup* at the end of the Third Pressing, as well as at the Patnīsaṃyāja oblations at the end of the model Iṣṭi, where Tvaṣṭar is a prominent figure.

In the Pātnīvatapaśu a stunted[25] sacrificial post (yūpa) is erected in front of the Gārhapatya,[26] the wife's realm—in ordinary animal sacrifices the yūpa is placed in front of the Āhavanīya in the east. To it an uncastrated[27] male animal is bound, but after the fire-circuit (paryagnikaraṇa) has been performed, the animal is released, with the same lexeme (ut √sṛj) as is used for the wife in Manu's Cups and the cow in the Arghya reception. Compare one account of this:

> BŚS XVII.15 (296: 5) agreṇa gārhapatyaṃ pātnīvatam ucchritya tasmiṁs tvāṣṭraṁ sāṇḍam ajaṃ paśum upākaroti taṃ paryagnikṛtam utsṛjyājyena saṁsthāṃ karoti
>
> Having erected the (yūpa) for '(Tvaṣṭar) with the wives' in front of the Gārhapatya, he attaches to it a be-testicled goat (as) animal victim for Tvaṣṭar. He releases it after the fire-circuit has been made and finishes the ritual with ghee.

The ritual is a mirror image of the myth. There a *female* (Manu's wife) was bound for sacrifice and released at the last moment not merely by a male, but by Indra, the most virile of the gods. Here a pointedly *male* victim is bound for sacrifice in the *female* realm and again released just in time. Though the ultimate agent of its release is not specified (the immediate agent is, of course, a priest), the presence of the yūpa in the wife's area might suggest that the release is due to female influence: she has the choice of continuing the sacrifice or not.

This suggestion is strengthened by a fragment of a myth found in the TS:[28]

> TS VI.5.8.4–5 devā́ vái tvā́ṣṭāram ajighām̐sant sá pátnīḥ prā́padyata tā́ṃ ná práti prā́yachan tásmād ápi // vádhyam prápannam ná práti práyachanti
>
> The gods wished to kill Tvaṣṭar. He took refuge with the wives. They did not hand him over. Therefore, (people) do not hand over even one worthy of killing who has come for refuge.

Again the story concerns a type of "guest," a fugitive to whom the host offers sanctuary. The hosts in the myth are wives, just as the "host" of the animal victim in the Pātnīvata sacrifice is the wife in front of whose fire the victim is tethered. By implication this wife is the real releaser of the victim in the Pātnīvata sacrifice, and she therefore also wields the power of life and death (however attenuated that power may seem in this case) in the same way that Indra exercises the power over *her* life in the Manu's Cups story. The exchange of hospitality roles also reflects the mirror image quality of the two episodes: in Manu's Cups Indra the *guest* is the agent of release, while in the Pātnīvata-paśu ritual (and associated mythic fragment) it is the *host*. The ascription of power to the (female) host may function somewhat like the cheerful denouements of the epic Exploited Host stories—to give the host some hope in what seems like a thankless role.

Let us look at the śrauta ritual more generally. Now that we have situated the wife as sacrificial victim in the Manu's Cups story within a context of hospitality and exchange relations (derived in part from examination of gṛhya and dharma texts), we have a model with which to reevaluate certain elements of the solemn ritual, some episodes involving the Sacrificer's Wife in the śrauta ritual, which we have examined previously.

Recall the various mediations and exchanges the wife performs in ritual. She and the Soma-buying cow symbolically trade identities: when the Sacrificer "marries" the Soma-cow, the wife receives the cow's footprint from the marital "seventh step," and the wife and the cow exchange glances. The cow is then used to purchase the soma, who is both honored guest and, ultimately, sacrificial substance. By this chain of superimpositions,

> wife → cow → victim [/soma].

In a number of other rituals involving animal sacrifices, the wife is brought into physical contact with the victim: she bathes the limbs of the dead animal in the ordinary Animal Sacrifice (Paśubandha); the queens prepare the paths for the knives to cut up the victim in the Aśvamedha; and, most dramatically, in the same ritual the chief queen mimics sex with the dead horse before it is cut up. Again the wife can be equated with the victim: she stands for the victim in the human realm.

In this ritual material, however, the exchange between wife and victim is carried through only partially and symbolically, by superimposing an expendable object (in each case an animal) over the wife. She is implicitly homologized to the victim, but she always remains at least one step away. But the myth of Manu's Cups carries this notion to its logical extreme. The demon-killing voice, that undestroyable force, exchanges its way through various items, the cups and the bull, until it lodges in the wife, who is then bound up as real sacrificial victim. The myth tears away the ritual screen, which shielded us (and the wife) from the brutal starkness of the *identity of wife and victim.*[29]

The myth also lays bare the mechanism responsible for this identity. It is hospitality relations that shape the plot. When strangers and guests ask Manu for something, he must respond, and his wife is thus a hostage, almost slaughtered, to his role as unstinting host. He cedes control to his visitors. The same mechanisms are at work in the śrauta ritual, but again somewhat hidden. As has often been pointed out, the clear model for the structure of śrauta ritual is the hospitable reception of guests: the gods come to the ritual ground, are offered a meal and entertained, and sent off at the end well-fed.[30] We have examined some of the clear elements of guest reception and the wife's participation in them, especially the guest reception of soma (Ātithya) and the Foot-washing water for the gods. The homologies between guest reception and solemn ritual are paraded at great length and quite explicitly in AV IX.6, Whitney's "Exalting the entertainment of guests." Each element of hospitality, down to the fetching of mattress and pillow (vs. 10), is equated with a particular set part of the śrauta ritual, as this introductory generalization makes clear:

> AV IX.6.3 yád vā́ átithipatir[31] átithīn pratipáśyati devayájanaṃ prékṣate
>
> When the lord of guests [host] looks on his guests, he sees a place of worship to the gods.

A similar set of elaborate parallels is found in ĀpDS II.7.1–10.

But the potential violence always inherent in the hospitality relation is also perceptible in śrauta ritual, albeit dimly. King Soma, the guest so hospitably received, is symbolically slaughtered; the animal victims are also addressed as if they were guests, after their deaths (see earlier discussion)—such are the anxieties of the guest. And the Sacrificer/host must expend his wealth, by providing all the ritual implements, all the offerings, as well as lavish Dakṣiṇās for the priests. He must kill his livestock, as animal victims in the more elaborate rites. So far, these parallel the first two trials of Manu. And what of his third, the sacrifice of his wife? The Sacrificer in śrauta ritual does not actually have his wife killed, of course. However, not only does the sacrificial victim stand in for her in some fashion, as we just discussed, but the last major act of the Soma Sacrifice—the Pātnīvata cup and the business with the Foot-washing waters—makes it clear that the wife is symbolically a sexual offering to the gods. When she pours the Foot-washing waters associated with divine guest reception over her thigh in a sexually charged setting, she is offered as a sexual token to the visiting gods just as surely as Oghavatī was to her Brahman houseguest.

The lessons of this: Ritual and hospitality cannot be separated. Moreover, the wife functions as central figure in both, as mediator and symbolic offering. And further, these roles of hers are inextricably connected with her sexuality.

The connections so described seem to lead, bleakly and inescapably, to her final role as victim, symbolic or real. Fortunately this result can be averted, but only through the good will of the other participants, which cannot always be counted upon. Again, the Manu's Cups story makes the covert explicit. Just as hospitality relations get our Pauline perilously tied to the stake, they also work to free her. When the god Indra comes as stranger and guest, the protocol of guest reception affords the escape mechanism, enables him to free Manu's wife without violating the system (and without Manu's help). When Indra sees Manu's wife tied to the ritual victim's post like a sacrificial animal, he orders "Set her free," with exactly the phrase a guest would use for the hostly cow in the Arghya guest reception. He thus uses *hospitality* machinery to avoid a *ritual* sacrifice, which had been set in motion by the last set of *guests*. (He also disposes of these demonic priests with a sophistic use of the same hospitality machinery.)

Manu's Cups thus dramatizes the risk inherent not only in hospitality but in ritual performance. Every relationship established between strangers, whether mortal or immortal, creates danger at its seams, makes a potentially perilous breach in the magic circle that surrounds oneself and one's household. When we invite the gods to our sacrifice, we must hope that they will be "good guests," that they will accept what we have to give but not ask too much, that they will recognize the appropriate limits on guestly behavior, since we as hosts cannot set those limits.

Heesterman has frequently[32] argued that the Vedic śrauta ritual is a sterile, mechanical enterprise, safe but ultimately unsatisfying because it has lost the agonistic quality he ascribes to it in its origins. But viewed from the perspective of hospitality, the ritual seems anything but safe. When you open your house to gods, you cannot be certain what will happen. The rewards are great but so are the risks, and the often fantastical elaboration of the rites with all the fussy arguments over every detail seems an attempt to keep the party from getting out of hand. You cannot call the cops when it is immortals who are tearing up the furniture.

D. Manu's Cups Revisited II: The Vocabulary of Hospitality

I have, in the last few sections, teased out the implications of the brief and initially enigmatic Manu's Cups story by reference to the much more expansive and much more explicit treatments of hospitality in both epic narrative literature and prescriptive ritual and legal texts. In other words I have sought similar themes and narrative patterns. But there is another way to figure out Manu's Cups—in fact the method I employed when I first embarked on my study of the story—through close attention to vocabulary and to the rhetorical or linguistic structure of the narrative. In this very compressed story, several key terms signal themes in a remarkably economical way, themes which must be presented much more verbosely in similar narratives in the Mahābhārata.

The condensed verbal style of the early Vedic mythological texts relies heavily on the impact of individual words and phrases, which evoke entire semantic complexes in the attentive audience. The epic style is more leisurely and exuberant, and its scale is too large to be able to deploy single words quite as tellingly as in the lapidary style of early Vedic. As latter-day interpreters, we must attempt to develop a sense for the kind of verbal effects a text may strive for. The difference between Vedic and epic styles is at least comparable to that between Pindar and Homer, or perhaps Wallace Stevens and Walt Whitman.

The following sections are intended partly as a methodological demonstration, to show how sensitivity to linguistic usage can be a sufficient interpretive strategy in confronting a difficult text. The vocabulary studies that follow should also establish the complex semantic parameters of the lexical field relating to hospitality and change the commonly accepted interpretation of some crucial terms.

Let me begin with the first question about the Manu's Cups story that I formulated long ago: why does Manu immediately accede to the demands of the strangers to hand over his possessions and finally his wife?[33] We have long since decided that his role as host forced him to agree to his guests' demands. But how is the importance of the hospitality relation established within this short narrative? There is no quoting of dharmic maxims, no explicit and sententious pedagogy—merely dialogue and action. But within this dialogue there are verbal clues. In all three versions the two Asuras approach him with elaborate and formulaically repeated requests. The relevant passages follow; in none of them does Manu hesitate or question the request.

> MS IV.8.1 (106: 8) tā́ abrūtāṃ máno yájvā vái śraddhā́devo 'sīmā́ni nau pā́trāṇi dehī́ti tā́ni vā́ ābhyām adadāt
> . . . tā́ abrūtāṃ máno yájvā vái śraddhā́devo 'sy anéna tva [*sic*] ṛṣabhéṇa yājayāvéti téna vā́ enam ayājayatām
> . . . tā́ abrūtāṃ máno yájvā vái śraddhā́devo 'sy anáyā tvā pátnyā yājayāvéti
>
> The two (Asuric Brahmans) said, "Manu, you are a worshiper with Śraddhā as your deity. Give us these cups." He gave them to the two. . . .
> . . . They two said, "Manu, you are a worshiper with Śraddhā as your deity. We will perform worship for you with this bull." With it they performed worship for him. . . .
> . . . They two said, "Manu, you are a worshiper with Śraddhā as your deity. We will perform worship for you with this wife."

> KS XXX.1 (181: 7) tā asurā abruvann imāni manukapālāni yācethām iti tau prātaritvānā abhiprāpadyetāṃ vāyave 'gnā3i vāyava indrā3 iti kiṃkāmau stha ity abravīd imāni nau kapālāni dehīti tāny ābhyām adadāt
> . . . tau prātaritvānā abhiprāpadyetāṃ vāyave 'gnā3i vāyava indrā3 iti kiṃkāmau stha ity abravīd anena tvarṣabheṇa yājayāveti

. . . tau prātaritvānā abhiprāpadyetāṃ vāyave 'gnā3i vāyava indrā3 iti kiṃkāmau stha ity abravīd anayā tvā patnyā yājayāveti

The Asuras said to these two (Asuric Brahmans). "Beg these cups of Manu." The two approached (as) Prātaritvans, (saying) "Ahoy Agni, for Vāyu; ahoy Indra, for Vāyu." (Manu) said, "What do you want?" "Give us these cups." He gave them to the two.

. . . The two approached (as) Prātaritvans, (saying) "Ahoy Agni, for Vāyu; ahoy Indra, for Vāyu." (Manu) said, "What do you want?" "We will perform worship for you with this bull." [And they did.]

. . . The two approached (as) Prātaritvans, (saying) "Ahoy Agni, for Vāyu; ahoy Indra, for Vāyu." (Manu) said, "What do you want?" "We will perform worship for you with this wife."

ŚB I.1.4.15 táu hocatuḥ / śraddhā́devo vái mánur āváṃ nú vedāvéti táu hāgátyocatur máno yājáyāva tvéti kénéty anénarṣabhéṇéti táthéti . . .

.16 . . . kilātākulī́ haivócatuḥ śraddhā́devo vái mánur āváṃ nv èvá vedāvéti táu hāgátyocatur máno yājáyāva tvéti kénéty anáyaivá jāyáyéti táthéti

These two (Asuric Brahmans) said, "Manu has Śraddhā as his deity (they say). Let's go find out." They went and said, "Manu, we will perform worship for you." "With what?" "With this bull." "OK."

(The Asuric Brahmans) Kilāta and Ākuli said, "Manu has Śraddhā as his deity (they say). Let's go find out." They went and said, "Manu, we will perform worship for you." "With what?" "With this wife." "OK."

The special relationship that exists between Manu and the two strangers, the relationship that forces Manu to act as he does, is signaled by salient vocabulary. In the KS passage the two Asuras are called prātaritvan, literally 'coming or going in the early morning', and they are urged to yāc 'ask for, beg' the cups. In all three passages Manu bears the epithet śraddhā́deva 'having Śraddhā as his deity'.[34] I will now examine each of these loaded words, beginning with the last, which contains the much misunderstood term śraddhā́.

1. *Śraddhā*

Manu's epithet śraddhā́deva 'having Śraddhā as his deity' seems the verbal 'open sesame' that compels Manu to give in the MS and ŚB.[35] In the MS the Asuric Brahmans formulaically address Manu before each request with máno yájvā vái śraddhā́devo 'si ("Manu, you are a worshiper with Śraddhā as your deity."). This appears to be almost like a charm or magic word to compel him to act according to the canons of śraddhā́. The ŚB is perhaps even more telling; the Asuric Brahmans address each other with ŚB I.1.4.15 śraddhā́devo vái mánur āváṃ nú vedāva ("Manu is [supposed to be] one with Śraddhā as his deity. Let's find out.") and then go and make their requests. Since Manu is truly śraddhā́deva, he must grant the requests. This particular term seems to trigger the host's obligation to grant the wishes of his guest.

This characteristic of Manu seems to have been proverbial, as he also appears in the Mahābhārata with the epithet śrāddhadeva (MBh XII.122.39).

Moreover, Manu's father Vivasvant is given the same epithet in the story of his failed birth as Mārtaṇḍa (MBh XII.329.44). Though this story is familiar from other sources, dating back to the RV,[36] the short prose MBh version introduces a few novel features. The goddess Aditi is cooking food for the gods, to strengthen them to smash the Asuras. Budha (the planet Mercury) comes to her while she is thus engaged and begs some of the food, a request she refuses:

> MBh XII.329.44 (3) aditiṃ cāvocad bhikṣāṃ dehīti
> (4) tatra devaiḥ pūrvam etat prāśyaṃ nānyenety aditir bhikṣāṃ nādāt
> He said to Aditi, "Give me alms."
> Aditi, (thinking) "This is to be eaten first by the gods, not by another," did not give alms.

The rejected visitor curses Aditi (in a sentence omitted from the CE),

> MBh XII.876* aditiḥ śaptā aditer udare bhaviṣyati vyathā
> Aditi was cursed: "There will be a pain in the belly of Aditi."

and the egg containing Vivasvant is killed (aṇḍam māritam [5]) by Budha.

> XII.329.44 (6) sa mārtaṇḍa vivasvān abhavac *chrāddhadevaḥ*
> He became Mārtaṇḍa ['stemming from a dead egg'] Vivasvant *Śrāddhadeva*.

This seems a purposely ironic detail. The birth of Vivasvant, Manu's father, was botched because of his mother's *violation of hospitality*. Manu himself in the Vedic prose story is a helpless dispenser of *automatic hospitality*. He must embody excessively the quality whose lack doomed his father's development. The word that links these stories is śraddhādeva/śrāddhadeva.

Śraddhā seems to express obligations in the realms both of hospitality and of ritual, in addition to those conceptual values ordinarily ascribed to it. The word śraddhā́ is a charged one in the ancient Indian religious tradition. Ordinarily rendered 'trust, confidence' or, less happily, 'faith', it often expresses the trust a worshiper has in the gods and in the efficacy of the ritual. There is no doubt that śraddhā́ and its associated verb śrád-dadhāti express such a meaning from the beginning of the Vedic period (and indeed from Indo-European times, given their cognates in Avestan zraz-dā, Latin crēdō, Old Irish cretid), as shown in the following AV passage expressing an intellectual belief in the existence of the gods:

> AV XI.2.28 yáḥ śraddádhāti sánti devā́ íti
> Who trusts/believes, "The gods exist."

But, as has long been recognized,[37] this intellectual trust in the efficacy of the worship has concrete manifestations, especially in generosity, gift-giving in ritual context, Köhler's 'Spendefreudigkeit' ('joy in [ritual] giving'), and is especially closely allied with the Dakṣiṇā or 'priestly gift' that the Sacrificer presents to the officiating priests.

The elegant little work of Köhler's on this word has clearly shown how 'trust' first in the gods and then in the power of the ritual gets expressed by frequent and lavish ritual performances *and* by munificent presents to the human performers of the rituals. The development from 'trust' to Köhler's 'Spendefreudigkeit' is thus less bizarre than might first appear. In this sense, in our story Manu has Śraddhā as his deity because he sacrifices without stint. He is, according to Köhler, "der Held der Opferfreudigkeit," "the hero of joy in offering."[38]

But Thieme suggested long ago (1938, p. 39) another use of śraddhā́—a suggestion that to my knowledge he never expanded upon—namely that the idiom expresses the *trust* or *agreement* between *strangers* in a *hospitality relation*, particularly (I would add) strangers belonging to the Aryan community—the guest trusted not to disturb the peace of the household, the host not to harm the guest.[39] Under this interpretation, śraddhā́ may refer to the host's obligation to provide for his guests' needs and desires, and Manu would hand over his possessions because his trust in hospitality relations compelled him to.

There is additional evidence in the texts for śraddhā́ in the sphere of hospitality. Although *giving* under obligations of hospitality may sometimes be difficult to separate from *giving* under ritual obligations, a number of passages can be identified in which there is no formal *ritual* context, but only one of guest/host relations. Let us begin with a passage from the Chāndogya Upaniṣad, also perhaps containing the term śraddhādeva. Here the context is unambiguously one of dispensing hospitality.

> ChU IV.1.1 jānaśrutir ha pautrayāṇaḥ śraddhādevo [corrected from śraddhādeyo by e.g. Böhtlingk, Senart] bahudāyī bahupākya āsa / sa ha sarvata āvasathān māpayāṃ cakre sarvata eva me 'tsyantīti
>
> Jānaśruti Pautrayāna was (one) having Śraddhā as his deity, giving much, having much cooked (food). He had lodging places built everywhere, (thinking) "Everywhere (people) will eat my (food)."

The Mahābhārata similarly contains numerous passages in which śraddhā is associated with the giving of hospitality or dispensing of food, in addition to the striking story of Vivasvant's birth just related. Let us examine two in which the hospitality context is especially clear. First, in the Fifth Book in the torrent of proverbial wisdom that Vidura pours out upon the insomniac Dhṛtarāṣṭra, we find one of the common clichés treating hospitality, a gnomic śloka that pops up with some regularity in Sanskrit literature—most English-speaking Sanskritists probably first make its acquaintance in one of the selections from the Hitopadeśa in Lanman's Sanskrit Reader.

> MBh V.36.32[40] tṛṇāni bhūmir udakaṃ vāk caturthī ca sūnṛtā
> satām etāni gṛheṣu noccidhyante kadā cana

Grass, (a place on) the ground, water, and (as) the fourth, pleasant speech.
These never lack in the houses of the good.

An aside about this passage: it appears to be a versification of two sūtras in the Gautama Dharma Sūtra, one of the oldest, if not the oldest of the extant dharma texts, but in GDS it is the minimal hospitality offered to a viparīta, either 'one who acts perversely' or 'one who is contrary (to those previously mentioned, namely, honored guests)'.

GDS V.35 viparīte tu tṛṇodakabhūmi
36 svāgatam antataḥ

But for the contrary/perverse (just) grass, water, ground, and lastly a welcome.

It is perhaps a sign of the gradual lowering of hospitality requirements that this maxim is quoted so often in later literature as an expression of the greatest hostly generosity! It has undergone a sort of hospitality grade inflation.

In any case, what interests us about the MBh passage is the verse that immediately follows:

MBh V.36.33 *śraddhayā parayā* rājann upanītāni satkṛtim
pravṛttāni mahāprājña dharmiṇāṃ puṇyakarmaṇām

According to the highest śraddhā, o king, (these) are presented as producing hospitality (satkṛti)
by those who possess dharma and meritorious actions, o very wise one.

The phrase śraddhayā parayā is translated by van Buitenen "with total faith," but this makes no sense in context. Nor in this nonritual context can we see Köhler's 'joy in ritual offering'. The context here is only and entirely that of ordinary hospitality, and śraddhayā parayā must mean "in accordance with the highest canons/practices of hospitality."

This small point in Vidura's sententious outpourings is confirmed by a more leisurely and discursive passage in the Third Book of the MBh, in the story of Mudgala, who is presented as the very type of virtuous giver (MBh III.246). Indeed Mudgala seems as put upon by guests as Manu is, and his patience with them comes from the same source: śraddhā.

Mudgala, a man of the usual virtues, himself lives only on rice, but is celebrated for his generosity in giving food to Brahmans. He is in fact described (twice in the twenty-verse story) as atithivratī (III.246.4, 15), literally 'observing a vow with regard to guests'. He regularly feeds hundreds of Brahmans at his twice-monthly New and Full Moon Sacrifices, but his food miraculously increases to meet the demand, because of his virtue. Once a particular ascetic, Durvāsas, whom we have met before, comes to one of these celebrations, abusively and rather madly demands food, eats it all, smears the leftovers on his body, and goes away. This happens at six successive sacrifices, but Mudgala cheerfully and unstintingly keeps providing Durvāsas food, though he himself goes without. Finally, after this test, Durvāsas praises Mudgala for his generosity, and Mudgala gets a divine reward, in the fashion of the usual denouement of Exploited Host stories.

The crucial point for us is how Mudgala's action is described when he first gives food to Durvāsas:

MBh III.246.15 prādāt sa tapasopāttaṃ kṣudhitāyā *tithivratī*
unmattāya *parāṃ śraddhāṃ* āsthāya sa dhṛtavrataḥ

He gave (the food) gained by (his own) austerity to the hungry, maniacal (Durvāsas)—he [Mudgala] *observing a vow with regard to guests* and being firm in his vows, practicing *the highest śraddhā*.

Van Buitenen translates "gave the . . . food . . . to . . . the madman *whom he trusted completely*," but there is no question of trusting the guest here. Mudgala is constrained by his atithi-vrata, his 'vow about guests', to practice hospitality no matter what the cost to himself. He is in exactly the same position as Manu, who surrenders his most precious possessions without complaint at the abrupt demands of strange Brahmans. Manu is śraddhādeva 'having Śraddhā as his deity'; Mudgala practices parā śraddhā 'highest śraddhā'. Śraddhā in these contexts can hardly be anything but the expression of extraordinary hospitality.

Similarly, in the Nakulākhyāna, which we have already examined, the extreme generosity of the hungry family to their guest (atithi) is several times characterized as resulting from śraddhā: they are śraddhādamasamanvita 'filled with the discipline of śraddhā' (XIV.93.12) and practice śraddhā parā 'highest śraddhā' (vss. 63, 68); their gifts are śraddhāpūta 'purified by śraddhā' (vs. 73).

Another likely passage in the MBh comes from the Nala episode. When Nala first appears in Damayantī's chambers, she says to him

MBh III.53.1 praṇayasva *yathāśraddhaṃ* rājan kiṃ karavāṇi te

and then offers herself and all her possessions to Nala. Van Buitenen translates "show your feelings in all good faith," whereas Köhler (p. 6) wants to see here an instance of śraddhā 'desire': "nach (Herzens-)Lust." But Damayantī's question kiṃ karavāṇi te is the standard opening in the hospitality ceremony, as we have seen, and the passage should be rendered: "manifest (your needs/wants) according to hospitality procedure; o king, what shall I do for you?"

Yet another clear hospitality context occurs in a passage relegated to an Appendix in the CE:

MBh XIV, App. I, No. 4.1020: sarvātithyaṃ ca yaḥ kuryād *yathāśraddhaṃ* nareśvara

And who would perform every attention to his guest *according to hospitality*, o king . . .

If śraddhā can mean 'hospitality', this can explain the derivation of a word referring to an important cultural institution, namely the Śrāddha ceremony, the (usually) monthly offering to the ancestors (Pitṛs) elaborately described in the gṛhya and dharma texts, as well as in the MBh.[41] The name of this ceremony is usually explained as somehow connected with the offerer's *faith* in the Brahmans or in the ritual's efficacy,[42] but this seems a convoluted way to derive this term, especially when one reads the descriptions of the rite. For by far the greater part of the treatments of this ceremony, particularly in dharma and epic texts, concerns *not* the actual offerings to the Pitṛs, but rather the meal offered to the attending Brahmans.[43] The Śrāddha ceremony consists in essence of inviting a group of Brahmans to dinner, of offering them hospitality; this is what distinguishes it from the śrauta equivalent, the Piṇḍapitṛyajña ceremony (as Köhler saw). So a direct derivation of the term as meaning 'related to hospitality' seems a better path than connecting it with some putative 'faith'.

The close association between hospitality and the Śrāddha ceremony is shown clearly in the visit of Utaṅka to King Pauṣya, which degenerates into a cursing match, as we saw earlier. Utaṅka, having accomplished his business with Pauṣya's wife (which we will examine shortly), presents himself to Pauṣya, who exclaims

> MBh I.3.123 bhagavaṃś cirasya pātram āsādyate / bhavāṃś ca guṇavān atithiḥ / tat kariṣye śrāddham
>
> Sir, after a long time a worthy vessel is met with. Your worship is a quality guest. So I will perform Śrāddha.

The unexpected guest is here the only trigger necessary for the Śrāddha feast; there is no mention of the ancestors, and Utaṅka in his rather ungracious acceptance of the offered Śrāddha only mentions food, which he wants offered as soon as possible:

> MBh I.3.124 kṛtakṣaṇa evāsmi / śīghram icchāmi yathopapannam annam upahṛtaṃ bhavateti
>
> I am in a hurry. I want food brought by you quickly, whatever is around.

That even the nonterrestrial recipients of the piety of the Śrāddha ceremony considered the feasting the primary purpose of the rite may be shown by a little episode in MBh XIII.92, one of the lengthy passages devoted to the Śrāddha in this text. Here the gods and the Pitṛs get indigestion from the offerings at one of the original Śrāddhas and finally have Agni take part in the meal to help digest the food. Their distress is described thus:

MBh XIII.92.3 nivāpair dīyamānaiś ca cāturvarṇyena bhārata
tarpitāḥ pitaro devās te nānnaṃ jarayanti vai
4 ajīrṇenābhihanyante te devāḥ pitṛbhiḥ saha

By the offerings given by the four varṇas, o Bhārata,
the gods and Pitṛs were satisfied. They could not burn up (/digest) (all) the food.
The gods and Pitṛs were afflicted with indigestion.

The word tarpitāḥ 'made satisfied' recalls the question asked to the invited Brahmans by the host of the Śrāddha ceremony at the close of the meal in the MŚS:

MŚS XI.9.2.9 tṛptāḥ stha [*sic*] iti pṛcchet tṛptāḥ sma iti pratyāhuḥ
"Are you satisfied?" he should ask. "We are satisfied," they should answer.

Both human and nonhuman participants thus feast till satiation.

Let me pick out only two additional aspects of the Śrāddha ceremony relevant to our concerns. At the end of the ceremony, when the well-fed Brahmans are sent home, the host begs this benediction of his ancestors, according to Manu:

MDŚ III.258 visṛjya brāhmaṇāṃs tāṃs tu . . .
. . . yāceteman varān pitṝn
259 dātāro no 'bhivardhantām. . . .
śraddhā ca no mā vyagamad [*sic*] bahu deyaṃ ca no 'stv iti

Having dismissed the Brahmans, he should beg these boons of (his) Pitṛs:
"Let givers increase among us. . . . Let not śraddhā depart from us; let there be much to be given by us."[44]

The significance of this expressed wish is given in a somewhat later verse:

MDŚ III.275 yad yad dadāti vidhivat samyak śraddhāsamanvitaḥ
tat tat pitṝṇāṃ bhavati paratrānantam akṣayam

Whatever one who is filled with śraddhā gives properly, accordingly to rule (in this world),
that becomes in the other world an unending, imperishable (possession?) of the Pitṛs.

The concrete manifestation of śraddhā is *giving* in this world, not 'faith' in the next, and the giving has just been accomplished by feeding the Brahmans.

The other detail in this ceremony of interest to us is the question of *who* is eligible to be invited to the Śrāddha feast. The Brahmans selected should be learned, should not be physically flawed, should not engage in various tainted or declassé practices or occupations, and so on. Indeed the provisions concerning who can and cannot be invited take up a large proportion of the space devoted to the Śrāddha ceremony in a number of texts.[45] This preoccupation with the qualities of the guests is explained by a śloka in Manu, to which I will return:

MDŚ III.149 na brāhmaṇaṃ parīkṣeta daive karmaṇi dharmavit
pitrye karmaṇi tu prāpte parīkṣeta prayatnataḥ

(Bühler:) For a rite sacred to the gods he who knows the law will not make (too close) inquiries regarding an (invited) Brahmaṇa,
but when one performs a ceremony in honor of the manes [i.e. a Śrāddha], one must carefully examine (the qualities and parentage of the guest).[46]

The first provision in most of the legal texts is that the chosen should not be related to the host by blood, or by ties of friendship, tutelage, or priestly service, unless no one else can be found. Compare, for example,

MDŚ III.138 na śrāddhe bhojayen mitram . . .
nāriṃ na mitraṃ yaṃ vidyāt taṃ śrāddhe bhojayed dvijam

At a Śrāddha he should not entertain a friend.
A twice-born whom he knows neither as foe nor friend he should entertain at a Śrāddha.[47]

Indeed, it is even forbidden to *make* friendships or alliances with those invited to a Śrāddha. The following passage contains one of our earliest injunctions against networking:

MDŚ III.140 yaḥ saṃgatāni kurute mohāc chrāddhena mānavaḥ
sa svargāc cyavate lokāc chrāddhamitro dvijādhamaḥ

The man who makes connections at a Śrāddha because of folly
is expelled from heaven. One who has friends (made at) a Śrāddha is the lowest of the twice-born.[48]

In other words, the Brahmans who are bidden to the Śrāddha ceremony exactly fill the role of the demanding guests of Manu and of Mudgala: they are functionally *strangers*, with no connection to their host beyond their shared membership in the Aryan community. One's duty of śraddhā, unquestioning hospitality, is manifested most nakedly with regard to strangers. This is reflected in these dharmic provisions against inviting any of one's connections to the Śrāddha ceremony or making any new ones there.

And this is precisely the point of the Śrāddha: naked hospitality. Although it might at first seem incongruous, even frivolous to join a celebration of hospitality relations (the Śrāddha feast) with a solemn memorial service in honor of the family dead, in fact this connection is particularly apt. The offering to the ancestors is, as it were, a commemoration of the *vertical*/diachronic ties that bind the Aryan community—the succession of generations—whereas the Śrāddha hospitality feast celebrates the *horizontal*/synchronic *extension* of the Aryan community, all those who are bound by the obligations of guest-friendship. This is perhaps also why more attention is paid to the worthiness of the invited guests in this rite than in one dedicated to the gods: they must represent the very type of the proper Aryan.

The preceding section is not designed to deny that the important and multivalent term śraddhā also has applications in the realm of ritual. Oldenberg,

Bloomfield, Köhler, and others have amply demonstrated that śraddhā often expresses 'Spendefreudigkeit' in the context of ritual, beginning already in the RVic hymn dedicated to the goddess Śraddhā (RV X.151), and this value is seen especially clearly in the close textual connections between śraddhā and the Dakṣiṇā, the ritual 'gift' given to the priest by the Sacrificer.

My intention has been only to show that śraddhā is also used in the context of nonritual hospitality: it is a duty owed to any guest (atithi). But these uses of the term are not contradictory, for, as we discussed, ritual and hospitality cannot be separated. On the one hand, śrauta ritual is the ultimate hospitality ceremony, offered to the gods; on the other, every guest can be a god in disguise, at least in theory.

We have also noted that the wife is central to the hospitality system, in some sense embodies these obligations and is often depicted as an exchangeable token in such contexts. It is in light of this that the otherwise surprising identification found at AB VII.10 śraddhā patnī "the wife is śraddhā" can be interpreted.[49] The wife is indeed 'hospitality' incarnate.

Thus, the innocent-looking term śraddhádeva applied to Manu in several versions of the Manu's Cups story would immediately signal to an alert audience what Manu's behavior is likely to be when faced with a pair of demanding guests. He would have no choice but to yield.

2. *Prātaritvan*

Let us now examine an epithet of these guests, to see what thematic complex *it* makes available to the hearers of the story: the word prātaritvan 'early coming', found in the KS version.

> KS XXX.1 (181: 7) tā asurā abruvann imāni manukapālāni yācethām iti tau prātaritvānā abhiprāpadyetām . . .
> . . . tau prātaritvānā abhiprāpadyetām . . .
> . . . tau prātaritvānā abhiprāpadyetām . . .
>
> The Asuras said to these two (Asuric Brahmans). "Beg these cups of Manu." The two approached (as) Prātaritvans . . .
> The two approached (as) Prātaritvans . . .
> The two approached (as) Prātaritvans . . .

It is highly probable that the use, indeed formulaic repetition, of this term here is significant, because otherwise it occurs with near-vanishing rarity. The word occurs in only three places that I know of: its three repetitions in the KS passage, twice in the first two verses of RV I.125, and once in the Nirukta.

The RVic passage is thus crucial for our understanding of the term, and, unfortunately, this passage shows just about as little clarity as outré RVic passages usually do. However, with philological care we can make some headway. The hymn is entitled by Geldner "Lob des freigebigen Opferers" [Praise of the generous Sacrificer] and begins with a short dialogue (vss. 2–3) between a householder (the Sacrificer) and a recent arrival. Just as in the KS, prātarítvan in the RV passage seems to identify this latter as a particular kind of visitor or guest, and just as in the KS, the reciprocal slot, the host, is also filled—by the householder. In KS the host is, of course, Manu; in the RV the host is otherwise unidentified. After the joint exchange, the hymn turns into a general praise of the liberally giving Sacrificer, the provider of Dakṣiṇās (vss. 4–7), all of this quite possibly in the mouth of the Prātaritvan.

The beginning of the hymn is situationally more limited. After a first verse describing the good effects of entertaining a Prātarítvan, the nameless host announces the same sentiment (vs. 2), and the Prātarítvan confirms the sentiment and bids his host to sacrifice (vs. 3).

RV I.125.1 prātā́ rátnam prātarítvā dadhāti tám̐ cikitvā́n pratigŕ̥hyā nídhatte
téna prajā́ṃ vardháyamāna ā́yū rāyás póṣeṇa sacate suvī́raḥ

In the early morning (prātár), the Prātaritvan establishes a treasure. A perceptive (man), receiving him (as guest), lays (the treasure) in himself.
Increasing his own progeny and life with it, possessing good men, he is accompanied by thriving of wealth.

RV I.125.2 sugúr asat suhiraṇyáḥ sváśvo br̥hád asmai váya índro dadhāti
yás tvā́yantaṃ vásunā prātaritvo mukṣī́jayeva pádim utsināti

[The host:] He will have good cows, good gold, good horses—for him Indra (will) establish lofty vigor—
he who, o Prātaritvan, binds you up like a bird (?) with a snare (?), you coming hither with goods.

RV I.125.3 ā́yam adyá sukŕ̥tam prā́tar ichánn iṣṭéḥ putráṃ vásumatā ráthena
aṃśóḥ sutám pāyaya matsarásya kṣayádvīraṃ vardhaya sūnŕ̥tābhiḥ

[The Prātaritvan:] I have come hither today, early in the morning, seeking one who performs (sacrifices) well, the son of my desire, (I) with a goods-filled chariot.
Make (Indra?) drink the pressed (soma) of the exhilarating stalk; strengthen the men-ruling (Indra?) with lovely (presents).

Hillebrandt[50] interpreted the Prātaritvan as an itinerant priest, a priestly vagabond, who offers his services—presumably performing sacrifices on a piecework basis for whatever householder, potential Sacrificer, he can persuade to employ him. And, indeed, Hillebrandt's interpretation fits the RVic passage well: as we just saw, in verse 3 the early arriving visitor orders *the ritual* to begin, and in the rest of the hymn he promises much in exchange for the sacrifice and, especially, for the liberal distribution of Dakṣiṇās. So it seems that this morning arrival must be capable of acting as priest.

Itinerant priest also fits the KS passage. The two Asuric Brahmans, posing as Prātaritvans, declare to Manu that they will *perform sacrifice* for him (anena tvarṣabheṇa/anayā patnyā yājayāva ("we will perform sacrifice for you with this bull/with this wife"). It is by this proposal that they get control of both bull and wife. From this it would seem that Prātaritvans were both *strangers* and *priests*, peddling priestly services for their livelihood.

This dual identity would impose a double obligation on Manu. As strangers they are entitled to a hospitable reception, and as priests performing on Manu's behalf they should receive a Dakṣiṇā or priestly gift (as well as the wherewithal to perform the sacrifice, in this case the sacrificial victims).

Before we focus on these visitors' role as guests, let us probe more deeply into their priestly nature. There may be another reason why Manu agrees to these barbarous sacrifices with apparent alacrity. Let us return to the Prātaritvan of the RV. Oldenberg,[51] though not entirely rejecting Hillebrandt's interpretation of this word, points out that the Prātaritvan arrives *bringing* wealth, though he is also demanding it in the form of a Dakṣinā. In verse 1 the Prātaritvan "establishes a treasure" (rátnam . . . dadhāti), which increases the life, progeny, and wealth of the householder who receives the Prātaritvan. In verse 2 the Prātaritvan is described as "coming hither with goods" (āyántaṃ vásunā), and in verse 3 he agrees that he has done so; indeed his goods fill a chariot (ā́yam . . . vásumatā ráthena). Why does the Prātaritvan have to travel about selling his services if he is already rich?

Here of course we must guard against being too literal, for surely on the one hand the ever increasing treasure (of vs. 1) and even the chariot full of goods (in vss. 2–3) simply stand for the well-being and riches that will accrue to the householder when he worships the gods and, incidentally, materially rewards the priest who performs the worship. It is the usual praise of the liberal patron and promise of tit for tat that is so familiar in the RV and indeed is reiterated in the more conventional second half of this very hymn.

Hence we can dismiss this objection rather easily, but perhaps prematurely—for Oldenberg has suggested another possibility, which can be integrated with the first, namely that the Prātaritvan, the bestower of treasure, is really a god, the "Genius of the morning Dakṣiṇā-giving." Geldner echoes Oldenberg with the possibility that the figure is actually Indra himself, wandering the earth incognito. I would simply combine the two interpretations: the human Prātaritvan, the itinerant priest as interpreted by Hillebrandt, acts out a divine role. The householders he visits acquiesce to his ritual performance so readily not only because they will derive benefit from any ritual performed on their behalf, but also because the human Prātaritvan symbolizes or embodies other, more powerful morning visitors, namely the gods who attend the morning worship. In other words, they may be entertaining a deity unaware, and even if not, they are receiving his earthly representative.

The strongest piece of evidence for this is an epithet very close, semantically and formally, to prātarítvan, namely prātaryā́van. The two differ in formation only in that the derived root √yā 'go, drive' has been substituted for the simple root √i 'go'. The epithet prātar-yā́van is always applied to gods or to their chariot, and it appears especially in passages calling the gods to worship here on earth. It is most especially characteristic of the Aśvins (RV II.39.2, V.77.1) or of their chariot (RV X.40.1, X.41.2). For the chariot:

RV X.41.2 prātaryújaṃ nāsatyā́dhi tiṣṭhathaḥ *prātaryā́vāṇam* madhuvā́hanaṃ *rátham*
víśo yéna gáchatho yájvarīr narā kīréś cid yajñáṃ hótṛmantam aśvinā

O Nāsatyas [Aśvins], you two mount the early-yoked, *early-coming*, honey-conveying *chariot*,
by which you come to the worshiping folk, o men, to the worship even of a humble man, (as long as) it has a Hotar, o Aśvins.

For the Aśvins themselves there is the remarkably insistent sequence in V.77.1–2:

RV V.77.1 prātaryā́vāṇā prathamā́ yajadhvam purā́ gṛ́dhrād áraruṣaḥ pibātaḥ
prātár hí yajñám aśvínā dadhā́te prá śaṃsanti kaváyaḥ pūrvabhā́jaḥ
2 prātár yajadhvam aśvínā hinota ná sāyám asti devayā́ ájuṣṭam
utā́nyó asmád yajate ví cā́vaḥ pū́rvaḥ-pūrvo yájamāno vánīyān

Worship first the two early-coming ones. They will drink (here) before the nongiving, greedy one (invites them).
For the Aśvins receive their worship early in the morning. (Early) the poets with the early share praise them.
Early do ye worship. Impel the Aśvins hither. (Worship) is not at evening, (when it is) unpleasing to divinity.
Another than us (will) worship, when it has dawned. The earlier the worshiper (worships), the more he wins.

But prātaryā́van is also used of the gods in general, on their way to the Soma Sacrifice:

RV VIII.38.7 prātaryā́vabhir ā́gataṃ devébhir jenyāvasū
índrāgnī sómapītaye

O Indra and Agni, possessing noble goods, come hither with the early-coming gods to the soma-drinking.

Given the very restricted divine contexts in which prātaryā́van appears and its formal similarity to prātarítvan, it is scarcely credible that the latter would not have been to some degree assimilated to the former: the itinerant human priest Prātaritvan seen as representing or embodying the divine visitors to the early worship, the Prātaryāvan. And indeed this confusion is found (if confusion it is) in the Nirukta passage, a verse of unknown origin in which the Aśvins are called prātar*itvan*.

Nir. IV.17 imé sutā́ índavaḥ prātárítvanā́ [*sic*] sajóṣasā *pibatām aśvínā tā́n
These (soma) drops are pressed. Let the early-coming Aśvins drink them together.

So the human Prātaritvans of RV I.125 and KS XXX.1 may well represent divinities to their hosts, but *which* divinities? In the case of RV I.125, the

Prātarítvan probably has the image of Indra, as Geldner has already suggested. The householder announces in verse 2 that Indra will establish all good things for the one who receives the Prātarítvan, and it is probably Indra, under the epithet kṣayád-vīra 'ruling men', who is worshiped in verse 3. We know from the RV that Indra is in the habit of going about the earth in search of a soma presser (apparently in the early morning). (Cf. e.g. RV V.30.1, V.31.12, VII.98.1, VIII.91.2.)

In the KS story it is even clearer which gods are being impersonated. As we just noted, the epithet prātaryā́van is especially characteristic of the dual divinities, the Aśvins. In the KS passage there are *two* Prātaritvānau, the two Asuric Brahmans, and the likelihood that they represent the Aśvins, are in some sense the wicked mirror image of the Aśvins, is increased by the fact that in the MS version of the passage the two Asuras are addressed by their suffering brethren with a very Aśvinesque command—the Aśvins are the twin physicians of the gods:

> MS IV.8.1 (106: 8) tā́ abruvaṁś *cíkitsataṃ nā* íti
>
> (The rest of the Asuras) said to these two (Asuric Brahmans), "*Heal us!*"

Why are the Aśvins especially known as prātaryā́van? Because they are among the earliest arrivals at the Soma Sacrifice. The Pressing Day of the Soma Sacrifice begins well before dawn. The first pressing of the day is called the *Prātaḥ*savana 'Early Morning Pressing'; it is preceded by a lengthy recitation known as the *Prātar*anuvāka, 'Early Morning Litany'—which indeed is supposed to begin even before the stirrings of birds are heard. In the Brāhmaṇas and śrauta sūtras it is explicitly stated for whom the Prātaranuvāka is intended. Compare, for example,

> AB II.15 devebhyaḥ *prātaryāvabhyo* hotar anubrūhīty āhādhvaryur ete vāva devāḥ *prātaryāvāṇo* yad agnir uṣā *aśvinau*
>
> "Hotar, recite to the *early-coming* gods," says the Adhvaryu. These are the *early-coming* gods: Agni, Uṣas, and the *Aśvins*.

The prātaryāvan 'early-coming' gods, including the Aśvins, are thus the audience of the Prātaranuvāka. Although Indra is not among these, he must arrive relatively early, as the first soma libation directed at particular divinities at this pressing is the cup to Indra and Vāyu.[52] Their presence at the first pressing may account for the otherwise opaque greeting of the Asuric Brahmans to Manu in the KS version: vāyave 'gnā3i vāyava indrā3 "Ahoy Agni, for Vāyu; ahoy Indra, for Vāyu," a formulation I have not yet been able to trace or parallel in the ritual literature. It may be a variation on the opening mantra accompanying the libation, the unremarkable and predictable vāyave tvā "thee for Vāyu."[53]

Thus, by examining the employment of the word prātaritvan, which makes one of its rare appearances in KS XXX.1, we get some hint as to why Manu obligingly hands over his belongings to his visitors. He would naturally think he was entertaining the Aśvins, the very type of 'early-coming' gods, and this would prompt him to accede to their demands: it is surely a bad move to refuse a god anything. Once again careful attention to the deployment of vocabulary allows us surprising access to latent semantics.[54]

As I have already extensively discussed, in the Mahābhārata the possibility of divine visitation underlies other apparently unmotivated acquiescence to inconvenient requests. The motif of the greedy guest who reveals himself as Dharma (vel sim.) and rewards his long-suffering hosts is the almost universal plot twist in the Exploited Host stories we have examined—the hope offered to a real-life host that hospitality will ultimately be its own reward, an incentive to good hostly behavior. The RV and KS passages I have just discussed make it clear that this theme of the visiting god-in-disguise is as old as the earliest Indian literature. We can only marvel that the KS passage announces this theme, with all its implications for the story, with such remarkable verbal economy: a single epithet thrice repeated is enough to capture and apply the thematic complex to the narrative.

3. Meni

Though the two Asuras manage to persuade Manu of their divine identity and good intentions, as we know they have no such thing: they violate the basic requirements of the hospitality relation. This violation is signaled by another term, mení. This word is found in the MS version, when the Asuras attempt to destroy the first two lodging places of the Asura-killing voice, namely the cups and the bull.

> MS IV.8.1 (106: 10) . . . tā́ny agnínā sámakṣāpayatāṃ tā́n jvālā́n ṛṣabháḥ sámaleṭ táṁ sá *menír* ánvapadyata tásya ruvató yā́vantó 'surā upā́śṛṇvaṁs tā́vantas tád áhar nā́bhavan . . . téna vā́ enam ayājayatāṃ tásya śróṇim ánavattaṁ suparṇá údamathnāt sā́ *manā́yyā upástham ā́padyata tā́ṁ sā́ *menír* ánvapadyata tásyā vádantyā yā́vantó 'surā upā́śṛṇvaṁs tā́vantas tád áhar nā́bhavan
>
> They burned them with fire. A bull licked up the flames. *Meni* came after/entered him. As many Asuras as heard him bellowing ceased to exist on that day. . . . With it [the bull] they performed worship for him. An eagle stole its haunch, (still) unoffered. It dropped in the lap of Manu's wife. *Meni* came after/entered her. As many Asuras as heard her speaking ceased to exist on that day.

This word used to be rendered by 'missile, weapon' in the standard dictionaries, but more recently has been interpreted as 'vengeance, revenge' (cf. Mayrhofer, *KEWA* s.v., with lit.) and connected to the root √mī 'exchange'. However, I have recently established[55] that the term instead refers to the *power or embodiment of negative or thwarted exchange*. I will not repeat my arguments here, but simply point to a few contexts in which the violation of proper hospitality or exchange relations entails meni.

In both MS (II.4.5 [42: 17]) and KS (XII.3 [166:15]) the performance of a certain ritual is recommended for someone who is conjuring against (abhi √car) another, but this ritual is not to be accompanied by a Dakṣiṇā. Thus the conjurer creates meni:

KS XII.3 (166: 15) abhicaran yajeta na dakṣiṇāṃ dadyān menim evainaṃ kṛtvābhiprayuṅkte menir hy adakṣiṇaḥ

One 'conjuring against' should worship (with this ritual). He should not give a Dakṣiṇā. Thus having made it [ritual] a meni he gains control. For (a ritual) without a Dakṣiṇā is a meni.

In other words, when the proper gift exchange mandated by normal ritual behavior does not occur, the ritual itself becomes a dangerous and destructive entity—which is precisely what someone practicing black magic would want.

A similar transformation happens to the "Brahman's cow," in the AV hymn[56] given this same name by Whitney (AV XII.5). Most of this hymn is devoted to the dreadful features the Brahman's cow displays to the Kṣatriya who takes her[57] (AV XII.5.5 tā́m ādádānasya brahmagavī́ṃ jinató brāhmaṇáṃ kṣatríyasya "of the Kṣatriya taking the Brahman's cow, overpowering the Brahman"). Four times in the hymn (vss. 16, 23, 39, 59), the cow is called a meni, for example

AV XII.5.16 meníḥ śatávadhā hí sā́ brahmajyásya kṣítir hí sā́

She is a hundred-killing meni; she is destruction for the Brahman-overcomer.

Again the issue is the violation of exchange relations: either the Kṣatriya has stolen a cow from the Brahman or, more likely (see n. 57), has failed to give it to him (probably as a ritual Dakṣiṇā). Cheated of her proper place in the ritual economy, the ordinarily benign cow changes into a ferocious creature, a force for destruction.

The meni of the Manu's Cups story is a similar force. The Asuras have offended against proper exchange relations by abusing their position as guests to gain control over the host's possessions. They have no right to what they have taken; they certainly have no right to *destroy* it. And so the object of the illegitimate exchange (the "Asura-killing voice") becomes a meni, embodying the power of such botched exchange relations, and *is exchanged* through the other vessels: bull and wife.

The Asuras do not understand this mechanism. In fact their downfall occurs because they do not understand the system of ritual economy at all. They think that if they sacrifice/destroy something, it will be gone. But in the Vedic conception of both ritual and natural circulation, nothing is lost: it is simply transformed or displaced. The system of exchanges that binds the world of men also works in the natural world and in the relations between men and gods. The 'voice' cannot be destroyed, but is transferred to another vehicle. Since the Asuras effect this transfer illegitimately, they unleash the power of negative exchange (meni), which travels unscathed through a series of vessels: when the *cups* are burned, it enters the *flames* which are licked by the *bull*; when the bull is sacrificed, it lodges in his *hip*, which is transferred by an *eagle* to the *wife*. Meanwhile the Asuras continue to die.

4. *Yāc*

We have recently explored how Manu's epithet śraddhā́deva compels him to give away his most precious possessions. Let us now turn to another term of compulsion, the verb √yāc 'ask for, beg', an action which the rest of the Asuras urge on their two representatives in the KS version of the tale.

> KS XXX.1 (181: 6) atha tarhi triṣṭāvarutrī āstām asurabrahmau tā asurā abruvann imāni manukapālāni *yācethām* iti
>
> At this time there were two Brahmans of the Asuras, (named) Triṣṭa and Avarutri. The Asuras said (to them), "*Beg* these cups of Manu."

Examining this term will allow us to see the exact mechanism by which the Asuras get control of what they desire.

In some ways √yāc is the most interesting of our terms, because it embodies the anxieties of both host and guest. On the one hand, it is one of the most powerful triggers of liberality: by the act of yāc-ing one can *compel* someone to give. On the other, the yāc-er puts himself in the power of the one approached and tacitly accepts inferior status. So, at the very least yāc-ing can be embarrassing or shameful; worse, it can also put one under duress or into danger.

√Yāc in later texts is a standard word for the begging of food (and money) by students and wandering ascetics, and throughout Sanskrit literature, beginning in early Vedic, the verb is in a reciprocal relation with the root √dā 'give', in passages too numerous to mention. Just note one early example in the AV:

> AV XII.4.1 *dádāmī́ty* evá brūyāt . . . vaśā́ṃ brahmábhyo *yā́cadbhyaḥ*
>
> "*I give* (her)," he should say to the Brahmans *begging* (his) cow.

This fifty-three-verse hymn never strays far from this initial theme: the perils and wickedness of not surrendering a vaśā cow when a Brahman asks for her.[58] Throughout the verb of asking is √yāc (vss. 1, 2, 12, 13, 19, 20, 22, 24, 25, 26, 31, 36, 48, 50). In the AV hymn, at any rate, the price of refusing a Brahman's yāc is disaster, creatively and extensively described.

The strong compulsion to *give* in response to a yāc is something of a theme in Middle Vedic literature. I cite one passage from a lengthy debate in the ŚB about whether paying reverence to Agni constitutes begging.

ŚB II.3.4.7 utá vái *yā́can dātā́raṃ* lábhata evótó bhartā́ bhāryàṃ nā́nubudhyate sá yadā́ivā́ha bhāryò vái te 'smi bibhṛhí méty áthainaṃ vedā́thainaṃ bhāryàṃ manyate

On the one hand, the one *who begs* gets himself a *giver*. On the other hand (sometimes) a supporter does not recognize a dependent. But when he [the begging dependent] says, "I am your dependent. Support me," then he [the giver/supporter] knows him and realizes he has to be supported.

The first clause can be translated "the one who begs finds or gets a giver," but the verb √labh conveys an element of force or compulsion—remember that with the preverb ā, √labh is the standard term for binding an animal for sacrifice. So a better translation might be "the one who begs really takes or captures for himself a giver," with emphatic evá to draw attention to the verb. The passage then continues with a tactic to use on a reluctant or forgetful giver. I will have occasion to refer to this again.

The reciprocal relation between yāc and dā and the element of compulsion in this relation are found also in the MBh, for example in Yayāti's reply to the supplicating Śarmiṣṭhā, who wants him to sleep with her:

MBh I.77.20 *dātavyaṃ yācamānebhya* iti me vratam āhitam
tvaṃ ca *yācasi* māṃ kāmaṃ brūhi kiṃ karavāṇi te

"One must *give* to *beggars*"—such is my established vow.
And you are *begging* a favor from me. Speak! What shall I do for you?

There are others in this text with the same vrata ('vow'). The young Somaśravas has sworn such a vow, as his father Śrutaśravas tells Janamejaya:

MBh I.3.15 asya tv ekam upāṃśuvratam / yad enaṃ kaś cid brāhmaṇaḥ kaṃ cid artham abhi*yācet* taṃ tasmai *dadyād* ayam

But he has one private vow. If any Brahman should *beg* any object from him, he would *give* it to him.

The most remarkable example in the MBh is Karṇa, the bastard elder brother of the Kaunteyas, who takes the Kurus' side. The son of the sun god Sūrya and the as yet unmarried Kuntī, Karṇa was born with built-in earrings and built-in armor, which confer invulnerability on him. However, when Indra, disguised as a Brahman, comes to beg this paraphernalia from him, Karṇa tears off earrings and armor and gives them to him—not only doing severe damage to his body, of which they formed a part, but also ensuring his own death in battle, since he has surrendered his protective invulnerability.

The story is told briefly in Book I (104.17ff.), but at great and dramatic length in Book III (III.284–86, 293–94). The sun god Sūrya, Karṇa's father, comes to him, warns him of Indra's plan, and implores him not to give his possessions away.[59] But Karṇa is adamant: he will adhere to his legendary generosity and give away even his life if he is *begged* for it. For if he does not, he risks losing his "eternal fame" (śāśvatī kīrti MBh III.284.35). He gives an impassioned speech (III.284.23–39) on the merit of everlasting fame even at the price of death, as opposed to the ignominy of continued life with loss of fame. It is a speech that could have issued from the mouth of Achilles—the marginal and ambiguous figure of Karṇa seems an embodiment of traditional, inherited, Indo-European ideals. And the action on which all this hinges is Karṇa's insistence on unquestioned giving to people who beg. I will give here only a few excerpts from this extraordinary passage.

MBh III.284.12 viditaṃ tena śīlaṃ te sarvasya jagatas tathā
yathā tvaṃ bhikṣitaḥ sadbhir *dadāsy* eva na *yācase*
13 tvaṃ hi tāta *dadāsy* eva brāhmaṇebhyaḥ *prayācitaḥ*
vittaṃ yac cānyad apy āhur na pratyākhyāsi karhi cit
. . . 15 tasmai *prayācamānāya* na *deye* kuṇḍale tvayā

[Sūrya:] Your practice is known by the entire world,
how when the good ask for alms, you *give*; you do not *beg*.
You *give*, when *begged*, to Brahmans any possession whatsoever, so they say. You never refuse, my dear.
. . . (But) you must not *give* your earrings to Indra, when he *begs*.

MBh III.284.25 vrataṃ vai mama loko 'yaṃ vetti kṛtsno vibhāvaso
yathāhaṃ dvijamukhyebhyo *dadyāṃ* prāṇān api dhruvam
26 yady āgacchati śakro māṃ brāhmaṇacchadmanāvṛtaḥ
. . . bhikṣitum
27 *dāsyāmi* vibudhaśreṣṭha kuṇḍale varma cottamam
na me kīrtiḥ praṇaśyeta triṣu lokeṣu viśrutā
28 madvidhasyāyaśasyaṃ hi na yuktaṃ prāṇarakṣaṇam
yuktaṃ hi yaśasā yuktaṃ maraṇaṃ lokasaṃmatam
29 so 'ham indrāya *dāsyāmi* kuṇḍale saha varmaṇā
yadi māṃ valavṛtraghno bhikṣārtham upayāsyati
30 . . . kuṇḍale me *prayācitum*

[Karṇa:] This whole world knows my firm vow, o sun, that *I would give* even my life to the Brahmans.
If Indra comes to me disguised as a Brahman to ask alms,
I will give, o best of the wise, my earrings and my excellent armor,
lest my fame, heard throughout the three worlds, should disappear.
For, for someone like me, a (course) lacking glory that saves one's life is not proper.
Proper is a death provided with glory, celebrated by the world.
So, *I will give* to Indra the earrings along with the armor,
if the slayer of Vala and Vṛtra approaches me, on an errand of alms, to *beg* my earrings.

And so it goes, on and on, in this vein. Sometime later (III.293f.) Indra does come, beg for the earrings[60] and armor, and when Karṇa cannot dissuade Indra from this request, he tears them off and hands them over. Karṇa seems in exactly the same position as Manu—in answer to a yāc he cannot refuse even a deadly request. The only difference is that in the MBh Karṇa's determination is presented as a purely personal vow, a vrata—just as Mudgala's extreme hospitality resulted from an atithi-vrata—whereas Manu's behavior in the earlier texts seems more regulated by cultural norms. But the MBh explanation seems just an after-the-fact rationalization of stubbornly, indeed recklessly traditional conduct.

Investigating the verb √yāc also gives us access to the role of women in the partnership of complementary oppositions of begging and giving—for even as women are the ordinary dispensers of hospitality to guests, it is typically housewives who are approached by mendicants and students on their begging rounds and who provide the asked-for food. The following fragment of a dialogue between a Brahman and a housewife shows the same strong relationship between √yāc 'beg' and √dā 'give' that I established above and depicts the woman as structural partner of the beggar.

MBh III.197.8 dehīti yācamāno vai

(The Brahman,) begging, (said) "Give!"

And I have already quoted a similar exchange between the goddess Aditi and a beggar:

MBh. XII.329.44 (3) aditiṃ cāvocad bhikṣāṃ dehīti
(4) tatra devaiḥ pūrvam etat prāśyaṃ nānyenety aditir bhikṣāṃ nādāt

He said to Aditi, "Give me alms."
Aditi, (thinking) "This is to be eaten first by the gods, not by another," did not give alms.

The gṛhya and dharma literature even provides us with the standardized beggars' verbal formulae for addressing the women approached:

JGS I.12 bhavatpūrvayā brāhmaṇo bhikṣeta bhavati bhikṣāṃ dehīti bhavanmadhyamayā rājanyo bhikṣāṃ bhavati dehīti bhavadantyayā vaiśyo dehi bhikṣāṃ bhavatīti kṣāṃ ca hiṃ ca na vardhayed bhavatpūrvayā vā sarve

A Brahman should beg with (the word) 'Lady' at the beginning (of the utterance): "Lady, give alms." A Rājanya [Kṣatriya] with 'Lady' in the middle: "Give, Lady, alms." A Vaiśya with 'Lady' at the end: "Give alms, Lady." He should not draw out (the final syllables) *kṣām* or *hi* [of the words 'alms' and 'give' respectively]. Or all (varṇas) (may put the word) 'Lady' at the beginning.[61]

When a student is first initiated, he is broken into the begging round gently: he begins with his mother or other female relatives and kindly disposed women.[62]

MDŚ II.50 mātaraṃ vā svasāraṃ vā mātur vā bhaginīṃ nijām
bhikṣeta bhikṣāṃ prathamaṃ yā cainaṃ nāvamānayet

(The newly initiated student) should first beg alms from his mother, or his sister, or his own mother's sister, or some woman who will not disdain (to give to) him.

Since the age of initiation may be as low as seven (and for Brahmans is usually specified as no later than eight), this practice seems a remarkably humane way to introduce the child to his duties.

Thus in daily life the woman continually enacts the *giver* role, the necessary opposite to that of *beggar*. Although this may seem a mere accidental result of practicalities—who, after all, is likely to be in the kitchen when the beggar comes around—the constant depiction of woman as giver must be carrying a further message. As we will see, the giver/beggar relationship is one of fundamental inequality. The giver, by virtue of his action, acquires power over the beggar, sometimes power of life or death. Given the ideological implications of "giving," it is remarkable that women should be cast as "givers," should be invested with the vocabulary of the giver/beggar relationship which elsewhere bestows power on the giver, should participate in what we might call "discourses of power"—even when all they do is hand over a bowl of rice.

In light of this we may reconsider the statement we met long ago in the ritual texts: "The wife is mistress of the household goods." In mundane life the wife does in fact make daily decisions about the disposal of household goods, and determine whether or not to give alms to a constant stream of beggars.[63] Thus we meet another unresolved contradiction affecting the woman: between her limited (to nonexistent) right to own property (as stated by the dharma texts, as we saw earlier) and her continually reenacted role of giver, which would seem to imply control over what is given. This will be discussed further.

E. Exploited Guests and Reluctant Recipients

1. *Shame*

I have, heretofore, concentrated on the vulnerability of the host/giver, unprotected (and unprotectable) from the boorish or even murderous behavior of a demanding guest/beggar. But the anxieties of hospitality are not only on one side. Let us now examine the other facet of yāc: the uncomfortable or even dangerous position in which it puts the *beggar*. First, though begging is a characteristic activity of Brahmans and clearly a lucrative one, it can also be somewhat shameful or embarrassing. In the Viṣṇu Smṛti the final blessing asked for in the Śrāddha ceremony, after the verse cited earlier, is

> ViSmṛ LXXIII.30 [≅ MBh XII.29.114abd] annaṃ ca no bahu bhaved atithīṃś ca labhemahi
> *yācitāraś* ca naḥ santu mā ca *yāciṣma* kaṃ cana
>
> May there be much food for us; may we receive (many) guests.
> Let *beggars* come to us; let us not *beg* anyone.

Kṣatriyas often proudly boast that they are *givers*, not *beggars*.[64] Let us assemble a few passages to that effect from the MBh. In the first book there is a little cat fight between Devayānī, daughter of a Brahman, and Śarmiṣṭhā, daughter of a king. The latter taunts the former with

MBh I.73.10 *yācatas* tvaṃ hi duhitā stuvataḥ pratigṛhṇataḥ
sutāhaṃ stūyamānasya *dadato* 'pratigṛhṇataḥ

You are the daughter of one who *begs*, praises, and receives (presents).
I am the offspring of one who is praised, who *gives*, and does not receive.[65]

When Bhīma steals lotuses for Draupadī from Kubera's garden, he disdains to ask for them, with this explanation:

MBh III.152.9 na hi *yācanti* rājāna eṣa dharmaḥ sanātanaḥ

For kings don't *beg*—that is the age-old dharma.

Similarly, when Yayāti, his merit exhausted, falls from heaven, the kings among whom he lands offer him the fruits of their sacrifice, but he refuses, with the explanation

MBh V.119.19 nāhaṃ pratigrahadhano brāhmaṇaḥ kṣatriyo hy aham

I am not a Brahman, whose wealth comes from accepting (presents). I am a Kṣatriya.

And Draupadī laments some ill-treatment she has received while disguised with

MBh IV.15.16 ye *dadyur* na ca *yāceyuḥ* . . .
teṣāṃ māṃ māninīṃ bhāryām

(He insulted) me, the proud wife of those who *give* and do not *beg*.

Indeed, one of the arguments Karṇa uses in his attempt to dissuade Indra from taking his earrings is that Indra, as lord of creatures, should not be begging from Karṇa, but giving to him (III.294.15). If Karṇa accedes, Indra will appear laughable.

MBh III.294.16 yadi *dāsyāmi* te deva kuṇḍale kavacaṃ tathā
vadhyatām upayāsyāmi tvaṃ ca śakrāvahāsyatām

If I *give* you, o god, the earrings and the armor,
I will become vulnerable, but you, o able one, will become ridiculous.

Though begging is specifically the Brahmans' province, they too can find the experience demeaning and may even evade or refuse a gift freely given. Such is the case in the curious story of Śaibya Vṛṣādarbhi and the ṛṣis embedded in the Bisastainyopakhyānam (XIII.94). Sometime in the past Śaibya had given his son away as a Dakṣiṇā to his priests (ṛtvij) (XIII.94.8 dakṣiṇārthe 'tha ṛtvigbhyo dattaḥ putro nijaḥ kila)—a present they clearly had accepted. In a time of famine the son died, and the priests, tormented by hunger, set about cooking him up in a pot (vs. 10 . . . ṛṣisattamāḥ/apacanta tadā sthālyāṃ kṣudhārtāḥ).[66] Śaibya comes upon the group still cooking as he wanders on the road, and he offers them an abundance of gifts:

MBh XIII.94.13 pratigrahas tārayati puṣṭir vai pratigṛhṇatām
. . . 14 priyo hi me brāhmaṇo *yācamāno*
dadyām ahaṃ vo 'śvatarīsahasram

Acceptance (of presents) will get (you) through. Accept prosperity.
A *begging* Brahman is a pleasure to me.
I *would give* you a thousand she-mules.

He then details other gifts he wishes to give them (dadāni 'I will give/let me give' appears in vss. 15 and 16, its synonym prayacchāmi in vs. 16).

But the ṛṣis indignantly refuse him:

MBh XIII.94.17 rājan pratigraho rājño madhvāsvādo viṣopamaḥ

O king, the acceptance (of presents) from a king is the worst of poisons, (though) sweet as honey.

This principle is not entirely dharmically supported. The relevant provisions in Manu (IV.84–91) seem simply to forbid accepting presents from *bad* or badly born kings (cf. also MBh. XIII.60.5 na tu pāpakṛtāṃ rājñāṃ pratigṛhṇanti sādhavaḥ), though he does say that accepting food from a king impairs the receiver's vigor (MDŚ IV.218). The ambivalence about accepting gifts is displayed by the internal contradictions in these texts.

So outraged are the ṛṣis by Śaibya's offers that they march off into the wilderness, even leaving behind the not yet cooked flesh (apakvam . . . māṃsam vs. 21) of what was, after all, Śaibya's son. He pursues them still, trying to ply them with figs stuffed with gold, but they still refuse. Finally he gets angry at their intransigence, and the story veers off in another direction.

In another, briefly narrated story the Reluctant Recipients are outsmarted by their host. Two Asuras approach Viṣṇu, who bids them welcome and offers them a boon (MBh III.194.19), but they themselves wish to be the benefactors:

MBh III.194.20 āvāṃ varaya deva tvaṃ varadau svaḥ surottama
dātārau svo varaṃ tubhyam

Ask us for a boon, o god. We are boon-givers, o best of gods.
We will give a boon to you.

He accepts (vs. 21 pratigṛhṇe varam) and chooses the right to kill them, which he then does.

The clearest example of the Reluctant Recipient is found in the Jāpakopākhyānam (MBh XII.192), which recounts a protracted clash of wills between King Ikṣvāku, who is anxious to give, and a Brahman, who declines to accept. Ikṣvāku visits the Brahman in the course of his Tīrtha Grand Tour. The

Brahman gives him the usual guest reception (XII.192.35–37). When he asks Ikṣvāku the usual hostly question (37 kiṃ karomīha), the king replies:

MBh XII.192.38 rājāhaṃ brāhmaṇaś ca tvaṃ yadi ṣaṭkarmasaṃsthitaḥ
dadāmi vasu kiṃ cit te prārthitaṃ tad vadasva me

If I am a king and you are a Brahman, established in the Six Duties [of a Brahman, one of which is pratigraha 'accepting presents', cf. MDŚ X.76–77],
I will give you some good thing. Tell me something you want.

But the Brahman refuses to receive anything and, in fact, attempts to turn the tables by himself offering the king a present.

MBh XII.192.39 dvividhā brāhmaṇā rājan dharmaś ca dvividhaḥ smṛtaḥ
pravṛttaś ca nivṛttaś ca nivṛtto 'smi pratigrahāt
40 . . . ahaṃ na pratigṛhṇāmi kim iṣṭaṃ kiṃ dadāni te

There are traditionally two kinds of Brahmans and two kinds of dharma, o king—
the inclined and the disinclined, and I am disinclined to accepting presents.
. . . I will not accept (anything). What (do you) want? What shall I give you?

The king, of course, cannot accept.

MBh XII.192.41 kṣatriyo 'haṃ na jānāmi dehīti vacanaṃ kva cit
prayaccha yuddham ity evaṃ vādinaḥ smo dvijottama

I am a Kṣatriya and don't even know the word 'Give!'
We are the ones who (only) say, "Give (me) battle!," o twice-born one.

After some confused wrangling[67] the Brahman actually manages to maneuver the king into begging for a gift—presumably because the Brahman is verbally sharper than his opponent. (As the king says, vāgvajrā brāhmaṇāḥ "Brahmans have word-cudgels," vs. 45.) The request is made with the full vocabulary of gift exchange that we have been examining:

MBh XII.192.43 *yāce* tvāṃ *dīyatāṃ* mahyaṃ japyasyāsya phalaṃ dvija
. . . 47 yat tad varṣaśataṃ pūrṇaṃ japyaṃ vai japatā tvayā
phalaṃ prāptaṃ tat *prayaccha* mama *ditsur* bhavān yadi

[The king:] I *beg* you. Let the fruit of this (prayer-)muttering *be given* to me, o twice-born.
The muttering accomplished by you muttering for a hundred years—
give that accumulated fruit, if your worship *desires to give* to me.

Nonetheless, the king almost gets out of accepting the gift when it turns out that the Brahman does not know how much his muttering is worth (vs. 51), but again the Brahman befuddles the king with his speech (many ślokas on satya) and finally accuses him of performing an untruth:

MBh XII.192.70 kasmāt tvam anṛtaṃ vākyaṃ dehīti kuruṣe 'śubham
71 yadi japyaphalaṃ dattaṃ mayā neṣiṣyase [*sic*] nṛpa

. . . 72 saṃśrutya yo na ditseta *yācitvā* yaś ca necchati
ubhāv ānṛtikāv etau

Why do you make the untrue and disagreeable speech 'Give!'
if you do not want the fruit of muttering given by me, o king?
. . . The person who, having promised, would not give and the one who, *having begged*, does not want—
Both are liars.

Although again the king attempts to escape the gift by bringing up his Kṣatriya nature (vs. 73), the Brahman points out that the king is the guest (and hence the beggar, by definition).

MBh XII.192.74 . . . nāpi te gṛham āvrajam
ihāgamya tu *yācitvā* na *gṛhṇīṣe* punaḥ katham

I didn't come to your house.
You, having coming here, *having begged*—how can you not *accept* in turn?

Their increasingly pointless and acrimonious quarrel is interrupted by the arrival of two others, Virūpa and Vikṛta, involved in a similar dispute. Virūpa is attempting to repay Vikṛta for the gift of a cow, which Virūpa had begged (yāc again) from him previously (vs. 92), but Vikṛta refuses the repayment. After charges and countercharges in this embedded vignette, we return to the Brahman and the king. Threatened by the Brahman's curse (vs. 109), the king finally gives in and agrees to accept the Brahman's gift, though he does wring a small concession from the latter—to accept in return some water that has fallen on the king's hand (vss. 111, 113).

The horror and humiliation of receiving, rather than giving, is thus dramatized at rather tedious length in this story. The tensions between host and guest, between giver and recipient, between Brahman and Kṣatriya are fully displayed, though as a sort of mirror image to the same tensions in the Exploited Host tales.

2. *Nonacceptance*

The consequences of begging can be worse than loss of face or a bit of derisive laughter, as we will see. This will be easier to understand if we return specifically to the hospitality relation for a moment. It turns out that a guest, by *accepting* hospitality, also accepts a relationship with the host and whatever else that implies.

Recall first the formulaic guest reception scenes we discussed long ago. They often have a feature I have so far not mentioned. The scenes often have two parts: the water, food, seat, and so on are offered by the host, and then they are *accepted* by the guest, usually with the lexeme prati √grah. The full formula seems to be as in MBh I.54.14 pratigṛhya ca tāṃ pūjām "having accepted this honor."[68]

However, sometimes the second step is aborted, the hospitality is rejected. Age-old custom is clearly not violated lightly. Refusal of hospitality brings shame, and worse, to the host, as one of Vidura's gnomic verses tells us:

MBh V.38.3 yasyodakaṃ madhuparkaṃ ca gāṃ ca
na mantravit *pratigṛhṇāti* gṛhe
lobhād bhayād arthakārpaṇyato vā
tasyānarthaṃ jīvitam āhur āryāḥ

(A man) in whose house a mantra-knower *does not accept* the water, the Madhuparka, and the cow,
because of greed, fear, or niggardliness of circumstances—
his life is worthless, so say the Ārya.

Rejection of hospitality serves almost as an official declaration of enmity. We have this from the lips of Kṛṣṇa himself. When he, Bhīma, and Arjuna enter the house of King Jarāsaṃdha with the intention of killing him, they refuse the hospitality of that insistently polite king. When he indignantly asks why, Kṛṣṇa replies with

MBh II.19.50 kāryavanto gṛhān etya śatruto *nārhaṇāṃ* vayam
pratigṛhṇīma tad viddhi etan naḥ śāśvataṃ vratam

When we come to a house on business of a hostile nature,
we *do not accept the honor*. Know this: it is our eternal vow.

Other characters who reject hospitality because of hostile relations include
King Kārtavīrya, who refuses the welcome of Jamadagni's wife (MBh III.116.20) and then ransacks the hermitage and steals a calf.
Rāvana, who scorns Sītā's offer of a meal (MBh III.262.31–32) and then attempts to abduct her.
The Purohita of Daśārṇa, sent to declare war[69] on Drupada, who rejects the cow and the Arghya water proffered to a specially honored guest (MBh V.193.16–17).
Sudhanvan, discussed earlier, who refuses Prahlāda's hospitality because he is engaged in a quarrel with his son (V.35.20–21).
Rejection under these circumstances is in fact required by the legal code.[70]

ĀpDS II.6.19 dviṣan dviṣato vā nānnam aśnīyāt . . .

One should not eat the food of someone he hates or who hates him.

This dharmic provision is effectively dramatized in the MBh in Kṛṣṇa's peace-seeking embassy to the Kurus referred to earlier. As noted there, he is received with elaborate and elaborately described hospitality by whomever he calls on. At Duryodhana's he is offered a meal, but he declines it. Duryodhana takes offense and berates him for his refusal; Kṛṣṇa flashes back, ending with the following statement:

MBh V.89.32 sarvam etad abhoktavyam annaṃ duṣṭābhisaṃhitam
kṣattur ekasya bhoktavyam iti me dhīyate matiḥ

All this food is inedible and spoiled.
Only (the food) of Vidura can be eaten—my mind is made up.

Kṛṣṇa's rejection of Duryodhana's dinner is not an act of personal pique. It is an announcement of hostile relations, whereas acceptance of food indicates the acceptance of at least temporary alliance. Kṛṣṇa is declaring his estrangement from Duryodhana, but he remains in charity with Vidura.

The message conveyed by rejected hospitality explains a curious insistence in ritual texts on the dangerous qualities of a rejected Dakṣiṇā (the priestly gift). As we saw earlier, in a number of parallel stories, beginning in Vedic prose, a rejected Dakṣiṇā is transformed from a tranquil cow (the prototypical Dakṣiṇā) into a savage female beast—a hyena (sālāvṛkī) in KS XXVIII.4 and ĀpŚS XIII.7.12, a lioness (siṃhī) in AB VI.35 and ŚB III.5.1.21, a tigress (vyāghrī) in MS IV.8.3 (110: 8). If taken back by the giver, she destroys him or his herds. The rule, as given by KS, is

KS XXVIII.4 (159: 1) tasmād dakṣiṇā pratinuttā na pratigṛhyā na goṣu cālayet sālāvṛky evainaṃ bhūtvā praviśati sainaṃ nirdahati

Therefore a Dakṣiṇā (once) rejected is not to be accepted back, nor should he allow (her) to wander among the (other) cows. Having become a female hyena, she approaches him and burns him up.

Presumably the enmity that causes the gift to be rejected enters the gift itself, transforming it into an embodiment of hostility that ravages the giver.[71]

3. *Danger: The Beggar in the Power of the Giver*

Let us now return to the predicament of the beggar.[72] Kṛṣṇa has the power to reject the offer of hospitality, as do others in the epic. But a beggar seems *not* to have this power. Though one who yāc's seems to be able to compel his target to give, this ability has its dark side, for the beggar cannot reject what he has asked for, and by accepting it, he tacitly acknowledges a relation with the giver.

Having to accept what is given can have its awkward moments, as in the comic story of Agastya and Ilvala. Agastya and a few companions go to Ilvala to beg some funds. Ilvala receives them graciously and offers them a meal—consisting of his brother Vātāpi, cooked. This is another story (like that of Śibi and his son) in which cannibalism symbolizes the charged and dangerous nature of the hospitality relation.

MBh III.97.2 teṣāṃ tato 'suraśreṣṭha *ātithyam* akarot tadā
sa saṃskṛtena kauravya bhrātrā vātāpinā kila

Then the best of the Asuras made the *Guestly offering* to them,
with his well-prepared [cooked] brother Vātāpi, o Kauravya.

Though very disturbed, the visitors clearly cannot refuse the meal, so Agastya eats, digests, and expels the brother as a fart before any dire consequences can occur. (Ilvala had the power to summon the dead back to their bodies, and it was his custom to cook his dead brother and feed him to Brahmans, then call him back during the digestion process, thereby splitting open the unfortunate feaster [MBh III.94.5–10].) Only at this point does Ilvala ask the formulaic question of his guests: (III.97.8) brūta kiṃ karavāṇi vaḥ "Tell (me): what can I do for you?"

But there are worse things about begging than being offered the occasional unsavory meal. By begging one not only enters into and acknowledges a relation with the giver, but this relation is fundamentally unequal. The beggar in some sense puts himself into the power of the giver and acknowledges his superiority. Recall ŚB II.3.4.7. The beggar got himself a giver, but at the cost of saying "I am your dependent; you are my supporter." The lengthy debate in which this passage is embedded depicts a sycophantic toady yāc-ing his master, flattering and fawning on his superior until the superior thinks himself compelled or bound to give. There is a certain amount of rather comic dithering about how best to go about the business of yāc-ing, so as not to annoy the one so approached. In other words, when you yāc someone, you are tacitly or openly acknowledging their superiority and their power over you, as well as their possession of the thing begged.

The acknowledgment of the power of the one you beg, as well as a nervous desire not to offend, can already be seen in a RVic passage containing the verb yāc:

RV VIII.1.20 mā́ tvā . . . sádā *yā́cann* ahám girā́ . . . sávaneṣu cukrudhaṃ
ká *ī́śānaṃ* ná *yāciṣat*

Let me not annoy you [Indra] at the soma pressings, when I'm always *begging* you with song.
Who wouldn't *beg* (his) *master*?

The RVic hymn concerning the Prātaritvan, which we have already examined, also may refer to the power of host over guest. Consider the curious last pāda of the householder's verse:

RV I.125.2cd yás tvāyántaṃ vásunā prātaritvo mukṣī́jayeva pádim utsinā́ti

(That host will thrive) who, o Prātaritvan, binds you up like a bird (?) with a snare (?), you coming hither with goods.

Our interpretation of this pāda is somewhat hampered by the fact that we have no idea what either mukṣī́jā or pádi means, but as Oldenberg pointed out (*Noten*, ad loc.), though we do not know the meanings of these words, the sense is pretty clear. The householder is *tying up* (ud √sā) the priestly visitor like some small animal (probably)—a rather jarring way of describing a supposedly benign hospitality relation. On this model, in the Manu's Cups story Manu would be 'tying up' the Asuric Brahmans by receiving them and allowing them to sacrifice for him. They come into his power by compelling his hospitality.

The Asuric Brahmans learn the extent of the power of the giver to their sorrow. After Manu has surrendered his wife to the Asuras, they sprinkle her and perform the fire-circuit, then go off to collect the rest of the ritual necessities. Indra recognizes the danger, disguises himself as another Brahman, reminds Manu of his devotion and Śraddhā, and offers to sacrifice for him, using the two Asuric Brahmans as the sacrificial animals. Manu is momentarily nonplussed, and the dialogue continues:

> MS IV.8.1 (107: 11) *ī́śe* 'hám̐ brāhmaṇáyor ítī́śiṣe hī́ty abravīd *átithipatir* vā́vā́tithīnām *īṣṭā* íti
>
> "Am I *master* of the two Brahmans?" "Indeed you are *master*," said (Indra), "A *lord of guests* [host] is *master of his guests*."

The sacrifice is then set in motion and the two Asuras destroyed. This ingenious exchange sets on its head the lordship ascribed to the *guest* in one of the later legal texts:

> ViSmṛ LXVII.31 yathā varṇānām̐ brāhmaṇaḥ prabhur yathā strīṇām̐ bhartā tathā gṛhasthasyātithiḥ
>
> Even as the Brahman is lord of the (other) classes, even as the husband (is lord) of wives, so is the guest (lord) of the householder.

And so the denouement of Manu's Cups shows the other side of the hospitality relation—the anxiety of the guest. By accepting hospitality and asking for gifts, the guest has delivered himself into the power of his host, if only temporarily. The host has not only the ceremonial title atithi-pati 'lord of guests', but the real power expressed by the verb √īś 'be master of'. Although no doubt Manu's power to dispose of his guests in this final fashion depended on their own prior violations of hospitality, the uneasy circumstances of *any* guest are clear here in Indra's clever and sophistic pronouncement. The careful regulation of hospitality relations spelled out in later texts, evident beneath the surface in Vedic texts, and paralleled in kindred traditions, responded to the tense and ambiguous reality that must have existed in this realm.

V

Women and Marriage

A. Marriage and Exchange

It may seem curious to have postponed for so long the discussion of the most obvious social institution affecting women in ancient India, namely marriage, but this delay was deliberate. By examining the roles women play in the pure and controllable hypothetical world of the ritual, we can identify some of these same conceptual positions in the messier realm of reality (or reality as depicted by our texts: we are always at some degrees of removal).

Perhaps even more important, our recent explorations of the tensions between strangers in the Aryan community and the anxieties inherent in the hospitality relationship required of members of that community provide us with information crucial to understanding the dynamics of marriage in this society. The creation of marital alliances is one response to the uneasy nature of the contacts between mutually obligated strangers. But, as our examination of the fraught nature of gift-exchange has also shown, the exchange at the heart of marriage will create tensions of its own, which need their own institutionalized means of resolution. In what follows, we will consider the results of these built-in anxieties on the structure and functioning of the system of marriage.

I have had occasion several times before to refer to marriage as the fundamental exchange relation in ancient India, the relation that allows women to serve in symbolic exchange roles throughout the religious sphere.[1] As Rubin has so aptly characterized women's role in the Lévi-Straussian concept of marital exchange in general:

> If it is women who are being transacted, then it is the men who give and take them who are linked, the women being a conduit of a relationship rather than a partner to it. . . . If women are the gifts, then it is men who are the exchange partners. And it is the partners, not the presents, upon whom reciprocal exchange confers its quasi-magical power of social linkage.[2]

The marriage alliance is a crucial one in the formation of linkages between noncontiguous portions of the Aryan community[3]—thus providing *synchronic* social cohesion—and an appropriate marriage is also the foundation for a proper continuation of the family, a *diachronic* consideration. A marriage thus serves the same functions as the Śrāddha ceremony discussed earlier, but in a much more permanent fashion, linking the males of the Aryan community in both horizontal and vertical bonds. It is no surprise then that in early Vedic the god Aryaman, guardian of 'custom' and 'civilization' and in some sense the embodiment of the Aryan community, has marriage under his special protection.[4] Nor should it be surprising that so much of the Mahābhārata, especially its crucial first book, should concern the making of marriages.

I do not have space in this work to embark on a full treatment of marriage in early India, and indeed much of the crucial material has been assembled elsewhere.[5] What I want to concentrate on is the marital exchange relation itself, in particular the assimilation of the bride to an exchange token and the way in which this token is then given—or taken. We have recently examined the anxieties of gift exchange in general. These anxieties can become heightened when the 'gift' is also a maiden and exchanging her creates a marriage.

1. Maiden as Commodity

Let me begin by examining a few episodes where the maiden as commodity is most nakedly evident.[6] The first is one version of the famous story of the old seer Cyavana and his young bride Sukanyā. This tale is found in the ŚB (IV.1.5), the JB (III.120–28), and the MBh (III.122–24) and is already present (darkly, as usual) in the RV. In all three versions, when the faithful[7] Sukanyā refuses to abandon her decrepit husband for the young and beautiful Aśvins, the latter make him young again, and Sukanyā is thus rewarded for her loyalty. But the versions differ in the exact details of how Sukanyā ended up married to Cyavana in the first place. In both ŚB and JB the marriage stems from trouble started by young men belonging to the clan of Sukanyā's father, Śaryāta Mānava. When the lads pelt the ascetic with clods of earth (and worse), Cyavana uses his powers to cause dissension in the clan, and Śaryāta realizes he must placate the seer.

In ŚB Śaryāta simply offers his daughter to Cyavana as appeasement, but the JB has a more interesting scenario. Śaryāta goes to Cyavana to ask forgiveness, and Cyavana demands Sukanyā (JB III.122 sa vai me sukanyāṃ dehi "give me Sukanyā"). Śaryāta at first refuses and tries to deflect the seer to a more acceptable gift, but Cyavana is adamant. So Śaryāta goes back to consult the rest. Their deliberations are purely economic. Family sentiment is not involved, and their decision goes in favor of Cyavana's demand:

> JB III.122 ekaṃ vai dve trīṇi paramam anayā dhanāni labhemahy athānayeha sarvam eva lapsyāmahe hantāsmā imāṃ dadāmeti
>
> [They deliberated:] "One (measure of) wealth (or) two, at most three would we get with her. But in this case we will get *everything* with her. Blast it, let's give her to him."

At issue clearly is the expected bride-price. Her kinsmen have obviously calculated her worth in the bridal market (with some shrewd assessment of possible fluctuations in that market) and decide that Cyavana's offer is an unexpectedly good deal. The numbers add up, and they do give her to him (though they attempt to allow her to escape—which would let them bargain her away to another husband), after which the story continues as in the other versions.

The MBh story of Mādhavī does indeed contain multiple bargainings of the same girl, an opportunity that Śaryāta missed. In this story a young Brahman named Gālava at the end of his studentship keeps asking his guru Viśvāmitra what he would like for a guru-gift. The guru gets irritated at this continual questioning and finally demands an outrageous return—eight hundred moon-white horses, each with a black ear—which, of course, Gālava cannot afford. But he is stuck with the bargain, and begins a begging round to kings known to be rich. The first on his list is the famous Yayāti, who, however, is in comparatively narrow financial straits. Though he cannot give the horses himself, he gives Gālava the means to acquire them. This "means" is Yayāti's own daughter, Mādhavī, whom Gālava is to *exchange for the horses*:

MBh V.113.12 . . . sutā me pratigṛhyatām
13 asyāḥ śulkaṃ pradāsyanti nṛpā rājyam api dhruvam
kiṃ punaḥ śyāmakarṇānāṃ hayānāṃ dve catuḥśate

[Yayāti said:] "Take my daughter.
Kings will surely give their kingdom as her bride-price.
Why not eight hundred black-eared horses?"

So Gālava sets off with a valuable commodity to exchange, and he hawks her with merchandizing zeal:

MBh V.113.20 kanyeyaṃ mama rājendra prasavaiḥ kulavardhinī
21 iyaṃ śulkena bhāryārthe haryaśva pratigṛhyatām
śulkaṃ te kīrtayiṣyāmi tac chrutvā saṃpradhāryatām

[Gālava said:] "This maiden of mine, o best of kings, will increase your lineage with offspring.
Take her for a wife, o Haryaśva, at (this) bride-price.
I will mention the price to you. Consider it carefully when you hear it."

But all of India seems to be suffering a recession. The first king he offers the girl to, Haryaśva, looks her over as if she were a horse herself (MBh V.114.2–4), noting her good points and her breeding potential, and agrees to hear the price:

MBh V.114.4 brūhi śulkaṃ dvijaśreṣṭha samīkṣya vibhavaṃ mama

[Haryaśva said:] "Tell me her bride-price, o best of the twice-born, with some consideration for (the extent of) my property."

Unfortunately Gālava has miscalculated that extent, as Haryaśva has only two hundred of the horses. He suggests a deal, that he should beget only one son on the girl, in exchange for the two hundred. At this point Mādhavī herself speaks for the first time, suggesting a remarkable commercial scheme that will net Gālava all of his horses while taking account of the depressed market in girls. Like so many other Mahābhārata maidens, Mādhavī possesses conveniently renewing virginity: after each childbirth she will become a virgin again. So she suggests that Gālava accept Haryaśva's cut-rate offer and repeat it with three other kings:

MBh V.114.11 sa tvaṃ dadasva māṃ rājñe pratigṛhya hayottamān
12 nṛpebhyo hi caturbhyas te pūrṇāny aṣṭau śatāni vai

[Mādhavī said:] "Give me to the king, taking the best of horses.
From four kings you will have the full eight hundred."

And so it happens. Gālava hands her over to a king; they disport themselves and finally have a son; then Gālava comes to collect the newly virgin Mādhavī and peddles her to the next one. The third king, Uśīnara, Gālava attempts to persuade into a double deal: two sons for four hundred horses, but Uśīnara only has the usual two hundred and must settle for one son (MBh V.116). With this the world's supply of moon-white black-eared horses is exhausted (MBh V.117.3–9), and Gālava takes the collected six hundred and presents them to his guru, along with Mādhavī in lieu of the other two hundred.

MBh V.117.11 aśvānāṃ kāṅkṣitārthānāṃ ṣaḍ imāni śatāni vai
śatadvayena kanyeyaṃ bhavatā pratigṛhyatām
12 asyāṃ rājarṣibhiḥ putrā jātā vai dhārmikās trayaḥ
caturthaṃ janayatv ekaṃ bhavān api narottama
13 pūrṇāny evaṃ śatāny aṣṭau turagāṇāṃ bhavantu te

[Gālava said:] "Here are six hundred horses in fulfillment of your expressed desire.
For the other two hundred, let your grace take this maiden.
Three dharmic sons have (already) been begotten on her by priestly sages.
Let your grace beget the fourth, o best of men.
Thus you should have (the equivalent of) the full eight hundred horses."

The guru has the gallantry to suggest that Gālava should have given him the girl in the first place (so he could have had four sons), but accepts her services for one son, as well as keeping the horses (MBh V.117.15–16).

Gālava is thus finally quit of his gift-giving obligation, thanks to Mādhavī's industry, and he returns her to her father Yayāti, who holds a bridal self-choice (svayaṃvara) for her (MBh V.118). It is perhaps not surprising that Mādhavī bypasses all the assembled suitors and chooses the forest as her bridegroom (V.118.5 vanaṃ vṛtavatī varam), where she proceeds to live alone, practicing austerities among the gentle beasts. She had surely had enough of men!

This tale is chilling in its frank dealing with numerical equivalence relations between women and commodities, the unembarrassed selling of a girl by a stranger who got her in a trade,[8] and the repeated details of the financial negotiations. But it is only an extreme example of the general treatment of marriage in ancient India: in both legal and narrative texts the crucial issue in marriage is the *transfer* of the bride from the paternal to the conjugal domain, and the costs and benefits entailed for both parties in this transaction.

2. *The Eight Forms of Marriage*

As is well known, Sanskrit legal texts classify marriage into eight types.[9] What distinguishes these types from each other are the occasion and circumstances under which the bride comes into the groom's possession. Though this is not the place for a complete treatment of this marital typology, in what follows I want briefly to examine the different exchange relations that characterize the different marriage types and then discuss in detail one of these types, the difficult case of marriage by abduction, which throws unexpected light on the anxieties of gift exchange we have noticed in other contexts.

Before doing this, however, we should have available a conspectus of the marriage types, which can be conveniently abstracted from Manu:

MDŚ III.27 ācchādya cārcayitvā ca śrutiśīlavate svayam
āhūya dānaṃ kanyāyā *brāhmo* dharmaḥ prakīrtitaḥ

The gift of a maiden, (the father) having adorned and honored (her) (with ornaments, etc.), and having himself invited (the bridegroom), to a man of Vedic learning and good character—that is called the *Brāhma* rite.

MDŚ III.28 yajñe tu vitate samyag ṛtvije karma kurvate
alaṃkṛtya sutādānāṃ *daivaṃ* dharmaṃ pracakṣate

The gift of a daughter, having ornamented her, to a priest correctly performing a rite, when the ritual has been set out—they call that the *Daiva* rite.

MDŚ III.29 ekaṃ gomithunaṃ dve vā varād ādāya dharmataḥ
kanyāpradānaṃ vidhivad *ārṣo* dharmaḥ sa ucyate

The gift of a maiden according to rule, on having received from the bridegroom a pair or two of oxen by law—that is called the *Ārṣa* rite.

MDŚ III.30 sahobhau caratāṃ dharmam iti vācānubhāṣya ca
kanyāpradānam abhyarcya *prājāpatyo* vidhiḥ smṛtaḥ

The gift of a maiden, after having addressed (the pair) with the words, "Together do ye both practice dharma," and having honored (her)—that is known as the *Prājāpatya* rule.

MDŚ III.31 jñātibhyo draviṇaṃ dattvā kanyāyai caiva śaktitaḥ
kanyāpradānaṃ svācchandyād *āsuro* dharma ucyate

The gift of a maiden voluntarily (to one) who has given wealth to her relations and to the maiden as far as possible—that is called the *Āsura* rite.

MDŚ III.32 icchayānyonyasaṃyogaḥ kanyāyāś ca varasya ca
gāndharvaḥ sa tu vijñeyo maithunyaḥ kāmasaṃbhavaḥ

The mutual union by desire of a maiden and the bridegroom is to be known as the *Gāndharva* (rite) devoted to sexual intercourse and arising from lust.

MDŚ III.33 hatvā chittvā ca bhittvā ca krośantīṃ rudatīṃ gṛhāt
prasahya kanyāharaṇaṃ *rākṣaso* vidhir ucyate

The abduction by force of a maiden, weeping and wailing, from her house, after smashing and cleaving and breaking (her relatives and household), that is called the *Rākṣasa* rule.

MDŚ III.34 suptāṃ mattāṃ pramattāṃ vā raho yatropagacchati
sa pāpiṣṭho vivāhānāṃ *paiśācaś* cāṣṭamo 'dhamaḥ

When (a man) approaches in secret (a maiden) who is asleep, intoxicated, or inattentive,
that most evil of marriages is the *Paiśāca*, the eighth and lowest.

The texts differ in their views of the legality and desirability of the marriage types. They almost all condemn the last one and applaud the first three or four, but are ambivalent and contradictory about those in the middle.[10] These attitudes can, in my opinion, be correlated with the amount and type of *exchange* involved in each type.

The condemned Paiśāca "marriage" is of course simply rape of a girl who is too incapacitated to defend herself or to summon others to do so. It is important to note that the rape occurs in secret (rahas): though the man *takes* the girl, he does not take her *from* anyone. There is no exchange because there is no other responsible party. This lack explains its nearly universal illegality in contrast to the two marriages above it in the scale, the Rākṣasa and the Gāndharva, which many texts allow, at least for some varṇas.[11] I will discuss the Rākṣasa marriage at great length below. Suffice it to say here that though it too looks like rape, indeed aggravated rape, it remains inside the law, however precariously, because there *are* other parties—the wounded family and the wailing bride—who (unwillingly) participate in the transfer, and their absence makes the abduction illegal, as we will see.

Similarly, in the Gāndharva marriage the two participants agree mutually (anyonya) and willingly (icchayā), and so, no matter how hasty and lust-driven the encounter, it may count as a legal marriage. What makes its legality shaky is not the sexual impetus, but the issue of whether the girl has the legal standing to enter into such an agreement, to *give herself* away. Clearly under some circumstances she does, and this freedom seems to apply here as well. I will return to this question below.

Let me now turn to the first five, rather less exciting types. What sets these five off from the others is the type of exchange that characterizes all of them. Each involves the *gift* of the maiden (by her father or other responsible guardian). Note the nearly synonymous expressions found in Manu: dānaṃ kanyāyāḥ (Brāhma), sutādānām (Daiva), kanyāpradānam (Ārṣa, Prājāpatya, Āsura),[12] and Manu's dictum that this gift is what creates the bridegroom's mastery over the bride (MDŚ V.152 pradānaṃ svāmyakāraṇam). Both the paternal and the conjugal representatives are willing parties in an exchange of property, which establishes a particular type of linkage between them. As we saw above, the *giving* of a gift implies a conscious and willing *recipient*, who by accepting the gift acknowledges a relationship of obligation with the giver. Both roles have their risks, especially that of the recipient, but the relationship forged thereby may be a benefit for both parties. The classification of these marriage types as 'gifts' invests them with all the qualities associated with ordinary gift exchange—in concentrated form, since the 'gift' is a potentially valuable one (if she is fertile) and the ensuing relationship likely to be long lasting.

3. Bride-Price and the Selling of the Daughter

Having noted what these five types have in common, let us now try to characterize their differences. Our first and easiest task is to distinguish the first four from the fifth, which may not properly be associated with them at all. As mentioned in note 12, no other text besides MDŚ defines the Āsura marriage as gift (in the presentation of the marital typology), and it is fairly clear why: this marriage type involves a śulka 'bride-price' given by the bridegroom to the family of the bride and the bride herself.[13] This might politely be called a countergift (and originally probably was, as we will see), but most texts treat it rather as a sales price and the Āsura marriage as straight selling of a daughter. ViSmṛ XXIV.24 has perhaps the bluntest statement: krayeṇāsuraḥ "(A marriage) by purchase (is called) Āsura (marriage)."

Yet the earliest use of the word śulka in a marriage context involves *reciprocal exchange* between bride and bridegroom, in a mutually contracted marriage which is also a cautionary tale about the dire effects of lack of exchange:

> JB I.145 imau vai lokau saha santau vyaitāṃ tayor na kiṃcana samapatat te devamanuṣyā aśanāyann itaḥpradānād dhi devā jīvanty amutaḥpradānān manuṣyās te bṛhadrathantare abrūtāṃ ye nāv ime priye tanvau tābhyāṃ vivahāvahā iti . . . tābhyāṃ vyavahetām uṣān evāsāv amuto 'syai *śulkam* akarod dhūmam ita iyam amuṣyai varṣam evāsāv amuto 'syai *śulkam* akarod devayajanam ita iyam amuṣyai
>
> These two worlds [heaven and earth], being (originally) together, went apart. Nothing whatever came to either one of them (from the other). The gods and men went hungry, for the gods live from what is given from here [earth], men from what is given from yonder [heaven]. The Bṛhad and Rathantara (Sāmans) said, "Let us arrange a marriage by means of these two dear bodies of ours." They arranged a marriage by means of them. Yonder (heaven) made saline soil (as) a *śulka* for this (earth) from yonder; this (earth) made (sacrificial?) smoke (as a *śulka*) for yonder (heaven)[14] from here. Yonder (heaven) made rain (as) a *śulka* for this (earth) from yonder; this (earth) (made) the place of worship (as a *śulka*) for yonder (heaven) from here.[15]

Here the śulka is clearly not a *bride*-price originating from only one side of the exchange relation, but a wedding gift that elicits a complementary countergift. Each gift completes the other, and the traffic in gifts from here to yonder and yonder to here knits together the two worlds again and makes life possible. If śulka was originally used thus in a marriage context, then the acceptance of a śulka by the bride's father was not at first tantamount to a sale.

This evolution in the meaning and practical value of the śulka may in part account for the extreme ambivalence about this marriage type displayed in the dharma texts. It is roundly condemned in theory in the legal texts and in the epic,[16] as in

> MDŚ IX.98 ādadīta na śūdro 'pi śulkaṃ duhitaraṃ dadan
> śulkaṃ hi gṛhṇan kurute channaṃ duhitṛvikrayam

Even a Śūdra should not take a bride-price when giving his daughter.
For in taking a bride-price he commits covert daughter-selling.

But as we have seen already in the stories of Sukanyā and Mādhavī, a bride-price[17] is a routine element in a father's deliberations about marrying off his daughter, and it is not merely a token gift. Mādhavī was on offer for the fantastic sum of eight hundred moon-white, black-eared horses. Nor is bridal sale in the epic restricted to the mythic past. Mādrī, the second wife of Pāṇḍu and mother of the twins Nakula and Sahadeva, was such a purchase:

MBh I.105.4 . . . mādrī madrapateḥ sutā
5 . . . pāṇḍor arthe parikrītā dhanena mahatā tadā
vivāhaṃ kārayām āsa bhīṣmaḥ pāṇḍor mahātmanaḥ

Mādrī, daughter of the lord of Madras, was bought for a great sum for Pāṇḍu's sake.
Bhīṣma thus arranged the marriage for great-souled Pāṇḍu.

Much later in the text (MBh XIII.44.18ff.) Bhīṣma and Yudhiṣṭhira engage in a complicated legal discussion about competing claimants for a girl, one of whom has already given a śulka—a discussion that implicitly assumes that a śulka can be a normal and respectable part of the marriage negotiations. Even Manu, whose high-minded rejection of bridal purchase has already been cited, elsewhere allows the bridegroom a two-for-one deal on a śulka, when the father has engaged in deception:

MDŚ VIII.204 anyāṃ ced darśayitvānyā voḍhuḥ kanyā pradīyate
ubhe te ekaśulkena vahed ity abravīn manuḥ

"If after (the father) has displayed one maiden, another is given to the bridegroom,
he may marry them both for one bride-price." So Manu said.

And just before a verse condemning the acceptance of śulkas (MDŚ IX.98), he treats the case of a man who dies after giving a śulka: the girl in this case is handed on to his brother.

MDŚ IX.97 kanyāyāṃ dattaśulkāyāṃ mriyeta yadi śulkadaḥ
devarāya pradātavyā yadi kanyānumanyate

In the case of a maiden for whom a bride-price has been given, if the giver of the bride-price dies,
she is to be given to the brother-in-law if the maiden agrees.

In an earlier text (MS I.10.11 [151: 3]) the Sacrificer's Wife (patnī) is said to have been "bought by her husband" (pátyuḥ krītā́), a passage that contradicts the BDS provision that a purchased woman is not a real wife (patnī) and cannot participate in ritual:

BDS I.21.2 . . . krītā dravyeṇa yā nārī sā na patnī vidhīyate/sā na daive na sā pitrye dāsīṃ tāṃ kaśyapo 'bravīt

A woman bought for money does not count as a patnī. She (cannot take part) in (ritual) to the gods or the Pitṛs. Kaśyapa called her a slave.

Despite the continually expressed disapproval of the bride-price, then, it is hard to escape the conclusion that it was a common custom, if slightly distasteful to the delicate-minded. The objection to the śulka was presumably not the simple fact that the groom offered the bride's family something in exchange for her. Reciprocal exchange, gift and countergift, are, after all, a central ideal of the culture. Rather, it seems likely that a bride-price of sufficient value would truncate exchange relations rather than establishing them. If the groom gives something worth as much as the bride (however this is calculated), he is quit of further obligations to her family, and one of the aims of marriage, to make long-term alliances among families, is frustrated. In other words, sale/purchase, with equivalence of value on both sides, produces a fleeting relationship, finished as soon as the transfer is complete. Because the two items exchanged are of equal worth, there is no lingering inequity to require a continuing relationship between the trading partners. This is an inappropriate model for marital exchange, where the *imbalance* of giver and recipient creates the desirable tension of as yet unfulfilled reciprocity.

4. *Types of Marriage by Gift*

Let me now turn to the first four marriage types, which unequivocally involve the gift of the bride. These are somewhat hard to distinguish from each other and conceptually can almost be collapsed. In fact MGS I.7.11 seems to do just that, suggesting that an approved girl should be given according either to the Brāhma or the Śaulka rule (saṃjuṣṭāṃ dharmeṇopayaccheta brāhmeṇa śaulkena vā).[18] The latter is clearly the Āsura marriage I have just discussed; the former probably refers globally to straightforward kanyādāna ('gift of a maiden'), whatever its particular manifestation. The Brāhma marriage in fact seems to be the unmarked type of "gift"-marriage, with the three others displaying particular, usually minor variations.

The easiest type to understand is the Daiva, the gift of a girl to a priest performing a ritual:

MDŚ III.28 yajñe tu vitate samyag ṛtvije karma kurvate
alaṃkṛtya sutādānāṃ daivaṃ dharmaṃ pracakṣate

The gift of a daughter, having ornamented her, to a priest correctly performing a rite, when the ritual has been set out—they call the Daiva rule.

The point here is not simply that the girl has made a respectable match, a man of the cloth rather than young man with more dubious moral credentials. Something else is involved than teas at the vicarage and jumble sales. The girl is being given *as a Dakṣiṇā*; she is part of the priestly gift or fee, as at least one legal text makes clear:

BDS I.20.5 dakṣiṇāsu nīyamānāsv antarvedy ṛtvije sa daivaḥ

(The gift of a maiden) to an officiating priest within the vedi when the (other) Dakṣiṇās are being led away, that is the Daiva (marriage).

Though some apologists[19] have attempted to deny the Daiva bride's status as Dakṣiṇā, a kind of superior cow, given in payment for ritual services rendered, it is hard to escape this conclusion. That women formed part of patrons' gifts to their skilled servitors (priests or poets) is clear from the RV, where they frequently figure in Dānastutis (the 'praise of the gift' [and its giver] with which a canny poet often ends his hymn). The word used there is frequently vadhū́ 'bride', as in

RV VIII.19.36 ádān me paurukutsyáḥ pañcāśátaṃ trasádasyur *vadhū́nām*
máṃhiṣṭho aryáḥ sátpatiḥ

Trasadasyu Paurukutsya, most generous, noble lord of substance, has given me fifteen *brides*.[20]

A woman as part of a priest's Dakṣiṇā is clearly found in the MŚS treatment of the "ritual for the acceptance of gifts," which prescribes what to say and what to do when given various kinds of Dakṣiṇās, the first of which is a woman (puruṣī):

MŚS XI.1.4 prajāpataye tveti puruṣīṃ pratigṛhṇīyād dhastinaṃ puruṣaṃ bhūmim . . .
2.1 puruṣīṁ haste gṛhītvā . . .

(Saying) "Thee for Prajāpati," he should accept a woman, an elephant, a man, land . . .
Having grasped the woman by the hand . . .

Lumping a girl in with livestock, gold, chariots, and the other assorted items often making up Dakṣiṇās (e.g. embroidered pillows, used clothing) gives the 'marriage' here a slightly tawdry air, and may account for Kṛṣṇa's dismissal of "gift"-marriage in the MBh (a passage to which I will return):

MBh I.213.4 pradānam api kanyāyāḥ paśuvat ko 'numaṃsyate

Who approves of the gift of a maiden, (as if she were) cattle?

The Ārṣa marriage presents us with a different interpretive problem, in that it appears to involve sale and to resemble the disapproved Āsura marriage already discussed.

MDŚ III.29 ekaṃ gomithunaṃ dve vā varād ādāya dharmataḥ
kanyāpradānaṃ vidhivad ārṣo dharmaḥ sa ucyate

The gift of a maiden according to rule, on having received from the bridegroom a pair or two of oxen by law—that is called the Ārṣa rite.

Not surprisingly, the difference between Ārṣa and Āsura marriages is hotly debated among the commentators, and the texts go to some length to deny that the pair of oxen (gomithuna) is in any way a śulka,[21] as in Manu's statement:

> MDŚ III.53 ārṣe gomithunaṃ śulkaṃ ke cid āhur mṛṣaiva tat
>
> Some people call the pair of oxen at the Ārṣa wedding a śulka, but falsely.

The bovine pair is only a token of respect (arhaṇam) towards the maiden (MDŚ III.54).

This interpretation seems a later rationalization of the embarrassing existence of an apparent bride-price in this "gift"-marriage. I think the explanation is somewhat different and requires taking into account several other factors. On the one hand the identity of the gift suggests a ritual function. The *pair* (mithuna) of oxen is likely to be an emblem of fertility and a model for the newly married couple: as we saw above, the word mithuna is used especially of productive sexual pairings. Moreover, it is possible that the oxen are destined to be sacrificed for the wedding feast (just as a cow is offered for slaughter to a guest, as we saw). This possibility is strengthened by the fact that the transfer of the pair is made in the middle of the wedding ceremony, according to BDS:

> BDS I.20.4 pūrvāṃ lājāhutiṃ kṛtvā gomithunaṃ kanyāvate dattvā grahaṇam ārṣaḥ[22]
>
> (If) after making the first offering of parched grain and having given a pair of oxen to the maiden's guardian, (the bridegroom) receives (her)—that is the Ārṣa marriage.

Moreover, as discussed earlier, the objection to the bride-price in the Āsura marriage was not that the bridegroom gave something in exchange for the bride, but that, if the bride-price was considered equivalent in value to the bride, it stopped the flow of exchange. Here the pair of oxen would clearly not be worth as much as a maiden (if a beautiful girl is worth eight hundred special horses), and so the countergift encourages exchange relations rather than arresting them.[23]

We come finally to the Prājāpatya marriage, whose special features are the most difficult to distinguish of the four "gift"-marriages. Indeed several texts omit it in their typologies (e.g. ĀpDS; VāsDS; probably MBh I.96). The mark of a Prājāpatya marriage, according to most texts (MDŚ III.30; YājñSmṛ I.60; GDS IV.7; BDS I.20.3; ĀśvGS I.6.3),[24] is the mantra that accompanies the ceremony: sahobhau caratāṃ dharmam "Together do ye both practice dharma." The reference is clearly to the joint duties of husband and wife in ritual—a topic I have already extensively discussed—but it is puzzling because wives married according to other legal types also share ritual duties with their husbands. Commentators have attempted to account for this inconsistency by suggesting that the husband in a Prājāpatya marriage undertook not to marry an additional wife,[25] but there seems no early evidence for such an interpretation. Moreover, in the epic sahadharmacarin/-cāriṇī 'joint-dharma-practicing' seems to be a byword for an observant wife of whatever type (cf. e.g. MBh I.145.31; I.App. I, No. 100.98; XII. App. 19.129, 136; XIII.134.7, 32).[26] Similarly, in the Rāmāyaṇa when Rāma has won Sītā in marriage by demonstrating valor as bride-price (vīryaśulka, a term to which I will return), Sītā's father addresses him thus:

R I.72.17 abravīj janako rājā kausalyānandavardhanam
iyaṃ sītā mama sutā *sahadharmacarī* tava
pratīccha caināṃ bhadraṃ te pāṇiṃ gṛhṇīṣva pāṇinā

King Janaka said to (Rāma), the increaser of the joy of Kausalyā [Rāma's mother]:
"Here is Sītā my daughter, your *joint-dharma-practicer.*
Please accept her; grasp (her) hand with (your) hand."

It may be that in the Prājāpatya type a verbal marriage *formula*, establishing a particularly important wifely role—that of ritual partner—has been extracted from the ordinary marriage ceremony and identified as a separate marriage *type*. It is, however, at least possible that the Prājāpatya marriage was originally a marriage of mutual agreement, like the Gāndharva marriage, arising not from lust as in the latter type, but from a mutually felt desire to embark on ritual responsibilities.[27] The emphasis on the word saha 'joint' might then indicate that the marriage was originally conceived as an equal venture, a partnership between two independent parties. Such a marriage might have as a model the JB marriage of heaven and earth, with mutual exchange of śulkas, discussed earlier. Unfortunately we have insufficient evidence to support such an intriguing view.

I have examined the various exchange mechanisms that characterize most of the different legally defined marriage types in ancient India. Let us now turn to the thorniest of these types, the Rākṣasa marriage or marriage by abduction, whose legality in the face of its brutality is baffling. An extended treatment of this marriage type will show how the politics of exchange relations not only allow but *require* this marriage type, and also how the violence is controlled and made dharmic within the marital system.

B. Marriage by Capture

As we have seen, the Rākṣasa (lit. 'demonic') marriage—marriage by capture or abduction—was defined with unblinking violence as

MDŚ III.33 hatvā chittvā ca bhittvā ca krośantīṃ rudatīṃ gṛhāt
prasahya kanyāharaṇaṃ rākṣaso vidhir ucyate

The abduction by force of a maiden, weeping and wailing, from her house, after smashing and cleaving and breaking (her relatives and household), that is called the Rākṣasa rite.[28]

The texts usually agree, sometimes reluctantly, in considering this type of marriage legal for Kṣatriyas, along with the more peaceable Gāndharva type, marriage by mutual agreement. It is sometimes instead tellingly called Kṣātra 'warrior's' marriage (e.g. VāsDS I.29, 34).

The lurid nature of this marriage type has guaranteed frequent discussion in the secondary literature,[29] but it is usually treated there as an uncontrolled and barbarous survival of a precivilized social stage[30]—wild and unpredictable behavior to be expected from the violent Kṣatriyas, but only precariously adapted into dharmic orthodoxy. However, examination of the Rākṣasa marriages depicted in the Mahābhārata shows that, despite the violence and outward chaos, the procedure followed in a Rākṣasa marriage is fixed and orderly and mimics in general outline and in many details the ordinary marriage ceremony as presented in the gṛhya sūtras. Conversely, that tranquil ceremony contains some features that evoke the more harried atmosphere of the abduction-marriage. Some conclusions to be drawn, and *not* drawn, from this overlap will be discussed later.

1. *'Demonic' (Rākṣasa) Marriages in the Mahābhārata*

I will begin with the most discursive depiction of a Rākṣasa marriage, Bhīṣma's abduction of Ambā and her two sisters on behalf of his brother Vicitravīrya, which is narrated at length twice in the Mahābhārata (I.96, V.170).[31] Bhīṣma, wishing to find his brother a wife (or wives), hears about the upcoming svayaṃvara (bridal 'self-choice') of the three sisters. He comes to the svayaṃvara, sweeps the girls onto his chariot, and carries them away, after defeating the assembled forces. The central part of the narrative in V.170 is as follows:

V.170.11 so 'ham *ekarathenaiva* gataḥ kāśipateḥ purīm
apaśyaṃ tā mahābāho tisraḥ kanyāḥ svalaṃkṛtāḥ
rājñaś caiva samāvṛttān pārthivān pṛthivīpate
12 tato 'haṃ tān nṛpān sarvān *āhūya samare* sthitān
ratham āropayāṃ cakre kanyās tā bharatarṣabha
13 *vīryaśulkāś* ca tā jñātvā *samāropya ratham* tadā
avocaṃ pārthivān sarvān ahaṃ tatra samāgatān
bhīṣmaḥ śāṃtanavaḥ kanyā haratīti punaḥ punaḥ
14 te yatadhvaṃ paraṃ śaktyā sarve mokṣāya pārthivāḥ
prasahya hi nayāmy eṣa miṣatāṃ vo narādhipāḥ
15 tatas te pṛthivīpālāḥ samutpetur udāyudhāḥ
yogo yoga iti kruddhāḥ sārathīṃś cāpy acodayan

11 I came *on a single chariot* to the city of Kāśipati.
I saw, o strong-armed one, the three well-adorned maidens
and the assembled earthly kings, o earthlord.
12 Then, *having challenged in battle* all the kings standing there,
I *made* the maidens *mount the chariot,* o bull of the Bharatas.
13 Having recognized that *their bride-price was a manly deed,* once I had *made them mount the chariot,*

I proclaimed to all the kings assembled there,
"Bhīṣma Śāṃtanava takes these maidens," again and again.
14 "Do ye all make the highest effort with (all your) ability to free (them), o earthlords.
For I lead/marry them by force before your eyes, o leaders of men."
15 Then the earthlords flew up together, with weapons raised.
With *"the yoke, the yoke,"* they angrily spurred on their charioteers.

There follow several verses (16–21), in which Bhīṣma defeats them all and goes home with the young women.

I have underlined what I consider the crucial thematic elements in the passage and tabulate them as follows:

1. Abductor's journey on a single chariot (ekarathena, vs. 11).
2. Abductor's verbal behavior: challenge (āhūya, vs. 12), repeated announcement of identity (vs. 13), announcement of intention and specific challenge (vs. 14).
3. Abductor makes maiden(s) mount chariot (vss. 12, 13).
4. Abductor offers fighting as a bride-price (vīrya-śulka, vs. 13); fights and defeats the assembled kings (vss. 15–21).

That these are not random elements in the narrative is clear from their appearance in some other narratives of Rākṣasa abductions. The two most discursive are the other version of Bhīṣma's abduction in I.96 and the story of Duryodhana's abduction of Citrāṅgada's daughter at *her* svayaṃvara in XII.4. In this latter story Duryodhana attends the svayaṃvara with Karṇa as his companion. When the maiden fails to choose him, the insulted Duryodhana forces her onto his chariot, challenges and defeats the assembled kings, and returns with her and Karṇa to his own city. Not only the general outline but also the salient details of these two stories follow those of the first narrative examined, as the following outline demonstrates.

1. Journey on single chariot

Bhīṣma: I.96.4 sa . . . rathenaikena . . . jagāma
"He came on a single chariot."
[cf. vs. 18 prayāntam ekam
"(him) driving forth alone"]

Duryodhana: XII.4.4 rathena kāñcanāṅgena karṇena sahito yayau
"He drove, together with Karṇa, on a gold-bodied chariot."

2. Verbal behavior: challenge and announcement of intent

Bhīṣma: I.96.12 tā imāḥ pṛthivīpālā jihīrṣāmi balād itaḥ
te yatadhvaṃ paraṃ śaktyā [= V.170.14c]
vijayāyetarāya vā
sthito 'haṃ pṛthivīpālā yuddhāya kṛtaniścayaḥ
"I intend to take these very (maidens) by force from here, o earthlords.

Do ye all make the highest effort with (all your) ability to defeat me—or the reverse.
I stand with resolution made for battle, o earthlords."

Duryodhana: XII.4.13 ājuhāva narādhipān
"He challenged the kings."

3. Causing to mount the chariot
Bhīṣma: I.96.7 ratham āropya tāḥ kanyāḥ
"having made the maidens mount the chariot"

13 sarvāḥ kanyāḥ . . . ratham āropayat svakam
"He made all the maidens mount his own chariot."

Duryodhana: XII.4.13 ratham āropya tāṃ kanyām
"having made the maiden mount the chariot"

4. Fighting
Bhīṣma: I.96.14–39

Duryodhana: XII.4.15–20

Even brief and incidental references to Rākṣasa abductions contain the same items. The following single verse references to the abduction of Rukmiṇī by Kṛṣṇa contain the *chariot*, the *fighting*, and the *abduction* itself:

MBh III.13.28 tathā parjanyaghoṣeṇa *rathenā*dityavarcasā
avākṣīr mahiṣīṃ bhojyāṃ *raṇe nirjitya* rukmiṇam

So, *on your chariot*, whose sound is Thunder's and whose splendor is the Sun's,
you carried off / married a Bhojyan[32] wife, *having defeated* Rukmin [her brother] *in battle*.

V.47.68 yo rukmiṇīm *ekarathena* bhojyām
utsādya rājñāṃ viṣayaṃ *prasahya*
uvāha bhāryāṃ yaśasā jvalantīm

Who, *on a single chariot, having destroyed* the territory of the kings *by force*,
carried off / married the Bhojyan [see n. 32] Rukmiṇī (as) wife, she flaming with glory.

All these features have counterparts, obvious or covert, in the ordinary wedding ceremony, as we will see by going step by step through the abduction narratives.

2. *Ceremonial Aspects of Rākṣasa Marriage*

Let us return to Bhīṣma and first remember that Bhīṣma's Rākṣasa marriage is only marriage by proxy: he abducts the young women as brides for his brother, Vicitravīrya.[33] Now the first (albeit optional) act in many gṛhya sūtra treatments of marriage is that the prospective bridegroom sends 'wooers' (vara[ka], saṃbhala; 'Brautwerber') as proxies to present his case to the bride's family.[34] Bhīṣma thus functions as a particularly violent 'wooer' for Vicitravīrya.[35]

These proxy wooers appear already in the RV in the somewhat enigmatic wedding hymn (X.85),[36] where the Aśvins are called vará (vss. 8, 9), in contrast to Soma, the vadhūyú 'bridegroom' (vs. 9), at the mythological wedding of Soma and Sūryā. The wooing journey of the Aśvins, *on a chariot*, is the subject of at least two verses in this hymn:

> RV X.85.14 yád aśvinā pṛchámānāv áyātaṃ tricakréṇa vahatúṃ sūryā́yāḥ . . .
> 15 yád áyātaṃ śubhas patī vareyáṃ sūryā́m úpa
> kváikaṃ cakráṃ vām āsīt kvà deṣṭrā́ya tasthathuḥ
>
> When, o Aśvins, you two drove with a three-wheeled (chariot) to the wedding of Sūryā to ask[37] for her . . .
> when you drove, o lords of beauty, to Sūryā to woo (her),
> where was your single wheel; where did you stand for the pointing out?

The 'pointing out' (deṣṭrā́ya) of verse 15 is obscure. Geldner (ad loc.), for example, thinks it refers to their 'pointing out' a place for Sūryā to stand in their already crowded chariot; O'Flaherty (1981, p. 272, n. 15) suggests that they are pointing out the path to the groom's house or "the path to the secret sun in heaven." But I think it has to do with the particular task of the proxy wooers when they come to the bride's house in the gṛhya sūtras. They announce their presence to the bride's father and family and then proclaim the names of the prospective bridegroom, identify him—point him out, so to speak. The fullest account of this is given in the ŚGS. When the wooers arrive, bearing flowers, fruit, and other auspicious tributes (ŚGS I.6.2), they proclaim three times ayam ahaṃ bho "Here I am, sir" (I.6.3), then (I.6.4) facing west while the family faces east, they recite the gotra names of the bridegroom and thus perform the formal wooing of the young woman.

> ŚGS I.6.3 ayam ahaṃ bho iti triḥ procya
> 4 udite prāṅmukhā gṛhyāḥ pratyaṅmukhāḥ āvahamānā gotranāmāny anukīrtayantaḥ kanyāṃ varayanti
>
> Having proclaimed three times "Here I am, sir,"
> When this has been said, the household facing east, the 'conveyors' facing west, reciting the gotra names, they woo the maiden.

The careful description of the east-west stationing of the two parties reminds us of the RVic question to the Aśvins: kvà deṣṭrā́ya tasthathuḥ "Where did you stand for the pointing out?" More important, the whole procedure reminds us exactly of Bhīṣma's actions when he abducts the sisters. From our pragmatic point of view Bhīṣma wastes time and draws unnecessary attention to himself by announcing "again and again" (punaḥ punaḥ: like the three times in the ŚGS) his full name and intentions: V.170.13 bhīṣmaḥ śāṃtanavaḥ kanyā harati "Bhīṣma Śāṃtanava takes the maidens." But in my view this proclamation is an essential part of the Rākṣasa marriage, a formal and ceremonial step corresponding to that in the gṛhya descriptions. Without it the act is simply a lawless abduction, not a marriage.[38]

The same proclamation is found elsewhere in early Indo-European literature. According to Livy (I, 58), the rape of Lucretia was preceded by just such an announcement. The rapist wakes the sleeping Lucretia and, curiously, gives his full name before proceeding:

> tace, Lucretia. *Sextus Tarquinius sum*; ferrum in manu est; moriere, si emiseris vocem.
>
> Quiet, Lucretia. *I am Sextus Tarquinius.* My sword is in my hand. You will die if you utter a sound.

Thus far Bhīṣma's abduction and the ordinary wedding ceremony parallel each other in their salient points: the chariot journey of the wooer(s), the announcement ('pointing out') of the wooer and the bridegroom and their intentions. Even the challenge that Bhīṣma and Duryodhana issue to the assembled kings may find its parallel, or rather its mirror image, in the wedding ceremony. Bhīṣma issues his challenge with the verb ā √hū (V.170.12 . . . tān nṛpān sarvān āhūya samare . . . "having challenged all the kings in combat"), as does Duryodhana in XII.4.13 ājuhāva narādhipān ("he challenged the kings"). This lexeme, of course, means not only 'challenge' (as here), but also 'invite'; in the latter value it is the verb used in the legal texts' description of the highest form of marriage, the Brāhma, for the bride's father's *inviting* the chosen suitor. For example,[39]

> MDŚ III.27 *āhūya* dānaṃ kanyāyā brāhmo dharmaḥ prakīrtitaḥ
>
> The giving of a maiden on *having invited* (the suitor) is called the Brāhma rite.
>
> MBh I.96.8 *āhūya* dānaṃ kanyānāṃ guṇavadbhyaḥ . . .
>
> The giving of maidens to men of quality, on *having invited* (them) . . .

In Bhīṣma's and Duryodhana's cases, the *un*invited suitor invites/challenges the bride's family and protectors to 'officiate' at the wedding through fighting—as a mirror-image substitute for having the family invite him to sue for the girl.

The next crucial step in the abduction schema, causing the maiden(s) to mount the chariot, may seem simply a practical necessity. How else is the abductor going to get them out of there? But the insistent repetition of it—both versions of Bhīṣma's episode mention it twice—should alert us that it has additional significance. Indeed, the mounting of the chariot figures largely in the ordinary marriage ceremony as well, all the way back to the Rig Veda. The chariot of the bride Sūryā is described several times in the wedding hymn, sometimes in elaborate metaphorical conceits (RV X.85.10–12, 16). Twice she *mounts* the chariot (or wagon) for her wedding journey, both times with the same verb used in the Bhīṣma and Duryodhana passages:

RV X.85.12 áno manasmáyaṃ sūryā́rohat prayatī́ pátim

Sūryā, going forth to her husband, *mounted* the wagon made of mind.

RV X.85.20 sukiṃśukáṃ śalmalíṃ viśvárūpaṃ híraṇyavarṇaṃ suvṛ́taṃ sucakrám *ā́ roha* sūrye amṛ́tasya lokám

O Sūryā, the (chariot) having kiṃśuka flowers (on it), made of śalmala wood, having all beauties, the color of gold, well-turning, well-wheeled—
mount (it)—the world of the immortal one.

Moreover, the gṛhya sūtra accounts of the wedding ceremony almost all give elaborate descriptions of the chariot journey to the new home, at the conclusion of the formal ceremonies at the bride's family home. The chariot seems no mere practical conveyance, given the care with which it is prepared and addressed.[40] For example, in the MGS there are separate mantras accompanying the harnessing of the horses and the cleaning of the chariot, and others addressed to the horses, to the wheels, and to the seat (MGS I.13.1–5). In most gṛhya sūtras the climax of this preparation comes when the groom *causes* the bride *to mount* the chariot. For example,

BGS I.5.4 athaināṃ dakṣiṇe haste gṛhītvā svaratham *āropya* svān gṛhān ānayati

Then, having taken her by her right hand, *having made her mount* his own chariot, he leads her to his own home.[41]

That the chariot should be invested with such meaning in the wedding ceremony is not surprising. It is only when the bride mounts his own chariot (svaratha) that the groom takes actual charge of her, rather than the symbolic charge he has acquired during the previous parts of the ritual.[42] She is now ensconced on a tiny island of *his* property in the midst of all of that of her family—the alien turf on which he has so far been acting. The importance of this must have led to the hyperbole of the RVic treatment, where, as we saw, the chariot at the moment the bride mounts it is called amṛ́tasya loká "the world of the immortal one." We should keep in mind that the RVic wedding hymn has no or almost no reflection of what we think of as the crucial parts of the later wedding ceremony—the seven steps, the circumambulation of the fire, the taking of the hand, the stepping on the stone, the joint gazing at the Pole Star—but it does have verses and verses devoted to the wedding chariot.

Thus, in the MBh abduction scenes, when the maiden is made to mount the chariot, this act is done not merely to ensure a quick getaway, but also serves as the single ceremonial action standing for and telescoping the entire wedding ceremony as performed under less trying circumstances. Again this feature has analogues elsewhere in the Indo-European world. Greek depictions of abduction (especially the abduction of Persephone) frequently involve a chariot, and some Hellenists have suggested that the groom's lifting of the bride into a chariot in ordinary Greek weddings is the survival or copy of an abduction motif.[43]

The final salient feature of the abduction scenes—the actual fighting—has, not surprisingly, fewer obvious counterparts in the wedding ceremony, but there are some, nonetheless. First consider the term Bhīṣma applies to the maidens at V.170.13: vīrya-śulka 'having a manly deed (vīrya) as a bride-price'. The vīrya is the fighting that Bhīṣma is about to engage in, and it serves as substitute for a more material śulka, like cows or gold, to be expected in so many epic weddings we have examined. In this way the fighting is brought within the orthodox system of gift and countergift, and the abduction made equivalent to other types of marriages (e.g. Ārṣa and Āsura) where such gifts change hands.

But Bhīṣma's statement and subsequent actions are also a pun on this term vīrya-śulka. Note the full phrase, V.170.13 vīryaśulkāś ca tā jñātvā "*recognizing* that they had a vīrya as a śulka." The svayaṃvara that Bhīṣma interrupted was a particular type, called the vīryaśulka svayaṃvara, a pseudo self-choice in which the maiden "chooses" the man who has best accomplished a feat of strength or manly skill set by her father. Arjuna won Draupadī in such a svayaṃvara, as Rāma did Sītā. (On this type, see Schmidt 1987, chap. 3.) What Bhīṣma says (and does) is "You want vīrya—I'll show you vīrya!" His bold defeat of the assembled kings puts in the shade whatever pallid and controlled test of valor had been devised for the svayaṃvara. (What the test was is never stated.)

Even *within* the orthodox wedding ceremony there are details that seem almost reminiscences of agonistic encounters. Perhaps the most striking is found in the KauśSū. At the very end of the ceremony, just before the mounting of the chariot, the bride is 'ungirded'—the cord (yoktra) that had been previously tied around her is untied (KauśSū 76.28). There follow two curious sūtras:

> KauśSū 76.29 aparasmin bhṛtyāḥ saṃrabhante
> 30 ye jayanti te balīyāṃsa eva manyante
>
> Servants grapple with each other over it [yoktra?] [or: in the distance (?)/later (?)]. Whichever ones win are considered the stronger.[44]

This little vignette, seemingly connected to nothing else in the ceremony and without parallels elsewhere (as far as I am aware), appears a dim and controlled reference to the conflict that might accompany some departures of bride and groom.[45]

Once the chariot has been mounted and the bridal journey begun, more texts seems to reflect possible conflict or difficulty. Several gṛhya sūtras prescribe a mantra if the bride cries at this point (rudatyām, cf. e.g. ĀśvGS I.8.4; ŚGS I.15.2). √Rud 'weep' is exactly what the bride (and in some versions her relations) is supposed to do at a Rākṣasa abduction (see MDŚ III.33 quoted earlier), and though even a conventionally married bride might well shed some tears on leaving her family and familiar haunts, the action seems especially appropriate to violent abduction.[46]

Indeed, the entire chariot journey seems fraught with dangers, and numerous special difficulties are anticipated and allotted their own mantras—from the breaking of an axle or other part of the chariot (e.g. ŚGS I.15.9–10; PārGS I.10.1–2; GobhGS II.4.3; ĀpGS II.6.4; MGS I.13.17) to the passing of a cemetery (ŚGS I.15.15; GobhGS II.4.2; ĀpGS II.6.4; MGS I.13.12) or big trees (GobhGS I.4.2) or trees with milky sap (ĀpGS II.6.5). Journeys, of course, were always dangerous, but the concentration on the perils of the wedding journey again may reflect a consciousness that getting away was the hardest part of a marriage by capture.

In discussing these points of contact between the ordinary marriage ceremony and abduction, I certainly do not wish to suggest that abduction was originally the usual or only type of marriage, which was then civilized and transformed into the ceremony we have. Nor do I want to suggest that the abduction was a mere charade—a regular ceremony with some theatrical combat. Rather I am only trying to show on the one hand that the Rākṣasa marriage has important *ceremonial* elements that parallel some in the regular marriage ritual, and on the other that *marriage* by abduction must have been legitimate and usual enough, at least in theory, to allow harmless copies of some of its elements to infiltrate nonviolent pairings.

3. Illegal Abductions

Having established what appear to be the features of a properly accomplished Rākṣasa marriage, it is instructive to look at examples that do not qualify as such, but simply as lawless abductions. The most thoroughly treated is the attempted abduction of the Mahābhārata's chief heroine, Draupadī, the Pāṇḍavas' wife, by Jayadratha in the Āraṇyaka Parvan (III.248–56). What is remarkable about this episode is not how *much* it deviates from the pattern we have established, but how little. All goes almost according to orthodoxy until nearly the last step.

Draupadī has been left essentially alone at the hermitage (III.250.3 ekā hy aham) while the Pāṇḍavas go hunting; her only companion beside her maid is the priest Dhaumya. King Jayadratha passes by. He is vivāhakāma (III.248.6) 'desirous of marriage', not simply out for sport, when he is attracted by the beautiful Draupadī. He is, however, "surrounded by a great retinue appropriate to a king, along with many kings" (vs. 7 mahatā paribarheṇa rājayogyena saṃvṛtaḥ / rājabhir bahubhiḥ sārdham), whereas our orthodox abductors arrived on a single chariot, hence accompanied at most only by their charioteer/ 'wooer'. Moreover, Jayadratha puts aside thoughts of marriage and decides simply to 'take' Draupadī. It is significant that the usual verb for 'abduct' in the Rākṣasa marriage, namely √hṛ, is not used. The verb instead is ā √dā:

III.248.13 vivāhārtho na me kaś cid imāṃ dṛṣṭvātisundarīm
etām evāham *ādāya* gamiṣyāmi svam ālayam

There is no reason for marriage for me now that I've seen this exceedingly lovely one.
Having taken her, I will go[47] to my own home.

Nevertheless, his next actions seem scrupulously correct. He dispatches his friend King Koṭikāśya as a sort of wooer, to find out who Draupadī is, who her protector is, and if she will come to him. In appropriate wooer fashion, Koṭikāśya *introduces himself and points out by name* Jayadratha, along with many of his retinue (III.249). After Koṭikāśya reports to him, Jayadratha goes off to call on Draupadī in the hermitage, though with six companions (III.251.8 ātmanā saptamaḥ), still too many for a proper Rākṣasa abduction.

The first hint of his intentions, after formal greetings on both sides, is his invitation (/command) to *mount his chariot*:

> III.251.14 ehi me *ratham āroha* sukham āpnuhi kevalam
>
> Come, *mount my chariot*. Attain complete happiness.

and to become his *wife* (III.251.18 bhāryā me bhava). Despite her contemptuous refusal, he renews his suggestions about the *chariot*:

> III.252.12 sā kṣipram ātiṣṭha gajaṃ rathaṃ vā
>
> Quickly mount my elephant or chariot.

Draupadī again refuses, warning him that Kṛṣṇa and Arjuna will come after her *on a single chariot*:

> III.252.14 yasyā hi kṛṣṇau padavīṃ caretāṃ
> samāsthitāv *ekarathe* sahāyau
>
> (I), whose trail the two Kṛṣṇas would follow,
> they standing as companions together *on a single chariot*.

She thus suggests that they will perform a correct (re)abduction, by following the conventions of Rākṣasa single combat. (On the reabduction, see V.B.4.)

Nonetheless, Jayadratha resorts to crude force (vss. 22–24) and succeeds finally in having her *mount the chariot*:

> III.252.22 sā tān anuprekṣya viśālanetrā
> jighṛkṣamāṇān avabhartsayantī
> provāca mā mā spṛśateti bhītā
> dhaumyaṃ pracakrośa purohitaṃ sā
> 23 jagrāha tām uttaravastradeśe
> jayadrathas taṃ samavākṣipat sā
> tayā samākṣiptatanuḥ sa pāpaḥ
> papāta śākhīva nikṛttamūlaḥ
> 24 pragṛhyamāṇā tu mahājavena
> muhur viniḥśvasya ca rājaputrī
> sā kṛṣyamāṇā *ratham āruroha*
>
> 22 Wide-eyed, she watched them about to grab her—scolding, (yet) afraid, she proclaimed, "Don't touch me!"
> She shrieked out to her priest, Dhaumya.

23 Jayadratha grabbed her by her upper garment. She threw him down.
The evil one, his body thrown down by her, fell like a tree with its roots cut.
24 But, being grabbed by the one with great speed,
in an instant the princess, gasping, being dragged, *mounted the chariot*.

The passage is notable for its graphic depiction of the struggle to get Draupadī onto the vehicle. In the other abduction passages we have examined the mounting is handled without textual fuss—even in the case of Bhīṣma, who had to manage *three* unwilling women in the midst of a crowd of irate warrior-suitors. Since the audience is meant to condemn Jayadratha's action, this passage permits itself a realistic glance at the violence necessary to force a desperate and protesting woman onto a small vehicle. In the Rākṣasa marriage passages, where the abduction is considered legal,[48] the potential violence is suppressed: the chariot mounting is handled so serenely that one imagines the abductor politely extending a hand to help the abductee up.[49]

When Draupadī seeks help from the priest Dhaumya (vs. 22 above), his reply is the most telling piece of our evidence. Rather than saying, as our modern sensibilities might expect, "you cannot abduct this virtuous wife" or "stop this outrageous violence against an innocent woman," he says instead

III.252.25 neyaṃ śakyā tvayā netum *avijitya mahārathān*
dharmaṃ kṣatrasya paurāṇam avekṣasva jayadratha

This (woman) cannot be led/married[50] by you, *without (your) having conquered great-chariot (fighters)*.
Look to the ancient *dharma of the warrior*, o Jayadratha.

Dhaumya does not condemn or forbid the abduction per se, but rather states that it *would* be legal if Jayadratha engaged in combat, in other words if he gave a vīrya as a śulka.[51]

When the Pāṇḍavas return and learn from her maid of Draupadī's abduction, they pursue Jayadratha's host. It is when they see Jayadratha and Draupadī *on his chariot* that they become frenzied:[52]

III.253.25 krodhaḥ prajajvāla jayadrathaṃ ca
dṛṣṭvā priyāṃ tasya rathe sthitāṃ ca
26 pracukruśuś cāpy atha sindhurājam

Their anger blazed forth, having seen Jayadratha and their dear one standing on his chariot.
They shrieked forth then at Sindhurāja [Jayadratha].

After the battle, in which the Pāṇḍavas are of course victorious, Jayadratha helps Draupadī *down from his chariot* (III.255.33 draupadīm avatārya), and Yudhiṣṭhira has her *remounted on their chariot*:

III.255.34 draupadīṃ dharmarājas tu dṛṣṭvā . . .
mādrīputreṇa vīreṇa ratham āropayat tadā

Dharmarāja, having seen Draupadī,
had her caused to mount [lit.] the chariot by the hero, Mādrī's son.

With this act the reabduction is formally complete; she is their wife again, because she is on their chariot.

But Draupadī is not content. She wants Jayadratha killed, because he is a bhāryābhihartā nirvairaḥ (III.255.46). Though this phrase may mean, as van Buitenen takes it, "a wife-snatcher without a cause," or perhaps "without a quarrel (to legitimate it)," I am inclined to interpret nirvaira as 'without heroism': "a wife-abductor who did not perform the *manly deed* (vīrya)" required to make the abduction legal. Certainly when Bhīma and Arjuna track down Jayadratha, who is in flight on foot, Arjuna addresses him

III.255.58 anena vīryeṇa kathaṃ striyaṃ prārthayase balāt
How can you seek a woman by force with *this* manly deed?

in apparent sarcastic reference to the vīrya that should have won Jayadratha the woman.

Thus it is the lack of a fight that distinguishes Jayadratha's condemned and craven wife-stealing; most of the other elements of a Rākṣasa marriage were correctly performed. This lack of direct challenge and fighting seems also to be what condemns some other, briefly mentioned abductions as unlawful. These were the work of the villainous (and soon to be killed) Śiśupāla. In reciting Śiśupāla's evil deeds just before cutting off his head, Kṛṣṇa mentions three abductions or attempted abductions—of the wife of Babhru (II.42.10), of Bhadrā Vaiśālī (II.42.11; this performed as 'wooer' on behalf of Karūṣa), and the apparently unsuccessful 'seeking' (prārthanā) of Rukmiṇī, Kṛṣṇa's own wife (II.42.15)[53] (whom Kṛṣṇa had himself legitimately married in a Rākṣasa marriage, as we learned earlier). In none of Śiśupāla's incidents is fighting mentioned. Moreover, Śiśupāla abducted Bhadrā while 'concealed by his magic power' (māyāpraticchannaḥ II.42.11), and the offense against Rukmiṇī seems to have been one done 'secretly' or 'out of sight' (parokṣam II.42.13). Again the sneakiness of the abductions, not the acts themselves, is what merits the scorn.

As it turns out, Hara had already made this point elegantly and forcefully in 1974 (esp. pp. 304–5)—an article I came upon only after I had reached the same conclusions. He too sees that abduction without a fight is just "a disgraceful act of robbery," and cites Dhaumya's words (III.252.25) quoted earlier, as well as a number of telling Rāmāyaṇa passages concerning Sītā's abduction. For further on his discussion, see V.B.4.

The requirement that fighting will legitimate an abduction may also be found in a cognate tradition, in an enigmatic provision in the Hittite law code.

I § 37 (29) ták-ku SAL-an ku[(-iš-k)]i pít-te-nu-uz-zi EGIR-an-da-m[a-aš-ma-a]š [ša]r-di-i̯a-aš pa-iz-zi

(30) ťak-ku 2 ĹU^{MEŠ} na-a-š-m]a 3 LÚ^{MEŠ} ak-kán-zi šar-ni-ik-zi[(-i)]l NU.GÁL [(z)]i-ik-u̯a UR!.BAR.RA ki-ša-at

If someone carries off a woman and a "Hilfstrupp" goes after them,
If two or three men die, there is no compensation. "You have become a wolf."

The usual interpretation of this law is that the *šardiyas* ('Hilfstrupp') is the abductor's. If any of his companions die, there is no compensation for them because the abductor has become an outlaw ('wolf') and thus too far outside society to participate in its legal system. His deed is so outrageous that the usual compensatory strategies cannot be employed.[54]

But I wonder if instead the *šardiyas* is a kind of posse, a Hilfstrupp for the woman's injured family, and the abductor's killing some of this posse in fact redeems the abduction, serves as his vīrya-śulka. Under this interpretation the absence of compensation would refer to the abduction itself. Since the fighting proved the abduction legal, the woman's family receives no damages. Calling the abductor 'wolf' would be roughly equivalent to the Sanskrit term rākṣasa 'demonic' describing an acceptable if violent form of marriage. I am not a Hittitologist, however, and I offer this interpretation very tentatively.

4. Reabduction and Counterwooing

The existence of legal abduction, with definable requirements, thus sets up an interesting countersituation. If abduction is legitimated by careful attention to certain ceremonial steps and, especially, by an act of extreme valor, then an abduction that lacks these features is illegal and should allow its victims legal redress. And so it does, as we have just seen in the illegal abduction of Draupadī. There her husbands could follow the abductor and reabduct their wife; had Jayadratha's original action been correctly performed, they presumably could not legally have pursued the pair.

What is most remarkable about reabduction is that it, too, follows the punctilious procedure of the ordinary wedding ceremony, as replicated in the legal abduction. This methodical care can be seen beneath the apparent chaos of the reabduction of Draupadī. We have already noted that Draupadī warned Jayadratha that Arjuna and Kṛṣṇa would follow *on a single chariot*, the appropriate vehicle for bridegroom and abductor alike. We have also indicated that the Pāṇḍavas offer an extraordinary vīrya as the legitimating act of heroism to reclaim their wife. The five of them alone attack and defeat the whole of Jayadratha's army (MBh III.255), chariots, elephants, foot soldiers and all. We have also seen them *remount* Draupadī *on their chariot*.

The crucial step in the wedding/abduction that we have not so far discussed in the reabduction is the wooing: the announcement of name and lineage and intention to marry/abduct. This turns out to be the most noteworthy feature of the reabduction because it is the least predictable. We might expect an outraged husband to pursue, attack, and reclaim his wife, but not necessarily to announce formally his identity and intention to do so. And the way in which this announcement is handled makes it more remarkable still. The Counterwooing (as I term it) is performed *by Draupadī to Jayadratha*. In other words, the abducted woman identifies her husbands (structural wooers) to her abductor, who is structurally her guardian at the moment and who corresponds in a perverse way to the bride's father, to whom the wooing announcement is ordinarily made.

When Jayadratha sees the Pāṇḍavas approaching, in this moment of panic and danger, he turns to Draupadī and asks for the equivalent of an introduction:

MBh III.254.3 āyāntīme pañca rathā mahānto
manye ca kṛṣṇe patayas tavaite
sā jānatī khyāpaya naḥ sukeśi
paraṃ-paraṃ pāṇḍavānāṃ rathastham

These five great chariot(-warrior)s are coming hither,
and I think they are your husbands, o Kṛṣṇā [Draupadī].
Recognizing (them), o fair-haired one, proclaim to us
in sequence each one of the Pāṇḍavas standing on the chariot.

She agrees, with a verse that emphasizes her *legal responsibility* to respond

MBh III.254.5 ākhyātavyaṃ tv eva sarvaṃ mumūrṣor
mayā tubhyaṃ pṛṣṭayā *dharma eṣaḥ*

But all of this must be proclaimed to one about to die,
(proclaimed) by me to you, since I was asked. *That is the law* (/dharma).

and then gives a sequence of elaborate identifications (III.254.6–20), with archaic syntactic figures and intricate descriptions, pointing to each of the Pāṇḍavas in turn and detailing his glory, as in the following treatment of Yudhiṣṭhira. Notice that his lineage is neatly included with his name at the end.

MBh III.254.6 yasya dhvajāgre nadato mṛdaṅgau
nandopanandau madhurau yuktarūpau
etaṃ svadharmārthaviniścayajñaṃ
sadā janāḥ kṛtyavanto 'nuyānti
7 ya eṣa jāmbūnadaśuddhagauraḥ
pracaṇḍaghoṇas tanur āyatākṣaḥ
etaṃ kuruśreṣṭhatamaṃ vadanti
yudhiṣṭhiraṃ dharmasutaṃ patiṃ me

6 At the top of whose standard sound the two drums,
the sweet Nanda and Upananda suitably formed—
him who knows the decisions concerning his own law and purpose
do the busy people always follow.
7 Who is pure and bright as gold,
large-nosed, slender, long-eyed—
him they call the best of the best of the Kurus,
Yudhiṣṭhira, son of Dharma, my husband.

This scene, which at first seems an inappropriate and lengthy intrusion in this dramatic episode, occupies nineteen Triṣṭubh verses; these verses are so-called "irregular" Triṣṭubhs and, as such, belong to the oldest, Kṣatriya core of our surviving Mahābhārata, as convincingly argued by M. C. Smith in her recent book.[55] On metrical evidence this episode belongs to the heart of the text.

In fact the scene, or its prototype, is probably a good deal older than the Mahābhārata. I have recently discussed the Counterwooing (and the Counter-abduction) as an inherited Indo-European epic theme.[56] Draupadī's identification of her husbands is uncannily like the Teikhoskopia, the famous scene in the Iliad in which Helen identifies certain Greek heroes for Priam and the other Trojan elders (Il. 3.166–235); both episodes serve the same purpose in their respective reabduction narratives—to announce and legitimate the fighting to come between original husband(s) and abductor.[57] Each episode depends on a shared model of legal and illegal abductions and the appropriate and allowed response to them; each assumes that the legitimating action must involve open combat between the abductor and the woman's protector(s).

5. A Test Case: Arjuna and Subhadrā

This conclusion, namely, that force is necessary to make a Rākṣasa marriage legal, at first seems to cause serious problems when we examine another Rākṣasa marriage in the Mahābhārata, celebrated and applauded as such, which appears to deviate more markedly from the norm than even Jayadratha's outrageous conduct—particularly in the absence of a battle. This is Arjuna's abduction of Subhadrā, Kṛṣṇa's sister (I.211–13). Nonetheless, despite its apparent lack of orthodoxy this episode is illuminated by being set within the structure of proper Rākṣasa marriages, as just established.

In this episode Arjuna falls in love with Subhadrā (whom he sees at a festival), and Kṛṣṇa urges him to abduct her, citing the Kṣatriya's right to marriage by capture and the uncertain outcome of a svayaṃvara:

I.211.22 prasahya haraṇaṃ cāpi kṣatriyāṇāṃ praśasyate
vivāhahetoḥ śūrāṇām iti dharmavido viduḥ
23 sa tvam arjuna kalyāṇīṃ prasahya bhaginīṃ mama
hara svayaṃvare hy asyāḥ ko vai veda cikīrṣitam

"Taking by force is also prescribed for Kṣatriyas,
as a grounds for marriage of heroes," so the dharma-knowers know.
So take my fair sister by force, o Arjuna.
For who knows what she's likely to do at a svayaṃvara.

Arjuna follows this advice, snatching Subhadrā on the road when she is returning from a pilgrimage. He does this with so little of the ceremony we have come to expect that Hopkins (1889, p. 358) says, "he simply runs off with her."

But the major elements *are* there; they must just be unearthed. First let us see which of our elements appear undisguised. The journey on the single chariot is certainly there. In fact Arjuna's elopement chariot merits two verses of description (I.212.3–4; beginning with rathena kāñcanāṅgena, the phrase used of Duryodhana's chariot in his abduction; see XII.4.4 quoted earlier), and Arjuna's equipage another (vs. 5). Since the amount of description given to an object in the Mahābhārata is often an index of how symbolically important it is, we should pay attention to this elaboration.

The mounting of the chariot is also there in its usual verbal form. It is the sole action of the actual abduction that is narrated:[58]

I.212.7 tām abhidrutya kaunteyaḥ prasahyā*ropayad ratham*

Racing up to her, the son of Kuntī forcibly *made her mount the chariot.*

We also know that she was not alone or defenseless (as Draupadī was), for her (armed) bodyguards see her abduction and raise the alarm back in the city:

I.212.9 hriyamāṇāṃ tu tāṃ dṛṣṭvā subhadrāṃ sainiko janaḥ
vikrośan prādravat sarvo dvārakām abhito purīm

On seeing Subhadrā being abducted, the military host,
shrieking out, all ran to the city of Dvārakā.

The presence of this sainiko janaḥ "martial force, military host," who witness (dṛṣṭvā) and raise the hue and cry (vikrośan) may almost be enough to keep Arjuna's Kṣatriya honor and make the abduction legal. Note Bhīṣma's insistence that the kings *watch* his actions, quoted above:

V.170.14 prasahya hi nayāmy eṣa *miṣatāṃ vo* narādhipāḥ

For I lead/marry (them) by force, *before your eyes*, o kings.

Moreover, the verb √kruś 'shriek' seems to serve almost as a technical term for raising the alarm in these circumstances. The verbal definition of Rākṣasa marriage in Manu (III.33 quoted earlier) requires that the abducted woman be krośantīm 'shrieking'. In the story of Draupadī's abduction not only does she shriek at the time, though to no avail (III.252.22 dhaumyaṃ pracakrośa purohitaṃ sā "she shrieked forth to the priest Dhaumya"), but the pursuing Pāṇḍavas do also when they see Jayadratha (pracukruśuḥ III.253.26 quoted earlier).[59]

But where are the wooer, the self-identification, the announcement of intentions, the challenge, and, most important, the fighting, the act of bravery, whose absence rendered Jayadratha a contemptible sneak?

For these we must focus on the figure of Kṛṣṇa, who performs these functions both before and after the fact. As Subhadrā's brother, Kṛṣṇa is the family member to whom Arjuna *announces his intentions* before the abduction. In fact, as we saw above, his intentions were actually suggested to him by Kṛṣṇa. But as Arjuna's friend, Kṛṣṇa acts also as the proxy *wooer*; at the very beginning of the episode he offers to speak to his father about the match (I.211.17), and later he persuades his angry kinsmen to accept the marriage.

At that point, after the abduction, when the warriors gather to denounce Arjuna and plan revenge against him, Kṛṣṇa performs the remaining ceremonial necessities. Having pronounced that the action was in his opinion lawful[60]

I.213.5 ataḥ prasahya hṛtavān kanyāṃ dharmeṇa pāṇḍavaḥ

Hence the Pāṇḍava forcibly abducted the maiden according to dharma.

he then *announces Arjuna's name and lineage*:

I.213.7 bharatasyānvaye jātaṃ śaṃtanoś ca mahātmanaḥ
kuntibhojātmajāputraṃ ko bubhūṣeta nārjunam

Who would not esteem Arjuna, born in the line of Bharata and of great-souled Śaṃtanu, son of the offspring of Kuntibhoja?

The challenge, after the fact, comes next. Kṛṣṇa simply says

I.213.8 na ca paśyāmi yaḥ pārthaṃ vikrameṇa parājayet
9 . . . ko nu tena samo bhavet

I do not see anyone who could defeat Pārtha by force. . . .
Who would be equal to him?

This postponed challenge is its own answer, of course. No one could defeat him; no one would be his equal, and Arjuna's vīrya, the '*act of heroism*' that wins the bride need not be actualized, so self-evident is its outcome.[61] It is no accident, I am sure, that the first of Arjuna's unbeatable attributes that Kṛṣṇa mentions is this context is his *chariot*: I.213.9 sa ca nāma rathas tādṛṅ madīyās te ca vājinaḥ "Such a chariot, and my horses!"

The apparent anomalies of Arjuna's Rākṣasa marriage are thus accounted for in two ways. On the one hand, Arjuna's valor is so obviously potent that it need not be proven. On the other, he already has secured the approval and cooperation, indeed collusion, of the bride's brother. Kṛṣṇa's dual role as bridegroom's wooer and bride's relative allows some of the formal elements of the Rākṣasa marriage to be displaced from the actual moment of abduction.

The precise relationship between Subhadrā and Kṛṣṇa is significant, because the brother of the bride plays a special role in marriage. The sad plight of the brotherless maiden is already alluded to in the Rig Veda several times (e.g. I.124.7, IV.5.5; cf. also MBh XIII.44.14; and Schmidt 1987, chap. 2), and Geldner, for example (ad RV I.124.7), suggests that brothers were the obvious matchmakers for sisters. Without a brother, a young woman had to look for a husband on her own.[62] If brothers find husbands for their sisters, then Kṛṣṇa has simply done his job, and the peculiar features of this Rākṣasa marriage fall into place.

6. *Rākṣasa Marriage and the Politics of Exchange*

What conclusions can be drawn about the Rākṣasa marriage? We should start with what we do not know: we have no way of knowing how widespread abduction was, at what period, or even whether it existed at all. Different scholars have dealt with this problem in different ways. Louis Dumont ([1966] 1970, p. 115), for example, simply denies that marriage by capture ever existed, without citing evidence for this view.[63] As noted earlier, others (Hopkins, Dumézil, Sternbach) have dealt with its seemingly barbarous aspects by banishing it to a remote past—brides used to be abducted in a precivilized state, but such behavior is now only a literary (and somehow a legal) memory.

Hara (1974, pp. 304–5) rightly disputes this convenient chronological distancing. Though he does not commit himself to the "reality" of Rākṣasa abduction, he does clearly show that it conforms entirely to the expressed contemporary ideals about the conduct of the warrior (Kṣatriya) class (kṣatra-dharma), particularly the central importance of fighting and the need to take whatever is wanted by force. As Hara ingeniously argues, the latter ideal, taking by force, is a necessary consequence of an even more fundamental tenet of Kṣatriya existence: the ban on accepting gifts—which I discussed at length in IV.E.

Hara has thus identified the crucial issue in Rākṣasa marriage, this most peculiarly depicted institution—a thoroughly rule-governed, inherently unruly act, legally sanctioned illegality. It is the only solution to the enduring dilemma of the warrior class. All the mechanisms of normal adult life for the Kṣatriya require that he be married. Indeed, as I have discussed, the basic exchange relation found in marriage in turn establishes the other systems of social linkage. But most other codified types of marriage in ancient India involve the *gift* of the maiden by the father to the bridegroom. Since the Kṣatriya's ideology bars him from accepting gifts, he is thus theoretically prevented from participation not only in marriage but in society itself.

Rule-governed abduction is the uneasy solution to this structural conundrum. By violently snatching the maiden, he does not betray his class ideals by accepting gifts. But by following the formal structure of ordinary marriage and by interacting, albeit violently, with the bride's family, he signals his participation in reciprocal social exchange. On the one hand, all aspects of life should be regulated by dharma, and so must the Kṣatriya's idealized marriage type, with violence both required and confined, with almost ludicrous versions of the ceremonial steps in an ordinary wedding marking the progress of the chaotic event. On the other hand, no matter how sedate the actual marriage of a Kṣatriya was (and many, perhaps all of them, were and had always been planned and agreed upon in advance), the ideology of the class still demanded abduction as a *model*. Hence the incorporation of abduction motifs into the thoroughly controlled wedding ceremony. Such was the warrior's dilemma—and its solution. The thematic similarities adduced from cognate Indo-European traditions suggest that the warrior may have been pondering and solving the same puzzle for several millennia.

C. Maidenly Self-Determination

In my brief discussion of Gāndharva marriage, I touched on the issue of maidenly independence: How does the Gāndharva marriage, a marriage of mutual agreement between the parties without intervention by parental or priestly authorities, fit into the system of exchange that otherwise seems to dominate marital arrangements? In particular, does the girl in question have the legal standing to effect an exchange, to *give herself* away? This question is worth pursuing, partly because it highlights some internal contradictions in the ancient Indian legal tradition and the dangers of uncritical quotation of the legal sources.

There is probably no passage about women in ancient India so often quoted as Manu's dictum about female independence:[64]

MDŚ IX.3 pitā rakṣati kaumāre bhartā rakṣati yauvane
rakṣanti sthavire putrā na strī svātantryam arhati

Her father guards (her) in childhood. Her husband guards (her) in youth.
Her sons guard (her) in old age. A woman is not fit for independence.

Taken at face value, this provision would seem to prevent females from any participation in legal decisions affecting them, as there would always be a male in official control over a woman, whatever her stage of life. The succession of husband after father in this law parallels the "gift" of the bride by father to husband in the marriage laws and suggests that there is no transition phase during which the girl can take legal responsibility for herself.

Indeed, MDŚ V.152 states that the *gift* (of the girl by her *father*) is the source of (*her husband's*) lordship over her (pradānaṃ svāmyakāraṇam). It is no doubt because the girl is assimilated to an exchange token in marriage, as property given and received, that her husband also has the right to give her away in turn. The question I raised long ago—why does Manu have the right to dispose of his wife to the visiting Asuric Brahmans who beg for her?—finally finds its answer here. His *acceptance* of her as gift at marriage gives him dominion over her: possession pure and simple.

In this connection, it is useful to consider the most shocking (or, at least, most famous) treatment of woman as chattel in all of Indian literature: Yudhiṣṭhira's staking (and losing) of his wife Draupadī in the dicing match in MBh II. Here the legal issue is not whether he had the right to do so in general, but whether in the particular circumstances he had forfeited that right. Before he offers up Draupadī as a bet, he has staked and lost *himself*. As she astutely realizes even before she is dragged into the assembly, a man who has lost his independence and become someone else's property has no property rights of his own. If a wife in general counts as property, in this case he no longer owns her and had no right to stake her.

Yet there is also a feeling that the "ownership" of the wife is somehow different, and perhaps, though lost himself, he still had lordship over her. This question is raised and evaded numerous times in the aftermath of the dicing (e.g. II.59.4; 60.7–8, 40; 61.23, 31–32; 62.25–26; 63.18), often using forms of the root √īś 'be master of', which, as we saw, was also crucial in the Manu's Cups story. The question is, in fact, never resolved: the issues it raises are too disruptive to confront directly, and Dhṛtarāṣṭra simply short-circuits the legal debate and manages to annul the effects of this first dicing match by fiat.

It is ironic that the legal point that might have freed Draupadī from threatened servitude in this scene is the doctrine that defines wives most strictly as possessions, as *objects* exactly parallel to the material goods and livestock that a slave cannot own. A more flexible and humane doctrine, which put wives into a different category, a relationship of dependence, but one between two *subjects*, would probably have allowed the barbaric result: the husband gambled the wife into slavery. It is probably the unacceptability of both these positions that keeps the debate from proceeding to resolution.[65]

In the dicing scene a central issue is the *legal standing* of the participants. One must have svātantryam 'independence' in order to have sway over others, and, as we saw above, MDŚ IX.3 explicitly denies women such legal standing. But in fact this provision, so often quoted and employed as the *point de depart* for discussion of the woeful plight of ancient Indian women, is contradicted continually, not only by the practice depicted in the literary texts, but in other provisions in the legal codes, indeed in the Mānava Dharma Śāstra itself. Under certain conditions a girl not only can but *must* assume legal responsibility for herself.

1. *Finding a Husband: The Father's Responsibilities*

The legal texts differ—but not too much—on the proper age for marriage. By sometime between three months and three years after her menarche, a father should find a husband for his daughter.[66] Otherwise he is guilty of bhrūṇahatya 'embryo-murder'. Compare, for example,

BDS IV.1.11 dadyāt . . . kanyāṃ nagnikām . . .
. . . noparundhyād rajasvalām
12 trīṇi varṣāṇy ṛtumatīṃ yaḥ kanyāṃ na prayacchati
sa tulyaṃ bhrūṇahatyāyai doṣam ṛcchaty asaṃśayam
13 . . . ekaikaikasminn ṛtau doṣaṃ pātakaṃ manur abravīt

He should give the maiden, while she is still naked[67] (of pubic hair) . . .
He should not keep (her) (at home) (after) she (begins to) menstruate.
Whoever does not give away a menstruating maiden within three years
incurs fault equivalent to embryo-killing, no doubt.
. . . Manu said that at each menstruation (the father incurs) a fault deserving of hell.

The anxiety produced by this unavoidable natural deadline is detectable in many epic stories. For example, the realization of Bhīma, Damayantī's father, that she is prāptayauvanā 'having reached youth/marriageable age'[68] (MBh III.51.7) is not an idle observation but a goad to serious action. He immediately makes plans to find her a husband. Maidens themselves were aware of the grave implications of their physical changes, as when the young Kuntī (later mother of the three oldest Pāṇḍavas) feels shame that she has had her first menstrual period and is still a virgin:

MBh III.290.3 . . . sā dadarśartuṃ yadṛcchayā
vrīḍitā sābhavad bālā kanyābhāve rajasvalā

She saw her period (had come) unexpectedly.
The child became ashamed of menstruating while in a maidenly state.

Another epic heroine, Śarmiṣṭhā, has similar worries:

MBh I.77.6 dadarśa yauvanaṃ prāptā ṛtuṃ sā cānvacintayat
7 ṛtukālaś ca saṃprāpto na ca me 'sti patir vṛtaḥ
kiṃ prāptaṃ kiṃ nu kartavyam

Having reached 'youth', she saw her menstrual period and set to thinking:
"My period has arrived, and no husband has been chosen for me.
What's happened; what's to be done?"

The plan she devises I will discuss shortly.

There are several options available to a father when a suitor has not presented himself for a girl in the danger period. One is that of Mātali (MBh V.95–102), who grumblingly embarks on a tour of the world to find a husband for his daughter. I have already discussed Yayāti, who allowed Gālava to hawk his daughter around the kingdoms of India. But perhaps the most popular solution in the epic[69] is to arrange for a svayaṃvara or 'self-choice', an institution we have already met several times, in which a group of eligible suitors is assembled and the girl gets her choice among them, at least theoretically. It is likely that the svayaṃvara was not simply a way to get the pick of eligible bachelors, but was resorted to when the girl otherwise had no serious prospects. So at least Kuntī's situation suggests. In a passage absent from the CE (but found in Calcutta), Kuntī's lack of suitors precipitated her father's arranging the svayaṃvara:

MBh I.1129* tāṃ tu tejasvinīṃ kanyāṃ rūpayauvanaśālinīm
nāvṛṇvan pārthivāḥ ke cid atīva strīguṇair yutām
tataḥ sā kuntibhojena rājñāhūya narādhipān
pitrā svayaṃvare dattā duhitā rājasattama

This maiden, (though) glorious, abounding in beauty and youth,
and exceedingly endowed with womenly virtues, no earthlords wooed.
So, King Kuntibhoja, her father, having invited the kings,
gave his daughter at a svayaṃvara, o best of kings.

As the svayaṃvara has been extensively discussed elsewhere,[70] I will not do so here. I will simply note that, though the *name* of this marriage type suggests that the girl has some measure of independent control, in fact she has very little. All occurs under the aegis of her father, who issues the invitations and thus controls the pool of suitors. Moreover, despite the name, few svayaṃvaras actually involve free *choice* (as Damayantī's does). Instead they are mainly of the vīryaśulka type discussed earlier, in which the suitors compete at a test of valor set by the father and the girl is trotted out at the end to dutifully "choose" the winner. This solves the father's problem but scarcely allows independent action on the part of the daughter.

To find such action we must consider what the law texts prescribe when the father fails in his duty to secure his daughter a husband. They permit—indeed, command—the girl to emancipate herself, to seek her own husband. The BDS, whose views on paternal responsibility were quoted earlier, immediately continues:

BDS IV.1.14 trīṇi varṣāṇy ṛtumatī kāṅkseta pitṛśāsanam
tataś caturthe varṣe tu vindeta sadṛśaṃ patim

Three years let a menstruating (maiden) wait for her father's command.
But after that, in the fourth year, let her find for herself a husband like (herself).

Manu makes a similar provision:

MDŚ IX.90 trīṇi varṣāṇy udīkṣeta kumāry ṛtumatī satī
ūrdhvaṃ tu kālād etasmād vindeta sadṛśaṃ patim
91 adīyamānā bhartāram adhigacched yadi svayam
nainaḥ kiṃ cid avāpnoti na ca yaṃ sādhigacchati

Three years a girl should wait, once she has started menstruating,
but after that time she should find a husband like (herself).
If, not having been given (by her father), she should approach a husband by herself,
she incurs no sin, nor does the one whom she approaches.

How a maiden on her own might accomplish this is demonstrated by Śarmiṣṭhā's actions after she makes the disquieting discovery quoted earlier. She simply propositions the husband of her mistress and friend Devayānī, begging him with the magic word √yāc discussed in IV.D.4:

MBh I.77.13 sā tvāṃ *yāce* prasādyāham ṛtuṃ *dehi* narādhipa

Propitiating you, I *beg* you: *grant* me my fertile season, o best of kings.

She confuses him with an array of sophistic arguments, and he gives in, acknowledging the compulsion of the √yāc (vs. 20, also I.78.31ff.). Though this liaison causes a certain amount of domestic upheaval, Śarmiṣṭhā's crude approach produces the desired result: sons.

The emancipation of a maiden has important economic consequences: the father is both absolved of further responsibility for the girl and deprived of any further (financial) interest in her. The groom need not pay the father a bride-price, but the girl cannot take her ornaments along with her. If she does, she is considered a thief. In other words, a girl who must find her own husband because of her father's inaction forfeits her membership in her natal family.

> MDŚ IX.92 alaṃkāraṃ nādadīta pitryaṃ kanyā svayaṃvarā
> mātṛkaṃ bhrātṛdattaṃ vā stenā syād yadi taṃ haret
> 93 pitre na dadyāc chulkaṃ tu kanyām ṛtumatīṃ haran
> sa hi svāmyād atikrāmed ṛtūnāṃ pratirodhanāt
>
> A maiden who has made her own choice should not take the ornaments given by her father,
> her mother, or her brother.[71] If she should take them, she would be a thief.
> But the (groom) taking a maiden who (has begun) menstruating should not give a bride-price to the father.
> For he neglected his lordship (over her) because he obstructed (the fulfillment) of her fertile periods.

Despite these rather dramatic legal pronouncements, I think it unlikely that ancient India was full of lone adolescent girls tramping the roads in search of husbands. In fact, the existence in the RV of the term amā-júr 'growing old at home (fem.)' suggests that spinsterhood in the bosom of the family was a possible, if not particularly appealing, state. However, the legal, narrative, and ritual texts concur in giving an unmarried girl some latitude for finding a husband on her own or for actively participating in the family quest.

2. *Finding a Husband: The Maiden's Ritual Options*

Let us begin with the ritual remedies and look first at the earliest and the most remarkable. As Schmidt has deftly argued,[72] the Apālā hymn in the RV (VIII.91) depicts a young girl approaching puberty performing a coming-of-age ritual for herself. She is alone and uses the equipment and mantras of the most solemn of Vedic solemn rituals, the Soma Sacrifice, to attract the god Indra and, ultimately, a husband. This ritual setting is noteworthy because a young, unmarried girl should not have studied the Veda and, even as a married woman and ritual participant, she will not be allowed to drink the soma (as we have already seen). Apālā thus teeters on the edge of blasphemy, and it is her almost desperate appropriation of forbidden ritual that emphasizes her anxiety about her state.

Though not identified as such in the text, Apālā's activity belongs to the class of rituals known as pati-vedana 'husband-finding', several examples of which are preserved in other texts. The first explicit reference to these is in the AV, which contains two husband-finding charms (AV II.36, VI.60). VI.60 speaks eloquently of the spinster's plight:

> AV VI.60.2 áśramad iyám aryamann anyā́sāṃ sámanaṃ yatī́
> aṅgó nv àryamann asyā́ anyā́ḥ sámanam ā́yati [*sic*]

This (girl), o Aryaman, has become weary going to the assembly [wedding celebration] of other (women).
Surely now, o Aryaman, other (women) will come to her assembly.

It invokes Aryaman, patron god of marriage, and Dhātar, the 'Arranger', to provide the girl in question with a husband.

II.36 more clearly involves ritual activity, for the speaker of the hymn identifies himself as a performer of this very ritual

AV II.36.2 dhātúr devásya satyéna kṛṇómi pativédanam
By the truth of the god Dhātar [the Arranger] I perform the husband-finding.

and a range of ritual equipment is deployed and addressed, including a boat (vs. 5), gold, bdellium, and "aukṣá" (?)[73] (híraṇya, gúggulu, aukṣá, vs. 7), an unidentified plant (vs. 8), and perhaps most peculiar, an animal's lair (ākhará):

AV II.36.4 yáthākharó maghavaṃś cā́rur eṣá priyó mṛgā́ṇāṃ suṣádā babhū́va
evā́ bhágasya juṣṭéyám astu nā́rī sáṃpriyā pátyā́virādhayantī
Just as this pleasant lair became dear to the well-settled[74] wild beasts, o generous one, so let this woman be enjoyable to Fortune, mutually dear, not at variance with her husband.

Unfortunately it is difficult, even with the aid of the KauśSū rubrication of the hymn (KauśSū 34.12ff.), to determine what is really going on, much less why: what is the symbolism of this odd conjunction of elements? For example, according to KauśSū 34.14, the lair (of vs. 4) and the items in verse 7 are employed together:

KauśSū 34.14 mṛgākharād vedyāṃ mantroktāni saṃpātavanti dvāre prayachati
(Having placed) on an altar (made from soil/sand taken) from a wild animal's lair the items [gold, bdellium, aukṣa] mentioned in the mantra, smeared with the dregs of ghee, he holds them out (to hang) on the door (Caland) [/ gives them (to the maiden) at the door (Bloomfield, ad AV II.36)].

What *is* clear—and important—is that the girl is an active participant in the ceremony. This is also the case in the pati-vedana of śrauta ritual, which occurs at the end of the third of the "Four-monthly" (Caturmāsyāni) seasonal rituals, namely, the Sākamedha. Toward the close of the Sākamedha the ritual participants take an unusual detour: they leave the ritual ground proper and proceed toward the north to a crossroads.[75] Here they make an apotropaic offering to the dread god Rudra, who is urged to go back home to the north, leaving the cattle and family of the Sacrificer unharmed. The particular form of Rudra invoked is Rudra 'Tryambaka' ('Rudra possessing three Ambikās'[76]), and in fact the entire ritual complex is known as the Traiyambakahoma. The figure of Ambikā is also called upon and identified as Rudra's sister:

VS III.57[77] eṣá te rudra bhāgáḥ sahá svásrā́mbikayā tám̐ juṣasva svā́hā

This is your share, o Rudra. With your sister Ambikā enjoy it. Hail!

A cake is offered to Rudra in (/on?) a mole-hill (ākhūtkhara), and the mole (ākhu)[78] is identified as Rudra's totemic animal:

MS I.10.4 (144: 4)[79] ākhúm̐ te rudra paśúm̐ karomi

I make the mole your animal, o Rudra.

It is within this curious, somewhat sinister ritual performed outside consecrated ground in an inauspicious, indeed dangerous place[80] that the 'husband-finding' spell is performed. More offering cakes figure in this ritual: the cakes number one more than there are members of the Sacrificer's family, with the extra cake identified with the as-yet-unborn descendant.

ŚB II.6.2.4 té vái pratipuruṣám̐ / yā́vanto gṛhyā̀ḥ syús tā́vanta ékenā́tiriktā bhavanti tát pratipuruṣám eváitád ékaikena yā́ asya prajā́ jātā́s tā́ rudríyāt prámuñcaty ékenā́tiriktā bhavanti tád yā́ evā́sya prajā́ ájātās tā́ rudríyāt prámuñcati

The (cakes) (are) per person. There are as many as there are members of the household, plus one more. By the one each per person he releases his (already) born descendants from the power of Rudra. By the one in addition he releases his unborn descendants from the power of Rudra.

A group of people, apparently the Sacrificer with members of his household,[81] circle the fire.[82] According to a number of texts, they go first three times from right to left, slapping their left thighs, then three times from left to right (the ordinary pradakṣiṇa of the fire) slapping their right thighs:

BŚS V.16 (152: 2) athaitam agnim̐ triḥ pradakṣiṇam̐ pariyanti dakṣiṇān ūrūn upāghnānāḥ

Then they go around the fire three times to the right, slapping their right thighs.[83]

This ceremonial parade reminds us of two similar spectacles we have already discussed: the servant maids who circle the fire on the Mahāvrata day of the Gavāmayana and the introductory ceremonies at the Aśvamedha, immediately after which the queen lies with the horse. Recall that in the Mahāvrata ritual a group of eight female slaves (dāsī) carrying water jars circle the mārjālīya singing, making ritual exclamations, slapping their thighs, and stamping their feet.[84] Meanwhile ritual copulation between a whore and a chaste student is occurring near by.

At the Aśvamedha, after the killing of the horse, the king's wives approach it, and as the Mahiṣī prepares for her ordeal, the others (sometimes accompanied by hundreds of female slaves) perform a series of ritual circuits. Let us reexamine one version of this:

ĀpŚS XX.17.13 tā dakṣiṇān keśapakṣān udgrathya savyān prasrasya dakṣiṇān ūrūn āghnānāḥ sigbhir abhidhūnvatyas triḥ pradakṣiṇam aśvaṃ pariyanti

Tying up the right side of their hair and loosening the left, slapping their right thighs and fanning with their hems, they go around the horse three times to the right.[85]

There follow three leftward circuits, and a final three to the right.

It is not only the ritual *activity* of the Aśvamedha that reminds us of the performance at the crossroads in the Sākamedha. Recall the name of that part of the Sākamedha, the Traiyambakahoma. In the Aśvamedha the mantra that accompanies the entrance of the queens, according to most texts,[86] is

ambe ambāly ambike
na mā nayati kaś cana
sasasty aśvakaḥ

O Ambā, Ambālī, Ambikā.
No one is leading me.
The horsikins is sleeping.

As we saw above, the three vocatives are taken as variants on affectionate words for 'mother', but together they also add up to the 'three Ambikās' of Rudra Tryambaka and its vṛddhi derivative, the Traiyambakahoma.[87] This verbal coincidence further invites us to connect the Aśvamedha and this part of the Sākamedha. But what links the odd apotropaic addendum of the latter with the great royal celebration of fertility and regal power?

I think this link must be seen in the daughter of the household, identified throughout the texts as pátikāmā 'having desire for a husband'. While the others in the household circle the fire, reciting a mantra already found in the RV[88]

RV VII.59.12 tryàmbakaṃ yajāmahe sugándhim puṣṭivárdhanam
urvārukám iva bándhanān mṛtyór mukṣīya mā́mṛ́tāt

We worship Tryambaka, the fragrant increaser of prosperity.
Like a cucumber from its stem, may I be released from death, not from immortality,

the maiden joins the circle, performing the same actions and reciting a variant of the same mantra, substituting pativédanam 'husband-finding' for puṣṭivárdhanam 'prosperity-increasing',[89] and a different version of pāda d.[90]

The KS describes the whole scene:

KS XXXVI.14 (81: 8) [cf. MS I.10.20 (160: 11)] tryambakaṃ yajāmaha iti pariyanti yā patikāmā syāt sāpi parīyāt pativedanam evāsyai kurvanti

(Saying) "We worship Tryambaka . . . ," they go around. The one desirous of a husband should also go around. Thus they perform a pati-vedana [husband-finding] (ritual) for her.

In considering this episode, we should keep in mind how circumscribed female roles are in ritual, especially śrauta ritual, and therefore how unusual it is for an unmarried young woman to be participating at all (even if the action does not take place on the ritual ground itself), spouting Vedic mantras adapted from the Rig Veda itself. The models furnished by the circumambulations at the Mahāvrata day and the Aśvamedha make the maiden's participation all the more remarkable, for, as we saw, those performances increased almost to frenzy the air of abandon created by the illicit and dangerous sexual unions at those two rituals. That a presumably chaste and guarded daughter of the Sacrificer is encouraged, indeed required, to swirl around the fire slapping her thighs and begging for a husband, as if attending upon a ritual copulation, suggests that sexual display rather than maidenly modesty contributed to the marital negotiations. The girl is made to perform a role as out of character as it is shameful—just like the usually sheltered queens in the Aśvamedha with their prurient banter and public sex.

Her role in the ritual is not finished, though what follows is enigmatic (at least to me). The other participants pelt the girl with cakes, in one fashion or another, and then they all return to the ritual realm proper, for a conventional oblation to the eminently respectable goddess Aditi, a motherly figure.

According to MŚS, after the circular parade they all throw up their cakes, catch them, and then throw them at the Sacrificer and the husband-seeking daughter.

> MŚS I.7.7.8 tān ūrdhvān udasyodasya . . . pratilabhante
> 9 tān yajamānāya samāvapanti patikāmāyai ca
>
> Having repeatedly tossed them straight up, they catch them again.
> They throw them all at the Sacrificer and the one with desire for a husband.

The cakes are left behind, high in a tree, when they turn back to the ritual ground. BŚS V.16–17 has the other participants scatter the cakes in the hands of the Sacrificer, who transfers them to the hands of his wife, and it is she who gives them to her daughter.[91] The volley of cakes may serve as a premature shower of fertility, like the rice at modern American weddings. (The cakes are in fact made of rice.) This suggestion is strengthened by the previously mentioned fact that the number of cakes equals the number of household members, plus one that represents the as yet unborn.

There are a few other loose ends in this ritual that we might attempt to tie up. First is an apparent connection between the two pati-vedana rituals we have examined, the magical one of the AV and KauśSū and the śrauta version in the Sākamedha. The former compares the pleasant lair (ākhará) of a wild animal to the would-be wife (AV II.36.4 quoted earlier) and uses soil from a lair in the ritual itself (mṛgākhara KauśSū 34.14 also quoted earlier). The latter offers a cake to Rudra on a mole-hill (ākhūtkara[92]) just before the husband-finding ritual gets under way. The association of these two fairly rare words ākhara and ākhu (which are probably etymologically connected) with two forms of husband-finding seems unlikely to be coincidental, especially since burrowing animals and burrows may not be the first semantic association one makes with marriage. The burrow and its maker may symbolize the cozy home to be made by the newly married couple, but perhaps more likely, given the rampant sexual symbolism elsewhere in the ritual,[93] the burrow may obliquely refer to the woman's sexual organs.

The other puzzle is the third term of comparison of the 'three Ambikās,' namely the three abducted sisters in the MBh (mentioned in n. 87). Though the connection seems hard to gainsay, especially because the sisters also occur in a marriage context, one might think that the epic maidens would provide bad role models for the husband-seeking girl of the Sākamedha. After all, the oldest of them, Ambā, lost her fiancé because of the abduction, and she remained a defiant spinster, whose murderous anger ultimately caused the death of Bhīṣma, her abductor. Even Ambikā and Ambālikā, though they settled happily enough into their married life after their unexpected abduction (see e.g. MBh I.96), might not have chosen this particular method of pati-vedana if they had had their druthers.

Yet perhaps it is not so surprising that these three maidens with their dubiously contracted (and in one case unachieved) marriages should be associated with a shunned god (Rudra) on the one hand and a marriage-minded girl on the other. If this girl needs a pati-vedana ritual, it is likely that the conventional husband-finding tactics have not yet worked. The performance of the ritual in an inauspicious place to an inauspicious god suggests that it is not a carefree maidenly festival, but a somewhat grim ceremony designed to remove whatever obstacles are preventing the normal progression to marriage. The evocation of the ambivalently viewed sisters would, as so often in Vedic ritual, identify some of the potential marital problems and banish them, along with Rudra, in standard apotropaic fashion.[94]

3. *Finding a Husband: Sāvitrī*

The famous epic heroine Sāvitrī also performs what appear to be pati-vedana rituals.[95] Her involvement in them gives us some insight into what prompts the ritual performance. Sāvitrī, the daughter of King Aśvapati, comes of age as a beautiful and accomplished maiden, but her very excellence seems to frighten men (many modern women will recognize this plight), and she lacks a suitor:[96]

> MBh III.277.27 tāṃ tu padmapalāśākṣīṃ jvalantīm iva tejasā
> na kaś cid varayām āsa tejasā prativāritaḥ
>
> This (girl), of the lotus-petal eyes, blazing with splendor as it were,
> no one wooed—kept off by her splendor.

Sāvitrī's first response to this is ritual, and it seems that she undertakes the rituals herself, without urging from her parents:

MBh III.277.28 athopoṣya śiraḥsnātā daivatāny abhigamya sā
hutvāgnim vidhivad viprān vācayām āsa parvaṇi

Having fasted, with her head bathed, having approached the divinities,
having offered into the fire according to rule, she had the sages recite on the Moon-phase day.

She takes the remains of this sacrifice to her father (vs. 29). It is only then that he realizes that she has reached youth (vs. 31 yauvanasthāṃ tu tāṃ dṛṣṭvā), the time at which responsibility falls upon him to find her a husband, as we know.

But here the story takes a twist we have not seen before. As we saw, according to the legal texts the father has somewhere between three months and three years to fulfill his duty, after which time it falls to the maiden to find a husband on her own. But here without even a token effort on his part, he sends the girl out to do the job herself. She is forced into independent action, though her father remains affectionate, concerned, and willing to perform his ceremonial role once the hard part is over:

MBh III.277.32 putri pradānakālas te na ca kaś cid vṛṇoti mām
svayam anviccha bhartāraṃ guṇaiḥ sadṛśam ātmanaḥ
33 prārthitaḥ puruṣo yaś ca nivedyas tvayā mama
vimṛśyāhaṃ pradāsyāmi varaya tvaṃ yathepsitam

[King Aśvapati:] "Daughter, it is time for your 'giving away', and no one has made wooing to me (for you).
Seek a husband by yourself, one like you in good qualities.
Whatever man you aim at—let me know,
and having investigated, I will give (you to him). Choose however you want."

He urges her to hurry, so that *he* will not incur blame for failure to marry her off (vss. 35–36)! And away she obediently goes. (He at least supplies her with an escort.) When she returns and reports her choice, her father is obliged to honor it and give her away to Satyavant, though he has objections to the young man (because he is to die within the year). Sāvitrī is quite emphatic in her determination to make the marriage. She does not ask her father's permission, but announces her fixed intention with the powerful rhetorical trio of thought, word, and deed.

MBh III.278.26 sakṛd vṛto mayā bhartā na dvitīyaṃ vṛṇomy aham
27 manasā niścayaṃ kṛtvā tato vācābhidhīyate
kriyate karmaṇā paścāt pramāṇaṃ me manas tataḥ

[Sāvitrī:] "Once has my husband been chosen by me. I will not choose a second.
Once resolved by my mind, it is announced by my speech.
Afterwards it will be done by my action. My mind is my authority."

In this story 'self-choice' is taken one step further. In the classical svayaṃvara (like Damayantī's), the girl chooses her own husband but only from a pool preselected by her father and assembled at his dwelling. Here Sāvitrī not only chooses for herself (note the emphatic svayam 'by yourself' in vs. 32 quoted earlier) but conducts the search. The candidate(s) are not brought to her; she must go into the world, unprotected by her parents.

However, the exchange aspects of the marriage itself remain conventional. Though she *chooses*, her father *gives*. In verse III.277.33 quoted earlier, Aśvapati promises to give her to whomever she chooses. After she has returned with the choice made, her father's friend and adviser Nārada several times tells Aśvapati that there is no objection to his giving her away (pradāna III.278.29, 31). Following this there is an elaborate description of the preparations for the wedding, including a visit by Aśvapati to the bridegroom's father. Aśvapati urges the *father* to accept her as daughter-in-law. Here even the groom is marginalized in the exchange relation, which is established between the two fathers:

MBh III.279.8 sāvitrī nāma rājarṣe kanyeyaṃ mama śobhanā
tāṃ svadharmeṇa dharmajña snuṣārthe tvaṃ gṛhāṇa me

[Aśvapati:] "This lovely maiden is mine, Sāvitrī by name, o kingly seer.
Accept her from me for a daughter-in-law, according to your own law, o knower of the law."

The parental deal is sealed, because each of the fathers wants an alliance with the other (III.279.12–13). Although Sāvitrī made an independent choice, it is ratified by both fathers because it serves dynastic ends. Following their agreement, the wedding is celebrated, with Aśvapati *giving away* the bride:

MBh III.279.16 dattvā tv aśvapatiḥ kanyāṃ yathārhaṃ ca paricchadam

Aśvapati, having given the maiden and appropriate paraphernalia [adornments as a dowry] . . .

4. *Ownership of the Self?*

So Sāvitrī, despite her gumption (which will be tested even more in saving her husband from death), does not resolve the question with which this section started: does a girl have legal standing to enter into a marriage by herself? Does the Gāndharva marriage, by mutual agreement, involve exchange relations as the other marriage types do? Does a maiden, in the absence of other guardian, "own" herself sufficiently to give herself away?

In answer to these questions we may cite three cases. The first is one we have discussed in another connection. Though it does not involve a real marriage, it does depict a Gāndharva-like situation. Remember Oghavatī, enjoined by her husband to give a guest whatever he demanded: the guest wanted her, and she conceded. The phrasing of the guest's wish is telling:

MBh XIII.2.53 *pradānenātmano* rājñi kartum arhasi me priyam

By the *gift of yourself*, o queen, you ought to do me a favor.

This expression exactly reproduces the previous instructions of her husband:

MBh XIII.2.42 yena yena ca tuṣyeta nityam eva tvayātithiḥ
apy *ātmanaḥ pradānena* na te kāryā vicāraṇā

Always by whatever means you might satisfy a guest,
even by the *gift of yourself*, you should not hesitate to do it.

Thus Oghavatī has the discretionary power to *give herself*, though this power has of course been temporarily bestowed by her husband.

Let us now turn to a story that *is* about a marriage, but not one of a Gāndharva type. This is the tale of the 'old maiden' (vṛddha-kanyā) (MBh IX.51), whose father died soon after she was born. The girl devoted herself to extreme asceticism, rather than seeking a husband:

MBh IX.51.7 sā pitrādīyamānāpi[97] bhartre naicchad aninditā
ātmanaḥ sadṛśaṃ sā tu bhartāraṃ nānvapaśyata

Not being given by her father to a husband, the faultless one did not seek (one).
She did not see a husband equal to herself.

Her tapas becomes ever greater, until she is too weak to move. However, despite her remarkable success at ascetic practices, she is told that she cannot achieve heaven because she has not been married (vss. 11–12). (Life *is* unfair.) To an assembly of sages she announces that she *will give* her merit to anyone who will marry her:

MBh IX.51.13 tapaso 'rdhaṃ prayacchāmi pāṇigrāhasya sattamāḥ

(She said:) "I will give half of my tapas to the one who grasps my hand [marries me], o best ones."

So *she* is conducting the marital negotiations and giving the dowry, in loco parentis, as it were. When someone takes her up on the offer, she also *gives her hand* (vs. 16 tasmai pāṇiṃ dadau tadā). She clearly has the standing to bargain and to give herself in marriage; there is not even a courtesy stand-in to act as pseudofather in the ceremony.

Although not strictly relevant to our concerns, the rest of the story deserves telling. The man who agrees to marry her does so on condition that he only have to spend one night with her, as the emaciated ascetic hag was clearly not an appealing sexual prospect. As soon as she is married, she becomes ravishingly beautiful, and he is eager to change the terms. But for her it remains a marriage of convenience, a ticket to heaven, and after the single necessary night she replies to his suggestion:

MBh IX.51.19 yas tvayā samayo vipra kṛto me tapatāṃ vara
tenoṣitāsmi bhadraṃ te svasti te 'stu vrajāmy aham

The agreement I made with you, o sage, o best of ascetics,
by that I will abide, if you please. Good luck to you. I'm moving on.

Our last case will be the one where we might have looked first. If we are interested in the legal standing of the maiden in a Gāndharva marriage, it might be useful to consider an example of one. The most famous Gāndharva marriage in Indian literature is that of Śakuntalā and Duḥṣanta, first treated in the MBh (I.62–69) (and given a very different spin by Kālidāsa in the famous play). Though Kālidāsa's Śakuntalā is practically catatonic in her languor, the epic heroine is by contrast a shrewd bargainer and learned in the law. She only enters into a Gāndharva marriage after she feels she has made her legal position unassailable.

When Duḥṣanta comes to her hermitage and finds a beautiful maiden, unprotected, with her father conveniently off in the forest, he attempts to dazzle her with offers of rich baubles and, incidentally, his kingdom (MBh I.67.1–4). Then he proposes a Gāndharva marriage ("the best kind of marriage" I.67.4). She immediately counters with an appeal to conventional, parentally controlled marriage:

MBh I.67.5 phalāhāro gato rājan pitā me ita āśramāt
tam muhūrtaṃ pratīkṣasva *sa māṃ tubhyaṃ pradāsyati*

My father has gone from the hermitage here to gather fruit, o king.
Wait for him awhile. *He will give me to you.*

Duḥṣanta responds to the underlying issue in her request by assuring her that she has the right to bestow herself:

MBh I.67.7 ātmano bandhur ātmaiva gatir ātmaiva cātmanaḥ
ātmanaiv*ātmano dānaṃ* kartum arhasi dharmataḥ

You yourself are your own relative. You yourself are your own means.
You ought to make a *gift of yourself* by yourself according to law.

He thus claims that she can act simultaneously as the bride and the giver of the bride, i.e. her father. He then continues with a discourse on the forms of marriage (probably meant to muddle her little mind). When she can get a word in edgewise, she displays a mind thoroughly unmuddled: she returns to the question of her right to give herself. Accepting his arguments, she then uses this role of "giver" to set conditions on the marriage:

MBh I.67.15 yadi dharmapathas tv eṣa yadi cātmā prabhur mama
pradāne pauravaśreṣṭha śṛṇu me samayaṃ prabho

If this is a legal course and if I myself am my own master,
o best of the Pauravas, hear my terms of agreement in my *giving* (of myself in marriage), o lord.

When he solemnly agrees to her stipulations, she enters the marriage. It is hardly her fault that he later reneged and needed further legal remonstrance from Śakuntalā to acknowledge the marriage.[98]

Thus, the question with which I began—Does Gāndharva marriage fit theoretically in the system of exchanges that define other marriage types?—could have been answered immediately and simply by examining this last epic story. The Śakuntalā episode shows clearly that it was crucial to the jurists to define the Gāndharva marriage as an exchange, a *gift*, and this was done by the somewhat sophistic expedient of allowing the girl to give herself, an expedient that implicitly attributes to her a legal independence that is explicitly denied in other parts of the legal texts.[99] I did not answer the question in so efficient a fashion, however, because it seemed useful to display the *range* of independent activity available (at least theoretically) to a girl in a marital context. Without the support of this variety of means, Duḥṣanta's argument and Śakuntalā's acceptance of it might seem the mere convenience of the moment. Moreover, this range of action simultaneously allowed, indeed enjoined, on the one hand and forbidden on the other, once again displays the ambivalence that characterizes the ancient Indian view of women.

Texts concerning the types of marriage in ancient India thus show a thoroughgoing preoccupation with the type of *exchange* each involves, and the difficult cases of abduction (Rākṣasa) and mutual agreement (Gāndharva) test but do not pass beyond the limits of this exchange system. In all the exchanges there must be two parties, legally capable of acting as giver and recipient. Defining women as "givers" in the Gāndharva marriage may seem a male strategem to persuade reluctant girls into parentally unsanctioned beds, but the implications of affording women this legal standing are important, destabilizing and subverting the superficial consensus about women's place and behavior.

VI

Conclusion

It is my intention here *not* to summarize the "message" of this book, *not* to resolve the tensions we have explored, *not* to explain away some of the evidence in order to create a coherent picture with the rest. The conceptual position of women in ancient India was by nature *not* unified, not governed by a coherent set of principles and attitudes. It was contradictory, and these contradictions, found both in overt statements and in attitudes covertly reflected in narrative and ritual, are irreconcilable. We would achieve consensus only by ignoring half the evidence. Nonetheless, it may be useful to restate these contradictions, and the evidence for them, that we have explored in the course of this book—this time working backward.

Let us begin with marriage, the subject treated in part V. Marriage is the institution in which women's status as object is most clearly evidenced. She is a simple exchange token between two family groups (represented by their male members) that wish to make an alliance; indeed, her worth in the marriage market is sometimes rather crudely calculated in numerical terms. Most important, she is "given" by her father to her bridegroom, and this gift creates the husband's lordship over the wife, making her a piece of property that may be alienated at will (consider Yudhiṣṭhira).

Yet marriage is such a crucial social mechanism that woman's position as its central token endows her with a certain strategic importance. Not only is the web of mutual responsibilities that bind Aryan society in general established by marriage alliances, but the life of each individual Aryan male requires marriage as its centerpiece. He cannot fulfill his duty to his ancestors without producing legitimate sons. He cannot even worship the gods without a wife to participate in the ritual. There is, at this period, no alternative, monastic option for leading a full religious life.[1]

Thus the remarkable amount of space in dharma and gṛhya texts devoted to marriage: the choosing and wooing of the bride, the precise variety of exchange involved in the different marriage types, as I discussed, and the elaborate wedding ceremonies described at length in the gṛhya sūtras. Perhaps the most telling example of the importance of integrating marriage into the other requirements and goals of the society is one we examined in detail: the Rākṣasa marriage, in which the need to *give* the bride and thus establish reciprocal obligations between the two families conflicts with the Kṣatriya's principled refusal to *accept gifts*. A ceremonial, rule-governed abduction was the result of this incompatibility.

Women's value as a breeding machine also has some rather unexpected personal and social effects. Ancient India seems to have been almost neurotically aware of the importance of menarche as the beginning of a female's fertile life (which was no doubt brief enough, given the medical conditions prevailing). Each menstrual period wasted as a virgin represents the loss of a potential son. As we saw, the texts provide much testimony to the anxieties produced in the family of a newly adolescent girl. It is her father's responsibility to remedy the situation, to find her a husband to start using that periodic fertility. But since time was so limited, all means had to be employed to produce the desired result—including any the girl herself might control. If her father's efforts fail after a period of time, the legal texts recommend that she emancipate herself and find her own husband, and various narratives show girls doing just that.

So, the paradoxical result of viewing women as son-producing *objects* is again to endow them with some *subjecthood*: legal control over their own fate in some circumstances and, at least in narrative literature, a conception of women (actually teenage girls!) as possessing sufficient intelligence and resourcefulness to find a man and negotiate a marriage. The very fact that there is no respectable alternative to traditional marriage for women—no roles for the useful spinster or the cloistered nun—makes available to the young girl in search of a husband some of the mettle that permanently unmarried women display in other societies.

Moreover, though in marriage she is handed from one man to another like a piece of goods, wifehood gives her access to whatever active roles exist for women. Again the object becomes subject. She "has control over the household goods"; she gives (or refuses) alms to the ubiquitous begging students and itinerant Brahmans; she dispenses hospitality to more important visitors; most significant (for our purposes anyway), she becomes the ritual partner of her husband, the Sacrificer's Wife. Thus she plays a crucial role in knitting together her community. By producing sons, she ensures the linkage of generations and the continued veneration of the ancestors. By dispensing food and hospitality, she forges harmonious links between different segments of secular Aryan society. By her role in śrauta ritual (and by making such ritual possible), she links gods and men and allows the religious life of the community to proceed.

This is a very rosy picture of the life of an ancient Indian wife. Not only is it surely far rosier than the reality was (whatever that may have been), but it puts a deceptively positive spin on the *conceptual* position of this wife. As I have repeatedly emphasized throughout this book, all of the linkages just mentioned are perilous and anxiety-producing. Allotting the woman important roles there essentially makes her into cannon fodder. She incurs the danger, risks herself by putting herself in contact with the unknown, while the men in her life benefit from her efforts but stay out of direct danger (saving themselves for safer activities like dicing and warfare). Let me now briefly summarize some of the dangers presented by these linkages and the ways in which the wife is touched by them.

We spent much of part IV exploring the "anxieties of hospitality" and of gift-exchange, and the elaborate mechanisms Aryan society devised to control the risks inherent in these activities. The Aryans of ancient India and their Indo-European ancestors were bound to each other by ties of guest-friendship. Traveling strangers were to be received hospitably and, as guests, kept safe, and these guests had the contrary obligation not to bring hostility into the household of their host. These relationships of mutual (dis)trust and responsibility were often cemented and symbolized by the bestowal of gifts, which required, sooner or later, answering countergifts. Even a cursory reading of Homer shows a peripatetic society staggering around under the weight of fancy cauldrons, massive bows, and the like, given in token of hospitality.

One of the most enduring and powerful "gifts" for binding such relationships was that of a girl in marriage. The families became allied in a more tangible and permanent way than was possible in the fleeting visits between men, since the woman became a physical part of her new household without being severed from her original home. This is the most important way in which the woman incurs the risks of hospitality. She is in essence a permanent "guest," almost a hostage to the proper hostly behavior of a set of functional strangers, her in-laws. It is this ambiguous, potentially uncomfortable position of the wife—any wife, for this is a stuctural position, not an accidental product of particular circumstances—that fits her to embody and enact linkage in other parts of the hospitality system and in other spheres of action entirely. I discussed the general anxieties of hospitality in such detail in part IV partly to make clear how crucial a role marriage exchange, discussed in part V, plays in assuaging or controlling these anxieties, by forging permanent alliances between families.

Within the system of hospitality itself, we saw the woman giving alms to beggars and treating guests with appropriately hostly behavior. But as we also saw, this is not just a matter of pouring tea and making up beds. In story after story, the wife is forced into humiliating behavior or a demeaning position by a demanding guest. Her endurance (and her husband's endurance in watching it happen) brings each story to a happy ending. The most emblematic of these tales are the epic story of Oghavatī, who has sex with a guest in obedience to her husband's instructions, and the Brāhmaṇa story of Manu's wife, given in part II, which provided the impetus for this entire book.

Manu's wife brings us to the function of the wife in the religious life of the community, the role of Sacrificer's Wife. When Manu and his wife are performing ritual together, Manu agrees to the sacrifice of his wife when guests, stranger-priests, demand it. The shockingly contradictory images of wife as simultaneously active ritual *partner* and passive sacrificial *victim* are strikingly conveyed in this brief tale, and much of the very lengthy part III of this book was devoted to reconciling these two images or, rather, to showing that they imply each other.

I began part III by discussing the statutory need for a wife in solemn ritual, the structural role of Sacrificer's Wife—and how her somewhat destabilizing presence was regulated physically and temporally. The inherent contradictions of her role emerge strongly here. A ritual must have a wife, but it doesn't want too much of one. The powers that she contributes, which make her presence a requirement, also make her dangerous to have around. She is generally confined to one part of the ritual ground, allotted much less verbal and physical activity in the ritual than the other participants, and banished entirely when she is menstruating or in childbed. But her marginalization also provides a frame for the ritual. It begins and ends in her part of the ritual ground, and actions involving her open and close the ritual performance. She thus provides linkage between sacred and mundane, as we have seen her linking other realms.

I then discussed her considerable function as emblem of sexuality and producer of fertility. Again her role as wife in the "real" world is tapped for its contribution to the universe of ritual. As wife, she regularly enters periods of fertility and (with luck) produces sons in the aftermath; as Sacrificer's Wife she injects this sexual fertility into the orderly but potentially sterile world of ritual and (with luck) contributes to cosmic thriving and increase.

Her sexuality is harnessed in numerous ways in the ritual—from covert and decorous actions, like looking at melted butter or receiving straws from a broom, to the truly lurid, as enacted especially in the queen's copulation with the dead horse at the Aśvamedha. Women's sexuality is viewed with much ambivalence: it can be a destructive as well as a creative force. But the ritualists are adept at making use of everything available to them, and so representations of "negative" sexuality are also incorporated into ritual, to gain access to the forces erupting from taboo pairings (e.g. the adultery confessed to at the Varuṇapraghāsa) or sexual jealousy (the Rejected Wife in the royal rituals).

This sexual and (pro)creative function of the wife is crucially important in the *vertical*, diachronic linkage of Aryan society, the production of new generations bound to the old. But her role in creating the *horizontal*, synchronic bonds of Aryan society is just as critical: she is the ultimate exchange token, the embodiment of hospitality. Not surprisingly, this function, too, is represented in ritual—but this time the mutual obligations of guest-friendship are between mortals and gods, and the wife mediates between them in a dangerous no-man's-land. We saw this especially in the Soma Sacrifice, where the wife hospitably receives King Soma, soon to become sacrificial victim, and in the Animal Sacrifice, where the wife treats the recently sacrificed animal as if it were a guest. But her risks go beyond merely making contact with sacrificial victims. She herself becomes homologized to the victim, when she exchanges roles with the cow that will be used to buy the soma to be sacrificed. And in perhaps the most remarkable, dramatically sustained episode in the Soma Sacrifice, she offers herself to the gods, as a sexual token, at the explosive end of the ritual. Thus the narrative of Manu's Cups, in which the wife is tied to the victim's stake, is merely a more explicit rendering of various episodes in ritual itself, in which the wife covertly functions as victim, as *exchange token* between men and gods, as the *gift* men give to the gods in anxious expectation of a countergift.

I hope that after this work it will no longer be possible to treat the ancient Indian wife, ritual or otherwise, as a footnote, a minor figure on the fringes of activity, pitiable but irrelevant. I also hope that it will not be possible to uncomplicate her functions, neatly summarize her social and conceptual niche.

I have tried neither to overglorify her positive roles nor to wallow in her humiliations, but to present her as she appears to me: "the bearer of all paradox." She is both sacrificer and sacrificed, both giver and given, both subject and object. And an appreciation of her position at the center of these paradoxes gives us a powerful tool for exploring the tensions and points of strain in the social, cultural, and religious realms of ancient India as a whole.

NOTES

Introduction

1. By "ancient India" I refer to a period beginning with the advent of Sanskrit-speaking Indo-Europeans in c. 1500 B.C.E. and lasting until approximately the time of the emperor Aśoka (3d c. B.C.E.). This period encompasses the Vedas and their associated texts as well as the older legal texts and the older strata of the Sanskrit epics, particularly the Mahābhārata. It should be noted that the older, pre-Sanskrit Indus Valley civilization is specifically excluded here.

2. Stodginess to the outsider. Needless to say, as a philologist I have spent some of my happiest hours/days/weeks pursuing the precise grammatical identity of verb forms, the constraints on the distribution of particles, and similar issues.

3. The classic work on gift-exchange is, of course, Mauss, "Essai sur le don" (1923–24). Benveniste frequently treated Indo-European manifestations of hospitality and gift-exchange; see especially "Don et échange dans le vocabulaire indo-européen" (1951) and *Le Vocabulaire des institutions indo-européennes* (1969), bk 1, sect. 2, and passim. See also Watkins 1970, 345–50. For Indo-Iranian, Thieme has written extensively on hospitality and other relations between strangers; see especially *Der Fremdling im Ṛgveda* (1938) and *Mitra and Aryaman* (1957a).

4. See especially Thieme 1957b, p. 90. See also Heesterman 1985, pp. 30–31 and n. 34; 48 and n. 26; 92, n. 45.

The close relation between ritual and hospitality was thoroughly appreciated by the ancient Indians. For example, one of the five 'great worships' (mahāyajñāḥ) to be performed daily by the householder (MDŚ III.69ff., among many texts) is the reception of guests. Cf. e.g. MDŚ III.70 nṛyajño 'tithipūjanam "The worship of man is the honoring of guests."

For further discussion, see part III.E and part IV.

5. For the differential effects of well-organized vs. poorly organized social institutions on the power and influence of women, see e.g. Hackett 1985.

6. Investigation of such sources for information on women in India has been urged e.g. by Wadley 1988, pp. 24, 39f.; Kakar 1988, p. 46.

7. Jamison 1991, pp. 217–21.

8. This is the case in the earlier parts of the legal tradition. Later the king is charged with imposing the punishment.

9. E.g. Marglin 1985, Wadley 1988, Kakar 1988, and Carmody 1989, chapter 3, "Hindu women." In contrast, several older works can be consulted with profit. M. Winternitz, *Die Frau in den indischen Religionen. Teil I. Die Frau im Brahmanismus* (1920), provides a useful compendium primarily of legal material concerning women. For the epic, Hopkins, "The social and military position of the ruling caste in ancient India" (1889), with its "Appendix on the status of women" (pp. 330–72), though of course dated in many respects, collects much of the relevant material for the first time and discusses it sensibly. Meyer, *Das Weib im altindischen Epos* (1915)—and its

tled English version, *Sexual life in ancient India*, (1930)—displays more alysis than its gratingly sentimental style and diction lead one to expect. ample, I have met MDŚ IX.2–3 quoted (usually in the 1886 translation of argIin 1988, p. 43; Wadley 1988, p. 30; Carmody 1989, p. 51; Kinsley

tories also tend to get flattened out in these treatments, somewhat manipulated into what often seem the *investigator*'s notion of ideological narrative. To choose one example, the complex figure of Sāvitrī in the MBh, a spunky and defiant woman who pursues Death and bests him in verbal argument in order to restore her husband to life, is treated by at least three scholars as a pure type of the submissive Hindu wife (Wadley 1988, p. 32; Kakar 1988, pp. 55–56; Carmody 1989, p. 47 [here unaccountably called Savitu]). Her wifely devotion is certainly an important theme, but the story is more complicated and more interesting, as we will see in V.C.3.

12. The oldest and most important is the Rig Veda (RV), which contains 1,028 hymns addressed to various divinities. The next oldest is the Atharva Veda (AV), consisting for the most part of magical and healing spells on a popular level, contrasting with the high literary craftsmanship and solemnity of the RV. The Yajur Veda (YV) contains specifically ritual formulae, often quite short and cryptic. The Sāma Veda (SV) is primarily a rearrangement of material extracted from the Rig Veda and is of less interest than the other texts from the verbal point of view, though of immense ritual importance.

13. Or if they do, they have been adapted into the male-oriented ritual orbit. Nonetheless, some of the ritual-internal texts (e.g. those directed against cowives or toward winning the love of a man) purport to be women's texts, and some of the ritual-external texts (e.g. the Strīkarman section of the Kauśika Sūtra) purport to describe women's own rituals. Some of these will be discussed later.

14. I use the word "objective" with full awareness of its danger and a consequent limitation on its applicability. We can, of course, take no ancient text as a completely "objective" record; in the case of these ritual texts I imagine they depict idealized and orderly ritual to some extent, without the procedural shortcuts that were no doubt commonly taken or the chaos that probably often reigned in the more demanding rites. On the other hand, I can see no reason that they would distort, or at any rate exaggerate, the role of women in ritual performance (they may minimize it), especially in the types of details usually reported: e.g. where she sits, what kind of basket or pot she carries, when she covers her head or looks at the offering.

15. A few works treat the wife's ritual role, but none is particularly satisfactory. Chaudhuri devoted a number of articles in the late 1930s and early 1940s to women in Vedic ritual. The promisingly titled "The wife in the Vedic ritual" (1940), though collecting much pertinent material, is almost entirely descriptive; what little analysis it contains is directed toward establishing the ritual supremacy of the chief wife and, by extension, the monogamous bent of ancient Indian society—sometimes to the detriment of the evidence. Other articles by him display a similar mixture of useful data collection and propagandistic argumentation for the essential benevolence of ancient Indian treatment of and attitudes toward women. Chaudhuri 1938, 1939, 1941a, 1941b.

Winternitz 1920 devotes relatively little space (pp. 8–15) to the wife's ritual behavior, though he makes some penetrating observations. Thite 1975 is also sparing in his treatment of the ritual wife (pp. 197–99).

The only substantial recent treatment of which I am aware is that of F. M. Smith 1991. This article will be discussed in detail later; though I welcome its stimulating discussion of the evidence, I find I can concur with few of its conclusions.

16. Because of my conviction that some of our most important clues lie in the exact formulations—the vocabulary and constructions—of our texts, I will always quote the original as well as my literal translation. (All translations are my own, unless otherwise specified.) This is not a matter of pedantry but of the respect I think we owe to the composers of the texts we are trying to understand.

17. For an example of this type, see my discussion in Jamison 1991, part II, chapter 7 of the obstetrical vocabulary and concepts employed in a myth ostensibly about something else entirely, the removal of darkness from the sun.

18. This is, of course, a complex topic and deserves far more discussion. I do not want to enter here into questions of sexist language and how it may affect female speakers and their access to and experience of power, or of differences between men's and women's speech. Nor can I discuss here the more serious question (more serious for historical study) of how denying females access to education or to certain texts or solemn recitations may make the language (or some levels of language) more fully the property of males than females. My point here is simply that grosso modo women and men speak "the same" language, and that, given the limitations of our other sources, ignoring the evidence of language further impoverishes our conception of ancient modes of thought.

19. This is literally what the Sanskrit says.

20. This book is not a treatise on the general legal status of women in ancient India, although such a work deserves to be written. In the meantime, the monumental *History of Dharmaśāstra* (hereafter *HDŚ*) 1930–62 of P. V. Kane is indispensible, and works such as Winternitz 1920, Leslie 1991b can be consulted for various aspects of this issue—though the reader should be aware that none of these works is as delicate or evenhanded in assessing the evidence as I would like to see.

21. For example, in at least one legal treatise (BDS) the killing of a woman merits the same punishment as the killing of a Śūdra (the lowest division of society) or a cow, though if she is fertile when killed, her status soars to that of a Kṣatriya or even a Brahman (cf. BDS I.19.3, 5; II.1.10.10–12; and Jamison 1991, pp. 214–17). However, other texts consider the killing of any woman more seriously. For example, in MDŚ VIII.89 a false witness is threatened with residence in the worlds inhabited by murderers of Brahmans (brahmaghnaḥ) or of women and children (strībālaghātinaḥ), which might suggest that these two types of crimes are equivalent. Similarly MDŚ IX.232.

On the general legal equivalence of women and the Śūdras, see Kane, *HDŚ* II.594–95.

22. Gonda 1980, p. 200. But compare Kane, *HDŚ* II, pp. 293–95, 365–68 and see the story of Apālā, who performs a Soma Sacrifice by herself (Schmidt 1987, pp. 1–29; Jamison 1991, chapter 6, part A). Aspects of this story are discussed in part V.

23. See in general Winternitz 1920, p. 40; Gonda 1980 passim, for further references to the primary literature.

Childbirth is even more polluting. At least the mother, usually also the father, and possibly other relatives become polluted for some period after birth (e.g. MDŚ V.58, 61–62). One cannot recite the Veda after eating the food of a woman who has just given birth (MDŚ IV.112, 212), and cleansing is required if one touches such a woman (MDŚ V.85).

24. The celebration in honor of the ancestors. For further discussion, see IV.D.1.

25. Gāndhārī also seems to be present in the Sabhā during the dicing match and its aftermath (cf. MBh II.63.24, 66.28ff.), and Draupadī's mother-in-law Kuntī as well: she later recalls her sorrow on seeing Draupadī there (MBh V.88.48ff.).

26. Cf. GDS XVIII.1; VāsDS V.1–2; BDS II.3.44–45, etc.

27. This pattern was already discussed, though in saccharine language, by Meyer in

his chapter "The woman of energy"; compare e.g. "the woman . . . resolute, full of fire, passionate in comparison with the often so slack and sinewless man," "the tender, timid sex so often takes the leadership in the Indian love tales . . . The woman is active, the man often quite passive" (Meyer [1915] 1930, p. 437).

28. Nala and Damayantī: MBh III.50–78; Sāvitrī: MBh III.277–83; Śakuntalā: MBh I.62–69; Draupadī: MBh II.59–65 and throughout the text. All these stories are easily accessible in the excellent translation of van Buitenen (1973 [Book I], 1975 [Books II, III], 1978 [Books IV, V]). I will discuss aspects of the stories of Sāvitrī and Śakuntalā in part V, as well as an episode involving Draupadī.

29. Urvaśī: RV X.95; Yamī: RV X.10; Lopamudrā: RV I.179. All are translated in O'Flaherty 1981, though given the difficulty of these hymns, there is much in those translations with which I would disagree.

30. There are many Vedic and epic stories that turn on this problem, but perhaps the most pointed is that of Jaratkāru, the aged ascetic who must save his shrivelled-up ancestors by marrying and begetting a son. He does so, but puts outrageous conditions on his marriage and abandons his wife as soon as she gets pregnant (MBh I.41–44).

31. On the āśrama system in general, see Olivelle 1993.

32. This periodic restriction also has the practical result of concentrating sexual activity during the woman's most fertile period, and not 'wasting' sex on times when she is unlikely to get pregnant, but I do not think that this practical consideration is the only motive. On the proper days see e.g. MDŚ III.45–48, 50; IV.128.

33. Or to bypass sex altogether, as some stories do. But real life afforded few chances of miraculous birth.

34. In later Hinduism this pattern is also common, e.g. in the stories of the marriage of Śiva and Parvatī. See in general O'Flaherty [1973] 1981. O'Flaherty is insightful concerning the conflict between asceticism and procreation (68ff.) and the practical value of the āśrama system (57, 78f.), but curiously fails to discuss the woman's role in any detail.

35. Perhaps the ultimate example of this reversal is the story of Ṛṣyaśṛṅga, the innocent young son of a seer who has never seen a woman and is tricked into sex play. He fills the role of unbelievably ignorant ingenu(e) generally taken by virginal damsels in Western literature. This tale is found in various versions in both of the Sanskrit epics and in the Pāli Jātakas; it has recently been illuminatingly discussed in an unpublished paper by Louise Hope.

36. The story of King Bhaṅgāsvana in MBh XIII.12 illustrates this point. This king, cursed by Indra, bathes in a pond and emerges as a woman (and has a great deal of comic trouble figuring out how to mount his horse). But later, when Indra relents and allows him to choose either sex, s/he opts to remain female because

> MBh XIII.12.47 striyāḥ puruṣasaṃyoge prītir abhyadhikā sadā
>
> In intercourse with men women always get the superior pleasure.

The Tiresias answer, but Bhaṅgāsvana's story ends more happily.

37. It is also probably no accident that these women use their power to further males, particularly their husbands (or husbands-to-be)—the Barbara Bush syndrome. Damayantī is always mopping up after Nala's stupid behavior. Draupadī saves the Pāṇḍavas from slavery. Sāvitrī saves her husband from Death. Śakuntalā fights her husband, but for the sake of their son (and so ultimately for the sake of the husband, too). The most obvious exception is the RVic Urvaśī, who is sick of her mortal hus-

band, does not seem particularly interested in their son, and wants to return to carefree life with her sister Apsarases. It is instructive, and depressing, to follow how later versions of this story (ŚB XI.5.1, BŚS XVIII.44–45) tone down and distort this subversive independence and twist it into wifely devotion, until we arrive at the Urvaśī of Kālidāsa, who is almost as much of a lovesick vaporing wimp as his Śakuntalā.

38. I owe this phrase to a student in my course "Gender patterns in the ancient Indian religious tradition" given at the Harvard Divinity School in the fall of 1992.

Part II

1. Though, as Lévi points out (1898, p. 121), Manu the legislator may simply be a transformation of Manu the sacrificer, under new social conditions.

2. The Asuras are the implacable mirror-image rivals of the gods (Devas) in middle Vedic literature and figure in numerous myths of this period. See Jamison 1991, p. 31, and forthcoming a.

3. It is surely no accident that the earlier versions use the term for *ritual* wife (patnī), while ŚB has substituted the less precise jāyā (a term more associated with the wife's role in procreation; see Winternitz 1920, p. 6). In the MS/KS version the wife's participation in the ritual is a crucial risk factor for her, as we will see.

4. Both MS and KS also have shortened versions (MS IV.1.6 [8: 10] ≅ KS XXXI.4 [5: 13]/KapS XLVII.4), and the TS and TB also contain brief and garbled mentions of the story. These TB, KS, and MS passages are virtually identical and do not mention the wife.

TS VI.6.6.1 índraḥ pátniyā mánum ayājayat tā́m páryagnikr̥tām údasr̥jat táyā mánur ārdhnot

Indra performed a sacrifice for Manu with his wife. He released her when the fire-circuit was completed. With her/this (rite) Manu succeeded.

TB III.2.5.9 mánoś śraddhā́devasya yájamānasyāsuraghnī́ vā́k / yajñāyudhéṣu práviṣṭāsīt / té 'surā yā́vanto yajñāyudhā́nām udvádatām upā́śr̥ṇvann / té párābhavan

An Asura-killing voice entered the ritual implements of Manu, the Sacrificer, who had Śraddhā as his deity. As many Asuras as heard the ritual implements sounding perished.

KS XXXI.4 (5: 13) manor vai śraddhādevasya yajamānasyāsuraghnī vāg yajñāyudhāni praviṣṭāsīt teṣāṃ yāvanto 'surā upāśr̥ṇvaṁs te parābhavan

An Asura-killing voice entered the ritual implements of Manu, the Sacrificer, who had Śraddhā as his deity. As many Asuras as heard them perished.

MS IV.1.6 (8: 10) mánor vái śraddhā́devasya yájamānasyāsuraghnī́ vā́g yajñāyudhā́ni práviṣṭāsīt tásyā vádantyā yā́vantó 'surā upā́śr̥ṇvaṁs tā́vantas tád áhar nā́bhavan

An Asura-killing voice entered the ritual implements of Manu, the Sacrificer, who had Śraddhā as his deity. As many Asuras as heard it [voice] speaking ceased to exist on that day.

5. There is, of course, no complete translation of the MS, but a translation of most of this episode is found in Lévi 1898, pp. 119–20. I became aware of Lévi's treatment of this story only after I had arrived at my own interpretation, so that our versions, though very close, are independent.

6. This word will be discussed later.

7. This word will be discussed later. Lévi simply translates here "La voix entra en lui."

8. This version has also been translated, by Rau (1966, pp. 91–92). Again my rendering of the story was made independently, before I came across this article.

9. This word will be discussed later.

Part III

1. To construct the wife's function in śrauta ritual, I have fully excerpted the relevant materials from the following texts:

<u>śrauta sūtras</u>

Black Yajur Veda (BYV): Baudhāyana Śrauta Sūtra (BŚS)
Āpastambha ŚS (ĀpŚS), both belonging to the Taittirīya Saṃhitā (TS);

Mānava ŚS (MŚS)
Vārāha ŚS (VārŚS), both belonging to the Maitrāyaṇi Saṃhitā (MS)

White Yajur Veda (WYV): Kātyāyana ŚS (KŚS), belonging to the Mādhyaṃdina Śākhā

Rig Veda (RV): Śāṅkhāyana ŚS (ŚŚS)

<u>Brāhmaṇa-type texts</u>

Black Yajur Veda: Taittirīya Saṃhitā (TS),
Maitrāyaṇi Saṃhitā (MS)
Kāṭhaka Saṃhitā (KS)

White Yajur Veda: Śatapatha Brāhmaṇa (ŚB)

The predominance of Yajur Veda texts results from the fact that the Adhvaryu priest, the priest of ritual activity, represents this Veda, and most of the wife's role consists of action, not words.

Other śrauta sūtras and other Brāhmaṇas were consulted as seemed appropriate, as well as general works on śrauta ritual and treatments of particular rituals (e.g. Hillebrandt 1879, 1897; Caland and Henry 1906–7; Dumont 1927; Einoo 1988). Specific references will be given below.

2. The sections of Staal 1983 that deal with the lengthy preparations for the 1975 performance of the Agnicayana in Kerala convey particularly well the mobilization of social resources required, beginning months in advance with the craftsmen who produced the material implements for the ritual.

3. For example, in the otherwise indispensible treatment of Hubert and Mauss 1898, the wife's ritual participation is barely mentioned in a footnote (p. 41, n. 263):

> The wife of the sacrifier [H and M's term for yajamāna] is present at all the Hindu solemn sacrifices, standing in a special place, loosely bound, and is the object of certain

> rites, which communicate to her in some degree the emanations of the sacrifice and assure her fertility.

Hopkins, admittedly describing the epic situation, states (1889, p. 338):

> They [women] had no independent part in Veda-study or in sacrifice, merely helping their husbands in the manual part of the daily sacrifice, and (barring accidental representation [meaning what? SWJ]) being entitled, like the slaves, to merely a perfunctory acquiescent word during religious rites.

Cf. also Lévi 1898, p. 157.

Staal (1983, p. 314) also barely mentions the wife's activities:

> The ceremonies can only be performed on behalf of a yajamāna who is married and whose wife is present. On a few occasions, she participates actively in the rites or recitations.

But his relative neglect of the wife may reflect modern Nambudiri practice: as far as I can ascertain from Staal's treatment, the wife does not participate in certain actions, like the cleansing of the animal victim, where classical śrauta ritual requires her.

An exception to the prevailing dismissal of the wife's importance is found in van Buitenen's treatment of the Pravargya: "[G]enerally in śrauta ritual the wife has an important, sometimes crucial, part to play" (1968, p. 2).

4. Indeed in Pāṇini IV.1.33 patnī is defined as "(the woman) who jointly participates in ritual [yajñasaṃyoge] (with her husband)."

5. Interestingly enough the Sacrificer is not called a pati.

6. See Kane, *HDŚ* II.556ff, with references to the primary literature.

7. See Kane, *HDŚ* II.559f; Winternitz 1920, p. 14, both with references to the primary literature.

8. Cf. e.g. MŚS VII.2.1.23; ĀpŚS XXI.3.9–10; KŚS XII.2.15–17; VārŚS III.2.1.12–16.

9. The general provisions affecting a menstruating woman were discussed in I.5.

10. Anālambhukā 'untouchable' is a clear euphemism for menstruation. The commentary glosses it with malavadvāsāḥ 'having stained clothing'. It is noteworthy, however, that the idiom ā √lambh 'to touch, take' is also a common euphemism for 'taking' an animal victim for sacrifice.

11. On this yoking see III.B.2a.

12. Caland in his note on this passage suggests that the identification between the saṃnahana specified in the passage and the wife's yoktra is probable, on the basis of Rudradatta's commentary. I am certain of it, especially since saṃ √nah is the idiom used for the wife's original binding.

13. BŚS XXIX.11 (385: 7) sutye 'hani mārjālīye sikatopopte pariśrityopaviśed anyeṣv ahaḥsu patnīśālāyām evopaviśet prāgvaṁśaṃ na prapadyeta.

14. Though, as noted, this was managed in the 1975 Agnicayana. On the different provisions for different rituals, see Chaudhuri 1939, pp. 501–2.

15. Here it is not clear whether the wife is "indisposed" or is not there for some more permanent reason (like death).

Cf. also ĀpŚS II.6.4, which recommends leaving out a particular mantra at this time in the absence of a wife (patnyabhāve). Caland points out in his note to this passage that there is general disagreement about what to do without a wife: some authorities suggest that the Sacrificer undertake her duties, while others want to eliminate them entirely. This problem is further discussed e.g. in the commentary to ĀpŚS I.20.13.

16. For further on this passage, see Bodewitz 1976, pp. 111–21.

17. The ritualists are not so solicitous of her welfare elsewhere, however. As we will see, the wife is deliberately put into contact with the perilous forces of death.

18. For a more complex case of the exclusion of the wife from a ritual, see the discussion of the Pravargya in III.C.2.

19. Cf. Kane, *HDŚ* II.557, 683f.; Winternitz 1920, pp. 9–10; B. K. Smith 1986, pp. 81ff., 1989; for some discussion of the matters treated in the next paragraphs, see B. K. Smith 1989, pp. 154–60.

20. Though when her husband is away, the fires remain with the wife, and a priest is appointed to perform the Agnihotra. See Kane, *HDŚ* II.683–85, 1007–8; BŚS XXIX.9, 12.

21. Though cf. ĀpDS II.15.17 na strī juhuyāt "A woman should not make oblation" for what may be older and more general provision.

22. For other possible substitutes in a Sattra, see Kane, *HDŚ* II.1241–42.

23. Gṛhya or 'domestic' rituals require only one fire.

24. Oddly enough, both Sacrificer and wife get "demoted" at the Dīkṣā (consecration) of the great sacrifices. As we will see, the food the two are allowed during the consecration period is cooked on separate fires. But it is the *Sacrificer*'s food that is cooked on the Gārhapatya, while the wife's is prepared on the Dakṣiṇāgni or Southern Fire. Cf. MŚS II.1.2.41; ĀpŚS X.17.6; KŚS VII.4.24.

25. There is a coda involving a return to the Āhavanīya fire—the Samiṣṭayajus, on which see III.C.3.

26. Or, even when the other two fires are drilled independently or are brought from an external fire (as some schools allow), the Gārhapatya is established first.

27. Cf. also JB II.114, III.157; ŚB VIII.6.3.11; TB II.2.9.5.

28. The connection between the wife and the jaghana is also found in one text, in a small incident at the end of the Animal Sacrifice (Paśubandha). When the Patnīsaṃyājas are performed, the tail (jāghanī) of the victim is offered to these wives of the gods (e.g. ŚB III.8.5.6). ĀpŚS mentions that after the offering, the wife is handed the remains of the tail (after the offering material has been cut off), and she then passes it on:

> ĀpŚS VII.27.12 tāṃ patnyai prayacchati tāṃ sādhvaryave 'nyasmai vā brāhmaṇāya
>
> He gives it [the tail] to the wife, and she (gives) it to the Adhvaryu or another Brahman.

This procedure resembles the bestowal of sexual tokens on the wife that we will discuss later, and it seems likely that this rather distasteful object—the mutilated tail of a sacrificed beast—was meant to pass its fertile powers to the recipient. The connection between the tail and the penis is well-nigh a semantic universal, and in Sanskrit the word śepa can be used for both.

29. Except for the daily Agnihotra.

30. For a full treatment, see Hillebrandt 1897.

31. Again, except in the simple, daily Agnihotra.

32. VārŚS I.3.2.21 yoktreṇa patnī saṃnahyate; and see esp. the second alternative in BhārŚS II.5.3 (cited by Hillebrandt 1879, p. 59, n. 5) patnīm ūrdhvajñum āsīnāṃ saṃnahya tiṣṭhantīṃ vā *svayaṃ vā patny ātmānam* ". . . or the wife (girds) herself by herself."

33. Except for this first one, the following mantras are quoted in the KS versions. Variants in other texts will be noted as relevant. Corresponding to the quoted TS I.1.10.1, KS I.10 (5: 6) has the less explicit gerund saṃnahya 'having girded'.

34. For further on Indrāṇī, see sections III.D.3 and III.E.4.

35. ĀpŚS II.5.3 vācayatīty eke; BŚS I.12 (17: 19) (some mss.) athaināṃ vācayati.

36. F. M. Smith 1991.

37. Recall the BŚS passage quoted earlier, banishing menstruating women from ritual for just this reason:

> BŚS XXIX.11 (384: 2) vijñāyate brahmahatyāyai hy eṣā varṇaṃ pratimucyāsta iti tasmād dhavir nānvīkṣeta na spṛśed iti
>
> As is known from tradition, she is in the state of having put on the color of Brahman-murder. Therefore she should not look at or touch the oblation.

38. Consider the story of Śunaḥśepa (AB VII.13–18), also cited by F. M. Smith (p. 20, n. 3; p. 26, n. 18), where Varuṇa's noose is *thwarted* by Indra.

39. The equivalence of the wife's yoktra and the Sacrificer's upavīta has also been noted by Schmidt (1987, p. 25), following Eggeling (ad ŚB I.3.1.13), who indeed cites the TB passage given above in the text.

40. F. M. Smith cites this passage and recognizes the initiatory aspects of the rite (p. 24, with n. 9), in fact stating "she has now brought herself into a working relationship with the gods and can pursue meaningful ritual activity" (p. 25). This recognition makes it all the more curious to me that he otherwise sees the act in such a negative light, despite textual evidence to the contrary.

41. With AV XIV.2.

42. In certain texts: e.g. KauśSū 76.7; ĀpGS II.4.8; and see Kane, *HDŚ* II.532–33; Chatterjee 1978, pp. 108–9.

43. In forms of the marriage ceremony that lack a yoktra, the mantra accompanies the untying of one of two tufts of wool bound in the bride's hair (e.g. ĀśvGS I.7.16, 17), symbolizing her release and departure from her two parents. In KauśSū it accompanies both the loosing of the yoktra (76.7) and the release of a hair band (75.23).

44. In an often quoted RVic verse the bride is said to have three husbands before the man she actually marries:

> RV X.85.40 sómaḥ prathamó vivide, gandharvó vivida úttaraḥ
> tṛtī́yo agníṣ ṭe pátis, turī́yas te manuṣyajā́ḥ
>
> Soma possessed (you) first; a Gandharva possessed (you) next.
> Agni was your third husband; your fourth is human-born.

It may be no accident that the mantra of initiation that the woman speaks in our Iṣṭi has been altered from patyur anuvratā bhūtvā "having become avowed to the husband" to *agner* anuvratā bhūtvā "having become avowed to Agni," who may be thus serving as third and last bridegroom in her liminal initiation period.

45. Even the period between rituals or after them may require abstinence. For example, in the three months that intervene between the seasonal rituals (Cāturmāsyāni), the Sacrificer "should not 'approach' a woman" (na striyam upaiti), though he may optionally or by requirement have intercourse with his wife during her fertile period:

MŚS I.7.2.25 [= VārŚS I.7.1.1] na striyam upaiti . . . ṛtau bhāryām upaiti

He does not approach a woman. . . . He approaches his wife at her season.

ĀpŚS VIII.4.5 . . . na striyam upaiti
6 ṛtve vā jāyām

He does not approach a woman.
Or (he approaches) his wife at her season.

BŚS XXVIII.8 (356: 13) na striyam upeyāt kāmam ṛtau jāyām upeyād yady ajātaputraḥ syāt

He should not approach a woman, (except) optionally he may approach his wife at her season if he should not have sons.

After performing the great ritual of the Laying of the Fire(-altar) (Agnicayana), a Sacrificer must restrict (though not abandon) his sexual activity, and subsequent repilings introduce new restrictions:

ĀpŚS XVII.24.2 saṃvatsaram . . . na ca rāmām upeyāt
. . . 5 na dvitīyaṃ citvānyasya striyam upeyāt /
na tṛtīyaṃ citvā kāṃ cana / bhāryāṃ vopeyāt

For a year he should not approach a dark woman (/ lower class concubine?).
. . . Having piled (the fire altar) a second time he should not approach the woman of another. Having piled a third time, he should not (approach) any woman. Or he may approach his wife.

TS V.6.8.3–4; KS XXII.7 (63: 18); MŚS VI.2.6.25; VārŚS II.2.5.9 have identical provisions, and do not even allow the last option of sex within marriage. KŚS XVIII.6.28–30 also puts severer restrictions on sex with each piling of the altar: after the first performance he should approach only women of the three twice-born varṇas; after the second only those of his own varṇa; and after the third no woman at all.

46. This requirement is so crucial that the word brahmacarya means both 'study of the Veda' and '(state of) chastity'.

47. On miraculously renewing virginity as a topos, see V.A.1.

48. See I.5 on the power created by the retention of semen by chaste seers.

49. The ungirding of the wife at the end of the ritual may find a bizarre echo in AV IX.3, called by Whitney "To accompany the releasing of a house," a title that may convey some of the peculiarity of this hymn. The hymn is used in the KauśSū in a ceremony granting a priest a house as a Dakṣiṇā (see Bloomfield 1897, ad loc.), but I doubt if this was its original purpose. In fact most of the verses concern the *dismantling* of the house (śālā) by unfastening the knots and fetters (pāśa! vs. 2) that hold it together. The house is repeatedly called mánasya *pátnī* "mistress/wife of the building" (vss. 5, 6, 9) [the word for house, śālā, is grammatically feminine], once compared to a bride (vadhū́) about to be carried away (vs. 24), and is invoked as víjāvati prájāvati "o possessor of births and offspring" (vss. 13, 14), as well as compared to a womb for Agni (vs. 21). At the end, when completely dismantled, she is urged not to fasten her fetter to us (vs. 24 mā́ naḥ pā́śaṃ práti mucaḥ).

Though there is much I do not understand about this hymn, I would tentatively suggest that it concerns the dismantling of the temporary ritual structures (also called śālā) at the end of the Soma Sacrifice. Indeed the ritual use of the building is alluded to. In verse 19 it is called the seat of soma (somyáṃ sádaḥ); verse 7 makes a number of ritual identifications.

> AV IX.3.7 havirdhā́nam agniśā́laṃ pátnīnāṃ sádanaṃ sádaḥ
> sádo devā́nām asi devi śāle
>
> O divine house, you are the cartshed, the house for Agni/fire, the seat and site for the wives, the seat for the gods.

Though Bloomfield thinks that "The bestowal of sacrificial epithets upon the house are [*sic*] obviously intended to enhance its value in the eyes of the recipient," there is no reason to believe that these "epithets" are not accurate. The untying of the temporary ritual house would then be homologized to the ungirding of the wife, with the same increase of fertility and acquisition of blessings desired from this action.

50. During Iṣṭis both Sacrificer and wife must abide by somewhat less rigorous restrictions, which specify the amount and type of food they may eat (e.g. MŚS I.4.1.5; ĀpŚS IV.2.3–5; VārŚS I.1.2.2; BŚS XXIV.21 [205: 10], etc.), where they may sleep (MŚS I.4.1.11), and which forbid sex (ĀpŚS IV.1.2).

51. KŚS VII.2.19 rather sensibly makes this optional for the wife. According to Staal (1983, p. 317), at the 1975 Agnicayana the wife was ceremonially shaved on the back of her neck.

52. Since she is yoked at the beginning of the whole Soma Sacrifice and remains in this state throughout it, she does not require regirding for every Iṣṭi embedded in the larger ritual—a fact that is noted by many texts (BŚS VI.3 [159: 11]; MŚS II.1.3.22; ĀpŚS X.4.12; 13; 21.5).

53. Remember also that these are the divinities that the widow of a Sacrificer is allowed to worship in gṛhya fashion at her lone fire.

For this reason F. M. Smith (1991, p. 28) suggests (following Agnihotram Ramanuja Thathachariar) that these offerings might originally have been an independent ritual, performed by women alone. Smith argues that "the tempo and structure of the full- and new-moon sacrifices would not be significantly damaged" if the Patnīsaṃyājas were not there, and that in fact this rite "introduces an element of asymmetry" into the ritual. But if one accepts my argument (presented in the body of the text) for the crucial linkage function of the Patnīsaṃyājas at this point in the ritual and their use as a framing device, Smith's objections are invalidated. (I am leery in general about looking for the "original" and "independent" sources of segments of śrauta ritual, since we have no independent evidence and no controls on the sources we thus propose.)

54. Cf. e.g. KS XXXII.4 (22: 5); ŚB I.9.2.9–13; KB III.9. The sexual and procreative purpose of these oblations has been well discussed by F. M. Smith 1991, pp. 27–32.

55. ĀpŚS III.9.4. Sim. MŚS I.3.5.4; ŚŚS I.15.3; VārŚS I.3.7.6. These goddesses commonly represent moon phases, and their invocation in the New and Full Moon ritual is therefore not surprising. These three goddesses, along with Anumati, who is also a moon phase, also figure in a slightly more elaborate rite, the Devikāhaviṃṣi, the so-called 'oblations to the goddesses of low rank'. Here offerings are made to the male divinity Dhātar 'Placer' as well as the four females. This rite is found at the end of the Soma Sacrifice (see in general Caland and Henry 1906–7, p. 408) and at the beginning of the Rājasūya (e.g. ĀpŚS XVIII.10.1–3; see Heesterman 1957, pp. 41–45). This pairing of a male deity with a group of female ones shows the same configuration as

the Patnīsaṃyājas and seems to serve the same procreative purpose. See e.g. Caland's note ad ĀpŚS XIII.24.3; Heesterman loc. cit.

Sinīvālī occurs in other contexts as well, as we will see later.

56. See MŚS I.3.5.3; ĀpŚS III.9.3; BŚS I.20 (30: 11), XX.14 (32: 13); KŚS III.7.8; VārŚS I.3.7.5; ŚB I.9.2.12.

57. See most explicitly MŚS I.3.5.6.

58. MŚS I.3.5.5; ĀpŚS III.9.10; KŚS III.7.9; VārŚS I.3.7.7.

59. F. M. Smith (1991, pp. 30–31) comes to quite different conclusions: he believes that the wife "is undercut in the performative context" (p. 31) and that there is "a clear disparity" between the importance of the mythic wives of the gods and the "disenfranchisement" of the mortal wife of the Sacrificer (p. 30). Our difference of opinion arises in part, I think, from differing assessments of the power of mythic reference to add resonance to ritual activity.

For other ritual events in which the wives of the gods participate or are invoked, see discussion of the Pātnīvata soma-cup in III.F.4 at the end of the Soma Sacrifice and of the Pātnīvata Animal Sacrifice.

The connection between the earthly household couple and its divine counterpart, and the (re)establishment of the domestic partnership is also acted out in a small episode in the middle of another ritual, the Soma Sacrifice known as the Vājapeya ('Drink of Strength'?). The episode is the Sacrificer's mounting of the yūpa, the post to which the sacrificial animal is usually tied. The Vājapeya is performed for the attainment of overlordship (among other reasons), and the Sacrificer's climb up the post is a not particularly surprising symbolic dramatization of this attainment. What is somewhat surprising is that the wife at least verbally, and sometimes literally, shares in this climb.

Before this action the Sacrificer and his wife put on special garments, over their consecration clothes, and are led up to the post. Then they engage in dialogue:

> BŚS XI.11 (80: 2) [Cf. ĀpŚS XVIII.5.9–12; MŚS VII.1.3.3.] atha jāyām āmantrayate jāya ehi suvo rohāveti rohāva hi suvar itītarā pratyāhāhaṃ nāv ubhayoḥ suvo rokṣyāmīti yajamānas tvaṃ nāv ubhayoḥ suvo roheti patnī
>
> Then (the Sacrificer) addresses his wife: "Come, wife [N.B. jāyā, not patnī]. Let us two mount to the sun." "Indeed, let us two mount to the sun," the other replies. "Of us two I will mount to the sun," says the Sacrificer. "Of us two do thou mount to the sun," says the wife.

The first dialogic exchange is made three times (cf. ĀpŚS XVIII.5.11; MS I.11.8 [169: 14]). In most texts, as here, only the Sacrificer mounts, but in KŚS (XIV.5.6) both climb the ladder.

The reason why the wife's explicit participation (physically or verbally) is needed in this action is not altogether clear on first inspection. However, if the point of the ritual is to assure the Sacrificer a replica of his earthly life in heaven, as several texts seem to suggest (TB I.3.3.4; KS XIV.6 [205: 16]; MS I.11.8 [169: 15]), his wife must be there to reestablish him as a heavenly householder. The ŚB is especially clear on this point:

> ŚB V.2.1.10 tád yáj jāyā́m āmantráyate 'rdhó ha vā́ eṣá ātmáno yáj jāyā́ tásmād yā́vaj jāyā́ṃ ná vindáte náivá tā́vat prájāyaté 'sarvo hí tā́vad bhávati
>
> Now as to why he addresses his wife: His wife is half of himself. Therefore, as long as he does not find his wife, so long is he also not (re)born. For so long is he not whole.

60. A black antelope skin is also used for the seat of the Sacrificer at the Dīkṣā, so the grain is in some sense undergoing consecration, not merely being pulverized.

Other texts that specify the wife's role in the grain preparation include MŚS I.1.2.4, 2.2.16; KŚS II.4.14; ĀpŚS I.20.12; 21.8–9; VārŚS I.2.4.49, 69.

61. Note that both the yaḥ kaś cid of this passage and the anyaḥ of KŚS are masculine (unlike the specified feminine of dāsī and śūdrā). This does not *necessarily* mean that the substitute would be male, but probably indicates that if a female member of the household, especially a servant, is not utilized, a male participant in the ritual would do.

62. The commentary says anālambhukatvādinā nimittena "because of menstruation, etc."

63. On this story see e.g. Jamison 1991, pp. 204–8, which treats it from a different perspective.

64. MS III.7.9 (88: 6). Cf. III.8.7 (103: 16), IV.1.12 (15: 8); TS VI.2.1.1; TB III.3.4.2, etc., as well as the equivalent KS comment after describing an action of the wife:

> atho mithunam eva yajñamukhe dadhāti prajananāya
>
> Then he places sexual pairing in the mouth/front of the worship, for progeneration.

KS XIV.8 (207: 7), XXIV.4 (93: 19), XXIV.8 (98: 15), XXV.8 (113: 13), XXXI.9 (11: 7).

65. F. M. Smith 1991, p. 31 has a good photograph of the wife touching the Adhvaryu with a grass blade while he pours ghee.

66. This is also the solution of the WYV śrauta sūtra, KŚS VI.5.7–8. However, neither BŚS nor ĀpŚS, which both belong to the Taittirīya Śākhā, seems to follow the TS solution cited above. Rather, both Adhvaryu and Sacrificer seem to wield the two skewers simultaneously:

> BŚS IV.6 (117: 11) paśum adhvaryur vapāśrapaṇībhyām anvārabhate vapāśrapaṇī yajamānaḥ
>
> The Adhvaryu touches the animal from behind with the two omentum-skewers; the Sacrificer (touches from behind) the two omentum-skewers.

> ĀpŚS VII.15.7 vapāśrapaṇībhyāṃ paśum anvārabhete adhvaryur yajamānaś ca
>
> The Adhvaryu and the Sacrificer touch the animal from behind with the two omentum-skewers.

Perhaps the presence of the Adhvaryu makes this procedure a little safer, even though the Sacrificer seems only to have skewers between him and the dangerous victim. The MŚS gives yet another variant on this perilous moment: the Adhvaryu and the Sacrificer (with his skewers) take hold of the beast seriatim:

> MŚS I.8.3.24 yūpāt pramucya paśum anvārabhya . . .
> 26 tābhyāṁ yajamānaḥ . . . paśum anvārabhate
>
> (The Adhvaryu), having loosened the animal from the stake and taken hold of it from behind . . .
> With these two (skewers) the Sacrificer takes hold of the animal from behind.

The care with which the Sacrificer is separated from contact with the victim, even while alive, contrasts strikingly with the unconcern with which the wife is brought into dangerously direct physical contact with the dead victim. See discussion in III.D.1, F.5.

67. Cf. ĀpŚS X.30.5, KŚS VIII.1.2; KS XXIV.8 (98: 13); TS VI.2.1.1; ŚB III.4.1.6; and Caland and Henry 1906–7, p. 53. For more on the Ātithya offering see III.F.1. We also saw the wife performing anvārambhaṇa at the Patnīsaṃyājas. Cf. KŚS III.7.9, where the wife holds onto the Adhvaryu; BŚS I.20 (30: 15), where the Adhvaryu and patnī do so mutually (samanvārabhete); ĀpŚS III.9.8, which specifies Adhvaryu, Āgnīdhra, and patnī. Cf. also MŚS I.3.5.5, 10.

68. Cf. MS I.4.8 (56: 10), III.7.9 (88: 7), III.8.7 (103: 17), IV.4.5 (56: 1); TS VI.2.1.2, VI.2.9.2; KS XIV.8 (207: 7), XXIV.4 (93: 19), XXXI.9 (11: 6), XXXII.4 (22: 12); TB I.3.7.2, III.3.4.2.

69. The conflict created by the need for the presence of the wife in all rituals and the polluting quality of menstrual blood was solved in a similar way, by removing the wife only partly from the ritual arena. See III.A.3.

70. On negative views of women in general, see I.5, and on woman as 'untruth', III.E.1.

71. Cf. MS IV.1.12 (15: 7) quoted earlier; KS XXXI.9 (11: 6); TB III.3.4.2.

72. Cf. ĀpŚS II.6.1–4; BŚS I.12 (18: 4); KŚS II.7.4; VārŚS I.3.2.25; ŚŚS IV.8.1; and Hillebrandt 1879, pp. 60–61; Kane, *HDŚ* II.1041–42.

73. Visual contact often "counts" as physical contact in some sense, and forces are often transferred by this means. See III.F.2.

74. If the wife is absent, the initial heating on the Gārhapatya is omitted, and the whole procedure (without, of course, the wife's glance) occurs at the Āhavanīya. Cf. ĀpŚS II.6.4; ŚB I.3.1.20; KŚS II.5.18.

75. My emendation; von Schroeder's text reads enān, and Mittwede (1986) notes no suggested textual changes.

76. Cf. KS XXXI.9 (11: 8); TB III.3.4.2, which, curiously, places the butter on the *Gārhapatya* for purification. Somewhat different reasons for the move from Gārhapatya to Āhavanīya are provided by ŚB I.3.1.20.

77. See e.g. Hillebrandt 1879, pp. 134ff.; Eggeling, ŚB V, pp. xlvi–l; Kane, *HDŚ* II.2.1147ff.; and especially van Buitenen 1968.

78. Besides the control exerted on the wife during the ceremony, Śūdras and others not learned in the Vedas cannot watch it; the performer of this ritual must undergo a particularly elaborate year-long consecration; and its performance is usually forbidden to one who is performing a Soma Sacrifice for the first time.

79. Cf. ĀpŚS XV.5.1–2; KŚS XXVI.2.2–3; BŚS IX.5 (272: 16).

80. For the emphasis on seeing, cf. BŚS IX.4 (270: 18) yathā patnī na paśyati tathā "(They do it) such that the wife does not see (it])"; KŚS XXVI.2.3 patnyadarśanam "(Its performance is) not to be seen by the wife."

81. ŚB XIV.1.4.16 is almost identical, except that it seems that the priest, not the wife, uncovers her head.

82. Cf. BŚS IX.8 (276: 18).

83. Cf. e.g. Kane, *HDŚ* II.2, p. 1149, n. 2557: "The pravargya was an awful and mystic or recondite affair and so the wife was not to see it."

84. According to TĀr V.3.1, the maker of the pot is also in danger, and this is why the pot is made in an enclosed space.

85. The same fear, that the wife may come too close to ritual forces that will burn up her offspring, is expressed in MS I.4.8 (56: 12) concerning the location of the patnīloka.

86. Jamison 1991, pp. 228–42, esp. 240f.
87. See III.A.3.
88. As I have already noted, it is curious that the ritualists elsewhere have no such scruples about bringing the wife into this kind of danger—e.g. in the bathing of the dead animal victim that I will discuss in III.F.5. Perhaps in such cases the stakes were simply too high to allow only partial or attenuated contact between the forces and the wife who must animate and harness them.
89. Cf. VārŚS I.3.2.24.
90. The Hotar carries it when the procession of priests return for the Patnīsaṃyāja oblations, in which the broom again serves as support. Cf. MŚS I.3.4.30, 5.1; ĀpŚS III.8.1; BŚS I.20 (30:1); KŚS III.6.21; VārŚS I.3.7.1.
91. Cf. also VārŚS I.3.7.16; BhārŚS III.10 (quoted by Hillebrandt 1879, p. 163); MS I.4.8 (56: 2); TB III.3.9.11.
92. Or touches her navel with the head of the broom. See Hillebrandt 1879, p. 162; ĀśvŚS I.11.2 vedaśirasā nābhideśam ālabheta prajākāmā cet.
93. ĀpŚS III.10.5 gives a choice, and BŚS III.30 (105: 1) simply specifies that he strews going toward the east. The ŚB again gives an explicitly sexual interpretation of this action:

> ŚB I.9.2.24 yóṣā vái védir vŕ̥ṣā vedáḥ paścā́d vái parī́tya vŕ̥ṣā yóṣām ádhidravati paścā́d eváinām etát parī́tya vŕ̥ṣṇā vedénā́dhidrāvayati tásmād ā́ védeḥ sáṁstr̥ṇāti
>
> The vedi is a woman; the broom is a male. Coming around from behind a male approaches a woman. Thus coming around from behind, he makes her [the vedi] approached by the male broom. Therefore he strews (the grass) continuously up to the vedi.

One of the broom's features that allows it to be homologized to a male is its grammatical gender, which is masculine. The exegetical literature frequently constructs sexual couplings out of a pair of nouns with complementary genders. In this particular coupling of broom and altar the virtual homophony of the words (vedá and védi) highlights their difference in genders (masculine and feminine). Moreover, the hourglass shape of the vedi causes it often to be compared to a woman with a narrow waist (or, conversely, women of this configuration are compared with vedis).
94. And that bestows on the Sacrificer his title Āhitāgni, one 'having established fires'.
95. Krick in her exhaustive account of the Agnyādheya ritual (1982) likewise found this to be a unique detail (p. 199, n. 500). She considers it evidence of a special relation of the wife with the Southern Fire, without discussing the much more common connection of the wife with the Gārhapatya.
96. Jamison 1991, pp. 228–42.
97. = TS IV.1.5; VS XI.55–57; KS XVI.5 (225: 13), etc.
98. A beautiful goddess associated with easy birth, among other things. See III.B.3a.
99. Cf. e.g. MŚS VI.1.2.13; KŚS XVI.3.21; ŚB VI.5.3.1.
100. See e.g. discussions by Puhvel 1970; 1987, pp. 269–76 and passim; Sauvé 1970; and O'Flaherty 1980, pp. 149–61 and passim, as well as the previous literature cited in these works. For a discussion of the formal verbal aspects of the litany, see Watkins, forthcoming. I have been told that Gore Vidal incorporated some part of the Aśvamedha into a work of fiction, but I have so far been unable to trace the reference.

101. Griffith's attitude to the whole ritual is clear from his sympathy for the Mahiṣī (1899, n. to XXIII.18): "she has to pass the night in disgusting contiguity to the slaughtered horse," "[she] must submit to the revolting ceremony . . . "

102. ĀpŚS XX.18.4 na me yabhati kaś cana: non me futuit quispiam. Otherwise Caland does not flinch at the sexual descriptions, and his usual extraordinary philological skill has clarified much in these difficult verses. P.-E. Dumont (1927) shows a similar lack of prudery, though he has frequent recourse to Latin.

103. I will also not discuss the Indo-European parallels that have occupied so much space in the secondary literature. (See esp. Puhvel 1970.)

104. So the text of the CE. Correct to parivṛktyā.

105. The major exception among the ancient texts may be the TB, which rather prudishly leaves out the sexually explicit verses in the central part of the episode, substituting an out-of-place discussion of the needles used afterwards to signal the paths of the knives (TB III.9.4–5). When it rejoins the ritual, with the less explicit, but still suggestive bantering verses (III.9.5.1ff.), it interprets the whole thing as a political allegory depicting the relations between the crown (rāṣṭram) and its subjects (viś), an interpretive tactic also resorted to by the ŚB (XIII.2.9).

106. My treatment is deeply indebted to Caland (especially in his translation of the ĀpŚS version [1928], but cf. also ŚŚS XVI.3–4 [1953]), to P.-E. Dumont 1927, and to Watkins.

107. ĀpŚS XX.17.12; BŚS XV.29 (234: 6); MŚS IX.2.4.12; KŚS XX.6.12; VS XXIII.18; ŚB XIII.2.8.3; TB III.9.6.3. The mantra is quoted in Taittirīyan form (TS VII.4.19.1). Other texts have slight variants in the form of the initial vocative (VS XXIII.18 ámbe ámbiké 'mbālike; MS III.12.20 [166: 9] ámby ámbike ámbālike).

108. Others (cf. e.g. Caland, ĀpŚS XX.17.12) have interpreted nayati as 'lead (against my will)', but given the clearly sexual variant of this verse below, it seems more likely that √nī here, as often, refers pregnantly to marriage, as Watkins has interpreted it.

109. Cf. also MŚS IX.2.4.13; KŚS XX.6.13; ŚB XIII.2.8.4.

110. On this, see especially Watkins.

111. ĀpŚS of course gives only the pratīkas of the mantras, which are quoted here in their TS form.

112. In some texts this last mantra accompanies the actual copulation (KŚS XX.6.16; VārŚS III.4.4.15; ŚB XIII.5.2.2), and in VārŚS it is the Sacrificer (i.e. the Mahiṣī's husband) who says it. In BŚS (XV.29 [234: 9]) the last two lines of the first mantra (āham . . .) accompany the copulation.

113. At least in theory. One has to wonder, however, whether the wife (or some wives) merely feigned the action under the concealing blanket.

114. See Puhvel 1970, p.162, citing Kirfel 1951, p. 47. That suffocation was the means of death is clear from e.g. ĀpŚS XX.17.8–9. Kirfel sought to prove that the Puruṣamedha ('Human Sacrifice') was older than the Aśvamedha (and served as its model, rather than the reverse, as most scholars believe) and that the death-ejaculation of the sacrificed man was meant to impregnate the Mahiṣī—a far-fetched hypothesis that deserves rejection.

115. On this rare word, see Hoffmann 1976, p. 570, n. 2; and Mayrhofer, *EWA* s.v.

116. The word udañji occurs only here. Caland takes it to mean 'erect' (see ĀpŚS XX.18.4), but the force of the second -añji- in this compound is then lost. My translation is a rather weak attempt to capture it.

117. The second member of this compound, -dhāvana- can belong to either (/both) root(s) dhāv ('run/flow'; 'clean/rub').

118. The lexeme parā √vadh is rather rare, but suppletive parā √han occurs in a sexual context, again implying women's pleasure, in the RV:

RV V.56.3 mīḷhúṣmatīva pṛthivī́ *párā hatā́* mádanty ety asmád ā́

'*Hit*' like (a woman) with a 'generous' (husband), the earth goes away intoxicated from us.

119. This word only here. Caland tentatively suggests 'Vulva' (ad ĀpŚS XX.18.4), Watkins 'clitoris'.

120. ĀpŚS XX.18.4; BŚS XV.30 (234:14).

121. The śrauta sūtras of the MS omit this part entirely and have the Mahiṣī arise immediately (MŚS IX.2.4.16; VārŚS III.4.4.16).

122. Or their attendants.

123. Since this phrase is masculine, it presumably included some male participants in the ritual, such as the priests, or perhaps just the Sacrificer, who started the round of mockery.

124. Or her attendants.

125. ĀśvŚS (X.8.8–14) also pairs wives and priests, but only two sets: Hotar and Mahiṣī, Brahman and Vāvātā.

126. Directed by Adhvaryu to Kumārī in ŚB, as we saw. In BŚS XV.30 (234: 17) the Parivṛktī addresses the Mahiṣī with it, and it is part of the wives' discourse in ĀpŚS XX.18.6. It is not found in the ŚŚS. The TS version (VII.4.19n, which BŚS and ĀpŚS of course both use) has some variants, chief of which is the more "popular" looking dhā́ṇikā for dhā́rakā.

127. It is difficult in English to convey the heavy diminutivization in this phrase, where not only the word for 'bird' but the relative pronoun and the demonstrative have the diminutive suffix -ka-, needless to say a rarity in the pronominal system. In fact this suffix appears frequently in these erotic verses, which may reflect either affectionate sexuality or simply a more "popular" level of language than is usual in these solemn religious texts: the -ka- suffix spreads rapidly in Middle Indic.

Another "popular" linguistic feature in these verses is the frequency of *l*-forms, for *r*, e.g. galgalīti (VS XXIII.22, to √gir/gil 'swallow': r-intensive form in RV járgurāṇa-), tilāmi (XXIII.24) for tirāmi, sthūlá- (XXIII.28) for sthūrá-.

128. Of Kumārī to Adhvaryu in ŚB, as we saw. In ŚŚS and ĀśvŚS (see n. 125) the second half-verse is instead the second half-verse of the Mahiṣī's reply to the Hotar. This latter version is metrically better.

129. The ŚŚS (XVI.4.6) and ĀśvŚS (X.8.11) have instead

yiyapsyata [Āśv yī . . .] iva te mano [Āśv mukhaṃ] hotar mā tvaṃ vado bahu

You have the mind / mouth of someone desiring to fuck. Hotar, don't you say much to me.

As Hoffmann points out (1976, p. 572, n. 23), the VS vivakṣata(ḥ) is probably a euphemistic substitute for the cruder desiderative of √yabh found in the two śrauta sūtras.

130. In ŚŚS it is the Hotar's address to the Mahiṣī; in BŚS part of the address of the whole crowd.

131. In ŚŚS it is the Brahman who addresses the Vāvātā; in BŚS the Sacrificer the Mahiṣī. In VārŚS III.4.4.16 the other wives lead the Mahiṣī to this accompaniment.

132. The most interesting variant is that of the Taittirīyins (TS VII.4.19i), whose

second pāda reads veṇubhārám girā́v iva "like a burden of bamboo up a mountain." Bamboo is elsewhere homologized to a womb, because of its hollowness (cf. e.g. TS V.1.1.4; MS III.1.2 [2: 18]; ŚB VI.3.1.31–32), and winnowing baskets can be made of bamboo (ŚB I.1.4.19–22).

133. These verses do not appear in the Taittirīya texts (TS, and the sūtras ĀpŚS and BŚS).

134. This is the standard word for 'testicles'—here referring perhaps to the labia, as P.-E. Dumont suggests (1927, p. 181)? (Such an identification seems already assumed by Delbrück [1893, p. 135].)

135. The interpretation of the obscure second half of this verse may be aided by Hoffmann's (1963) discussion of the compound mṛgaśaphá 'deer's hoof', found in a maxim quoted in the ritual literature, but I am not certain how.

136. On this verse, see Hoffmann (1976, p. 573, n. 26).

137. In BŚS the Vāvātā addresses the Mahiṣī.

138. Or, as P.-E. Dumont takes it (1927, p.181), "despises the beast that gets fed." The word paśu refers exclusively to *domestic* animals, and part of the point seems to be the contrast between the wild deer and its tamed counterpart. In the second half of the verse we can assume that the Śūdra woman is considered *wild*, the women of the three Aryan varṇas as tame.

This *may* in turn make oblique reference to another feature of the Aśvamedha. Besides the horse, there are literally hundreds of other sacrificial victims, both wild and tame. But after the paryagni (fire-circuit: the circling of the bound victims with a fire brand) the *wild* animals are set free, while (most of) the tame ones are sacrificed.

139. Cf. KŚS XX.5.20–23, XX.7.10–15; also ŚSS XVI.4.7–8; ĀpŚS XX.19.6ff., etc. Many texts prescribe only one session.

140. See e.g. Kuiper 1960, with references to early literature; also Witzel 1987; Insler 1989–90; Thompson forthcoming.

141. This verse was obviously not picked entirely at random, since it is reminiscent not only in style, but also in content of the Aśvamedha riddles, in particular to

VS XXIII.24 mātā́ ca te pitā́ ca té 'graṃ vṛkṣásya rohataḥ

Your mother and your father climb to the top of the tree,

with both the treetop and the parent.

Several verses in the Kuntāpa sequence of hymns (to be discussed later) also contain riddling references to trees, fruit, and birds, with clear erotic intent, as in the Aśvamedha verse with this configuration. Cf. AV XX.127.4 [=ŚSS XII.15.1; RV Kh V.9.1], AV XX.136.7, AV XX.136.9 [=ŚSS XII.24.6; RV Kh V.22.5].

142. This is clearly brought out in Thieme's illuminating discussion of the three related verses, RV I.164.20–22 (1949, pp. 55–73). Cf. also Brereton 1985, for simultaneous riddling reference to both cosmic and ritual situations elsewhere in the RV.

143. For a heretofore unrecognized one, see Jamison 1981.

144. For some discussion see Jamison 1991, pp. 289–97.

145. AVŚ XX.127–36; the text (with significant variants) also found in RV Kh V.8–22 [see Scheftelowitz 1906]; ŚSS XII.14–25. The ritual employment of these hymns is given in AB VI.32ff.; KB XXX.5ff. For further discussion, see Bloomfield 1899, pp. 96ff.; Hauer 1927, pp. 267–78; Keith 1925, p. 400; Hoffmann 1940, p. 139 [=1975, p. 6].

The ritual usage of this sequence (to be discussed in III.F.4) will connect with the sexual drama of the Aśvamedha in some surprising ways and will further illuminate the Vṛṣākapi hymn we are about to discuss.

146. There is a slight grammatical problem with this interpretation. Since the compound is accented on its first member (vṛṣā́-kapi-), it might be expected to have bahuvrīhi (possessive) value, hence '*possessing* a bullish kapi', rather than simply 'bullish kapi'. On this basis Insler has recently suggested that the word does not refer to a monkey at all, but rather refers to a different entity that is characterized by the quality of a 'bullish kapi'.

However, the same character is called just kapi 'monkey' in verse 5; and furthermore vṛṣā́kapi- does not show correct bahuvrīhi accent either. The numerous bahuvrīhis with vṛ́ṣan- 'bull' as first member have accent on the initial syllable (e.g. vṛ́ṣa-kratu- 'having bullish will', vṛ́ṣa-ratha- 'having a bullish chariot', vṛ́ṣa-śuṣma- 'having bullish force', etc.). Wackernagel 1905, pp. 251, 266 takes vṛṣā́kapi as a determinative compound ('Mannaffe', 'grosser Affe'), not a bahuvrīhi, and, despite the formal difficulties, I also prefer to follow the traditional interpretation.

147. Insler has also recently treated this hymn in detail and reached very different conclusions from mine. We presented our separate versions at a symposium at the April 1994 meeting of the American Oriental Society, with stimulating commentary by W. Doniger and helpful discussion from the audience. Insler's views, as well as the contributions of Doniger and the audience, have forced me to refine my discussion of the hymn. Thieme 1985 also presents a new interpretation of the hymn.

In brief, Insler thinks the hymn depicts the tension arisen between Indra and Indrāṇī because Indra has lost sexual interest in his wife, and he considers Vṛṣākapi the name of "the animus" of Indra's penis (see n. 146 above); Thieme thinks the hymn was a bawdily encouraging song designed to rid a timid bride of her fear of first intercourse, as well as a fertility spell. Given the difficulties of this text, the more searching examinations of it the better, though I am not convinced by either of these. Since Insler's interpretation is not yet published, I will not discuss it in detail here, though I will make some reference to Thieme's.

148. There is much disagreement about who says which verses. Though the common opinion (e.g. Geldner ad loc.; Renou 1956, p. 91; O'Flaherty 1981, p. 259) seems to be that Indrāṇī speaks both 1 and 2, I am inclined to follow Thieme (1938, pp. 13–14) and assign vs. 1 to Indra.

149. I think this journey is also referred to, indeed enlarged on toward the end of the hymn in vss. 19–20, to which we will return.

150. If we can use such a loaded word for an ancient Indian character.

151. This, of course, is true for all of the postwar Mahābhārata. The Pāṇḍavas seem to live in a state of clinical depression for parvan after parvan.

152. Notice the reminiscence of the almost identical phrase, aryáḥ puṣṭéṣu, in vs. 1.

153. I would also suggest a fugitive connection to a disconnected phrase from the so-called Prattle of Etaśa section of the Kuntāpa hymn sequence, which contains a diminutivized feminine of this color adjective:

AV XX.129.3 [=ŚŚS XII.18.1; RV Kh. V.15.1] tā́sām ékā hárikniká (/hárikliká)
4 háriknike (/hároklike) kím icchasi

One of them is a little tawny one.
Little tawny one, what do you want?

The stylistic context of all three references is similar, but what this particular 'little tawny one' is doing is not clear.

154. Thieme (1985, pp. 242–43) ingeniously (if not entirely convincingly) connects vy àdūduṣat with the figure of the vidūṣaka in classical Sanskrit drama.

155. Two of the three occurrences of the noun kapí- 'monkey' in the AV (i.e. the oldest attestations of the simplex besides vs. 5 in this hymn) appear in conjunction with śván- 'dog' as here (AV III.9.4, IV.37.11). Indeed, in III.9.4 the monkey is called "the spoiler of dogs" (śúnāṃ kapír iva dū́ṣaṇaḥ), using the same root √dūṣ 'spoil' as in vs. 5. Unfortunately, the sense of the AV passages is utterly obscure to me.

156. Thieme (1985, pp. 240–41) argues that this verse cannot be spoken by Indrāṇī because the wife of the great god Indra would not be so undignified. Similarly, Insler denies that Indra's wife would ever consider having sex with a monkey. But who would think that the wife of a powerful earthly king would sleep with a dead horse?! The shocking discrepancy between regal wife and lowly beast, and regal wife and crudely obscene speech, are precisely the point of the coupling in the Aśvamedha—and, I would submit, of this RVic hymn as well.

157. Henceforth I will omit the final pāda of refrain ("Indra above all!") from both text and translation, but it should be remembered that each verse, whatever its contents, lurches back to this glorification of Indra.

158. Vedic Sanskrit has an exact equivalent of our ubiquitous teenage "like" insertion.

159. As Thieme (1985, p. 244) perceptively points out, though Indrāṇī's physical charms are being described as in vs. 6, the level of diction is very different. The adjectival formation type belongs to elevated poetic discourse and corresponds almost uncannily, as Thieme shows, to Greek descriptions of goddesses.

160. Most likely a reference to the Patnīsaṃyājas 'joint offerings (to the gods) with their wives', which we have discussed before. So Geldner, ad loc. Such an allusion would make it clear that she is used to functioning as Sacrificer's Wife in the less elaborate rites of the ordinary ritual calendar.

161. The *exact* meaning of this verse is somewhat difficult to fathom. Geldner (and, it appears from their translations, also Renou 1956, p. 93; O'Flaherty 1981, ad loc.) assumes that sma purā́ has domain over both clauses in the verse. This adverbial phrase is used with the present tense seemingly to indicate habitual past action with present relevance (Grassmann, sma 6; Delbrück 1888, pp. 278, 502), though the RVic examples are not altogether clear. Under this interpretation, mahīyate in pāda d would mean 'has been/keeps being glorified' (thus e.g. O'Flaherty's "she would go . . . she would be praised . . . ").

I think rather that the two clauses are contrastive: "she *used* to go . . . (but now) she *is* glorified"). The point is that Indrāṇī has always in the past behaved as a proper patnī in normal ritual, circumspectly attending the "joint offerings" and the like, but now, in the Aśvamedha, she has been alloted a much more visible and important role and consequently receives more glory than the wife in standard ritual.

162. Oldenberg's reconstruction (*Noten*, ad loc.) is especially busy, showing, I would say, an uncharacteristic lack of sensitivity on his part.

163. One could, if one wanted, connect this strategy to Hoffmann's "memorative" function of the injunctive mood (cf. Hoffmann 1967, passim).

164. I.179 ends with a Zauberspruch, just as X.86 does, but this puts the hymn in ritual, not narrative context.

165. The oblation is called 'watery' (ápya-), a designation that is not entirely clear, though several possible explanations come to mind. As we will see (III.F.5), in the śrauta Animal Sacrifice immediately after the victim is killed, he is washed with water by the wife (and the Adhvaryu). Hence, the 'watery' oblation may be the dampened

dead victim. It is also worth noting that horses in general are considered 'watery' and to have been born not in a womb but in water (apsujā́). (Cf. e.g. MS II.3.3 [30: 8]; TS II.3.12.2.)

Alternatively, this 'watery' oblation may be a soma libation, since ápya is also used of soma:

RV IX.86.45 agregó rā́j*ā́pyas* taviṣyate

(Soma) the king, *the watery one*, going in front, displays his strength.

166. Von Schroeder (1908, pp. 306–7) considers Vṛṣākapāyī a nonspeaking part, but does think she exists as a separate character and is addressed in the hymn.

167. We might note in passing the verbal similarity between *utā́hám admi* pī́va íd "And I eat only the fat meat" and Indrāṇī's boast in vs. 9 *utā́hám asmi* vīríṇī "And I have a man." But I do not know exactly what to make of it. We can complicate our problem further by adding to the mix the "fat maiden" of the Kuntāpa hymn sequence (kumārī́ . . . pīvarī́ AV XX.136.16).

168. On kukṣí- 'cheek', not 'belly', see Jamison 1987.

169. Geldner in his introduction to the hymn (RV III, p. 274) and his notes on vss. 12c, 15ab; Oldenberg, *Noten* ad X.86.12; Renou 1956, pp. 94, 246–47.

170. Most other scholars (Geldner, Oldenberg, Renou, O'Flaherty) assign vs. 16 to Indrāṇī, vs. 17 to Vṛṣākapi's wife.

171. If the horse's penis *is* actually erect as a result of its strangulation (see n. 114), the little aphorism just quoted would be literally true. But even if the horse's penis is flaccid, it has been brought into the woman's lap in a quasi-sexual act.

172. Cf. e.g. MŚS IX.2.2.9; KŚS XX.2.12, 3.20; ĀpŚS XX.7.13–14; TB III.9.17.2–4.

173. The Agastya/Lopāmudrā hymn (RV I.179), of course, depicts a scene inspired by the same paradox, and the Yama/Yamī hymn (RV X.10) is certainly thematically related, as I discussed in I.5.

As Brereton has pointed out to me, vss. 16–17 may also allow a completely opposite interpretation, *in addition to*, rather than *instead of* the one advanced in the body of the text. The penis that "hangs between the thighs" may be hanging between the thighs of the *woman* and so engaged in successful intercourse; the one that "has sat down" may be one that has lost its erection. So the conventional notions of power could also be read into these verses: sexual success = mastery; lack of it = lack of mastery. The multilayered interpretational possibilities for these verses are simply another example of the verbal virtuosity of the RVic bards.

Thieme (1985, pp. 246–47, n. 22) has yet another interpretation of these two verses.

174. A parasvant is also one of the ancillary victims at the Aśvamedha (see e.g. VS XXIV.28), though since there are numerous different animals in this list, it is well not to make too much of this.

175. This verse is universally (Geldner, Oldenberg [*Noten*, ad loc.], Renou, O'Flaherty) assigned to Indra, along with vs. 20, but rhetorically it follows directly on vs. 18, which begins ayám indra vṛṣā́kapiḥ, with Vṛṣākapi referred to in the third person. He then picks up the same ayám, but with first person verb. The use of strong deictics with the first person is marked usage, and often follows from rhetorical situations of this nature, as I have argued elsewhere ("A disguised speech act in the Rig Veda," paper presented at the Eighth World Sanskrit Conference, Vienna, August 1990).

176. The second member of this compound, -náṃśana-, is ordinarily assigned to the root √naś 'disappear', caus. 'make disappear, destroy' (so Geldner, Renou, O'Flaherty).

Oldenberg objects to this on morphological grounds and instead interprets it as belonging to √naś 'reach, attain', an assignment that Geldner vigorously opposes. I think the ambiguity is deliberate, and that the compound should be interpreted with both meanings simultaneously, as I will argue in the body of the text.

177. The verb here belongs to the root √sas, not the √svap of svapna in RV X.86.21, but this is actually a guarantee of its formulaic archaism, since √svap originally lacked a present, and √sas suppletively provided it. See Jamison 1982/83.

178. One problem with this verse that does not sufficiently emerge in English translation is that the verb ájagantana (ā́jagantana?) and the adjective údañcaḥ are both plural, when the two vocatives might lead us to expect a dual. Geldner suggests that the plural also includes the wives, but perhaps it refers to the many other victims of the Aśvamedha or to the crowd of ritual participants.

179. Though there is probably no etymological connection between the yūpa (the stake to which the victim is bound during the preliminary actions of the sacrifice) and the root √yup represented in the second member of the compound jana-yópanaḥ 'remover/eraser of men', their phonological similarity may have brought the yūpa to the mind of the audience.

180. Like I.179.6 at the end of the Agastya and Lopāmudrā hymn (Thieme 1963a). Thieme (1985, p. 247) also interprets this verse in a similar fashion.

181. See III.D.1:

TS VII.4.19.1 ā́hám ajāni garbhadhám ā́ tvám ajāsi garbhadhám

I will impel the impregnator; you will impel the impregnator.

TS VII.4.19.1 vṛ́ṣā vāṁ retodhā́ réto dadhātu

Let the bullish seed-placer of you two place the seed.

182. On another image of prodigious fertility and multiple births, see Jamison 1993.

183. On the morpho-syntactic relations between the two presents, see Jamison 1983, pp. 107–8.

184. For its employment in codified śrauta ritual, see III.F.4.

185. Delbrück (1900, p. 129) suggests that carasi is an elliptical expression for carasi mithunám "do/practice sexual pairing." If he is correct (as the immediately following VārŚS passage suggests), it would be parallel to the coy suggestiveness of the English sexual expression "do it."

186. MŚS I.7.4.11; ĀpŚS VIII.6.22; BŚS V.7 (136: 16); VārŚS I.7.2.29; HirŚS V.2 (Einoo 106). KŚS V.5.6 has rather ā √cakṣ 'announce'.

187. Cf. BŚS V.7 (136: 16). ĀpŚS VIII.6.21; VārŚS I.7.2.29; HirŚS V.2 (Einoo 106) simply substitute the plural number: "which ones/as many as she indicates," "those let Varuṇa seize . . . "

188. See Einoo 1988, p. 109.

189. For the secondary literature, cf. e.g. Keith 1925, p. 265; Macdonell and Keith 1912, pp. 396, 480; Oldenberg 1917, pp. 323–24; Lévi 1898, pp. 156–58; Hubert and Mauss 1898, p. 69, n. 395; p. 71, n. 410; F. M. Smith 1991, p. 26. Lévi (p. 157, n. 1) also suggests that the interrogation is a symptom of the priests' hatred of women.

Heesterman 1985, pp. 134–37 also sees the Varuṇapraghāsa as a rite of "guilt and atonement," and discusses the wife's role with much subtlety.

190. See n. 185: "does it with others" may be a more accurate translation.

191. See e.g. F. M. Smith 1991, p. 26.

192. The commentary to KŚS V.5.7–9 allows the answer "with no other" (nānyena) if she has no lover. Otherwise no text or commentary I have examined provides a method for denying the existence of a lover.

193. So already the commentary to ĀpŚS VIII.6.22: yadi saty eva jāre tam anuktvā.

194. It is possible that the lover's nonexistence would be expressed with

> *yaj jāram *a*santaṃ prabrūyāt
>
> If she should declare that a lover does not exist . . .

But the stem asant often seems to be specialized for 'untruth, lie' and might not convey simple nonexistence in this context. This is a place where our syntactic judgments are simply too crude to decide.

195. The cleverness of this purification has not been sufficiently appreciated. If her adultery has resulted in pregnancy, she will, of course, not menstruate.

196. In Sanskrit. The Pāli Jātakas seem to take a far more jaundiced view of women, and contain a number of stories in which a wife ingeniously evades the restraints her husband has attempted to put on her commerce with other men. This may reflect general folkloric attitudes, or a particularly Buddhist distaste for women.

197. Heesterman (1985, pp. 134–35) also sees that the wife's guilt or innocence is not really the point. He suggests instead that "it is the ambivalent relationship between the two families or clans whose connubial alliance is represented by woman" (135). Although this is an eloquent statement of an issue we will discuss at length below, I do not think it is applicable here. Heesterman's explanation requires a more contorted interpretation of some elements of the following offering to Indra and the Maruts than that ritual action will allow (see esp. pp. 135–36).

198. For another such figure, a hired scapegoat figure, consider the Ātreya Brahman, who functions as scapegoat at the end of the Aśvamedha: he submerges himself in water, has inauspicious mantras said over him, and is ceremonially driven off—with a rich prize of cows and so forth for his trouble. For discussion, see Jamison 1991, pp. 223–28.

199. The Pratiprasthātar also often has charge of the wife, e.g. in the Dīkṣā, where he does for the wife what the Adhvaryu does for the Sacrificer.

200. ĀpŚS VIII.6.3 suggests a different fashion of readying the barley, but still has the wife prepare the dishes. BhārŚS VIII.7.1 also specifies the wife. In HirŚS V.2 the husband and wife together perform this. See in general Einoo 1988, pp. 91ff.

201. ĀpŚS VIII.6.3 . . . patnī karambhapātrāṇi karoti 4. atrāpi meṣaṃ meṣīṃ ca karotīti vājasaneyakam.

202. See MŚS I.7.4.13–15; ĀpŚS VIII.6.23; BŚS V.7–8; KŚS V.5.10 [here the wife optionally offers alone]; VārŚS I.7.2.30; HirŚS V.2 (Einoo 106); MS I.10.11 (151: 10); ŚB II.5.2.23 [here the wife apparently offers alone, pace Eggeling].

203. For this complex procedure, see Einoo 1988, pp. 120ff.

204. For example, the always hypersexual Indra is transformed into a ram already in the RV (VIII.2.40; cf. I.51.1, I.52.1), an identification perpetuated also in the Brāhmaṇas (cf. e.g. JB III.234–36; and O'Flaherty 1985, pp. 58–60). In the Rāmāyaṇa story of Ahalyā, which we will examine in IV.A, when Indra is castrated for sexual transgression, he is made whole again with a ram's testicles (R I.48.6–10). After personal observation of a ram's physique and behavior, I am not surprised by the symbolic function of rams in ancient Indian myth and ritual.

205. See Jamison 1991, part II.6.

206. For a very different interpretation of the offering of ram and ewe, see Heesterman 1993, p. 193, n. 30.

207. Cf. MŚS VII.2.7.11; KŚS XIII.3.7; BŚS XVI.21 (267: 6), 22 (268: 7); ĀpŚS XXI.18.4, 19.9–12; VārŚS III.2.5.38–40; PB V.5.14–17; JB II.405; TS VII.5.9.3; KS XXXIV.5 (39: 3). The solar symbolism of the round white hide is fairly obvious and was already appreciated by the exegetes (cf. e.g. PB V.5.17).

208. See e.g. JB II.405 tayor āryeṇa varṇena śaudraṃ varṇaṃ jyāpayanti "Of these two they have the Śūdra defeated by the Aryan."

209. Cf. e.g. KS XXXIV.5 (39: 1); PB V.5.13 (and Caland's useful note thereon); VārŚS III.2.5.33; MŚS VII.2.7.12; KŚS XIII.3.3–5.

210. Cf. e.g. MŚS VII.2.7.13; VārŚS III.2.5.30. Other texts simply specify that they are found at the right door post of the shed (ĀpŚS XXI.17.18, 19.5). The other two contrasting pairs are also placed so that the "good" one is inside, the bad one outside the sacral area.

211. Gonda 1961 discusses this ill-matched pair at some length. See also Hauer 1927, pp. 246–67, Kaelber 1989, pp. 18–19.

212. Given the specifically sexual content of the rest of their dialogue, we should expect the 'un-Aryan things' (anārya) to fall in the same semantic realm. I know of no evidence that might further define it, but tentatively suggest that it refers to homosexual behavior, the 'un-Aryan' designation conveying some of the same exotic decadence as the English expression "Greek love."

213. Or, as the anonymous reader for Oxford University Press suggested, "the neglected is ill-done," comparing nirākṛti 'one who neglects religious duties'. The reader also pointed out the virtuosic manipulation of a sociolinguistic index, the r/l distinction, in this exchange. Even the titles of the two participants show this distinction: the student, brahma-cā*r*in, has the "high" Sanskrit r, the whore, puṃś-ca*l*ī, the "popular" l, in forms belonging to the same root (√car/cal). As the reader suggested, "the whore seems to mock the student by repeating the sound "r" in her comment": anā*r*yaka*r*mann avakī*r*ṇi duśca*r*itaṃ ni*r*ākṛ*r*tam.

214. "Other people" is masculine here, but may be so generically, without intending to specify the sex. On the other hand, if the VārŚS version quoted in the body of the text is correct on this point (as I think possible), a vocative jālmi 'o vile one (fem.)' may be a better reading than accusative jāram 'lover (masc.)'. I would prefer not having the -ana-stem nirmārjani governing the accusative jāram as the MŚS seems to require. If we do read jālmi (vel sim.) instead, the -ana-stem could simply govern the genitive parasya janasya, whose gender would then not be a problem: "o wiper-off (/masturbator?) of other men." As the reader also pointed out, jālmi is an attractive reading for another reason, as it shows the student deliberately insulting the whore by addressing her with the "low" l-sound. See n. 213 above.

DrāhŚS XI.3.10 also reads jālmi and also contains a genitive (grāmasya) dependent on mārjani 'wiper-off'. The full text of the DrāhŚS version of the curse is

> dhik tvā jālmi puṁścali grāmasya mārjani puruṣasya śiśnapraṇejani
>
> Fie on you, o vile whore, o wiper of the village, o washer of the penis of man.

215. It is not absolutely certain that this sexual act is between whore and student, since two sūtras concerning the battle of the Śūdra and the Aryan intervene. But since other texts specify their sexual pairing, and there are no other likely candidates, it seems rather probable.

216. Despite appearances this sūtra does not, in my opinion, introduce a new character. Instead, the place-name-derived 'Māgadhan' ('man from Magadha') seems to be the older designation for the male member of this couple. The Vrātya hymn in the AV, the first place in which the word puṃścalī́ occurs, gives four mystical (and incomprehensible) identifications of the 'whore' and the 'Māgadhan', each corresponding to one of the cardinal points; for example,

> AV XV.2.1 tásya prā́cyāṃ diśí śraddhā́ puṃścalī́ mitró māgadháḥ . . .
>
> Of him, in the eastern quarter, trust was the whore, Mitra (/the ally) was the Māgadhan . . .

This set of identifications seems to refer to exactly the ritual pairing we are discussing. Māgadhan for brahmacārin also is found in JB II.405.

Gonda, however, in the article just cited (1961, pp. 82 ff. [=1975, pp. 227ff.]), believes that the two pairs are different and may correspond to different stages in the development of the ritual. Similarly Hauer 1927, pp. 265–66, with citation of earlier literature. The correct solution is not particularly relevant to our problem, since whatever the exact identity of the pairs, they fulfill the same structural role.

217. Caland seems to think that they are both clinging to the doorpost, but given the middle voice of the participle āśliṣyamāṇau and the erotic tone of the whole, I think my interpretation is more likely.

218. With the emendations of Caland and Raghu Vira (1971).

219. The exact purport of this is not clear to me, and given the generally poor state of preservation of the Vārāha text and the deviations from the corresponding MŚS, it is likely that this is not the original insult. On the other hand, see n. 214 above for possible corrections that VārŚS, with DrāhŚS, suggests for the MŚS.

220. Although as with KŚS there are several sūtras between the dialogue and the sexual act, I find it hard to believe the same pair is not involved.

221. I assume that the plural refers to the participants and beneficiaries in the ritual and that they "speak all manner of speech and practice sex" vicariously, thereby getting the benefits without having to say or do anything improper themselves. Hauer, on the other hand, suggests that originally many, perhaps all the participants in the ritual (except for the officiating priests) engaged in sex (1927, p. 264). I find this hard to believe. Vedic ritual uses jolts of sex, and the suggestion of sex, with great finesse and sense of dramatic placement, while uncontrolled, orgiastic behavior would lessen the drama and blunt the clean lines of the ritual structure.

222. Or partly achieved. The Gavāmayana is not of the same importance as the Aśvamedha and so need not aim for quite so striking effects.

Gonda (1961, pp. 90–92 [=1975, pp. 235–37]) suggests that women who engage in "prolonged or customary cohabitation" (i.e. whores) are particularly tied to the fertility of the soil, and that sexual potency and supranormal powers are especially ascribed to ascetics. This is certainly true, as far as it goes, but it is the pairing of these figures that gives the Mahāvrata copulation its idiosyncratic punch.

223. Which makes Hauer's suggestion (n. 221) that all *but* the officiating priests engaged in copulation even less likely, as there would be hardly anyone present except such priests.

224. Cf. MŚS VII.2.7.8; KŚS XIII.3.17; BŚS XVI.21 (267: 9, 268: 2); ĀpŚS XXI.17.16, 19.3; ŚŚS XVII.3.12–16; PB V.6.8.

225. Cf. e.g. MŚS VII.2.7.10; KŚS XIII.3.20–26; BŚS XVI.21 (267: 11), 22 (268: 10), 23; ĀpŚS XXI.18.7, 19.18–20.5; VārŚS III.2.5.41–44.

226. Specifically the son of a younger sister of the father of the king/Sacrificer and one of a younger sister of his mother, according to ĀpŚS XX.3.7; VārŚS III.4.1.20; TB III.8.4.1.

227. KŚS XX.1.36–38 instead allows either an Āyogava (according to the commentary a person of mixed class) or 'a whore' (puṃścalū).

228. Krick 1972 suggests an ingenious alternative interpretation, that the dog is the ritual representative of the mythic dog Saramā, who will then function as leader for the horse to the land of the dead.

229. As the anonymous reader for Oxford University Press pointed out, the dog is despised as a scavenger and considered ritually impure, so that it may count as a sort of canine 'whore's son'.

Krick (1972, p. 29, n. 17) suggests that the whore's son has access, through his mother, to "chthonic powers" that immunize him against death, but I do not see any particular evidence for this.

230. Falk 1982; see also Jamison 1991, pp. 258–60.

231. On the Ratnins in general, see Heesterman 1957, pp. 49–57. The exact functions of various of these officials are uncertain, and the standard translations of some of them convey more of a Western medieval courtly flavor than is probably accurate.

TB I.7.3 follows this list exactly, save for inserting the Vāvātā 'Favorite Wife' between the Mahiṣī and the Parivṛktī. The Taittirīya śrauta sūtras for the most part follow this innovation (e.g. ĀpŚS XVIII.10.14; BŚS XII.5 [91: 16]). MS (IV.3.8) and KS (XV.4) essentially agree with the TS list, though the Rājanya is replaced by the king. Their order is also slightly different: after the senānī the order is

Saṃgrahītar
Kṣattar
Sūta
Grāmaṇī
Bhāgadugha
Akṣāvāpa

KS also substitutes the Purohita for the Brāhmaṇa, and the final offering takes place in the joint dwelling of the Akṣāvāpa and the Govyaccha 'cow-tormentor' (?). ŚB (V.3.1) has a different order at the beginning of the list and isolates the Parivṛktī at the end:

Senānī
Purohita (for Brāhmaṇa)
King
Mahiṣī
Sūta
Grāmaṇī
Kṣattar
Saṃgrahītar
Bhāgadugha

Akṣāvāpa and Govikartana ('Cow-carver'?)

Pālāgala ('Courier'? – note that this is the masculine of the fourth, low-class wife of the king, the Pālāgalī)

Parivṛktī

KŚS XV.3.3–14 follows ŚB, though substituting dūta 'messenger' for pālāgala.

232. Kūṭa (in accented texts kūṭá) is usually interpreted as 'horn*less*', but it seems to have the same morphological relationship to kū̂ṭa 'mallet, hammer' as kárṇa 'ear': karṇá 'eared.' Kūṭá should therefore either mean 'having horns like mallets, i.e. stubby or ill-formed' or, perhaps more likely, as with other adjectives of like formation, 'one-horned', thus also ill-formed. Karṇá appears parallel to kūṭá in a passage describing an unacceptable animal in MS:

> MS III.9.5 (122: 3) yáḥ kūṭó vā karṇó vā kāṇó vā śuṣkó vā́vartata
>
> Which one turned out to be (bad-)horned, (bad-)eared, one-eyed, shrivelled up . . .

233. Cf. e.g. MŚS IX.1.1.36; BŚS XII.5 (92: 1); KŚS XV.3.14; MS IV.3.8 (47: 12); TB I.7.3.4; ŚB V.3.1.13.

234. MS IV.3.8 (47: 15) agrees with KS save for the horns.

235. ŚBK VII.1.4.14 adds trístanā 'three-teated'.

236. Cf. MS IV.3.8 (47: 12); TB I.7.3.4.

237. Indra's romantic adventures are a standard topos in Vedic mythology, so that it would not be surprising to find a single wife of Indra filling several different wifely roles over the course of time.

238. Senā means both weapon and army in early Vedic.

239. It might be possible to interpret this locative absolute as an army/weapon raised *against* the Sacrificer, but the logic of the rest of the passage makes this the less likely possibility. That it is the Sacrificer's senā is also supported by the TS parallel:

> TS II.2.8.1 indrāṇyái carúm̐ nír vaped yásya sénā́saṁśiteva syā́t
>
> He [priest] should offer a caru to Indrāṇī (for him) whose senā is, as it were, 'unsharpened'.

The MS parallel (II.2.5 [19: 6]) is similar to KS, with sénāyām uttíṣṭhantyām.

240. Jamison 1991, pp. 93–96.

241. Unfortunately the same idiom is not used for 'avoided' and 'rejected'. The Avoided Wife is always pari √vṛj, while the Rejected Dakṣiṇā is either prati √nud ('pushed back') or simply 'not accepted' (na prati √grah).

242. Cf. KS VIII.17; MS III.8.4 (97: 1) and IV.12.1 (179: 9); TB II.4.2.7. The pādas are in different order, with different intermediate pādas and some variants in the various texts. I will thus quote the pādas I consider relevant independently, as I am not certain how (or if) they fit together.

243. The stretching forth of the bull's feet in RV X.102.4 may also remind us of the action urged on the dead horse in the Aśvamedha. When the copulation with the Mahiṣī is about to begin, she addresses it with

TS VII.4.19.1e táu sahá catúraḥ padáḥ sáṃ prásārayāvahai

Together let us two stretch forth our four feet.

However, if there is a thematic connection here, its exact significance escapes me.

244. The Sanskrit word order expresses this action iconically: the long genitive phrase referring to the bull opens the half-verse, followed by the verb. The sentence ends " . . . droppings Mudgalānī," where the niṣpádaḥ do literally touch her.

245. On the connection between birth and defecation in Vedic, see Jamison 1991, pp. 115–23.

246. It may be worth pointing to another female charioteer: in MBh V.183.15–17 the river Gaṅgā saves her hard-pressed son Bhīṣma (in his duel with Rāma) by taking the reins when his charioteer is killed. (Note that vs. 16 is an irregular Triṣṭubh and hence perhaps forms part of the older core of the epic [cf. M. C. Smith 1992, p. 135].)

247. On this part of the ceremony in general, see Heesterman 1957, pp. 123–26.

248. In the MŚS this occurs later than in the other texts, after the ritual game of dice.

249. In other words he says "X, son of Y; Y, son of X."

250. On the cattle raid in general, see Heesterman 1957, pp. 126–39.

251. MŚS IX.1.3.31; ĀpŚS XVIII.17.11; VārŚS III.3.4.6; MS IV.4.5 (55: 19); KŚS XV.6.32 does not specify a recipient. ĀpŚS precedes the bow exchange with a different kind of contact:

ĀpŚS XVIII.17.10 indrasya vajro 'sīti dhanurārtnyā patnīm aśvāṃś copanudati

(Saying) "You are Indra's cudgel," he taps the wife and the horses with the end of the bow.

HirŚS (cited by Caland, ad loc.) allows tapping of either wife or horses. For BŚS see discussion to follow.

252. Falk argues, I think correctly, that the BŚS version is earlier than that of the ŚB.

253. As we have already seen, the ŚB defines the Parivṛktī as childless.

254. Similar is "The king is dead. Long live the king."

Heesterman's interpretation of this ceremony (1957, p. 125) is similar to mine.

255. We should remember that during the first unction, the king is handed a bow and three arrows. Cf. e.g. ŚB V.3.5.29–30.

256. The classic treatment of this ritual in the secondary literature is the exhaustive work of Caland and Henry, *L'Agniṣṭoma* (1906–7).

257. For a rather different view of this Iṣṭi see Heesterman 1993, pp. 203ff.

258. Or such seems the most reasonable interpretation of these texts. Cf. Caland and Henry 1906–7, p. 53. Keith, however, translates the TS passage (pátny anvárabhate) "The wife (of the sacrificer) holds on (to the cart)," presumably following ĀpŚS X.30.5, which, however, seems aberrant to me.

259. MS III.7.9 (88: 7) pátnyā hástān nírvapaty eṣá vái pátnyā yajñásyānvārambháḥ.

260. Cf. KS XXIV.8 (98: 13); TS VI.2.1.1.

261. The KS and TS parallels also introduce the sexual motif in this context.

262. It is also striking that Manu gave away the cups unilaterally, if the wife is (also?) master of them, as the ritual texts imply.

263. (It is also a place name.) The literal meaning of the verbal lexeme pari √nah from which this noun is derived is 'tie around', and so the noun presumably originally referred to a box that was bound up for safe transit (or safekeeping).

264. The parallel passages (AV I.11.5; TS III.3.10.1) have instead of parīṇaham the obscure duals gavī́nike, gavīnyàu respectively. Could these possibly be related to the even more obscure "two splinters/fish in the cow's hoof" found in the Parivṛktī's verse in the Aśvamedha?

VS XXIII.28 yád asyā aṁhubhédyāḥ kṛdhú sthūlám upā́tasat
muṣkā́v íd asyā ejato gośaphé śakulā́v iva

When the stunted, thick (penis) has shuttled from her narrow slit,
her two balls stir like the two splinters (/fish) in a cow's hoof (?).

265. For another likely reason that the wife is said to control household goods, see IV.D.4.

266. On the symbolic nature of footprints in Vedic, see Thompson, 1995.

267. The suspension dots mark mantras that I have not quoted; otherwise all the ritual *action* is there.

268. On the curious form yāvat-tmūtam, see Mayrhofer *EWA*, sub *KNA V*.

269. Several texts omit the gazes between Soma-cow and Sacrificer and between wife and Sacrificer. MŚS unusually omits the wife's receiving of the pot, while in KŚS (VII.6.22) the Adhvaryu takes the pot back from the Sacrificer and himself gives it to the wife. Meanwhile (VII.6.23) the Neṣṭar has the wife recite a mantra.

270. For a wholly different interpretation of the Soma-cow's seventh step, see Heesterman 1985, pp. 65–67.

271. Cf. e.g. ŚGS I.14.5ff.; ĀśvGS I.7.19; PārGS I.8.1; GobhGS II.2.11ff.; KhGS I.3.26; HirGS I.20.9f., 21.1ff.; ĀpGS II.4.16f.; JGS I.21; MGS I.11.18.

272. For further discussion of this legal doctrine, see Kane, *HDŚ* II.538–39.

273. The mantra collection of the Āpastambha *Gṛhya* Sūtra, the so-called Mantrapatha (ĀpM, Winternitz 1897), has almost the identical formulation at *its* seventh step: the grammatically impossible I.3.14 sákhāyau saptápadā babhūva, with one manuscript reading rather abhūma, and one the more desirable saptápadāv abhūva (found also in BhārGS, according to Winternitz [p. xvii]). On the readings and his reasons for editing babhūva, see Winternitz (pp. xvi–xvii). The point here is that the Āpastambhins have essentially *identical* mantras (down to their grammatical disturbance) for the climax of the marriage ceremony in their gṛhya sūtra and the final step taken by Soma-cow and Sacrificer in their śrauta sūtra.

274. For a very different interpretation of the seventh step, see Heesterman 1993, p. 127.

275. See e.g. BŚS VI.14; MŚS II.1.4.8–10; ĀpŚS X.25.2ff.; KŚS VII.8.1ff.; ŚB III.3.3.1ff., etc. Each text varies slightly, but each clearly contains a scripted performance between the two participants, a little drama. On the whole sequence consult Caland and Henry 1906–7, pp. 43–48.

276. Cf. e.g. MS III.7.3 (77: 7); KS XXIII.10 (86: 3), XXIV.1 (90: 3); TS VI.1.6; ŚB III.2.4.

277. The text continues with instructions for the other cart. Cf. BŚS VI.24 (184: 15); MŚS II.2.2.15. Other texts (KŚS VIII.3.28–29; MS III.8.7 [103: 16]; KS XXV.8 [113: 13]; TS VI.2.9.1–2; ŚB III.5.3.13–16) also mention the anointing, but if the footprint has already been used elsewhere, another substance is clearly needed. ŚB and its śrauta

sūtra KŚS employ instead the ghee also used, just previously, for an offering made in the wheel track of the wagon. Both these texts elsewhere also mention the possibility of using a fourth of the footprint for this task as well (ŚB III.6.3.5; cf. KŚS VIII.6.31).

278. In MŚS II.2.4.25 it is in this *new* Gārhapatya that the other half of the Soma-cow's footprint is strewn, presumably as part of the activity for establishing the new patnīloka. This occurs at approximately the same time as the wife is led up to the new Gārhapatya. She sits down, saying

> MŚS II.2.4.19 athāham anugāminī sve loke viśa iha
>
> Then I, a follower, sit down in my own world here.

279. On this journey, see Heesterman 1993, p. 126 and n. 69.

280. Other aspects of this journey will be discussed later.

281. Cf. ŚB III.3.3.18.

282. This is the same mantra which the wife pronounces when she looks at the heated Mahāvīra pot in the Pravargya ceremony, as discussed earlier. There, too, the glance was sexual and procreative in intent. As we have seen before (in the girding of the wife and its connection with the marriage ceremony), the use of identical mantras can serve as a sort of cross-referencing system, to evoke the content and purpose of one ritual in the context of another one of apparently very different type.

283. On the fetching and parading of the Overnight waters, see Caland and Henry 1906–7, pp. 119–22.

284. Cf. Caland and Henry 1906–7, pp. 140–42; MŚS II.3.2.9–20; ĀpŚS XII.5.2–13; KŚS IX.3.3; BŚS VII.3 (203: 1).

285. See Caland and Henry 1906–7, pp. 142–44.

286. Cf. MŚS II.3.2.23; ĀpŚS XII.5.14. BŚS requires two different placements of the waters (VII.3 [203: 17], VII.15 [225: 11]). See Caland and Henry 1906–7, p. 144.

287. If to √vaś, or 'bellowing for' if to √vāś. (Both may well be meant.)

288. See n. 287 immediately above.

289. See MS I.6.12 (104: 10); KS XI.6 (151: 5), etc.; and Jamison 1991, pp. 204–8. For further on leftovers in ancient Indian religion, see Malamoud 1972.

290. The Āditya oblation is actually considered a preliminary offering, not part of the Tṛtīya Savana proper. See Eggeling ad ŚB IV.3.5.2. On the offering in general, see Caland and Henry 1906–7, pp. 330ff.

291. See e.g. MŚS II.5.1.11–12; ĀpŚS XIII.10.5–6; Caland and Henry 1906–7, pp. 334–35.

292. In BŚS (VIII.10 [247: 11]) the wife does not seem to perform this action, but merely 'grasps from behind' (anvārabdhāyāṃ patnyām) while it occurs. KŚS does not make it clear who performs it, but the wife 'looks' at the vessel (avekṣate patnī KŚS X.5.7) while it is going on.

293. TS III.2.8; ĀpŚS XIII.10.10; BŚS VIII.10 (247: 12); the WYV (VS VIII.5) uses some similar mantras.

294. I will not comment on some of the difficult and potentially corrupt features of these verses.

295. We encountered a similar though less elaborate fixation on the domestic partnership at the end of the paradigm Iṣṭi, at the Patnīsaṃyāja oblations, where the mantra brought husband and wife back together after their separation during the central part of the ritual:

MS I.4.3 (51: 4) sáṃ pátnī pátyā sukṛtéṣu gachatām̐ yajñásya yuktáu dhúryā abhūthām
āprīṇānáu vijáhatā árātīṃ diví jyótir uttamám ā́rabhethām

Let the wife come together with her husband among the well-performed (ritual actions?). You two have become the yoked team of the worship.
Pleasing each other, leaving behind hostility, you two have grasped the highest light in heaven.

The Third Pressing, as the last important part of the Soma ritual, occupies a structural position similar to that of the Patnīsaṃyājas and the other concluding actions in the Iṣṭi discussed earlier. The Pātnīvata oblation at the Third Pressing, which is almost identical to the Patnīsaṃyājas, makes the connection between the Third Pressing and the end of the Iṣṭi especially clear.

296. It is probably no accident that unmixed soma is called śukra 'pure'.

297. The figure of Apālā, a teenaged girl who presses soma and offers it to Indra from her mouth, is clearly meant to be viewed as an exception. On this story, see Schmidt 1987, pp. 1–29; Jamison 1991, pp. 149–72. For further on this story see also V.C.2.

298. For some of the conceptual dangers involved in gestation and birth, see Jamison 1991, pp. 183–242 passim.

299. A number of other offerings and recitations have taken place since the addition of the āśir.

300. The third, Soma, is present by virtue of being the ritual substance.

301. These are found in the prose texts of the YV, i.e. MS (IV.7.4); KS (XXVIII.8); TS (VI.5.8); and ŚB (IV.4.2).

302. Similar KS XXVIII.8 (162: 15); TS VI.5.8.3–4; and ŚB IV.4.2.9.

303. It is interesting that, at least in the MS mental universe, it is possible to imagine the gender tables turned: it is by mythological *accident*, not inherent nature, that men, not women, frequent the assembly.

KS shares the prevailing opinion about lack of strength (nirindriya), but adds perhaps the most bizarre mythic justification of gender differences, which is worth quoting for that reason:

KS XXVIII.8 (162: 20) upariṣṭāc chrīṇāti tasmāt stry akhalatir bhāvukā

He mixes (it) from the upper part. Therefore the woman is unlikely to become bald.

304. ŚBK V.4.4.9 is essentially identical, but substitutes strī́ḥ 'women' for pátnīḥ 'wives' in both places.

305. See MŚS II.2.1.40–41; ĀpŚS XI.3.13–14; BŚS VI.20 (179: 16); Caland and Henry 1906–7, p. 71. The reason for this recitation and for its particular position in the ritual are not clear to me.

306. Not all the cup was offered at the oblation, as the MŚS makes clear (II.5.2.14).

307. Cf. MŚS II.5.2.15–16; ĀśvŚS V.19.8; ŚB IV.4.2.18; TS VI.5.8.5–6.

308. Cf. ĀpŚS XIII.15.1 with Caland's note.

309. Recall the description of the coupling of the Mahiṣī and the dead horse in several texts:

BŚS XV.29 (234: 9) athaiṣā mahiṣy upasthe śepham ādhatte

Then the Mahiṣī places the penis in her lap.

ŚB XIII.5.2.2 áśvasya śiśnáṃ máhiṣy úpasthe nídhatte

The Mahiṣī puts the penis of the horse in her lap.

310. I have not found this exact provision in any other text, but in ŚŚS VIII.5.5 the Agnīd addresses the Neṣṭar with almost identical words (neṣṭar upahūyasva).

311. ŚBK is similar but not identical:

ŚBK V.4.4.12 táṃ ná pratyúpahvayeta néd asya hatásya níraṣṭasya pratyupahváyā íti

He should not invite him, (thinking) "Lest I should invite someone who is smashed and castrated."

It is decided nonetheless to invite him, but not because the possibility of his identity with the castrated women is denied. Rather, the priest has already offered soma in the Agnīd's hearth, and so it seems to be bad manners not to invite the Agnīd to drink it too. (So ŚB IV.4.2.16.)

312. ŚBM is essentially the same, but instead of the identifications

Neṣṭar = wife (pátnī) = female (yóṣā),

it has

Neṣṭar = female (yóṣā) = female (yóṣā),

which looks like the result of bad textual transmission.

313. Cf. KS XXVI.1 (122: 7), which is the source of the śruti quotation; also PB VIII.7.11.

314. For similar interpretations, see KS XXVI.1 (122: 3); MS IV.5.4 (67: 18); PB VIII.7.9–10.

315. Cf. MŚS II.5.2.22; ĀpŚS XIII.15.8; KŚS X.7.5.

316. The fourth Veda, the Atharva Veda, is of course marginally represented in śrauta ritual by the presence of the Brahman, who nominally belongs to the AV. However, unlike the other three Vedas, the AV text furnishes no verbal portion of the ritual, and in fact, the Brahman does not normally *act* in the ritual, but merely supervises silently.

317. TS VI.5.8.6; MS IV.5.4 (68: 5); ŚB IV.4.2.18. KS XXVI.1 (122: 4), by contrast, simply calls the Udgātar a bull (vṛṣan).

318. Cf. e.g. PB VII.10.16; JB I.88, I.259; MS IV.6.4 (84: 1).

319. Which in fact is realized as *hum* in recitation.

320. Similar ĀpŚS V.25.11 hiṅkṛtya vāgyataḥ striyam upeyāt. As Caland points out (ad loc.), "Das Hörbarmachen des Hiṅlautes vor dem Zusammensein der Vermählten ist aus den Gṛhyasūtras (vgl. z.B. Bhār. gṛhs. I.20 am Anf.) bekannt."

321. Cf. also JB III.70; as well as related passages like PB VI.8.5; TS II.5.7.1.

322. Not, however, in context of the ritual we are discussing.

323. On sniffing as a means of animation, see Jamison 1991, pp. 116–20.

324. We can also note that, according to the rest of the ŚB passage just cited, though

the Vasus and Rudras each have their pressing for their exclusive use, the Ādityas must share theirs, and the All Gods may be a way of referring to the interlopers at the Third Pressing.

325. The later Pūjā ceremony, of course, depends on a physical, manipulable representation of the god, but otherwise in many ways replicates—and makes manifest—the underlying structures of the more abstract and conceptual Vedic ritual.

326. Many of these same incidents, particularly the Pātnīvata cup and the sequence involving the Agnīd, Neṣṭar, wife, and Udgātar, have also been treated by F. M. Smith (1991, pp. 32–42). Though he cites many of the same passages and reaches some of the same conclusions (e.g. that the Neṣṭar plays both female and male roles, p. 40), we diverge on a number of issues. In particular, Smith suggests that this elaborate edifice may substitute for an earlier ritual scenario in which the wife engaged in ritual copulation with her husband and/or one or more of the priests (p. 41). Moreover, Smith neither examines the importance of certain ritual details like the identity of the water that the wife pours on her thigh, nor situates the incidents he discusses in the context of the Third Pressing. So despite a number of useful comments and insights, his treatment of these incidents does not, in my opinion, really crack their code.

327. The ritual form of that day is discussed in Jamison 1991, pp. 278–80.

328. See AB VI.27–36; KB XXX.1–8; ŚŚS XII.13–25; cf. also Bloomfield 1899, pp. 96–101, esp. 96 and 100; Keith 1920, pp. 32–33, 56–59.

329. This recitation also takes place on the Viśvajit day just mentioned, but at the Midday Pressing, as far as I can make out.

330. I assume that the Vṛṣākapi hymn was adapted to this purpose only after the Aśvamedha liturgy had become fixed. Deprived of its original ritual purpose, it found a new liturgical home in an elaborated version of the Third Pressing—conceptually allied to the Aśvamedha, but much more pallid.

331. Besides its status as an independent rite, the Animal Sacrifice (Paśubandha) also forms a part of a number of other rituals. For example, there are several animal sacrifices embedded in the Soma Sacrifice.

332. Cf. MŚS I.8.4.1ff.; ĀpŚS VII.18.1ff.; KŚS VI.5.26ff.; VārŚS I.6.5.11ff.; MS III.10.1 (128: 3); ŚB III.8.2.1ff.

333. Heesterman (1993, p. 15, n. 40) claims that the Sacrificer touches the dead victim once its dismembered body has been reassembled on the vedi, but in the passages he cites for this action (ĀpŚS VII.25.6; MS III.10.4 [134: 10]) the Sacrificer is not mentioned, and it seems clear that the Adhvaryu performs this task.

Part IV

1. For earlier discussion of this charged word, see III.F.4.

2. The MBh also contains a narrative concerning Ahalyā, Gautama, and sexual infidelity (XII.258), but the hospitality motif is absent. Instead the story turns on Gautama's order to their son to kill Ahalyā for her adultery. The son reflects on his conflicting responsibilities to father and mother, resolves not to carry out the command, and is rewarded by Gautama, who has since reconsidered.

3. Prof. F. Wilhelm has recently discussed hospitality issues in a forthcoming paper, entitled "Hospitality and caste system." I had the pleasure of hearing this paper at the American Oriental Society meeting in March 1991, and he has since kindly supplied me with a copy. Though our conclusions coincide on some details, they were reached independently, and our emphases are, in general, different.

4. Especially in *Der Fremdling im Ṛgveda* (1938).

5. Treatments of guest reception include the following: ViSmṛ 67.28ff.; ĀpDS II.6-9; GDS V.25ff.; VāsDS VIII.4ff. Cf. also Gonda 1980, pp. 207f., 210, 385f.

6. Substantially the same story is told at MBh II.61.60ff., but that version completely lacks the hospitality motif.

7. According to a verse omitted in the Critical Edition (193*): svayaṃvare sthitā kanyā keśinī nāma nāmataḥ "A maiden named Keśinī was engaged in her svayamvara . . . " Van Buitenen calls Keśinī the *wife* of Virocana (MBh III, p. 254, introductory remarks), but the agonistic quality of the exchanges between the two men make it more likely that they are competing for Keśinī's favor. Moreover she is called a kumārī at V.35.31 and a kanyā in the verse just quoted, both of which indicate an unmarried maiden.

On the institution of the svayaṃvara, see discussion in part V, passim.

8. The wording here is reminiscent of the Prātaritvan 'early-coming' visitors in the Manu story, for which see IV.D.2, but this is probably not significant.

9. As so often, the dispenser of hospitality is a woman.

10. A roll of twisted grass, typical seat of student or ascetic.

11. On the cow and Madhuparka as offerings for the most distinguished guests see e.g. ĀpDS II.8.5-7.

12. On the host himself washing the guest's feet see e.g. ĀpDS II.6.9, where it is also allowed to have two Śūdras do it. Presumably only the most distinguished of guests would receive the host's personal ministrations.

13. This episode is also treated by Prof. Wilhelm in the paper referred to in n. 3.

14. Durvāsas surely counts as the worst houseguest in Indian literature. We will examine another of his escapades in the MBh later, and he comes close to ruining Śakuntalā's life in the Kālidāsa play.

15. Again, note prātar 'early in the morning', which recalls the Prātaritvan of Manu's Cups. See IV.D.2.

16. Not all the manuscripts immolate the girls, but almost all do feature the burning of the furniture.

17. Notice the appearance of the 'leftover' (ucchiṣṭa) here again.

18. Kṛṣṇa is narrating this story to his son Pradyumna.

19. For another instance of smearing limbs with food, see the story of Mudgala in IV.D.1.

20. Recall the mantra pronounced over the husband and wife in the standard śrauta Iṣṭi: "You two have become the yoked team of the ritual."

21. Though many of us, after a lifetime of houseguests, have stories not too much less dramatic!

22. Compare Vyāsa's dismissal of the cow in the guest reception quoted earlier (MBh I.54.14).

23. Cf. JGS I.19; ĀśvGS I.24.30-33; PārGS I.3.26-30; ŚGS II.15.1ff, 16.1; GobhGS IV.10.18; KhGS IV.4.17, etc.

In several of the accounts the violent intent is even more vividly displayed. In JGS I.19 the announcer of the cow is "another (person) with a knife in his hand" (paraḥ svadhitipāṇiḥ; cf. PārGS I.3.26); in GobhGS IV.10.18 the announcer is a 'barber' (nāpitaḥ).

24. Some of the śrauta sūtras treat this ritual within the Soma Sacrifice, some in a separate section. For the ritual, cf. e.g. MŚS V.2.12; BŚS XVII.15; ĀpŚS XIV.5.9, 7.12-17; KŚS VIII.8.36-9.4; and for Brāhmaṇic treatments, see MS IV.8.1 (108: 3); KS XXX.1 (181: 1, 182: 12); TS VI.6.6.1, ŚB III.7.2.8.

25. Only reaching to the navel (adhonābhi MŚS V.2.12.36; yathādho nābhisaṃmitaḥ ĀpŚS XIV.5.9; avacīnaṃ nā́bhyāḥ MS IV.8.1 [108: 4]; nābhimātra KŚS VIII.8.36).

26. MŚS V.2.12.36; BŚS XVII.15 (296: 5). Other texts call this the Śālādvārya (KŚS VIII.8.36 '[the fire] at the door of the hut') or Śālāmukhīya (ĀpŚS XIV.7.12 '[the fire] at the mouth of the hut'), but the same fire is meant.

27. So specifically BŚS XVII.15 (296: 6); ĀpŚS XIV.7.13 (sāṇḍam 'with testicles'); ŚB III.7.2.8 (muṣkará 'id.').

28. The story is told apropos of the Pātnīvata *cup* (graha) at the end of the Third Pressing, a ritual I have already discussed at length. I am inclined to think that it has been displaced from its appropriate place (nearby) as commentary on the Pātnīvata-*paśu* because of the similarity of names.

29. Heesterman (1993, pp. 26ff. and passim) discusses the apparent identity of *Sacrificer* and sacrificed.

30. See references assembled in part I, nn. 3 and 4.

31. Outside of the Manu's Cups story the word átithipati 'lord of guests, host' is found in Vedic only in this hymn (vss. 18 and 53 besides this one).

32. See especially in Heesterman 1985, chapter 2 "Brahmin, ritual, and renouncer" (revision of identically entitled article in *WZKSOA* 8 [1964] 1–31); chapter 3 "The case of the severed head" (revision of identically entitled article in *WZKSOA* 11 [1967] 22–43); chapter 6 "Vedic sacrifice and transcendence," where, for example, he terms Vedic ritual "a fully technical and harmless procedure" (p. 87). Heesterman 1993 is entirely concerned with this topic. For further discussion of Heesterman's reconstruction of the history of Vedic ritual, see Jamison, forthcoming b.

33. Or "his possessions, *including* his wife." The power of men to give away, barter for, or exchange women as chattels will be explored in part V.

34. Though in the KS this epithet does not occur in the formulaic begging exchange, but when Indra realizes what the Asuras are planning against Manu śraddhādeva.

35. In KS also Indra gives him this epithet, and it occurs in the short versions of MS, KS, and TB.

36. On this see e.g. Jamison 1991, pp. 204ff.

37. Cf. e.g. Bloomfield 1896, p. 411; Oldenberg 1896; Hara 1963, esp. p. 139; and especially Köhler 1948/1973, p. 39 and passim.

38. Cf. also Lévi 1898, pp. 108–21, esp. 120–21, for a slightly different interpretation.

39. On śraddhā́ as a term with originally *social* content, see also Heesterman (1993, pp. 77–78).

40. Cf. also MBh III.2.52.

41. For a thorough treatment of this ceremony, see Kane, *HDŚ* IV.334–551.

42. By ancient commentators (see Kane, *HDŚ* IV.351f., with discussion of earlier literature) as well as modern ones (e.g. Keith 1927, p. 427). But it would seem rather peculiar if in all of Vedic ritual only this ceremony commanded enough 'faith' from its practioners to merit the name. Köhler (p. 50) is rather closer to my derivation in taking it as developed from the meaning 'Spendefreudigkeit gegenüber Brahmanen'.

43. Cf. Kane, *HDŚ* IV.181f. on later debates about which is more important: the offering to the ancestors or the feast for the Brahmans.

44. ViSmṛ LXXIII.28; MBh XII.29.114c.

45. E.g. GDS XV.16–30; MDŚ III.150–86; MBh XIII.24.13–32; XIII.90.5–32; cf. extensive discussion in Kane, *HDŚ* IV.383–96.

46. ≅ MBh XIII.90.2–4, 33.

47. Cf. ĀpDS II.17.4; GDS XV.12, 20; VāsDS XI.17; BDS II.14.6; MBh XIII.90.36.

48. Cf. GDS XV.12; MBh XIII.90.35.

49. This passage is a later addition to the text. On it see e.g. Bodewitz 1976, pp. 119–21, though Bodewitz's interpretation of the term śraddhā seems to me a retrogression.

50. Hillebrandt 1927–29, p. 264.

51. Oldenberg, *Noten*, ad loc.

52. Vāyu, plus or minus Indra, as first recipient of the soma drink is known already to the RV (I.134.1, 6; I.135.4; II.11.14; VII.92.1).

53. E.g. VS VII.7; TS I.2.3.3, 4.4.1; MS I.2.3 (12: 14); KS IV.2 (30: 1); ĀpŚS XII.14.9, etc. Rau (1966, p. 91, n. 62) comments of the Manu's Cups formula, "Wahrscheinlich der Anfang einer Opferlitanei," but does not identify it further.

54. Thieme (1938, p. 82A) deals briefly with the word prātarítvan, which he takes not as 'early-coming' but as 'early-*going*'. He makes the sensible point that ordinarily a guest does not *come* in the morning, but leaves then after spending the night. This fits well with the later regulations and definitions of guest status, and if prātarítvan were confined to simple hospitality contexts, I would agree with Thieme. However, he does not take into account the related prātaryā́van or the ritual contexts in which both words are found. Moreover he is forced into a tortured explanation of RV I.125.3a ā́yam adyá sukŕ̥taṃ prātár ichán as "Ich kam *heute*, wünschend einen Wohltäter am *Morgen*," with adyá and prātár referring to different days (today . . . tomorrow), while a more natural interpretation is "I came early today."

55. Jamison, forthcoming c.

56. I use the word 'hymn' loosely, as the text is primarily in prose.

57. Or probably rather 'keeps her', i.e. the Kṣatriya who does not give the cow to the Brahman on the appropriate occasions.

58. This hymn is followed immediately by AV XII.5, which I just had occasion to cite, in which the cow becomes a meni when she is taken from (or not given to?) a Brahman.

59. The story of Sūrya's visit to Kuntibhoja (III.287ff.), an Exploited Host narrative that we examined earlier, is related in the course of this episode. Conceiving Karṇa is the ultimate, somewhat dubious reward for Kuntī's unflagging service to Sūrya then.

60. The story of Utaṅka and Pauṣya, which has come up twice before, contains a prefiguring and somewhat farcical version of this great episode. The errand on which Utaṅka comes to Pauṣya is to *beg* Pauṣya's wife's *earrings* as a guru-gift for his teacher's wife. She gives them up readily in response to a yāc (I.3.108–18), without damage to her person—unlike Karṇa.

61. For these utterances cf. PārGS II.5.2–4; MDŚ II.49; ĀpDS I.3.28–30; GDS II.36; VāsDS XI.68–70; BDS I.3.16–17; ViSmr̥ 27.25. ĀśvGS I.22.6–8 is unusual in also allowing men to be approached, with the formula bhavān bhikṣāṃ dadātu "Let your honor give alms" (with the masc. honorific bhavān that corresponds to fem. bhavati 'Lady' in the normal formula).

62. See e.g. JGS I.12; MGS I.22.20; ŚGS II.6.5–6; ĀśvGS I.22.7; PārGS II.5.5–7; GobhGS II.10.42–43; HirGS I.7.16–17; VārGS V.28.

63. That she does make decisions about whether to give or not, not merely transfer food mechanically to whoever asks for it, is clear from Aditi's refusal quoted earlier. ĀpDS I.3.26 also threatens the loss of all sorts of merit to "women who refuse" (strīṇāṃ pratyācakṣāṇānām) to give to students.

64. Further implications of this principle will be discussed in part V.B.

65. Cf. BDS II.4.26.

66. This shocking piece of attempted cannibalism reminds us of the story of another of Śibi's sons, cooked by him as food for the demanding Brahman (discussed earlier), though the stories seem otherwise unconnected.

67. Vss. 42–47 do not appear to me to be in the correct order in the Critical Edition. I am inclined to read 44 after 41 and 42–43 after 46. (This is similar but not identical to the order in some mss. [D_7 T $G_{1.3.6}$].)

68. Note the frequent appearance of prati √grah in the scenes described above.

69. The formula of this declaration is dehi yuddham . . . mama (V.193.19) "give me battle," a counterpart of Ikṣvāku's prayaccha yuddham (XII.192.41) discussed earlier, which was presented as the only request a Kṣatriya knows how to make.

70. Though the opposite is not forbidden: one can give to one's enemies if begged. Cf. MBh V.33.99 dadāty amitreṣv api yācitaḥ "When begged, he gives even to his enemies."

71. For further on the rejected Dakṣiṇā, see Jamison 1991, pp. 192–96. Earlier I discussed the similarity between the rejected Dakṣiṇā and the "Avoided Wife."

72. The dangers of receiving gifts and hospitality have been frequently and illuminatingly discussed by Heesterman (see e.g. 1959, 1962, and 1993).

Part V

1. The Lévi-Strauss "exchangist" view of marriage and, specifically, the notion that in the standard marriage type the bride is "given" to the groom, have been disputed recently by J. Goody (e.g. 1990, pp. 167ff.). This is not the place—and I am not the person—to engage in a theoretical dispute over this issue, but if we take the testimony of the texts seriously, it is hard to avoid the conclusion that marriage is conceptually a part of the gift-exchange system in ancient India, as the discussion in the body of the text should demonstrate.

Goody's objections to the notion of marriage as gift seem to rest on a misunderstanding about the nature of gift-exchange in this society. He seems to believe that giving *severs* relations between the giver and the receiver, and *alienates* the gift from the giver. Therefore, marriage cannot involve gift, because the wife nonetheless retains a relationship with her natal family (see e.g. pp. 169f., 222ff., 249, 465ff.). However, as we have seen, giving *creates* rather than severs relationships, and the gift itself is a link between giver and recipient. This concept has been well expressed by Gonda (1954 = 1975, p. 175):

> To the gift, indeed, a mystic power is attached which establishes community: giver and receiver participate in the gift and, therefore, in each other. The man who gives places himself in relation to the man who receives: the man who receives unites himself to the man who gives [N.B. the gender]; the accepted gift often binds.

2. Rubin, "The traffic in women," in Reiter 1975.

3. Though marriage partners are generally supposed to belong to the same caste, there are prohibitions against belonging to identical subgroups within that caste (for details see e.g. Kane, *HDŚ* II.1. 436–38). The result of these prohibitions is to require a sort of controlled exogamy.

4. On the characteristics of Aryaman, with illuminating discussion of the earlier literature, see Brereton 1981, pp. 150–91.

5. See e.g. Kane, *HDŚ* II.1, chap. IX (pp. 427–541); Chatterjee 1978; Apte 1978.

6. The theme of woman as an item of exchange between men is not confined to ancient India or the ancient world in general. In the year of this writing (1993) there have been at least three mainstream Hollywood movies on this subject, one involving a man's proposition to pay a million dollars for one night with another man's wife (*Indecent Proposal*), the others the lending of a girl to a man in exchange for a favor (*Maddog and Glory*) or in payment of a gambling debt (*Honeymoon in Vegas*).

7. In the JB she is only a recent convert to loyalty, however. She begins by trying to escape from Cyavana by trickery.

8. Though Yayāti seems to give Mādhavī to Gālava in a strictly disinterested way, as alms, he casually remarks when he hands her over that he desires 'daughter's sons' (dauhitra MBh V.113.14), i.e. grandsons born to a daughter, to serve as male heirs of a sonless man. The four sons Mādhavī produces from her various liaisons count not merely as the sons of their several fathers but as part of Yayāti's lineage. (On the possibility of dual heritage and dual responsibility in this case, see Schmidt 1987, pp. 39-43.) In fact, when much later Yayāti loses his merit and falls from heaven, his four grandsons and Mādhavī donate their merit to him and he reascends (MBh V.119–21). So Yayāti stood to gain from Gālava's aggressive salesmanship as well.

9. The list of marriage types is a regular feature of dharma texts, e.g. MDŚ III.20–34; ĀpDS II.11.17–20, 12.1–3; GDS IV.6–15; BDS I.20, etc. It is also found occasionally in gṛhya texts (ĀśvGS I.6), and it is treated in the epic, not only in dharma passages (e.g. MBh XIII.44.3-9), but also in narrative (e.g. MBh I.96.8–11).

10. For a useful summary of the various views, see Kane, *HDŚ* II.1.521–22. A tabulated conspectus of legal doctrine follows:

MDŚ III.23: first six legal for Brahman
last four for Kṣatriya
same (except Rākṣasa) for Vaiśya and Śūdra
24 first four: Brahman
Rākṣasa: Kṣatriya
Āsura: Vaiśya and Śūdra
25 Paiśāca and Āsura never to be used; other three of the last five acceptable [for all?]
26 Gāndharva and Rākṣasa: Kṣatriya
39–41 first four produce good sons/last four bad sons

ĀpDS II.12.3 first three (Brāhma, Ārṣa, Daiva) good (in that order)

GDS IV.14 first four (Brāhma, Prājāpatya, Ārṣa, Daiva)
15 or first six (+ Gāndharva, Āsura)

BDS I.20.10 first four (Brāhma, Prājāpatya, Ārṣa, Daiva) in order: Brahman
12 6 and 7 (Āsura, Rākṣasa): Kṣatriya
13 5 and 8 (Gāndharva, Paiśāca): Vaiśya and Śūdra
16 Gāndharva: for everyone

ViSmṛ XXIV.27 first four (Brāhma, Daiva, Ārṣa, Prājāpatya): Brahman
28 also Gāndharva: Kṣatriya

MBh XIII.44.8 Paiśāca and Āsura: always illegal
.9 Brāhma, Kṣātra [Rākṣasa], Gāndharva: legal

Kane, *HDŚ* II.1.521 all smṛtis agree on first four (Brāhma, Daiva, Ārṣa, Prājāpatya)
almost all agree Paiśāca worst

11. Particularly Kṣatriyas. See MDŚ III.23–26; BDS I.20.12 (Rākṣasa); ViSmṛ XXIV.28 (Gāndharva).

12. Treatments of the marital typology in other texts are less consistent in their use of the term 'gift'. Only the Brāhma rite is consistently so described (in the texts I consulted [YājñSmṛ I.58; GDS IV.6; VāsDS I.30; BDS I.20.2; ViSmṛ XXIV.19; ĀśvGS I.6.1; MBh I.96.8, XIII.44.3]). The Daiva type is frequently classified as a gift; the Ārṣa and Prājāpatya types sometimes; and the Āsura never, outside of MDŚ, at least in the texts I checked. However, the absence of the word 'give' or 'gift' in any particular text is not necessarily significant, since in the condensed style of the sūtras it may be supplied for subsequent entries from the first member in the list, namely the Brāhma type. Nonetheless, the consistent lack of the term for the Āsura type in all texts besides Manu may be deliberate. Kane (*HDŚ* II.1. 517–18) considers the first four types (Brāhma, Daiva, Ārṣa, Prājāpatya) to involve kanyādāna 'gift of a maiden'.

13. Though the marriage *type* is not described as a gift outside of MDŚ, in describing (or condemning) the bride-price, some texts do use the word 'give':

> MBh XIII.95.72 dadātu kanyāṃ śulkena
>
> Let him (not) give a maiden for a śulka.

> BDS I.21.3 śulkena ye prayacchanti svasutāṃ lobhamohitāḥ
>
> Those who crazed with greed give their own daughter for a śulka . . .

Cf. also MGS I.7.11 saṃjuṣṭāṃ dharmeṇopayaccheta brāhmeṇa śaulkena vā "He should give an approved (maiden) by the Brāhma or Bride-price rule."

14. The two occurrences of fem. *amuṣyai* in this passage should surely instead be read as masc. *amuṣmai*. The akṣaras **ṣy** and **ṣm** are nearly identical, and the immediately preceding fem. *asyai* in both instances would have led to the confusion.

15. Versions of this story are also found in PB VII.10.1–4; AB IV.27. For further on the JB version, see Caland 1919, p. 46, as well as his partial translation at PB VII.10.3; and Hoffmann's important discussion (1960, p. 113).

16. Cf. MDŚ III.51–54; ĀpDS II.13.11; BDS I.21.2; MBh I.213.4, XIII.45.19–20, XIII.95.72. See also Kane, *HDŚ* II.1. 503–9, 519; Chatterjee 1978, p. 38; Apte 1978, pp. 145–48.

17. Explicitly called śulka in the Mādhavī story.

18. KāṭhGS XV.1–5 and XVI.1–5 gives further details on differences in the ritual associated with each. In the former the giver says "I shall give (her)" (dadāni) and the groom "I accept (her)" (pratigṛhṇāmi) three times to the assembled company (KāṭhGS XV.4). In the latter gold is exchanged during the ceremony, and the bride's father and the groom each refer to his own contribution in their formulaic exchange:

> KāṭhGS XVI.3 prajābhyas tveti pradadāti
> 4 rāyaspoṣāya tveti pratigṛhṇāti
>
> (The father) gives (her), (saying) "thee [girl] for offspring."
> (The groom) accepts (her), (saying) "thee [gold] for thriving of wealth."

19. See Kane, *HDS* II.1. 517 with n. 1205, on this point.

20. Cf. also RV VII.18.22, VIII.68.17, VI.27.8, I.126.3.

21. On this see Kane, *HDŚ* II.1. 518; Chatterjee 1978, p. 39.

22. So Cm, with other manuscripts having similar phrasing. Hultzsch, however, reads simply gobhyāṃ sahārṣaḥ "together with a pair of oxen—the Ārṣa" for gomithunam . . . ārṣaḥ.

23. Gonda seems to make some similar points in his discussion of Āsura and Ārṣa marriage (1954), but despite some elegant formulations about the function of gift-exchange, his treatment of the marriage types is rather vague and does not seem to lead to definite conclusions.

24. ViSmṛ XXIV.22 is exceptional in defining it simply as prārthitapradānena prājāpatyaḥ "By the giving (of a maiden) at (the bridegroom's) demand, the Prājāpatya (is accomplished)."

25. See Kane, *HDŚ* II.1. 518–19; Chatterjee 1978, p. 42.

26. See also MBh XII.258.34 (the story of Gautama and Ahalyā), where divorce is proclaimed to be illegal after pāṇibandhaṃ svayaṃ kṛtvā sahadharmam upetya ca "having performed the hand-joining by themselves and having embarked on joint dharma."

27. Hopkins (1889, pp. 359ff.) suggests that the Prājāpatya was an earlier form of the svayaṃvara (self-choice).

28. Cf. ĀpDS II.12.2; GDS IV.12; BDS I.20.8; VāsDS I.34; ViSmṛ XXIV.25; YājñSmṛ I.61; ĀśvGS I.6.8; VaikhGS III.1; MBh XIII.44.7, etc. See Sternbach 1943–44, p. 182 for further references.

29. Cf. e.g. Hopkins 1889, pp. 337, 348, 351, 358–62 and passim; Sternbach 1943–44, 1951; Hara 1974; Apte 1978, pp. 82, 84, 150 and passim; Chatterjee 1978, pp. 35ff.; Dumézil 1979, pp. 66–71 and passim; Arabagian 1984; Sergent 1984, pp. 186–87.

30. Cf. e.g. Hopkins 1889, pp. 337, 361; Sternbach 1943–44, 1951; Dumézil 1979, p. 70; and see, in contrast, Gonda's sensible remarks on "preconceived evolutionistic ideas with regard to the 'history' of marriage" (1954 = 1975, pp. 172–73).

31. Bhīṣma also mentions it in passing in XIII.44, where the story has been altered to fit his discourse on marriage dharma: only two young women are involved (XIII.44.37), each with a technical legal problem.

32. A pun. Bhojya is both a proper name, being the name of the family to which Rukmiṇī belonged, and an adjective meaning 'to be enjoyed' (including sexually).

33. Which makes it rather annoying that some discussions of this incident state that Bhīṣma "raped" the sisters. So Sergent 1984, pp. 186–87. Sergent's reference to Dumézil 1979 for this information is unfair to the latter, who merely calls it an "enlèvement" and makes it quite clear that the maidens are destined for Bhīṣma's brother—another indication that not only primary texts but even secondary literature is subject to crude and careless misreading.

In fact, it is almost heavy-handedly emphasized in the text that Bhīṣma did not lay a finger on them. Cf. e.g.

I.96.44 snuṣā iva sa dharmātmā bhaginya iva cānujāḥ
yathā duhitaraś caiva pratigṛhya yayau kurūn

Taking them, like daughters-in-law, like younger sisters, like daughters, the dharma-souled one went to the Kurus.

34. Cf. e.g. ŚGS I.6; JGS I.20; KauśSū 75.8–9, etc.; and Gonda 1980, pp. 387f.

35. Duryodhana seems to abduct Citrāṅgada's daughter for himself, but Karṇa, who accompanies him in this exploit (as the text repeatedly emphasizes), may somehow serve structurally as his 'wooer' or, at least, best man.

36. Also in the AV outside of the wedding hymn in XI.8.1, 2.

37. Both Geldner (ad loc.) and O'Flaherty (1981, p. 272, n. 13) take the middle voice of pṛchámānau as literally and narrowly self-beneficial: 'asking on behalf of oneself'. They interpret it as referring to or playing upon another possible mythic configuration in which the Aśvins are themselves the bridegrooms of Sūryā, not the wooers for Soma. However, in *this* hymn the Aśvins are emphatically just the wooers (cf. the nearby vs. 9 sómo vadhūyúr abhavad aśvínāstām ubhā́ varā́ "Soma was the bridegroom; both the Aśvins were the wooers"), and I think the middle voice has a more general domain here: 'asking on behalf of *our side*'. It is worth noting that in ŚGS I.6.4 (for which see below) the wooers are called 'conveyors (of the bride)', also in the middle voice (āvahamāna- i.e. lit. 'conveyors for themselves'). The polarization of '*bride*'s family/ supporters' and '*groom*'s family/supporters' is more significant than any distinction between, say, groom and groom's friend. Hence any action undertaken by anyone on the groom's side would be construed as self-beneficial/-involved, even if the immediate benefit accrues only to the groom. The interfamilial alliances resulting from the marriage will also benefit the groom's connections.

38. This announcement is a little less clear in the other narrative of the Bhīṣma abduction, but it is there. First, when Bhīṣma initially sees the sisters, the narrator identifies him by a variant of his full name, though elsewhere he is usually identified just as Bhīṣma, or by an epithet, or simply by 'he':

I.96.5 dadarśa kanyās tāś caiva bhīṣmaḥ śaṃtanunandanaḥ

Bhīṣma, the joy of Śaṃtanu, saw these maidens.

Then, during the roll call of the kings at the svayaṃvara (I.96.6 kīrtyamāneṣu rājñāṃ tu nāmasv atha sahasraśaḥ "then as the names of the kings were being recited by the thousands"), Bhīṣma takes this action:

I.96.6 bhīṣmaḥ svayaṃ tadā rājan varayām āsa tāḥ prabhuḥ

This must mean "Lordly Bhīṣma himself then formally wooed these (maidens), o king." (Note the pun on svayaṃvara.) Though varayati under other circumstances may mean simply 'choose', in marriage texts it is clearly a technical term for the proclamation of the bridegroom's name and intent—cf. varayanti 'they woo' in ŚGS I.6.4 just quoted (also MGS I.7.4). I therefore think that varayām āsa in I.96.6 marks Bhīṣma's self-identifying announcement.

He then goes on to give a dharma lesson, explaining the eight forms of marriage in wearisome detail (vss. 8–11, differing in some interesting respects from Manu and other legal treatments), before issuing the challenge quoted earlier (I.96.12). He cannot be accused of trying to sneak away with the girls without making himself known.

Duryodhana's announcement is also somewhat covert. He has, it seems, legitimately come to the svayaṃvara and only decides to abduct the young woman when she passes him over. Therefore, his name was probably included in the formal proclamation of the would-be suitors:

XII.4.11 tataḥ saṃśrāvyamāneṣu rājñāṃ nāmasu bhārata

Then when the names of the kings were being announced, o Bhārata . . .

When the young woman ignores him, he sets the abduction in motion, and at that point the narrator refers to him by his full name:

XII.4.11 (cont'd) atyakrāmad *dhārtarāṣṭraṃ* sā kanyā varavarṇinī
12 *duryodhanas tu kauravyo* nāmarṣayata laṅghanam

The fair-faced maiden passed over *Dhṛtarāṣṭra's son.*
Duryodhana Kauravya did not brook the insult.

Just as in Bhīṣma's case in I.96.5, the appearance of the full name embedded in the narrative substitutes for a direct speech, first-person announcement such as we got in V.170.13.

39. Cf. YājñSmṛ I.58; ViSmṛ XXIV.19. Note also that the kings at the svayaṃvara were invited there (e.g. V.170.10 rājānaś ca samāhūtāḥ "the kings invited together").

40. Nonetheless Apte (1978, p. 107) considers the journey "not an essential part of the marriage ritual." This judgment can be disputed on methodological grounds: we should pay serious attention to any element that gets considerable space in a text, no matter how extraneous it seems to *us*. Sūtra texts are especially parsimonious verbally, yet here lavish in their treatment of the bridal journey. The prominence of the wedding chariot already in the RV independently suggests its importance in the marriage ritual.

41. Cf. MGS I.13.6; KāṭhGS XXVI.4; VārGS XV.2; ĀśvGS I.8.1; KauśSū 77.1; ĀpGS II.5.22.

42. Prof. Kim McCone has also suggested to me that the acquisition of a chariot (and other property) may have signaled the coming of age of an Indo-European male and made him eligible to marry.

43. The prominence of the chariot journey in marriage ritual and its similarity to abduction motifs have been discussed with some regularity in recent work on Greek weddings. Cf. Sourvinou-Inwood 1973 ("Young Abductor" scenes represent non-mythological marriage theme, with Persephone's abduction as mythological model); 1987 (mock abduction and lifting of bride into chariot by bridegroom, p. 139); Jenkins 1983 (useful discussion of anthropological literature on abduction marriage); Seaford 1987 (abduction of Persephone on chariot, p. 112).

44. Note, in passing, the similarity of this phrase to Iliad 3.71 (quoted in n. 57) ὁππότερος δέ κε νικήσῃ κρείσσων τε γένηται "whoever wins and turns out to be stronger," in reference to the single combat of Paris and Menelaos over Helen.

45. Gonda (1980, p. 396), who translates "servants take hold of it," sees this rather as "a case of a contest generating beneficient energy, restoring productive power, prefiguring the outcome or result desired, or ensuring the success of an undertaking," but this interpretation seems unhelpfully vague and general.

46. Keith scornfully comments on this, "in which—absurdly—a trace of marriage by robbery has been seen" (1927, p. 375, n. 3), without giving references for the "absurd" opinion.

47. It may also be significant that he says gamiṣyāmi 'I will go', rather than using a form of √nī 'lead' or √vah 'convey', which are part of the vocabulary of ordinary (nonviolent) marriage and are also used in legal Rākṣasa abductions. For √nī in Rākṣasa marriage contexts, see Dhaumya's use of the verb later on (III.252.25), also Bhīṣma in V.170.14 prasahya hi nayāmy eṣa "I lead/marry (them) by force"; I.96.43 ānayām āsa kāśyasya sutāḥ "he caused the daughters of the king of the Kaśis to be led/married" (if ānayām āsa is, as I suspect, a haplologized periphrastic perfect to the causative). For √vah, the two passages concerning the abduction of Rukmiṇī quoted above: III.13.28 avākṣīḥ 'you conveyed/married'; V.47.68 uvāha 'he conveyed'.

48. N.B. whatever its consequences. We must remember that Bhīṣma's abduction of Ambā is ultimately disastrous for *him*: it causes (by a chain of circumstances too long to discuss here) his death.

49. That struggle might have been possible in those instances is suggested when the unhappy Ambā reflects after the fact that she should have jumped off in the melee:

V.173.4 mamāyaṃ svakṛto doṣo yāhaṃ bhīṣmarathāt tadā
pravṛtte vaiśase yuddhe śālvārthaṃ nāpataṃ purā

This is my own self-inflicted fault, that I did not fly/fall off Bhīṣma's chariot for the sake of Śālva [her fiancé, who rejects her after the abduction], while the destructive battle was going on.

50. Note the use of the verb √nī here; see n. 47.

51. It is because of Dhaumya's statement here and also those regarding Sītā's abduction in the Rāmāyaṇa (quoted by Hara 1974, pp. 304–5) that I do not think that the offense is the abduction of a married woman, rather than an unmarried one as e.g. Arabagian (1984, p. 112) has suggested.

52. Her position on his chariot is reiterated in III.254.2 (rathe sthitām).

53. It is not clear to me exactly how far Śiśupāla got in this case. On the one hand, Śiśupāla does not possess Rukmiṇī now, so he did not actually succeed in Rākṣasa *marriage*. On the other, immediately after Kṛṣṇa mentions this offense, Śiśupāla taunts him with

II.42.18 matpūrvāṃ rukmiṇīṃ kṛṣṇa saṃsatsu parikīrtayan
viśeṣataḥ pārthiveṣu vrīḍāṃ na kuruṣe katham
19 manyamāno hi kaḥ satsu puruṣaḥ parikīrtayet
anyapūrvāṃ striyaṃ jātu tvadanyaḥ . . .

18 Kṛṣṇa—narrating at length among the assembled kings how Rukmiṇī previously was mine—how can you not have shame?!

19 What man but you would think to announce in the assembly that his wife had previously been another's?!

It should be noted that the Critical Edition is dubious about this entire passage (though it includes it in the main text), as it does not occur in the Southern recension.

Śiśupāla's words imply that he had not merely asked for Rukmiṇī's hand and been rejected, but that he had enjoyed some sort of possession of her that might shame or embarrass her current husband. But the word used of Śiśupāla's relation to Rukmiṇī, prārthanā 'seeking', is also used of Jayadratha after his abduction of Draupadī is thwarted (remember III.255.58 anena vīryeṇa kathaṃ striyaṃ *prārthayase* balāt "How can you *seek* a woman by force with this manly deed?"), and so it may refer to an unconsummated abduction, where the husband may or may not feel his wife has been violated. Indeed, elsewhere in the MBh this lexeme seems to refer to irregular and unscrupulous approaches to unprotected women—e.g. what may happen to a man's wife and daughter after he dies (I.146.11–13, 16) or to a servant maid. When Damayantī is so disguised, one of her conditions for employment is that anyone who 'seeks' her will be punished (III.62.39).

In any case, despite Śiśupāla's taunts, Kṛṣṇa seems to feel no shame—his marriage to Rukmiṇī was a long and successful one. His equanimity contrasts with Rāma's rejection of Sītā after her abduction and that of Ambā's betrothed, Śālva, after hers.

54. The legal penalty for both murder and abduction in Hittite law is material compensation.

55. M. C. Smith 1992, esp. p. 129.

56. Jamison 1994.

57. Helen's scene occurs just before Menelaos, her previous husband, and Paris, her abductor and current husband, embark on *single combat* over Helen and her possessions.

> Il. 3.69–72 (≅ 90–92) *αὐτὰρ ἔμ' ἐν μέσσῳ καὶ ἀρηίφιλον Μενέλαον*
> *συμβάλετ' ἀμφ' Ἑλένῃ καὶ κτήμασι πᾶσι μάχεσθαι.*
> *ὁππότερος δέ κε νικήσῃ κρείσσων τε γένηται,*
> *κρήμαφ' ἑλὼν εὖ πάντα γυναῖκά τε οἴκαδ' ἀγέσθω.*
>
> But put me [Paris] and warlike Menelaos in the middle to fight about Helen and all (her) possessions.
> Whichever shall win and turn out to be the stronger, taking all the possessions and the woman, let him lead (them) home.

58. Though another part of the wedding ceremony may be covertly alluded to in the first half-verse of I.212.7: Subhadrā has just performed a ritual circumambulation of Mt. Raivata (pradakṣiṇaṃ giriṃ kṛtvā), which reminds us of the agnipariṇayana (a pradakṣiṇa or circumambulation of the fire), an important part of the standard marriage rite.

59. On the importance of witness, see also Hara 1974, pp. 304–5 and on the technical legal value of √kruś, see Watkins 1970, p. 324. Recall that Lucretia was specifically warned to keep quiet, under threat of death, which helps mark that incident as an unlawful procedure.

60. In fact he dismisses the other types of marriage as inferior in this case (I.213.2–5) and is especially contemptuous of marriages involving either gift or bride-price. I have had occasion to cite his remarks before:

> MBh I.213.4 pradānam api kanyāyāḥ paśuvat ko 'numaṃsyate
> vikriyaṃ cāpy apatyasya kaḥ kuryāt puruṣo bhuvi
>
> Who would approve of the giving of a maiden as if (she were) cattle,
> And what man on earth would sell his offspring?

61. Given that Subhadrā had a sainako janaḥ accompanying her, we assume that the men therein had the same reaction. They forbore to fight to protect their charge, when faced with Arjuna alone.

62. As Schmidt has clearly demonstrated (1987, chap. 2), the brotherless maiden is an unappealing marriage prospect for other reasons, since she is structurally likely to be made a putrikā or 'appointed daughter'. Her first-born son would be claimed by her own family, as a male heir able to perform ancestor worship for her sonless father.

The structural importance of the brother seems to be recognized in the gṛhya sūtra treatments of the wedding ceremony, where it is he who pours the roasted grain into the bride's hands, for the thrice-repeated Lājāhoma oblation, an important step in the ceremony (cf. e.g. JGS I.21; ĀśvGS I.7.8).

63. He seems in fact to claim that it never existed, in any culture, but ethnographic studies have found evidence of it, either real or staged, in a number of other cultures. Cf. e.g. Shore 1981; Ortner 1981.

64. See part I, n. 10. Cf. also MDŚ V.148.

65. We should also remember that Yudhiṣṭhira gambled away *his brothers* before he staked himself, and everyone, brothers included, accepts his legal right to treat *them* as

property, as he still owned himself when he did so. Women are not the only ones affected here.

66. Three months: GDS XVIII.20; ViSmṛ XXIV.40; three years: BDS IV.1.12, 14; VāsDS XVII.67–68; MDŚ IX.90. Cf. Schmidt 1987, pp. 22–23; Kane, *HDŚ* II.1. 439–47. It is clear in the earlier dharma texts that child marriage in its later form was not practiced. Cf. esp. Thieme 1963b and the discussion in Kane just cited. However, child marriage may have come into vogue in response to the pressures to arrange a marriage just at puberty that I am about to discuss.

67. Cf. Thieme 1963b [= 1984, pp. 435–43]; Schmidt 1987, pp. 15, 23.

68. On the technical meaning of yauvana in the life stages of females, see Thieme 1963b [= 1984, pp. 426ff., esp. p. 438].

69. And, it seems, restricted to Kṣatriyas, especially to kings' daughters. To name a few: Damayantī, Draupadī, Sītā, Kuntī, the girls whose svayaṃvaras were truncated by abduction (Ambā and her sisters, Citrāṅgada's daughter, and Subhadrā [her svayaṃvara only in the planning stages]).

70. See esp. Schmidt 1987, chap. III.

71. The gifts of father, mother, and brother are three of the six types of women's property, as defined by Manu somewhat later in the text. The other three types are connected with marriage:

MDŚ IX.194 adhyagnyadhyāvāhanikaṃ dattaṃ ca prītikarmaṇi
bhrātṛmātṛpitṛprāptaṃ ṣaḍvidhaṃ strīdhanaṃ smṛtam

What is given at the (bridal) fire, on the (bridal) journey, in token of affection,
what is acquired from brother, mother, and father—these are traditionally considered the six types of women's property.

72. Schmidt 1987, pp. 1–29. See also Jamison 1991, pp. 149–72.

73. Bloomfield (AV ad loc.) translates 'balsam' following Sāyaṇa, but in his note on the passage suggests rather 'bull's grease', which at least has the merit of derivational sense; Caland (1900 ad KauśSū 34.14) similarly translates it as 'fat from a steer'; Whitney (AV ad loc.) sensibly leaves it untranslated.

74. Following Whitney's emendation of suṣádā to suṣádām.

75. In a pinch these can be artificially manufactured by crisscrossing wagon tracks:

BŚS V.16 (151: 12) yady u vai na bhavaty anasā vā rathena vā viyānti

If there is no (crossroads), they drive transversely with a cart or a chariot.

76. The ŚB (II.6.2.9) gives a different etymology and interpretation of the term, taking the first element from strī́ 'woman', but this derivation is fanciful.

77. ≅ MS I.10.20 (160: 5); TS I.8.6.1; etc. On this offering see Einoo 1988, pp. 281–84.

78. 'Mole' (so BR, MonWms, Grassmann, Keith TS, etc.) seems the most likely interpretation of this term, especially if it is derived from √khan 'dig' (though see possible objections to this derivation in Mayrhofer *EWA* sub KHAN), but other renderings have been offered, esp. 'rat' (Whitney, AV VII.50.1; Griffith VS III.57, etc.; [see also BR, MonWms]).

79. Cf. KS IX.7 (100: 1), XXXVI.14 (81: 1); TS I.8.6.1, VI.6.4.4–5; VS III.57, etc.

80. Crossroads have bad associations in ancient India, just as in ancient Greece—remember Oedipus.

81. Cf. VārŚS I.7.4.64 . . . yajamāno 'mātyaiḥ sahāgniṃ paryeti "the Sacrificer together with members of the household goes around the fire."

82. Cf. e.g. MŚS I.7.7.6, where the marchers carry the cakes.

83. Cf. also Keith 1927, p. 322; Hillebrandt 1897, p. 118; Einoo 1988, pp. 284–90.

84. Cf. e.g. MŚS VII.2.7.10; KŚS XIII.3.20–26; BŚS XVI.21 (267: 11), 22 (268: 10), 23; ĀpŚS XXI.18.7, 19.18–20.5; VārŚS III.2.5.41–44.

85. Cf. also MŚS IX.2.4.13; KŚS XX.6.13; ŚB XIII.2.8.4.

86. ĀpŚS XX.17.12; BŚS XV.29 (234: 6); MŚS IX.2.4.12; KŚS XX.6.12; VS XXIII.18; ŚB XIII.2.8.3; TB III.9.6.3, some with vocative variant ambe ambike ambālike.

87. Neither of these, in turn, can be separated from the three sisters abducted by Bhīṣma in the Rākṣasa marriage discussed earlier: Ambā, Ambikā, and Ambālikā. Note that in the Aśvamedha mantra VS XXIII.18 has the variant ámbe ámbiké 'mbālike, which matches the MBh names and sequence exactly. What this means I will attempt to discern below.

88. The mantra is widespread. Cf. VS III.60; TS I.8.6.2; MS I.10.4 (144: 12); etc.

89. AV XIV.1.17 also substitutes aryamáṇam, the patron of marriage, for tryàmbakaṃ in pāda a.

90. Depending on text. The version of pāda d found in ĀpŚS VIII.18.3; BŚS V.16 (152: 8) is ito mukṣīya mā pateḥ "Might I be released *from here, not from a husband*," while VS III.60; ŚB II.6.2.14 have itó mukṣīya mā́mútaḥ " . . . from here, not from yonder." As ŚB explains, 'from here' means 'from her relatives' (jñātíbhyaḥ), while 'not from yonder' means 'not from husbands' (pátibhyaḥ). In any case the intent is clear: strictly marital vocabulary is substituted for the general wishes for prosperity and long life found in the original mantra.

91. VārŚS I.7.4.66–67 allows either the Sacrificer or the girl to receive the cakes. For further variations, see Einoo 1988, pp. 289–90.

92. ŚB II.6.2.10; KŚS V.10.11; ĀpŚS VIII.17.9; BhārŚS VIII.22.6; HirŚS V.5. Variants: MŚS I.7.7.4; VārŚS I.7.4.62 ākhukiri; VaikhŚS IX.10 ākhumūṣā. See Einoo 1988, pp. 278–81.

93. And given the fact that the idealization of the 'cozy home' is more characteristic of Victorian England than of ancient India.

94. This discussion assumes that some version of the epic story of Ambā and her sisters already existed in early Vedic and that these three girls were associated with the three Ambikās belonging to Rudra. Despite the difficulties involved in explaining the exact relation of the two sets of three females, I think this is more likely than assuming that a later epic poet simply made up the story of the abduction and its aftermath and named the female protagonists by plucking some designations out of the onomastic repository of Vedic ritual.

The discussion also assumes that Ambikā (along with the others) is viewed with suspicion, not welcome. Although the ŚB implies that Ambikā is a benevolent patroness of unmarried girls

> ŚB II.6.2.13 . . . yā́ ha vái sā́ rudrásya svásā́mbikā nā́ma sā́ ha vái bhágasyeṣṭe tásmād u hā́pi kumāryàḥ párīyuḥ
>
> Rudra's sister, whose name is Ambikā, is master of (good) fortune. Therefore the girls also go around (the fire),

other texts identify her as autumn (śarád) and attribute Rudra's special murderousness in autumn to her influence (cf. MS I.10.20 [160: 6]; KS XXXVI.14; TB I.6.10.4).

95. Another epic heroine, the previous incarnation of Draupadī, when she did not find a husband, "undertook austerities for the sake of a husband" (MBh I.157.8 tapas taptum athārebhe patyartham).

96. As she is also the *only* child of Aśvapati, her potential status of 'appointed daughter' may have put people off as well (see n. 62), though this obstacle is not mentioned in the story.

97. The Critical Edition prints *pitrā dīyamānāpi* here, but the verse makes better sense with a negated participle *adīyamānā*.

98. However, Mahābhārata I also contains a parallel story of a more timid maiden, Tapatī. When asked by a king to engage in Gāndharva marriage (I.161.13), she disavows all power over herself and dutifully cites Manu's views on women's lack of independence:

MBh I.161.14 nāham īśātmano rājan kanyā pitṛmatī hy aham
mayi ced asti te prītir yācasva pitaraṃ mama
. . . 16 na cāham īśā dehasya tasmān nṛpatisattama
samīpaṃ nopagacchāmi na svatantrā hi yoṣitaḥ

I am not mistress of myself, o king, for I am a girl with a father.
If you have pleasure in me, beg [note √yāc] my father for me. . . .
I am not mistress of my body, therefore, o best of kings,
I cannot come to you; for women are not independent.

This canny evasive action has the desired result: he waits and asks her father properly (in fact with a genuine proxy wooer [MBh I.163.1, 5–6]), and a legal gift marriage is concluded without ambiguity. Note that her reason for claiming lack of power over herself is that she has a father. This might suggest that fatherless girls could legally dispose of themselves—or were forced to.

99. Dumézil (1979, pp. 43–44) also wonders at the conflict between the woman's right to bestow herself in a Gāndharva marriage and the legal doctrine denying her 'independence'. He decides that the "autonomy" characteristic of Kṣatriyas is extended to women of that varṇa. But this seems a makeshift solution, as there seems to be no particular evidence for the *general* autonomy of Kṣatriya women.

Part VI

1. "The married householder, therefore, represents the ideal religious life within the vedic world." (Olivelle 1993, p. 55; cf. in general section 2.1 of that work.)

BIBLIOGRAPHY

Abbreviations of Texts

The order used is that of the Roman alphabet, with long vowels following the corresponding short vowels and *ś*, *ṣ* following *s*. Sanskrit text editions and references to translations are given in a separate section immediately preceding the main bibliography.]

AB	Aitareya Brāhmaṇa
AiĀr	Aitareya Āraṇyaka
AV	Atharva Veda
AVP	Atharva Veda Paippalāda
AVŚ	Atharva Veda Śaunaka
ĀpDS	Āpastambha Dharma Sūtra
ĀpGS	Āpastambha Gṛhya Sūtra
ĀpM	Āpastambha Mantrapāṭha
ĀpŚS	Āpastambha Śrauta Sūtra
ĀśvGS	Āśvalāyana Gṛhya Sūtra
ĀśvŚS	Āśvalāyana Śrauta Sūtra
BDS	Baudhāyana Dharma Sūtra
BGS	Baudhāyana Gṛhya Sūtra
BhārGS	Bhāradvāja Gṛhya Sūtra
BhārŚS	Bhāradvāja Śrauta Sūtra
BŚS	Baudhāyana Śrauta Sūtra
BYV	Black (Kṛṣṇa) Yajur Veda
ChUp	Chāndogya Upaniṣad
DrāhŚS	Drāhyāyaṇa Śrauta Sūtra
GDS	Gautama Dharma Sūtra
GobhGS	Gobhila Gṛhya Sūtra
HirGS	Hiranyakeśin Gṛhya Sūtra
HirŚS	Hiranyakeśin Śrauta Sūtra
Il.	Iliad
J.	Jātaka

JB	Jaiminīya Brāhmaṇa
JGS	Jaiminīya Gṛhya Sūtra
KapS	Kapiṣṭhala Saṃhitā
KāṭhGS	Kāṭhaka Gṛhya Sūtra
KauśSū	Kauśika Sūtra
KB	Kauṣītaki (or Śāṅkhāyana) Brāhmaṇa
KhGS	Khādira Gṛhya Sūtra
KS	Kāṭhaka Saṃhitā
KŚS	Kātyāyana Śrauta Sūtra
MBh	Mahābhārata
MDŚ	Mānava Dharma Śāstra
MGS	Mānava Gṛhya Sūtra
MS	Maitrāyaṇī Saṃhitā
MŚS	Mānava Śrauta Sūtra
Nir.	Nirukta
Pāṇ	Pāṇini
PārGS	Pāraskara Gṛhya Sūtra
PB	Pañcaviṃśa Brāhmaṇa (or Tāṇḍya Mahābrāhmaṇa)
R	Rāmāyaṇa
RV	Rig Veda
RV Kh	Rig Veda Khila
SV	Sāma Veda
ŚB	Śatapatha Brāhmaṇa
ŚBK	Śatapatha Brāhmaṇa Kāṇva
ŚBM	Śatapatha Brāhmaṇa Mādhyaṃdina
ŚGS	Śāṅkhāyana Gṛhya Sūtra
ŚŚS	Śāṅkhāyana Śrauta Sūtra
TĀr	Taittirīya Āraṇyaka
TB	Taittirīya Brāhmaṇa
TS	Taittirīya Saṃhitā
VaikhGS	Vaikhānasa Gṛhya Sūtra
VaikhŚS	Vaikhānasa Śrauta Sūtra
VaitŚS	Vaitāna Śrauta Sūtra
VārGS	Vārāha Gṛhya Sūtra
VārŚS	Vārāha Śrauta Sūtra
VāsDS	Vāsiṣṭha Dharma Sūtra
ViSmṛ	Viṣṇu Smṛti

VS	Vājasaneyi Saṃhitā
WYV	White (Śukla) Yajur Veda
YājñSmṛ	Yājñavalkya Smṛti
YV	Yajur Veda

Other Abbreviations

Abh. Preuss. Akad. d. Wiss.	*Abhandlungen der Preussischen Akademie der Wissenschaft*
ABORI	*Annals of the Bhandarkar Oriental Research Institute*
AJP	*American Journal of Philology*
AO	*Acta Orientalia*
BB	*Beiträge zur Kunde der indogermanischen Sprachen*
BEI	*Bulletin d'Etudes Indiennes*
BICS	*Bulletin of the Institute of Classical Studies* (London Univ.)
BR	Böhtlingk, O., and R. Roth, 1855–75
CE/Crit. Ed.	Critical Edition
EVP	*Études védiques et pāṇinéennes* [= Renou 1955–69]
EWA	*Etymologisches Wörterbuch des Altindoarischen* [= Mayrhofer 1986–]
HDŚ	*History of Dharmaśāstra* [= Kane 1930–62]
JHS	*Journal of Hellenic Studies*
IHQ	*Indian Historical Quarterly*
IIJ	*Indo-Iranian Journal*
Ind. Stud.	*Indische Studien*
Ind. Taur.	*Indologica Taurinensia*
JAOS	*Journal of the American Oriental Society*
KEWA	*Kurzgefasstes etymologisches Wörterbuch des Altindischen* [= Mayrhofer 1956–80]
KZ	*Zeitschrift für vergleichende Sprachforschung auf dem Gebiete der indogermanischen Sprachen*
MonWms	Monier-Williams, M. 1899
MSS	*Münchener Studien zur Sprachwissenschaft*
NIA	*New Indian Antiquary*
PAPS	*Proceedings of the American Philosophical Society*
s.v.	*sub verbo*
WZKM	*Wiener Zeitschrift für die Kunde des Morgenlandes*
WZKS	*Wiener Zeitschrift für die Kunde Südasiens*
WZKSOA	*Wiener Zeitschrift für die Kunde Süd- und Ostasiens*
ZDMG	*Zeitschrift der Deutschen Morgenländischen Gesellschaft*

Primary Sources: Text Editions

Titles in many cases have been abbreviated and transliteration conventions modernized.

AB — *Das Aitareya Brāhmaṇa*. Ed. Th. Aufrecht. Bonn 1879. (Repr. Hildesheim 1975.) [Trans. Keith 1920.]

AiĀr — *The Aitareya Āraṇyaka*. Ed. A. B. Keith. Oxford 1909. (Repr. New Delhi 1981.) [Includes trans.]

AV — *Atharva Veda Sanhita*. Eds. R. Roth and W. D. Whitney. 2d. corr. ed. M. Lindenau. Berlin 1924. (Repr. Bonn 1966.) [Trans. Whitney 1905, partial trans. Bloomfield 1897.]

Atharvaveda (Śaunaka), IV.1 *Kāṇḍas XIX, XX*. Ed. Vishva Bandhu. Hoshiarpur 1962.

ĀpDS — *Aphorisms on the sacred law of the Hindus by Apastamba*. Ed. G. Bühler. Bombay 1868. [Trans. Bühler 1898.]

ĀpGS — *The Āpastambha Gṛhyasūtra*. Ed. M. Winternitz. Vienna 1887. [Trans. Oldenberg 1892.]

ĀpM — *The Mantrapāṭha: Or the prayer book of the Āpastambins*. Ed. M. Winternitz. Oxford 1897.

ĀpŚS — *The Śrauta Sūtra of Āpastambha*. 3 vols. Ed. R. Garbe. Calcutta 1882, 1885, 1902. (Repr. New Delhi 1983.) [Trans. Caland 1921–28.]

ĀśvGS — *Indische Hausregeln, I. Āśvalāyana*. Ed. A. F. Stenzler. Leipzig 1864. [Trans. Oldenberg 1886.]

ĀśvŚS — *The Śrauta Sūtra of Āśvalāyana*. Ed. R. Vidyaratna. Calcutta 1874.

BDS — *Das Baudhāyana-Dharmasūtra*. Ed. E. Hultzsch. 2d ed. Leipzig 1922. [Trans. Bühler 1898.]

BGS — *The Bodhāyana Gṛhyasutra*. Ed. R. Shama Sastri. 2d ed. Mysore 1920.

BhārGS — *The domestic ritual according to the school of Bhāradvāja*. Ed. H. J. W. Salomons. Leiden 1913.

BhārŚS — *The Śrauta, Paitṛmedhika and Pariśeṣa Sūtras of Bharadvāja*. Ed. C. G. Kashikar. Poona 1964. [Includes trans.]

BŚS — *The Baudhāyana Śrauta Sūtra*. 3 vols. Ed. W. Caland. Calcutta 1904–24. (2d ed. New Delhi 1982.)

ChUp — [Chāndogya Upaniṣad: numerous eds. and trans. including] Ed. O. Böhtlingk. Leipzig 1889; ed. E. Senart. Paris 1930.

DrāhŚS — *Drāhyāyaṇa Śrauta Sūtra XI–XV*. Ed. Raghu Vira, *Journal of Vedic Studies* I (1934) 13–80.

GDS — *The Institutes of Gautama*. Ed. A. F. Stenzler. London 1876. [Trans. Bühler 1898.]

GobhGS — *Das Gobhilagṛhyasūtra*. Ed. F. Knauer. Dorpat-Leipzig 1884, 1886. [Includes trans., also trans. Oldenberg 1892.]

HirGS *The Gṛhyasūtra of Hiraṇyakeśin*. Ed. J. Kirste. Vienna 1889. [Trans. Oldenberg 1892.]

HirŚS [Partial ed.]*The Cāturmāsya Sacrifices, with special reference to the Hiraṇyakeśi Śrautasūtra*. Ed. V. V. Bhide. Poona 1979. [Partial trans. Einoo 1988.]

J. *The Jātaka*. 7 vols. Ed. V. Fausbøll. London 1877–97. (Repr. Oxford 1962–64.) [Trans. Cowell 1895–1907.]

JB *Jaiminīya-Brahmaṇa*. Eds. Raghu Vira and Lokesh Chandra. Nagpur 1954. [Partial ed. and trans. Caland 1919.]

JGS *The Jaiminigṛhyasūtra*. Ed. W. Caland. Lahore 1922. (Repr. 1984.) [Includes trans.]

KapS *Kapiṣṭhala-Kaṭha-Saṃhitā*. Ed. Raghu Vira. Lahore 1932. (2d ed. Delhi 1968.)

KāṭhGS *The Kāṭhakagṛhyasūtra*. Ed. W. Caland. Lahore 1925.

KauśSū *The Kauśika Sūtra*. Ed. M. Bloomfield, *JAOS* 14 (1890). (Repr. Delhi 1972.) [Partial trans. Caland 1900.]

KB *Das Kaushītaki Brāhmaṇa*. Ed. B. Lindner. Jena 1887. [Trans. Keith 1920.]

KhGS [Trans. Oldenberg 1886.]

KS *Kāṭhakam. Die Saṃhitā der Kaṭha-Śākhā*. 3 vols. Ed. L. von Schroeder. Leipzig 1900, 1909, 1910.

KŚS *The Śrautasūtra of Kātyāyana*. Ed. A. Weber. Berlin-London. 1859.

[Partial ed.] *Kātyāyana Śrauta Sūtra*. Ed. H. G. Ranade. Poona 1978. [Includes trans.]

MBh *The Mahābhārata*. 19 vols. Ed. V. S. Sukthankar, S. K. Belvalkar, and P. L. Vaidya, et al. Poona 1933–66. [Partial trans. van Buitenen 1973, 1975, 1978.]

MDŚ *Mānava Dharma-Śāstra*. Ed. J. Jolly. London 1887. [Trans. Bühler 1886; Doniger and Smith 1991.]

MGS *Das Mānava-gṛhya-sūtra*. Ed. F. Knauer. St. Petersburg. 1897. [Trans. Dresden 1941.]

MS *Maitrāyaṇī Saṃhitā*. 4 vols. Ed. L. von Schroeder. Leipzig 1881, 1883, 1885, 1886.

MŚS *The Mānava Śrautasūtra*. 2 vols. Ed. J. M. van Gelder. New Delhi 1961, 1963. [Includes trans.]

Nir. *The Nighaṇṭu and the Nirukta*. Ed. L. Sarup. 1920–27. (Repr. Delhi 1967.) [Includes trans.]

Pāṇ. *Pāṇini's Grammatik*. Ed. O. Böhtlingk. Leipzig 1887. [Includes trans.]

PārGS *Indische Hausregeln. II. Pāraskara*. Ed. A. F. Stenzler. Leipzig 1876. [Trans. Oldenberg 1886.]

PB [Pañcaviṃśa Brāhmaṇa] *Tāṇḍyamahābrāhmaṇa*. 2 vols. Ed. A. Chinnaswāmī Śāstrī. Benares 1935, 1936. (Repr. Benares 1987.) [Trans. Caland 1931.]

R *The Vālmīki-Rāmāyaṇa* (Crit. Ed.). 7 vols. Eds. G. H. Bhatt, P. L. Vaidya, et al. Baroda 1960–75. [Partial trans. Goldman 1984.]

RV *Die Hymnen des Rigveda*. 2 vols. Ed. Th. Aufrecht. Bonn 1877. (Repr. Wiesbaden 1968.) [Trans. Geldner 1951; partial trans. O'Flaherty 1981.]

RV Kh *Die Apokryphen des Ṛgveda*. Ed. I. Scheftelowitz. Breslau 1907.

SV *Die Hymnen des Sāma-Veda*. 2 vols. Ed. Th. Benfey. Leipzig 1848.

ŚB *The Śatapatha-Brāhmaṇa in the Mādhyandina-Śākhā*. Ed. A. Weber. Berlin-London 1855. (Repr. Benares 1964.) [Trans. Eggeling 1882–1900.]

ŚBK *The Śatapatha Brāhmaṇa in the Kāṇvīya recension*. Ed. W. Caland and Raghu Vira. Lahore 1926. (Repr. Delhi 1983.)

ŚGS *Śāṅkhāyaṇa Gṛhya Sūtra*. Ed. S. R. Sehgal. Delhi 1960. [Trans. Oldenberg 1886.]

ŚŚS *The Śāṅkhāyana Śrauta Sūtra*. Ed. A. Hillebrandt. Calcutta 1888. [Trans. Caland 1953.]

TĀr *Taittirīya Āraṇyaka*. 3 vols. Ed. A. Mahadeva Sastri and K. Rangacarya. Mysore 1900–2. (Repr. Delhi 1985.)

TB *The Taittirīya Brāhmaṇa*. 4 vols. Ed. A. Mahadeva Sastri. Mysore 1908–21. (Repr. Delhi 1985.)

TS *Die Taittirīya-Saṃhitā*. 2 vols. Ed. A. Weber. Leipzig 1871, 1872. [Trans. Keith 1914.]

VaikhGS *Vaikhānasasmārtasūtram*. Ed. W. Caland. Calcutta 1927.

VaikhŚS *Vaikhānasa-Śrautasūtram*. Ed. W. Caland. Calcutta 1941.

VaitŚS *Vaitāna Sūtra*. Ed. R. Garbe. London 1878.

VārGS *Vārāha-Gṛhyasūtra*. Ed. Raghu Vira. Lahore 1932.

VārŚS *Vārāha-Śrauta-Sūtra*. Eds. W. Caland and Raghu Vira. Lahore 1933. (Repr. Delhi 1971.)

VāsDS *Śrīvāsiṣṭhadharmaśāstram*. Ed. A. A. Führer. Bombay 1883. [Trans. Bühler 1898.]

ViSmṛ *Viṣṇusmṛti*. Ed. J. Jolly. Calcutta 1881. [Trans. Jolly 1900.]

VS *The Vājasaneyi-Sanhitā*. Ed. A. Weber. Berlin-London 1852. (Repr. Benares 1972.) [Trans. Griffith 1899.]

YājñSmṛ *Yājñavalkyadharmaśāstram*. Ed. A. F. Stenzler. Berlin-London 1849. [Includes trans.]

Secondary Sources

Apte, U. M. 1978. *The sacrament of marriage in Hindu society*. Delhi.

Arabagian, R. K. 1984. "Cattle raiding and bride stealing: The goddess in Indo-European heroic literature." *Religion* 14, pp. 107–42.

Atkinson, C. W., C. H. Buchanan, and M. R. Miles, eds. 1985. *Immaculate and powerful*. Boston.

Benveniste, E. 1951. "Don et échange dans le vocabulaire indo-européen," *L'Année sociologique*, 3ᵉ sér., II. [Repr. in *Problèmes de linguistique générale* I, 1966, pp. 315–26. Paris.]

———. 1969. *Le Vocabulaire des institutions indo-européennes*. Paris. [Eng. trans. E. Palmer, 1973, *Indo-European language and society*. Coral Gables, Fla.]

Bloomfield, M. 1896. "Contributions to the interpretation of the Veda. 7th Series." *AJP* 17, pp. 399–437.

———. 1897. *Hymns of the Atharva-Veda*. (Sacred Books of the East 42.) Oxford. [Repr. Delhi 1964.]

———. 1899. *The Atharvaveda*. Strassburg.

———. 1906. *A Vedic concordance*. (Harvard Oriental Series 10.) Cambridge, Mass.

Bodewitz, H. W. 1976. *The daily evening and morning offering (*Agnihotra*) according to the Brāhmaṇas*. Leiden.

Böhtlingk, O. and R. Roth. 1855–75. *Sanskrit-Wörterbuch*. 7 vols. St. Petersburg. [Repr. Delhi 1990.]

Brereton, J. P. 1981. *The Ṛgvedic Ādityas*. (American Oriental Series 63.) New Haven.

———. 1985. "Style and purpose in Ṛgveda 2.11." *IIJ* 28, pp. 237–62.

Bühler, G. 1886. *The laws of Manu*. (Sacred Books of the East 25.) Oxford.

———. 1898. *The sacred laws of the Āryas*. Part I *Āpastamba and Gautama*, 2d ed.; Part II *Vasiṣṭha and Baudhāyana*. New York. (American edition of Sacred Books of the East 2, 14.)

Buitenen, J. A. B. v. 1968. *The Pravargya*. Poona.

———. 1973. *The Mahābhārata, 1. The book of the beginning*. Chicago.

———. 1975. *The Mahābhārata, 2. The book of the assembly hall, 3. The book of the forest*. Chicago.

———. 1978. *The Mahābhārata, 4. The book of Virāṭa, 5. The book of the effort*. Chicago.

Caland, W. 1900. *Altindisches Zauberritual: Probe einer Uebersetzung der wichtigsten Theile des Kauśika Sūtra*. Amsterdam. [Repr. Wiesbaden 1967.]

———. 1904–13. *The Baudhāyana Śrauta Sūtra belonging to the Taittirīya Saṃhitā*. 3 vols. (Bibliotheca Indica 163.) Calcutta. 2d ed. New Delhi 1982.

———. 1919. *Das Jaiminīya-Brāhmaṇa in Auswahl*. (Verhandelingen der Koninklijke Akademie van Wetenschappen te Amsterdam, Afd. Lett., N. R. 19.4.) Amsterdam. [Repr. Wiesbaden 1970.]

———. 1921–28. *Das Śrautasūtra des Āpastambha*. 3 vols. Göttingen-Leipzig 1921; Amsterdam 1924, 1928. [Repr. Wiesbaden 1969.]

———.1926. *The Śatapatha Brāhmaṇa in the Kāṇvīya recension*. Revised by Raghu Vira. Lahore. [Repr. Delhi 1983.]

———. 1931. *Pañcaviṃśa-Brāhmaṇa. The Brāhmaṇa of twenty five chapters*. (Bibliotheca Indica 255.) Calcutta. [Repr. Delhi 1982.]

———. 1953. *Śāṅkhāyana-Śrautasūtra, being a major yājñika text of the Ṛgveda translated into English for the first time*. Nagpur.

Caland, W., and V. Henry. 1906–7. *L'Agniṣṭoma: Description complète de la forme normale du sacrifice de Soma dans le cult védique*. Paris.
Caland, W., and Raghu Vira. 1971. *Vārāha-Śrauta-Sūtra*. Delhi.
Carmody, D. L. 1989. *Women and world religions*. Englewood Cliff, N. J.
Chatterjee, C. K. 1978. *Studies in the rites and rituals of Hindu marriage in ancient India*. Calcutta.
Chaudhuri, J. B. 1938. "Position of mother in Vedic ritual." *IHQ* 14, pp. 822–30.
———. 1939. "The initiation of women." *IHQ* 15, pp. 101–21.
———. 1940. "The wife in the Vedic ritual." *IHQ* 16, pp. 70–98.
———. 1941a. "The position of the daughter in Vedic ritual." *NIA* 4, pp. 77–85.
———. 1941b. "The position of wives other than the first in the Vedic ritual." *IHQ* 17, pp. 180–95, 492–505.
Cowell, E. B., et al. 1895–1907. *The Jātaka*. 6 vols. Cambridge.
Delbrück, B. 1888. *Altindische Syntax*. (= Syntactische Forschungen V.) Halle an der Saale. [Repr. Darmstadt 1968.]
———. 1893. *Vergleichende Syntax der indogermanischen Sprachen* I. Strassburg.
———. 1900. *Vergleichende Syntax der indogermanischen Sprachen* III. Strassburg.
Doniger, W., and B. K. Smith. 1991. *The laws of Manu*. Harmondsworth.
Dresden, M. J. 1941. *Mānavagṛhyasūtra*. Groningen.
Dumézil, G. 1979. *Mariages indo-europeéns*. Paris.
Dumont, L. 1966. *Homo hierarchicus*. Paris. [Trans. M. Sainsbury, 1970 Chicago.]
Dumont, P.-E. 1927. *L'Aśvamedha: Description du sacrifice solonnel du cheval dans le culte védique d'après les textes du Yajurveda blanche*. Paris.
Eggeling, J. 1882-1900. *The Śatapatha Brāhmaṇa. According to the text of the Mādhyandina school*. 5 vols. (Sacred Books of the East 12, 26, 41, 43-44.) Oxford. [Repr. Delhi 1963.]
Einoo, S. 1988. *Die Cāturmāsya oder die altindischen Tertialopfer dargestellt nach den Vorschriften der Brāhmaṇas und der Śrautasūtras*. (Monumenta Serindica No. 18.) Tokyo.
Falk, H. 1982. "Zur Tiersucht im alten Indien." *IIJ* 24, pp. 169–80.
———. 1984. "Die Legende von Śunaḥśepa vor ihrem rituellen Hintergrund." *ZDMG* 134, pp. 115–35.
Geldner, K. F. 1951. *Der Rigveda. Aus dem Sanskrit ins Deutsche übersetzt und mit einem laufenden Kommentar versehen*. 3 vols. (Harvard Oriental Series 33, 34, 35.) Cambridge, Mass.
Ghadially, R. 1988. *Women and Indian society*. New Delhi.
Goldman, R. P. 1984. *The Rāmāyaṇa of Vālmīki*. Vol. I. *Bālakāṇḍa*. Princeton.
Gonda, J. 1954. "Reflections on the Ārṣa and Āsura forms of marriage," in Fs. L. Sarup, pp. 1–15 [= 1975, pp. 171–85].
———. 1961. "Ascetics and courtesans." *Adyar Library Bulletin*, pp. 78–102 [= 1975, pp. 223–47].
———. 1975. *Selected Studies* IV: *History of Indian Religion*. Leiden.
———. 1980. *Vedic ritual. The non-solemn rites*. Leiden.
Goody, J. 1990. *The oriental, the ancient and the primitive: Systems of marriage and the family in the pre-industrial societies of Eurasia*. Cambridge.
Grassmann, H. 1872–75. *Wörterbuch zum Rig-Veda*. Leipzig.
Griffith, R. T. H. 1899. *The hymns of the Yajur-Veda*. Benares.
Hackett, J. 1985. "In the days of Jael: Reclaiming the history of women in ancient Israel," in C. W. Atkinson, C. H. Buchanan, and M. R. Miles, eds., 1985.
Hara, M. 1963. "Notes on two Sanskrit religious terms." *IIJ* 7, pp. 124–45.

———. 1974. "A note on the Rākṣasa form of marriage." *JAOS* 94, pp. 296–306.
Hauer, J. W. 1927. *Der Vrātya*. Stuttgart.
Heesterman, J. C. 1957. *The ancient Indian royal consecration*. 's-Gravenhage.
———. 1959. "Reflections on the *dakṣiṇā*." *IIJ* 3, pp. 241–58.
———. 1962. "Vrātya and sacrifice." *IIJ* 6, pp. 1–37.
———. 1985. *The inner conflict of tradition, Essays in Indian ritual, kingship, and society*. Chicago.
———. 1993. *The broken world of sacrifice: An essay in ancient Indian ritual*. Chicago.
Hillebrandt, A. 1879. *Das altindische Neu- und Vollmondsopfer in seiner einfachsten Form*. Jena. [Repr. Graz 1977.]
———. 1897. *Ritualliteratur*. Strassburg.
———. 1927–29. *Vedische Mythologie*, 2d ed. 2 vols. Breslau. [Repr. Hildesheim 1965.]
Hoffmann, K. 1940. "Vedische Namen." *Wörter und Sachen* 21, pp. 139–61. [= Hoffmann 1975, pp. 6–28.]
———. 1960. "Der vedische Typus *menāmenam*." *KZ* 76, pp. 242–48. [= Hoffmann 1975, pp. 113–19.]
———. 1963. "YV mṛgaśaphá-, m." *KZ* 78, pp. 84–88 [= Hoffmann 1975, pp. 148–52].
———. 1967. *Der Injunktiv im Veda*. Heidelberg.
———. 1975. *Aufsätze zur Indoiranistik* I [= Kleine Schriften]. Ed. J. Narten. Wiesbaden.
———. 1976. *Aufsätze zur Indoiranistik* II [= Kleine Schriften]. Ed. J. Narten. Wiesbaden.
Hopkins, E. W. 1889. "The social and military position of the ruling caste in ancient India." *JAOS* 13, pp. 57–376.
Hubert, H., and M. Mauss. 1898. "Essai sur la nature et la fonction du sacrifice." *L'Année sociologique*, pp. 29–138. [Eng. trans., W. D. Halls, *Sacrifice: its Nature and Function*, 1964, Chicago.]
Insler, S. 1989–90. "The shattered head split and the Epic tale of Śakuntalā." *BEI* 7–8, pp. 97–139.
Jamison, S. W. 1981. "Astobhayat, anubhartrī́, and RV I.88.6." *AO* 42, pp. 55–63.
———. 1982/83. "'Sleep' in Vedic and Indo-European." *KZ* 96, pp. 6–16.
———. 1983. *Function and form in the* -áya-*formations of the Rig Veda and Atharva Veda*. Göttingen.
———. 1987. "Linguistic and philological remarks on some Vedic body parts" [Part II, 'kukṣí', pp. 71–81], in *Studies in memory of Warren Cowgill (1929–1985)*, pp. 66–91. Ed. C. Watkins. Berlin.
———.1991. *The ravenous hyenas and the wounded sun: Myth and ritual in ancient India*. Ithaca and London.
———. 1993. "Natural history notes on the RVic 'Frog' hymn." *ABORI* 52/53, pp. 137–44.
———. 1994. "Draupadī on the walls of Troy: Iliad 3 from an Indic perspective." *Classical Antiquity* 13, 5–16.
———. Forthcoming a. "Formulaic elements in Vedic myth," to appear in *Proceedings of the First International Conference on Vedic Studies* (Harvard University).
———. Forthcoming b. Review of Heesterman 1993. To appear in *Method and Theory in the Study of Religion*.
———. Forthcoming c. "Vedic mení, Avestan maēni, and the power of thwarted exchange," to appear in Fs. P. Thieme.

Jamison, S. W., and M. Witzel. Forthcoming a. "Vedic Hinduism" in *The Study of Hinduism*. Ed. Arvind Sharma (to appear, University of South Carolina Press). [Abbreviated versions of next item]

———. Forthcoming b. "Vedic Hinduism" in *New studies in Hinduism*. Ed. A. Sharma.

Jenkins, I. 1983. "Is there life after marriage? A study of abduction motif in vase paintings of the Athenian wedding ceremony." *BICS* 30, pp. 137–45.

Jolly, J. 1900. *The Institutes of Vishnu*. New York. (American edition of Sacred Books of the East 8.)

Kaelber, W. 1989. *Tapta Mārga: Asceticism and initiation in Vedic India*. Albany.

Kakar, S. 1988. "Feminine identity in India," in Ghadially 1988, pp. 44–68.

Kane, P. V. 1930–62. *History of Dharmaśāstra*. [*HDŚ*.] Poona. [2d ed. 1973–90.]

Keith, A. B. 1914. *The Veda of the Black Yajus School entitled Taittiriya Sanhita*. 2 vols. (Harvard Oriental Series 18, 19.) Cambridge, Mass. [Repr. Delhi 1967.]

———. 1920. *Rigveda Brāhmaṇas: The Aitareya and Kauṣītaki Brāhmaṇas of the Rigveda*. (Harvard Oriental Series 25.) [Repr. Delhi 1971.]

———. 1925. *The religion and philosophy of the Vedas and Upanishads*. 2 vols. (Harvard Oriental Series 31, 32.) Cambridge, Mass. [Repr. Delhi 1970.]

Kinsley, D. 1986. *Hindu goddesses: Visions of the divine feminine in the Hindu religious tradition*. Berkeley, Los Angeles, London.

Kirfel, W. 1951. "Der Aśvamedha und der Puruṣamedha," in *Beiträge zur indischen Philologie und Altertumskunde* [Fs. W. Schubring], pp. 39–50. Hamburg.

Köhler, H.-W. 1948/1973. *Śrad-dhā- in der vedischen und altbuddhistischen Literatur* [diss. 1948, ed. K. L. Janert and publ. 1973]. Wiesbaden.

Krick, H. 1972. "Der vieräugige Hund im Aśvamedha. Zur Deutung von TS VII 1, 11, 1(b)." *WZKS* 16, pp. 27–39.

———. 1982. *Das Ritual der Feuergründung (Agnyādheya)*. Ed. G. Oberhammer. (Österreichische Akad. d. Wiss., Philos.-Hist. Klasse, Sitzungsber., vol. 399.) Vienna.

Kuiper, F. B. J. 1960. "The ancient Aryan verbal contest." *IIJ* 4, pp. 217–81.

Lanman, C. R. 1885. *A Sanskrit reader*. Cambridge, Mass.

Leslie, J. (ed.) 1991a. *Roles and rituals for Hindu women*. London.

———. (ed.) 1991b. *Rules and remedies in classical Indian law*. Leiden.

Lévi, S. 1898. *La Doctrine du sacrifice dans les Brāhmaṇas*. Paris. [Repr. Paris 1966.]

Macdonell, A. A., and A. B. Keith. 1912. *Vedic index of names and subjects*. 2 vols. London. [Repr. Delhi 1958.]

Malamoud, C. 1972. "Observations sur la notion de 'reste' dans le brāhmanisme." *WZKS* 16, pp. 5–26.

Marglin, F. A. 1985. "Female sexuality in the Hindu world," in C. W. Atkinson, C. H. Buchanan, and M. R. Miles, eds., 1985.

Mauss, M. 1923–24. "Essai sur le don." *L'Année sociologique*, nouv. sér., I. [repr. 1950 (*Sociologie et Anthropologie*); Eng. trans. *The Gift* (trans. I. Cunnision) Oxford 1954; *The Gift* (trans. W. D. Halls) London 1990.]

Mayrhofer, M. 1956–80. *KEWA*. = *Kurzgefasstes etymologisches Wörterbuch des Altindischen*. 4 vols. Heidelberg.

———. 1986– . *EWA*. = *Etymologisches Wörterbuch des Altindoarischen*. Heidelberg.

Meyer, J. J. 1915. *Das Weib im altindischen Epos*. Leipzig. [Eng. version, 1930. *Sexual life in ancient India*. London.]

Minkowski, C. Z. 1991. *Priesthood in ancient India: A study of the Maitrāvaruṇa priest*. Vienna.

Mittwede, M. 1986. *Textkritische Bemerkungen zur Maitrāyaṇī Saṃhitā*. Stuttgart.

Monier-Williams, M. 1899. *A Sanskrit-English Dictionary*, 2d ed. Oxford. [Repr. 1956.]
O'Flaherty, W. D. 1973. *Asceticism and eroticism in the mythology of Śiva*. London-New York. [Repr. 1981 as *Śiva: The erotic ascetic*. New York.]
———. 1980. *Women, androgynes, and other mythical beasts*. Chicago and London.
———. 1981. *The Rig Veda: An anthology*. Harmondsworth.
———. 1985. *Tales of sex and violence. Folklore, sacrifice, and danger in the Jaiminīya Brāhmaṇa*. Chicago.
Oldenberg, H. 1886, 1892. *The Gṛhya-Sūtras*. 2 vols. (Sacred Books of the East 29, 30.) [Repr. Delhi 1964.]
———. 1896. "Śraddhá." *ZDMG* 50, pp. 448–50. [= 1967, pp. 26–28.]
———. 1909, 1912. *Ṛgveda. Textkritische und exegetische Noten*. Cited as *Noten*. (Abhandlungen der königlichen Gesellschaft der Wissenschaften zu Göttingen 11, 13.) Berlin. [Repr. Göttingen 1970.]
———. 1917. *Die Religion des Veda*, 2d. ed. Stuttgart. [Repr. Darmstadt 1970.]
———. 1967. *Kleine Schriften*. Ed. K. L. Janert. Wiesbaden.
Olivelle, P. 1993. *The Āśrama system: The history and hermeneutics of a religious institution*. Oxford.
Ortner, S. 1981. "Gender and sexuality in hierarchical societies," in S. Ortner and H. Whitehead, eds., 1981, pp. 359–409.
Ortner, S., and H. Whitehead, eds. 1981. *Sexual meanings: The cultural construction of gender and sexuality*. Cambridge.
Puhvel, J. 1970. "Aspects of equine functionality," in *Myth and law among the Indo-Europeans*, ed. J. Puhvel, pp. 159–72. Berkeley, Los Angeles, London.
———. 1987. *Comparative mythology*. Baltimore.
Rau, W. 1966. "Fünfzehn Indra-Geschichten." *Asiatische Studien* 20, pp. 72–100.
Reiter, R. 1975. *Towards an anthropology of women*. New York.
Renou, L. 1954. *Vocabulaire du rituel védique*. Paris.
———. 1955–69. *Études védiques et pāṇinéennes*. 17 vols. (Publications de l'Institut de Civilisation Indienne, Fasc. 1, 2, 4, 6, 9–10, 12, 14, 16–18, 20, 22–23, 26–27, 30.) Paris.
———. 1956. *Hymnes spéculatifs du Véda*. Paris.
Rubin, G. 1975. "The traffic in women: Notes towards a political economy of sex," in Reiter 1975, pp. 157–210.
Sauvé, J. L. 1970. "The divine victim: Aspects of human sacrifice in Viking Scandinavia and Vedic India," in Puhvel, ed., 1970, pp. 173–91.
Scheftelowitz, I. 1906. *Die Apokryphen des Ṛgveda*. Breslau.
Schmidt, H.-P. 1987. *Some women's rites and rights in the Veda*. Poona.
Schroeder, L. von. 1908. *Mysterium und Mimus im Rigveda*. Leipzig.
Seaford, R. A. S. 1987. "The tragic wedding." *JHS* 107, pp. 106–30.
Sen, C. 1978. *A dictionary of the Vedic rituals*. Delhi.
Sergent, B. 1984. "Three notes on the trifunctional Indo-European marriage." *JIES* 12, pp. 179–91.
Shore, B. 1981. "Sexuality and gender in Samoa," in S. Ortner and H. Whitehead, eds., 1981, pp. 192–215.
Smith, B. K. 1986. "The unity of ritual: The place of the domestic sacrifice in Vedic ritualism." *IIJ* 29, pp. 79–96.
———. 1989. *Reflections on resemblance, ritual, and religion*. Oxford.
Smith, F. M. 1991. "Indra's curse, Varuṇa's noose, and the suppression of women in Vedic *Śrauta* ritual," in Leslie 1991a, pp. 17–45.

Smith, M. C. 1992. *The warrior code of India's sacred song*. New York and London.

Sörensen, S. 1904. *An index to the names in the Mahābhārata*. London. [Repr. Delhi 1978.]

Sourvinou-Inwood, C. 1973. "The Young Abductor of the Locrian pinakes." *BICS* 20, pp. 12–21.

———. 1987. "A series of erotic pursuits: Images and meanings." *JHS* 107, pp. 131–53.

Staal, F. 1983. *Agni: The Vedic ritual of the fire altar*. 2 vols. Berkeley.

Sternbach, L. 1943–44. "The Rākṣasa-Vivāha and the Paiśāca-Vivāha." *NIA* 6, pp. 182–85.

———. 1951. "Forms of marriage in ancient India and their development." *Bhāratīya Vidyā* 12, pp. 62–138.

Thieme, P. 1938. *Der Fremdling im Ṛgveda*. Leipzig.

———. 1949. *Untersuchungen zur Wortkunde und Auslegung des Rigveda*. Halle.

———. 1957a. *Mitra and Aryaman*. New Haven.

———. 1957b. "Vorzarathustriches bei den Zarathustriern." *ZDMG* 107, pp. 67–104.

———. 1963a. "Agastya und Lopāmudrā." *ZDMG* 113, pp. 69–79. [= 1984, pp. 202–12.]

———. 1963b. "'Jungfrauengatte.' Sanskrit kaumāraḥ patiḥ—Homer. κουρίδιος πόσις—lat. maritus." *KZ* 78, pp. 161–248. [= 1984, pp. 426–513.]

———. 1984. *Kleine Schriften*, 2d ed. Wiesbaden.

———. 1985. "Bemerkungen zum Vṛṣākapi-Gedicht (RV 10.86)." *XXII. Deutscher Orientalistentag* [21–25 March 1983], *Ausgewählte Vorträge* (ed. W. Röllig) (*ZDMG Supplement VI*), pp. 238–47.

Thite, G. U. 1975. *Sacrifice in the Brāhmaṇa texts*. Poona.

Thompson, G. 1995. "The pursuit of hidden tracks in Vedic." *IIJ* 38, pp. 1–30.

———. Forthcoming. "The Vedic Brahmodya."

Vishva Bandhu. 1942–76. 5 vols. in 10 parts. *A Vedic word concordance (Vaidikapadānukramakoṣa)*. Hoshiarpur.

Wackernagel, J. 1905. *Altindische Grammatik*. Vol. II.1 *Einleitung zur Wortlehre. Nominalkomposition*. Göttingen. [Repr. 1957.]

Wadley, S. 1988. "Women and the Hindu tradition," in Ghadially 1988, pp. 23–43.

Watkins, C. 1970. "Studies in Indo-European legal language, institutions, and mythology," in *Indo-European and the Indo-Europeans*, ed. G. Cardona, H. M. Hoenigswald, and A. Senn, pp. 321–54.

———. 1995. *How to kill a dragon. Aspects of Indo-European poetics*. Oxford.

Whitney, W. D. 1905. *Atharva-Veda-Saṃhitā. Translated into English with a critical and exegetical commentary by William Dwight Whitney, revised and edited by Charles Rockwell Lanman*. 2 vols. (Harvard Oriental Series 7, 8.). Cambridge, Mass. [Repr. Delhi 1962.]

Winternitz, M. 1897. *The Mantrapāṭha: Or the prayer book of the Āpastambins*. (Anecdota Oxoniensia, Aryan Series Part VIII.) Oxford.

———. 1920. *Die Frau in den indischen Religionen. Teil I. Die Frau im Brahmanismus*. Leipzig.

Witzel, M. 1987. "The case of the shattered head." *Studien zur Indologie und Iranistik* 13/14, pp. 363–415.

SUBJECT INDEX

N.B.: Roman alphabetical order has been observed, but with long vowels following their short equivalents and sibilants in the order s, ś, ṣ. Many Sanskrit words are further identified in parentheses as rituals, gods, personal names (PN), and so forth.

Cow, 141-42, 261 n. 21
as Dakṣiṇā, 101-2, 104, 106-7
for guest, 158-59, 161, 170-71, 200, 292 nn. 11,22-23
milk of, mixed with soma, 82-83, 104, 126, 129-30, 133. *See also* Āśir
for purchasing soma. *See* Soma-cow
raid or race, 105-6, 108-9, 111-12
Cyavana (PN), 164-68, 208, 296 n. 7

Daiva marriage, 190, 196, 211-12, 215-16, 296 n. 10, 297 n. 12
Dakṣiṇā, 101-5, 108, 118, 173, 268 n. 49
maiden as, 215-16
rejected, 106-7, 201, 285 n. 241, 295 n. 71
and śraddhā, 178, 184-86
Dakṣiṇāgni (fire), 39, 51-52, 56, 62-63, 266 n. 24, 273 n. 95
Damayantī (PN), 15, 180, 262 n. 37, 301 n. 53
marriage of, 237-39, 246, 303 n. 69
Dancing, ritual, 65, 67, 98, 242-44
Darśapūrṇamāsa (ritual), 29, 37, 179, 269 n. 55
as paradigm Iṣṭi 42, 61, 116
Dharma (god), 155, 162, 164, 169, 189
Dharma texts, 8-9
begging formulae in, 194
guest-reception in, 157-58
marriage in, 253, 296 nn. 9-10
Śrāddha ceremony in, 181
Dhṛtarāṣṭra (PN), 159, 178, 237
Dialogue. *See also* Riddles
hymns, 16-17, 81
insulting, in ritual, 69-71, 74, 83-84, 88, 96-98, 146
at Soma-purchase, 122, 287 n. 275
at Vājapeya, 270 n. 59
Dicing, 13, 15, 108, 236-37, 286 n. 248. *See also* Yudhiṣṭhira
Dīkṣā. *See* Consecration
Dog, 78-79, 99, 278 n. 155, 284 nn. 228-29
Draupadī (PN), 196, 225, 262 n. 37, 303 n. 69, 305 n. 95
abduction of, 226-30, 301 n. 53
at Aśvamedha, 65-66
Duḥṣanta (PN), 249-50
Durvāsas (PN), 157, 164-68, 179-80, 292 n. 14
Duryodhana, 14, 159, 200-201
and Rākṣasa marriage, 220-21, 223, 298 n. 35, 299 n. 38

Eating, 48, 200-201
taboos on, 14, 37, 261 n. 23, 269 n. 50
Establishment of the Fires. *See* Agnyādheya
Excrement, 105-6, 109, 286 nn. 244-45
Expiation, 33, 71-72, 90-91, 93-95

Fertility, 41-42, 53, 62-65, 110, 143-44
in Aśvamedha, 82, 86-87, 95
and the broom, 48, 59-61
in Third Pressing, 126-27, 132-34, 139-45
Fingernails, 48, 101-2
Fire-altar. *See* Agnicayana
Fires, ritual, 31, 37, 39, 41. *See also* Āhavanīya; Dakṣiṇāgni; Gārhapatya
Fire-sticks, 62-63
Food and feeding, 14, 37, 166-69, 181-83, 292 n. 19
for guest, 116, 157, 162-64, 178-80
for sacrificial animals, 71, 93-95, 276 n. 138
Footprint, 287 n. 266
of Soma-cow, 119-20, 123-27, 172, 287 nn. 273-74, 277, 288 n. 278
Foot-washing, 119, 142-43, 161, 292 n. 12
Foot-washing water
in Animal Sacrifice, 146-48
for guest, 154, 156-60, 162
in Soma Sacrifice, 119, 127-28, 138-45, 173-74

Gandharvas, 123, 140, 267 n. 44
Gautama (PN), 156, 291 n. 2, 296 n. 26
Gavāmayana (ritual), 96-98, 145-46, 242, 283 n. 222
Gazing, 272 n. 73, 288 n. 292
between wife and Soma-cow, 119-21, 126, 172, 287 n. 269
at boiling milk, 57-59
at melted butter, 34, 55-57, 61-62, 125
of Udgātar at wife, 136, 139-41
Gālava (PN), 208-10, 238, 296 n. 8
Gāndharva marriage, 211-12, 218-19, 296 n. 10, 297 n. 11
and women's independence, 236, 247-50, 305 nn. 98-99
Gāndhārī (PN), 14, 261 n. 25
Gārhapatya (fire), 84, 266 n. 26
in Iṣṭi, 50-52, 56, 60-63, 272 nn. 74,76
in other rituals, 89, 111, 123-24, 171, 288 n. 278
and wife, 38-41, 266 n. 24, 273 n. 95
Gender switching, 137-38, 142, 262 n. 36, 289 n. 303, 291 n. 326
Ghee, 37, 55-57, 61-62, 125, 133-37
Gifts and gift-exchange, 5, 25, 115, 191-95, 254-55, 259 n. 3, 294 n. 60
dangers of accepting, 191, 195-203, 295 n. 72
marriage as, 207-50, 255, 295 n. 1, 297 nn. 12-13. *See also* Marriage
of oneself, 155, 212, 236, 247-50, 305 nn. 98-99. *See also* Gāndharva marriage

INDEX OF PASSAGES

N.B.: In texts (BŚS, KS, MS) where page and line numbers are parenthetically indicated, the line number refers only to the beginning of the citation, the relevant passage may extend over several lines.

CPSIA information can be obtained at www.ICGtesting.com
Printed in the USA
BVOW08s0354181215

430587BV00001B/28/P

9 780195 096637